THE FAITH OF A LIBERAL

THE FAITH
OF A LIBERAL

Selected Essays by

MORRIS R. COHEN

Essay Index Reprint Series

BOOKS FOR LIBRARIES PRESS
FREEPORT, NEW YORK

To the ever-blessed memory
of
MARY RYSHPAN COHEN
the dear companion of my life's journey
and
to our children, who, in life's diverse paths,
have remained loyal to the liberal faith
in which they were nurtured

ACKNOWLEDGMENTS

For permission to reprint articles included in this book, the author thanks the editors of the *Dial*, the *Nation*, the *New Republic*, the *Menorah Journal*, the *Modern Monthly*, the *Survey Graphic*, the *World Tomorrow*, the *Annals* of the American Academy of Political and Social Science, the *League for Industrial Democracy Monthly*, the *City College Quarterly* and the *Journal of the History of Ideas* (College of the City of New York), the *Philosophical Review* (Cornell University), the *Yale Review*, the *Columbia Law Review*, the *Harvard Law Review*, the *Illinois Law Review*, the *National Lawyers Guild Quarterly*, and the *University of Pennsylvania Law Review*. Two of the chapters are reprinted by special arrangement and with the permission of McGraw-Hill Book Company and the Viking Press, in whose publications they originally appeared.

CONTENTS

I. PROLOGUE

1. What I Believe — 3

II. HEROIC FIGURES IN THE LIBERAL TRADITION

2. Spinoza: Prophet of Liberalism — 13
3. Three Great Judges: Holmes, Brandeis, Cardozo — 20
4. Einstein and His World — 46

III. THE SUBSTANCE OF LIBERALISM

5. The Intellectual Basis of Individualism — 59
6. Liberalism and Irrationalism — 67
7. Calvinism without the Glory of God — 72
8. An Ethical Philosophy of Life — 78
9. Philosophy in Wartime—an Apologia — 84

IV. POLITICO-ECONOMIC ISSUES

10. The Legend of Magna Charta — 91
11. Socialism and Capitalism — 93
12. Why I Am Not a Communist — 110
13. Minimizing Social Conflicts — 119
14. The Symbols of Government — 136
15. The Industrial Discipline and the Governmental Arts — 148

vii

CONTENTS

16. Democracy Inspected   155

17. Freedom: Its Meaning   161

18. Economic Pieties   167

V. LAW AND JUSTICE

19. Constitutional and Natural Rights in 1789 and Since   175

20. The Sacco-Vanzetti Case Reweighed   193

21. A Scandalous Denial of Justice: The Bertrand Russell
    Case   198

VI. LITERATURE AND LITERARY
CRITICISM

22. Forces in American Criticism   213

23. Impressionism and Authority in Literary Criticism   227

24. Dante as a Moral Teacher   234

25. Heine   241

VII. HISTORICAL PERSPECTIVES

26. Parrington's America   249

27. America: Dream, Epic, and Reality   256

28. Liberalism and the Russian Mind   261

29. The Significance of Napoleon   266

VIII. EDUCATION

30. Education and the Changing Social Order   273

31. The Need for a Modern University   278

32. The Prestige of Ideas in America   283

33. In Defense of the Contemplative Life   288

34. On Teaching Philosophy   292

35. Huxley: The Prophet of a Great Hope   296

CONTENTS

IX. RELIGION

36. The Intellectual Love of God 307
37. A Note on Rabbi Joshua of Nazareth 320
38. Erasmus and Luther 322
39. Zionism: Tribalism or Liberalism? 326
40. Baseball as a National Religion 334
41. The Dark Side of Religion 337

X. PHILOSOPHIC CURRENTS

42. Vision and Technique in Philosophy 365
43. The Founder of Pragmatism 391
44. An Adventurous Philosopher 398
45. The New Philosopher's Stone 403
46. Philosophy in the Modern Curriculum 408

XI. SCIENCE AND MYTHOLOGY

47. A Classic That Survives 417
48. Mythical Science 420
49. Dogmatism in the Name of Science 425
50. The Open Mind 430

XII. EPILOGUE

51. The Future of American Liberalism 437
Index 471

I

PROLOGUE

1

WHAT I BELIEVE

IN THE PRIDE of youth I used to characterize myself as philosophically a stray dog, unchained to any metaphysical kennel. It seemed to me better to brave the muddy realities of the unprotected out-of-doors, the uncertain food, the attacks from the watchdogs of comfortable homes, and above all the chilling rains and winds of factual experience. For the roving way led through bracing airs over green hills to broad sunny plains and sparkling rivers flowing to distant seas. But as I approach the years of postrheumatic wisdom, I am beginning to find increasing refuge in the great palaces and parks of the classical philosophies.

I no longer despise those who, like our great poet-philosopher Santayana, set up a wall around their garden to shut off the disconsolate hills and the monotonous sea as well as the smoke and din of the market place. After all, no matter how small our plot of ground, we always have with us the fundamental elements—earth, air, sky, and rain. To the enterprising mind, the mystery of creation is as profound and as challenging here as elsewhere. The sun and stars, and the alternations of bright days and dark nights, persist through the changes of cosmic weather. And the human scene, likewise, offers the same elements of hunger and love, pride and foolishness, joy and suffering, throughout diverse ages and climes. I have thus learned to see virtue in the stably organized as well as in the wild or untamed intel-

Published in *The Nation*, Vol. 133, p. 128 (August 5, 1931).

lectual life. Nevertheless, I have never become completely at home in even the greatest of academic philosophies. I can never forget that there is a world outside of their boundaries, and their guards look askance at me because I never completely get rid of the out-of-door mud.

The central fact to which, it seems to me, prevailing creeds refuse to accord sufficiently serious attention is the obvious impossibility of attaining omniscience. Endowed as we are at birth with infinite ignorance, no amount of knowledge which we acquire in our finite existence can completely exhaust all the complex and temporally endless realms of being. This of course does not justify the absolute denial of all knowledge. No skeptic believes his own opinions to be as baseless as those of his opponent. To recognize ignorance, we must know something. But simple honesty requires us to admit that none of our creeds are entirely free from guesswork. This lack of omniscience is not cured by reliance on faith, intuition, or authority. For however certain we may *feel*, we never *know* that such faith, intuition, or authority will not in the end prove itself mistaken. Faith may influence the conduct resulting from our beliefs, but it cannot change the character of our ancestry or of the events that have already happened, and no one really believes that faith will enable him to escape death and other incidents of our common fate. Nor does the practical necessity of acting on our beliefs make them true. The misery of mankind testifies to our many poignantly unsolved problems.

To the inadequacy of our knowledge must be added the tremendous force of temporarily pleasant illusions, compared with which the love of truth is pitifully frail. Indeed, we may regard the attraction which illusion has for us as similar to that which a flame at night has for a moth. The sources of illusion are many: inherited forms of expression, fashions in respectable or approved opinions, the idols of our tribe or clique, of the market place, of our professional conventions, and the like. But the greatest of all is that vanity which is rooted in our very existence as individuals and which makes each one of us view himself as *the* privileged center of the universe. Is not the zenith directly

4

over *my* head? And is not everyone else and everyone else's point of view only a part of my wider vista?

In our daily life this shows itself in our self-centeredness, in our inability to do justice to others or to realize that they have feelings and rights like our own. We cannot fully see the interests of others because we identify our own with those of humanity or of eternal righteousness. Thus the working classes speak of themselves as the people, the middle classes as the public, and the upper classes as the country. In philosophy this fatal vanity shows itself in anthropomorphism, in making man the central aim or goal of the whole cosmic process—though no one disputes the evidence of astronomy and geology that the life of the human species is but an episode in the history of the cosmically tiny bit of dust, our earth, which has had a beginning and is therefore likely to have an end.

From this point of view the great line of division is not entirely between ancient religion and modern science. Fundamentalists, moralists, and "scientific" evolutionists are at one in pretending to have plumbed the depths of the universe and to have found that it is all planned in a quasi-human way for our "uplift." On the other hand great religious teachers, like the morally wise men of science, have taught the great lesson of humility—that there are always vast realms beyond our ken or control, and that the great blessing of inner peace is unattainable without a sense of the mystery of creation about us and a wisely cultivated resignation to our mortal but inevitable limitations. The necessary effort to understand and control external nature does not require the silly pretension that we can become the omniscient and omnipotent rulers of the universe.

The worst offenders in this respect are, indeed, those physicists and biologists who, in trying to reconcile science with the vague sentimentality which they call religion, abandon altogether the habit of demanding rigorous evidence, which is the essence of science, and indulge in utterly irresponsible statements based on complete ignorance as to the nature of religion, morality, and their history.

I do not wish to restrict the liberty of prophesying. A scientific specialist has a right to be a member of a church as of a political party, and to be as confident as a good husband or anybody else that his is the best possible choice. But he has no right to claim the authority of science for his opinion or conviction. The theory that atoms are composed of electrons cannot prove liberal Protestant theology, nor does the "curvature" of space establish the truth of the Christian moral code. It is sentimental vanity and not science to speak of man as the highest outcome of evolution. In point of sober fact every existing species is just as much the last stage of "evolution." And the probabilities are that man will disappear long before the bacteria and other "lower" forms which now feed on him, but which have a more ancient and more stable biologic existence. None of the facts of natural selection prevent the stupid from multiplying their kind or the cruel and ruthless from surviving in the brute struggle. Biology does not show us more righteousness in the world than that which human beings exercise; and the ancient observation is still true that rain, sunshine, and earthquakes, growth, disease, and death visit the just and the unjust alike.

There are many today who cry out that without the anthropomorphic illusion the value of life and all zest for it disappear. We may sympathize with the personal distress of those who cannot emotionally readjust themselves to new views. But we must not forget that anthropomorphism has been at the root of the superstitions that have made human life full of hideous terrors, so that emancipation from anthropomorphic religion has been hailed by many, from the days of Epicurus and Lucretius to those of Shelley and Bertrand Russell, as the most joyous and beneficent liberation. Certainly it is possible for a materialist like Democritus to be known as a cheerful philosopher, and for a thoroughgoing naturalist and opponent of anthropomorphism like Spinoza to be a model of serenity and of the intellectual love of God.

So long as we lack omniscience and omnipotence life will necessarily contain a tragic element. Death will continue to rob us of those we most dearly love, and unforeseen circumstances will frustrate our most cherished plans. But we cannot overcome this by willful illusion, any more than the ostrich (according to the slanderous account of ignorant mortals) can escape the

6

hunter by burying his head in the sand. And if we are told that some do attain bliss through ignorance, we reply that success in a lottery is no argument for lotteries. The safer way to peace and serenity is through the cultivation of intelligent courage and wise resignation. We need courage to look into our own heart and clear it of the foolish desires which make us sow vain hopes and devote needless toil and anxiety to raise bitter crops of disappointment. And we need resignation to learn to live in a world that is not formed just for our comfort. A wise Frenchman has well said that we need not throw to the dogs all that is not fit for the altar of the gods.

It is fashionable today to despise this ancient wisdom and to profess the belief that the progress of science will enable us to conquer nature completely so that we shall have a heaven on earth. Sober facts, however, give no support to this vain hope. Great as has been the contribution of science to human comfort, it has undoubtedly also served to increase our unsatisfied desires and our capacity for poignant suffering. Thus, despite the beneficent progress of medicine it is not at all certain that life has become on the whole less painful, and there is every indication that the habits developed by our machine age are reducing the span of years which the adult American can be expected to live. Moreover, it is possible that with the decline of liberalism and the gradual uniformity and standardization of ideas which modern machinery facilitates, we may choke that free intellectual variability which is the source of genuine progress in science. In any case the history of the human race offers a picture of an arduous and perilous journey in which each one of us drops out before the end is in sight. What makes it possible for us to carry on, instead of quitting as we can when we really want to, is not our guess as to the unknown goal, but rather the zest developed by our actual daily experiences, by our organic activities, by the light and warmth of the sun and air, and by the joys of human companionship. When the zest for life is really gone, all words of comfort or exhortation are vain. There is nothing to which to appeal. But wise reflection may fan the flame when it is low, illumine our labor, and increase the scope of our peaceful enjoyments.

The realization of the pathetic frailty of the knowledge or beliefs on which our life depends thus leads not to despair but to open-eyed courage. But it also points to a most intimate connection between scientific method and liberal civilization. Science is not, as it is popularly conceived, a new set of dogmas taught by a newer and better set of priests called scientists. It is rather a method which is based on a critical attitude to all plausible and self-evident propositions. It seeks not to reject them, but to find out what evidence there is to support them rather than their possible alternatives. This open eye for possible alternatives, each to receive the same logical treatment before we can determine which is the best grounded, is the essence of liberalism in art, morals, and politics. Conservatism clings to what is established, fearing that if we let go, all the values of life will perish. The radical or revolutionary, impressed with the evil of the existing order or disorder, recklessly puts all faith in some principle without regard for the hidden dangers which it may contain, let alone the cruel hardships which readjustments must involve. The liberal views life as an adventure in which we must take risks in new situations, but in which there is no guaranty that the new will always be the good or the true. Like science, liberalism insists on a critical examination of the content of all our beliefs, principles, or initial hypotheses and on subjecting them to a continuous process of verification so that they will be progressively better founded in experience and reason.

It is fashionable nowadays to belittle the reasons men give for their faith. "Who," asks James, "ever heard of anyone changing his religion because of a reasoned argument?" It is difficult to answer this because we have no way of counting all those who, though unwilling in the heat of argument to admit the force of their opponents' reasons, yet sooner or later are so affected by them as to use them against others. Reasons are themselves essential parts of our belief. And can we maintain that beliefs are of no influence in our lives?

On matters of human life and fate those addicted to much reasoning have not been generally placed in the foremost rank occupied by the great religious and moral teachers. Simple folk distrust those clever fellows who by reasoning seem to make the worse appear the better cause. We recognize the substantial unsoundness of certain conclusions before we are able to place our fingers on the exact fallacy in the argument that supports them. All this applies also to the seemingly more cautious and technical reasoning which passes as scientific method. Sound judgment often rightly rejects propositions in education or social science that are "proved" by formal definitions, statistical charts, graphs, and other paraphernalia. For superficial research workers, too readily impressed with their easily learned methods, often lack the native intelligence or breadth of view to prevent them from giving absurd interpretations to their statistical results. No amount of training in rational science can supply native intelligence where it is lacking. Yet training in reason is undoubtedly a necessary aid to all who can learn. How far it is necessary to make our reasons explicit depends on diverse circumstances. But we are generally safer if we have carefully reasoned out our position.

The prophet may deliver his burden with no warrant but the awful "Thus saith the Lord"; and the poet may impose his own passionate vision without any authority except the magic of his words. But men must use reason to weigh the truth of what rival prophets and poets have said. And he who helps them to reason more justly renders a service second to none in importance and beneficence.

Unless men reason they remain sunk in blind dogmatism, clinging obstinately to questionable beliefs without the consciousness that these may be mere prejudices. "To have doubted one's own first principles," said Justice Holmes, "is the mark of a civilized man." And to refuse to do so, we may add, is the essence of fanaticism.

The fanatic clings to certain beliefs and in their defense is ready to shut the gates of mercy on mankind, precisely because he cannot see any alternative to them except utter chaos or iniquity. Rational reflection, however, makes us see other possibilities and opens our minds to the thought that some of the moral or physical principles that seem to us self-evident may be only sanctified taboos or inherited conventions. The latter may be useful and necessary to save us the trouble of painful thought for which we have no time or inclination in the rush of our practical activities. But they may also be obstacles to a richer life.

Those who confuse life and external motion often claim that thought or reflection makes our action less resolute, and they urge us to stop thinking and do something. But that men's thoughtless or impulsive acts are always wiser than their reasoned conduct is hardly shown even in the case of Hamlet. To reflect that in the absence of omniscience all our principles of morality and conduct are but hypotheses need not prevent us from staking our lives on these anticipations of experience and from fighting as valiantly as we can for what we hold dearest. But it makes us more chivalric, tolerant, or sympathetic with those poor souls who risk their all on some other guess. I do not believe in the adequacy of the usual sentimental interpretation of the Golden Rule to love my neighbor as myself. My neighbor has a right to think the form of my love for myself quite foolish and to resent having it inflicted on him. Nor do I see any good in loving my neighbor's wife and children as my own. Love means discrimination and preference, and the obverse of that is natural aversion. Civil society depends not on blindness or insensibility to the loathsome traits of our fellow-mortals, but upon respecting their rights without taking them to our bosoms. This can be achieved only through sympathetic understanding. Co-operation with those from whom we differ is possible only if we rationalize our beliefs and thus make them intelligible to those having different backgrounds.

In general the value of rationality is similar in morals to that in science. It enables us to frame policies of action and ethical judgment fit for wider outlooks than those of immediate physical stimulus and organic impulse. In enabling us to anticipate the future and adjust ourselves to it in advance, it lifts us above the necessity of living from hand to mouth in the mere immediacy of the moment. It thus enlarges our being and gives us strength to contemplate new physical and moral possibilities without that vertiginous bewilderment which comes to creatures of mere routine when they face the unfamiliar.

II

HEROIC FIGURES IN THE
LIBERAL TRADITION

2

SPINOZA: PROPHET OF LIBERALISM

THOSE who have studied Spinoza in his historic setting are not likely to claim for him an opulence of original ideas comparable to that of Leibniz or Kant. As a genuinely humble, nonprofessional, but devoted seeker for the truth—his type still persists among lowly Jewish artisans—Spinoza never valued ideas for their novelty, and had no hankering to be the founder of a new system of philosophy. The tremendous impression which he has made on the imagination of mankind during the last century and a half is due rather to the singular purity of his light, and to the way in which many traditional ideas (and even their hackneyed expressions) are fused into a pure and coherent whole by the fire of his concentrated intellectual energy that kindles a lyric ardor for human well-being. In this respect Spinoza greatly resembles Dante. Like Dante, he could well have said: My work is in the field of ethics or practical philosophy. It is to trace the way from human bondage and misery to freedom and happiness; and if I touch on speculative matters, it is because I agree with Aristotle that intellectual vision is essential to the highest human life and that truly practical men must theorize.

It is because he so well exemplifies the faith that the way to human salvation is through reason and enlightenment that Spinoza may well be considered the philosopher-prophet of liberalism.

Published in *The New Republic*, Vol. 50, p. 164 (March 30, 1927).

If liberals have not always recognized this, their opponents—obscurantists, authoritarians, and enemies of enlightenment and scientific method—have amply done so. For since within a few weeks of the publication of the *Tractatus Theologico-Politicus,* they have never ceased to pay Spinoza the homage of their inveterate hatred—a hatred based on genuine fear.

The term liberalism is vague enough; but historically it is well identified with the policies which are the offspring of the philosophy of the Enlightenment, a philosophy which in the seventeenth century found congenial support in cosmopolitan Holland, the nursery of Grotius as well as of Spinoza.

As opposed to the policies of fear and suppression, based on the principle that nature is sin and intellect the devil, the policies of liberalism aim to liberate the energies of human nature by the free and fearless use of reason. Liberalism disregards dogmas and rules that hinder the freedom of scientific inquiry and the questioning of all accepted truths. Prophets, priestly hierarchies, sacred books, and sanctified traditions must submit their claims to the court of human reason and experience. In this way mankind is liberated from superstitious fears, such as that of magic or witchcraft, and from arbitrary and cruel restraints on human happiness. Liberalism in general thus means the opening up of opportunities in all fields of human endeavor, together with an emphasis on the value of deliberative rather than arbitrary forces in the governance of practical affairs.

The touchstone that enables us to recognize liberalism is the question of toleration. Do you believe in prohibiting the expression of opinions that are contrary to what you hold to be the truth in politics, morals, and religion? If you do, then admirable as you may otherwise be, you are not of the true liberal faith.

The doctrine of toleration involves significant practical and theoretic difficulties. The practical difficulty has never been stated more clearly than by Spinoza. It amounts to this: How can a government allow poisonous and subversive errors or immoral opinions to spread without thereby being derelict in its duty to protect and preserve the community? How can the state maintain its sovereignty without suppressing views hostile to its continued existence? In theoretic terms this amounts to the familiar taunt: How can you have a definite conviction and yet find ground to tolerate views that contradict it?

Spinoza's answer involves the distinction between demonstrated knowledge of necessary relations and ordinary beliefs as to existential issues on which we are only subjectively certain. The rationalist who maintains the ideal of rigorous demonstration is all the more ready to appreciate the fallibility of our ordinary beliefs. Experience confirms this, in showing how often men have been mistaken when they were convinced of having attained the final, absolute truth. Indeed, the history of physical science shows that, by questioning that which seems to us self-evident, our opponents can be of the greatest help in making us see more of the truth.

While our supreme interest in the truth thus forbids the suppression of opinion, the state cannot avoid the duty of regulating conduct in the interest of the common safety. Once the will of the state is expressed in law, it cannot allow variations of opinion or conscience to serve as an excuse for disobedience or rebellion. So emphatic is Spinoza in his insistence on the sovereignty of the state that he has often been wrongly interpreted as a political absolutist like Hobbes. But Spinoza is a follower not of the Hobbes of our conventional tradition, but of the Hobbes who wrote the *Leviathan*, primarily to exalt the state against the Kingdom of Darkness—i.e., the Roman Church as a temporal power and superstate. Spinoza, like most liberals, undoubtedly shares this view of the necessary autonomy of the state. History has shown this to be a much needed protection, not only against the abuses of clericalism, but also against the anarchic despotism of local potentates, trade guilds, and other effective tyrannies.

But while the state must thus maintain its sovereignty, wisdom dictates that it recognize the inherent limitations of its power. No earthly sovereign can do what he pleases. A government works only by means of external constraints, generally by the fear of punishment. It cannot compel people to respect and love that for which they have contempt or disgust. Moreover, to make men obey the law is not the supreme end of the state, though it is its principal method. The final end of the state is to make men free to develop their powers; and excessive regulation by a fallible earthly sovereign is likely to defeat that end, and thus do more harm than good. A good illustration of this is to be found in the field of sumptuary legislation. The following words of Spinoza sound peculiarly timely to us today: "Many attempts have been made to frame sumptuary laws. But these attempts have never succeeded in their end. For all laws which can be violated without doing anyone an injury are laughed at. Nay, so far are they from doing anything to control the desires and passions of men that, on the contrary, they direct and incite men's thoughts the more towards those very objects; for we always strive for what is forbidden and desire the things we are not allowed to have. And men of leisure are never deficient in the ingenuity needed to enable them to outwit laws framed to regulate things that cannot be effectively forbidden.

"My conclusion, then, is that those vices which are commonly bred in a state of peace, of which we are here speaking, can never be directly prevented, but only indirectly. That is to say, we can only prevent them by constituting the state in such a way that most men will not indeed live with wisdom (for that cannot be secured simply by law) but will be led by those emotions from which the state will derive most advantage."

More generally still: "He who tries to determine everything by law will foment crime rather than lessen it. Things which cannot be prevented must necessarily be allowed, even though some disadvantages may often arise therefrom. How many evils arise, for instance, from luxury, envy, avarice, drunkenness, and such like things. Yet these must be submitted to, because they cannot be prevented by legal regulations."

All this means that, in politics, as in all other human activities, the way to true peace and freedom leads through the path of wisely cultivated resignation. We must recognize that we are not like God, that there are powers outside of us greater than ourselves, and that absolute perfection is, therefore, denied to us humans in our practical efforts. This also involves, as a necessary corollary, the existence of risks in all human enterprise. It is the open recognition of the element of risk, together with the faith that human energy is worth liberating, that is the key to rational liberalism. If liberalism has not always been so understood it is because of the difficulty of distinguishing it from light-hearted optimistic libertarianism, or the doctrine that all restraint on the satisfaction of our natural desires is evil. The difficulty with this doctrine is that human impulses, unguided by rational reflection, conflict with one another and undoubtedly lead to ugliness, vice, disease, and death. Sanity involves some order and discrimination, rather than a promiscuous acceptance of all our impulses as good. That is why true liberalism values not only deliberative reason but also a certain amount of self-control as necessary for the mastery of life. This emphasis on the element of self-restraint has given Spinoza the appearance of an other-worldly ascetic. But this is entirely a misunderstanding. The wise man, according to Spinoza, will "refresh and recreate himself with moderate and pleasant food and drink, with the sweet smells and attractions of growing plants, with ornamentation, music, games, plays, and other things of this kind, of which anyone can make use without doing harm to another." Enjoyment as the satisfaction of human desires is, indeed, the very essence of the human good. Only it requires wisdom to liberate ourselves from natural brutish stupidity and enslaving passions. It is due to an inadequate consideration of the problem of evil, of our irrational passions, that eighteenth-century liberalism fell into bankruptcy and was assigned to the materialists, who restricted human enjoyment to immediate sensuous possession. Though Spinoza as a consistent naturalist disbelieves in the actual existence of disembodied spirits (such belief is really cryptomaterialism), it never occurs to him to banish reason from nature. Reason as a natural energy not only widens but intensifies human enjoyment, in the very process of ordering and taming our natural impulses.

From this point of view, the supreme aim of the state—to promote real freedom—can be achieved only through such an ordering of things as will strengthen the process of reason as a habit.

Spinoza's preference for democracy, and his opposition to all dictatorship and militarism, are due to the connection which he sees between obedience to law and the general opportunity for deliberation and consent to the law. Of course it is true that the goodness or badness of a law is determined by its content, rather than by the fact that it was passed by many or by one. But in regard to the obedience based on consent, democracies are more favorably situated than governments in which the law is felt to be more alien. There may, doubtless, be a great deal of actual disobedience to law, even in a democracy. But where there is an opportunity for open discussion to bring to light men's grievances, and where attention to the interests of the multitude is politically imperative, there is less likelihood of the law's being upset by insurrection or other violent upheaval. Democracies are better able to change the law when there is a general demand for it.

If it is objected that democratic states like the Dutch Republic are not as permanent as autocratic states like Turkey, Spinoza answers that monarchies are in fact disguised aristocracies, where courtiers or even courtesans frequently exert the real power. An absolute ruler is thus frequently kept in ignorance of the true state of affairs; and in general the element of fear for his personal safety deprives him of the necessary calm and deliberative outlook. Arbitrary power may spread more fear or uncertainty among good citizens than among those disposed to violate or evade the decrees of the sovereign. In short, a despotic government based on fear or blind obedience is a state of slavery, and its wretchedness is not relieved by its permanence.

As inequality produces jealousy and discord, the peace of the state requires that invidious distinctions be avoided as far as possible. "It is certain that if equality of citizens be once laid aside, liberty perishes."

Political liberalism as opposed to absolutism shows itself in its attitude to the moral right of revolution. No state, of course, can allow itself to be defied or overthrown without violating its duty to maintain order. Yet as men cannot be ruled by fear alone, he who replaces an existing order by one generally felt to be better is a savior of his country. He should not, however, complain if he is punished when he fails in his attempt.

The opponents of religious liberalism have condemned

Spinoza for robbing mankind of its most precious possessions—faith in God, in freedom and in immortality.

It is true that Spinoza rejects the idea of an anthropomorphic God, who will respond to our flattering prayers, reward us for our unsuccessful efforts, and in general compensate us for the harshness of the natural order and the weaknesses of our reason. But such a conception of the deity is too much a product of human weakness to find support in any philosophy that has a vigorous sense for evidence. If, however, religion consists in humility (as a sense of infinite powers beyond our scope), charity or love (as a sense of the mystic potency in our fellow human beings), and spirituality (as a sense of the limitations of all that is merely material, actual or even attainable), then no one was more deeply religious than Spinoza.

It is true that Spinoza does not believe in the freedom of the will, in the sense of arbitrary or causeless volition. Such freedom would rob life of order and significant certainty. But Spinoza does believe in the possibility of attaining freedom from irrational passion, and in the conquest of our weaknesses by the very act of understanding them. True freedom or release from bondage is possible only by breaking the inner chains that prevent our turning to the vision of peace.

Finally, Spinoza has little regard for the immortality which means the postponement of certain human gratifications to a period beyond our natural life. He does, however, believe in the immortality which we achieve when we live in the eternal present or identify ourselves with those human values that the process of time can never adequately realize or destroy.

THREE GREAT JUDGES

1. OLIVER WENDELL HOLMES

IT IS NOT EASY for a grateful and admiring friend of Justice Holmes to write objectively about his character and achievements. The attempt at a dispassionate analysis of his career seems bound to leave out the vital spark, his unique and outstanding personality, and at best to reduce him to the level of the one who is writing about him. But his own insistence that we view critically what we love and reverence, and the example of his unfailing courage, shame hesitation before an unpromising task. After all, Holmes's work has been before the public for several generations, his *magnum opus* was published more than fifty years ago, and we are bound to ask: What is his permanent or historic significance?

Holmes's life was in many respects a most apt illustration of the Hellenic ideal of the great-souled man who is a child of *eudaimonia,* or good fortune. All the gifts seemed to be his and well used. He was born into the New England intellectual aristocracy in that Golden Day when it still combined the Puritan discipline of plain living and high thinking with wide cosmopolitan interests and contacts, and he was favored with a brain and a body that enabled him to do a prodigious amount of concentrated work day after day without lessening his amazing and ever-youthful buoyancy.

The substance of this essay appeared in *The New Republic,* Vol. 82, p. 206 (April 3, 1935).

The various phases of his life—the fact that he was the son of a famous father, that he was thrice seriously wounded in the Civil War, that he became one of the world's greatest legal scholars, that he was an eminent judge for fifty years, serving his country with distinction even after his ninetieth birthday, and that he continued to the end to express his challenging faith in pithy and heroic phrases—all served to impress the imagination of the American people and to arouse for him unprecedented admiration and reverence. And yet, the frustration that fate has in store for all human effort did not spare him. Despite his great éclat, despite the fact that no other man ever brought to the judicial office his legal learning and general intellectual or philosophic power, he did not in his own lifetime exert any highly effective influence on the law and life of our country.* Except in the matter of civil rights, he has not, like Marshall or Taney, changed the current of our constitutional law, nor for that matter left any permanent impress on any other branch of our law, as lesser men, like Story, did in admiralty or conflict of laws. Holmes was a lone, though a titanic, figure, and the currents of our national life have swept by and around him. He was, indeed, one of the last great representatives of the individualistic liberalism of John Stuart Mill, of the faith in intellectual freedom and tolerance to which the majority still pays some customary lip service but which a large number, on the right and on the left, at heart despise.

Though the statistician, misled by the fallacy of supposing all cases to be equally important, may object, the popular conception of Holmes as a great dissenter is substantially just. On the important issues of our time—on social legislation regulating the hours of work, the minimum wage, child labor, the issuing of injunctions, the open shop and the like, and especially on the right to express opinions hateful to the majority or hostile to the government—almost all his impressive opinions were in dissent. In relatively few cases of social importance did he express the

---

* This essay was written in 1935, before the considerable changes in the personnel and fundamental attitude of the Supreme Court. Since then Holmes's views on constitutional law have been pretty generally followed by the majority of the Court, and expressed with particular clarity by Justices Black and Douglas.

view of a liberal majority of the court. For the most part his opinions, like those of other judges, were concerned with routine cases; and in some of these, for example, on the question of the liability of a railroad for accidents to those who cross its tracks, he represented the economic individualism of a century ago in a manner that few of his liberal-minded admirers have cared to extol. We must remember that Holmes was reared in the tradition of aristocratic individualism. This showed itself in a certain aloofness and detachment, illustrated in the fact that he did not read the daily newspapers, and rather took pride in that fact! Yet on some social issues his insight was rather in advance of the economists and even of the "social workers" of his generation. Thus, he very early saw that the problem of workmen's compensation must be viewed not as a question of individual fault but rather as one concerning the total social cost of production, including that of insurance. Traditional pious phrases could not prevent his disciplined mind from seeing that the interests of workers and their employers were not altogether identical but involved genuine conflict as real as that between competitors in business, and entitled to as much recognition by the law. Indeed, he came to realize that all legislation must favor some class at the expense of others.

The reason for Justice Holmes's dissents was stated by him as early as 1897: "When socialism first began to be talked about, the comfortable classes of the community were a good deal frightened." This "led people who no longer hope to control the legislatures to look to the courts as expounders of the Constitutions, and in some courts new principles have been discovered outside the bodies of those instruments, which may be generalized into acceptance of the economic doctrines which prevailed about fifty years ago, and a wholesale prohibition of what a tribunal of lawyers does not think about right." [1] Judges, he told us on another occasion, are elderly men and are likely to hate at sight any analysis to which they are not accustomed and which disturbs repose of mind. It is this inability on the part of judges to rise above their traditional but partisan views that has made

[1] "The Path of the Law," in Collected Legal Papers (1921), pp. 167, 184.

22

of our courts whited sepulchers from which has emanated little light or healing for a distressed nation but asphyxiation for many generous hopes or plans to relieve those who suffer from economic depression.

Holmes's failure, despite his great prestige, to induce the leaders of the bench and the bar in his own generation to accept his social and nonpartisan view of the judicial function, or to make them see the unanswerable fact that when the people of the United States adopted the Fourteenth Amendment they could not possibly have intended to prohibit all the social legislation that courts have vetoed in its name,* may be explained by the very fact that he was essentially a thinker and had no inclination or genius for effective leadership. He was personally respected, but his rigor of thought was caviar to the general, and could not appeal to a profession that is engaged primarily in helping the country's business and is called learned only by traditional courtesy. We may, however, also see in his failure the limitation of the old liberalism that appealed to intelligence against organized group interests. For though, of course, judges as a rule sincerely and ardently desire to be impartial and just, they are generally chosen from the leaders of the bar who have spent years in defending the interests of property. Such experience only strengthens convictions absorbed in youth and increases the natural resistance to new ideas. But it is well not to generalize too hastily about social tendencies or to lose hope for liberalism prematurely. To measure enduring influence in the realm of thought we need a longer time-span than that required for immediate practical effects. There are indeed some indications that, among some of our younger teachers of law, Holmes's ideas are taking root and may well grow to bear much fruit. But that will largely depend on the possibility of the growth of a genuine scientific spirit in our law schools. This requires unusually favorable conditions that will allow detachment and freedom from external pressure, not the least of which is the pressure either to make the study of the law immediately "practical" or to accept the loose conceptions of science that make so much of our social

* Only very recently has the Supreme Court in a manner caught up with Holmes's views on the Fourteenth Amendment.

science pompous pretense, devoid of genuine insight or substance.

Holmes's major contributions were at first in the field of legal history. Here he clearly achieved permanent results of great value that can be put beside the work of the great German, French, and English masters. There are paragraphs in his *The Common Law* that contain more substantial contributions to the understanding of primitive man (who is always with or within us) than volumes of Frazer's uncritical anthropologic gossip. But that was practically finished more than half a century ago, and the number of workers in this country who have followed his footsteps and have tried to build on his results can be counted on the fingers of one hand.

Holmes never abandoned his interest in legal history. But his judicial duties after 1882 shifted the center of his preoccupation toward the general policies of the law. The study of legal history has often made for conservatism—witness Savigny and Maine. It is not easy to resist the illusion that what has been must remain. And Holmes was not subject to the contrary illusion that what has persisted for ages can be safely ignored or easily wiped out by a resolution. He could not overlook those features of human life that have persisted since classical antiquity or since the invasion of the barbarians. But he saw that change is inescapable and that the law must therefore be constantly adopting new premises from life, eliminating or sloughing off mere survivals from the past. For this reason he could not share the common fetishism of the Constitution as an inspired or final revelation for all time. Life is an experiment and a constant search, and a Constitution cannot and should not prevent social changes that lawyers may regard as inadvisable.

He saw very clearly that the grounds of social policy have to take a somewhat inarticulate form. For the apprehension of new elements requires a sensitive perception and familiarity with new details and cannot be deduced from established principles. But the way to guard against reading our personal and debatable opinions into the law is by logical and juridical techniques which make our premises explicit and subject them to critical analysis and scientific verification. The need of questioning first principles is especially urgent in view of the widespread habit of taking refuge in seemingly self-evident moral maxims as excuses for not analyzing the actual facts. For these maxims, being familiar, produce the illusion of clarity. This confusion of law and morality aroused Holmes's most vigorous intellectual protest, and he urged that the law must be washed in cynic acid to separate it from its moralistic veneer. Had he participated in the recent decision of the gold cases [2] he could certainly have vigorously dissented from that part of the majority opinion which, confusing the moral and the legal, declared that Congress had no moral right to curtail contractual obligation, even though to pay in full would have involved unjust enrichment of the bondholders and perhaps the financial ruin of the country. Holmes believed in going back behind pious phrases to the actualities of life.

For this reason it is most unfortunate that a dictum of his, that the life of the law is not logic but experience, has been taken out of its context to support anti-intellectualists and others who in the interest of impressionism and sentimentalism oppose rigorous thought. Holmes, as a follower of Hobbes, opposed the traditional view (which goes back to Coke) that the law is nothing but reason and that all the judge does is to deduce it logically from fixed principles. The law as a growing body can never attain complete consistency but it must constantly seek it to realize its function. It must not narrow its vision but it must grasp its material firmly.

In his later years Justice Holmes impressed a growing number of people as a thinker who was giving immortal expression to basic ideas on human life and destiny. He certainly was a philosopher in the literal sense of the word—i.e., he was a devoted lover of wisdom, of seeing things in their widest vistas under the aspect of eternity. But he did not care for philosophic technique and his expressions were oracular, like those of seers such as Emerson, rather than organized and coherent doctrines. This makes it possible for different people to pick out sentences or paragraphs to suit their diverse purposes, so that his utterances become orna-

[2] Norman v. Baltimore & O. R.R., 294 U.S. 240 (1935); Nortz v. United States, 294 U.S. 317 (1935); Perry v. United States, 294 U.S. 330 (1935).

ments of discourse rather than methods of organizing and developing our insights in a rigorously logical manner.

He admired in others flashes of insight, aperçus, rather than doctrines developed with full rigor. This explains, in part, his lack of influence on the legal profession as a whole. For the method of relying on flashes of insight is one that cannot be followed by most people, who are not so extraordinarily gifted but need the steady light of reason. His hero was Montesquieu, who, although full of extraordinary insights, still is somewhat deficient on strictly verifiable facts in the realms of history, the influence of climate, and even details of Roman law. Unlike his colleague Brandeis, whom he greatly admired and even revered, he did not have the patience to acquaint himself with the hard facts of current economic life. As a result, he uncritically accepted the old economic dogma of capitalism: that through everyone's seeking his individual profit the good of all will best be served. This is but a revised form of the old optimistic Leibnizian doctrine of a pre-established harmony, which has its roots in the still older theologic doctrine that God cannot be the author of anything that is not in the long run good. That he accepted this doctrine quite naively and uncritically is shown by the fact that he never took notice of the paradox, under the capitalist system, of people on the verge of starvation when there is a glut in the wheat market, and multitudes lacking adequate clothes when there is a surplus of cotton that cannot be disposed of except at a ruinous loss—all this at a time when people are most anxious to work hard to produce the goods of life.

Despite this lack of strictly logical organization, there is an unmistakable direction in Holmes's thought.

Holmes came to intellectual maturity at a time when the work of Lyell, Darwin, Huxley, and the higher critics of the Bible was shaking men's faith in the old New England or Calvinistic theology. He was in the habit of saying that probably no generation departed so much from the preceding one as his from that of his father. Holmes remained throughout his life essentially an agnostic. Nevertheless, in all essentials the Puritan tradition continued to dominate his mind. Instead of the glory of a personal God he substituted the "unimaginable whole" of reality, which served equally well to teach the great lesson of humility. To accomplish anything in a world that is bigger than ourselves we must accept our human limitations. The great act of faith is thus to recognize that we are not gods. No one who knew Holmes or reads any of his writings can fail to note the tremendous impression that his military experience in the Civil War left upon him. Yet I feel that his glorification of the soldier's faith, the acceptance of the duties of the station in which we find ourselves or of the tasks that our daily jobs offer us, goes back to his Calvinistic background, as shown by his frequent use of the concept of destiny. He not only accepts the task that Fate assigns to us but glories in unquestioning submission to the dictates of Fate.

Holmes's military phraseology is but a convenient dress for this attitude of submission. Now while submission to the inevitable is a brute necessity—there is no use in kicking against the pricks, according to St. Paul—Holmes's belief that effort is "one of the ways in which the inevitable comes to pass" is really inconsistent with unquestioning submission. For effort has no meaning if devoid of intelligent direction. Indeed, the glorification of unquestioning submission is indistinguishable from the slavish attitude. Holmes had a contempt for people who set themselves up against the gods. He might have learned something from the Biblical account of Jacob winning a blessing from a god through struggle—if not from the story of Prometheus bringing blessings to humanity by defying Zeus.

The characteristic quality of Holmes's thought came from the combination of robust skepticism with a subtle or mystic sense of that which has not yet been or perhaps cannot ever be adequately expressed. Though we shall never be omniscient like the gods, we can and must constantly learn. Holmes saw with amazing clarity both the emptiness of dogmatic principles and the myopic shallowness of those who evade the business of thought by burying their heads in the sands of isolated and therefore meaningless facts. Facts presented vistas for him and he was interested in the long perspectives that they offered. But he did not (except in the field of legal history) originate fruitful hypotheses around which facts can rationally group themselves.

THE FAITH OF A LIBERAL

Though he admired the abstract thinker, he did not himself delight in prolonged abstract thought. He was essentially a moralist of the Stoic or pagan kind, sustained by inner courage to face a world in which there were no guarantees of success and where one had to risk his life on his daily guesses. He frequently referred to his view as that of a "bet-a-bit-arian."

Holmes's failure to articulate his philosophy fully and rigorously, probably due to the cultivated man's aversion to the details of logical technique, is shown by the fact that though he recognized that labor and capital have divergent interests and that labor is entitled to as much protection by law as are competing businesses, nevertheless he joined the majority of the Court in condemning labor's resort to the boycott in the Danbury Hatters' Case. Indeed, his position in this and other cases such as the Northern Securities Case, in which he showed himself friendly to large concentrations of capital, has caused some publicists to regard him as illiberal if not a downright Tory. But the issue is not so simple, even if we take account of the fact that as men grow older they generally become more conservative, and that the Sons and Daughters of the Revolution are not apt to favor revolution in principle. It is difficult to believe in free competition in all realms and yet see the necessity for restricting ruinous competition in a special field, even if the ruin affects large numbers of working people. Besides the difficulty of drawing a sharp line between liberals and those who are not liberal—as if liberalism were a simple, definite trait applicable to all fields—there is the difficulty of restricting the application of general maxims, especially those that are accepted on authority, hallowed by long usage, and sanctified by pious phrases that it never occurs to us to question. Holmes recognized that general maxims do not decide particular cases in the absence of minor premises which express the particular circumstances of the case.

Holmes's youth was spent in an atmosphere in which the abolition of the Corn Laws, the rise of the commercial classes, and the development of unrestrained competition were almost universally accepted as great liberal achievements. He continued, from force of habit, to use old phrases that assume a pre-established harmony between the individual desire for profit and the good of the whole community.

Holmes's reputation as a liberal thus has to be corrected not only by a realization of the backwardness of his fundamental economic views, which he inherited from the classical economists, but even more by the fundamental illiberality of his race theories, which he got from his rather naïve acceptance of Malthus and the popular Darwinian account of the struggle for existence and the survival of the fittest.

Indeed, for a thoroughly civilized man, which Holmes was in the best sense of the word, he shows a remarkable absence of sympathy or compassion for the sufferings and frailties of mankind. His morality is thoroughly pagan or Stoic in that respect. His emphasis is on the pagan virtues of courage, temperance, and justice, without any reference to the Hebrew-Christian view of God the Father, who is compassionate in His love for all men and sends down the beneficent rain on the just and the unjust alike. He is thus too ready to invoke the penalty of death in his theory of justice, and can think of no better remedy for the abuse of ownership than that the crowd will kill the man guilty of abusing the goods which the multitude needs. There are doubtless untold dangers in sentimental weakness, but Holmes shows rare courage or wisdom (the two are identical according to Plato)—courage to face an uncertain world in which there are no guarantees for the success of our efforts, no matter how noble in intention.

All the possibilities of economic and social reform, of alternatives to unbridled economic individualism, remained a sealed book to Holmes. The narrow outlook which the assumptions of classical economics left him was never expanded by acquaintance with the actual facts of our economic disorder.

Holmes's scant sympathy for social reform shows itself in expressions of contempt which fall far below his usual high-mindedness.[3] He does not realize the havoc that economic distress produces in human life when parents are unable properly to feed their young ones or to provide them with the training

---

[3] Cf. his reference to the ideal of socialized property as "humbug," in "Ideals and Doubts," Collected Legal Papers, p. 306.

necessary to bring to fruition their potential gifts. It is tempting to ascribe this lack of sympathy to the fact that Holmes himself, brought up in cultured affluence, never felt the demoralizing effects of poverty. But I think the real explanation is to be found in his militaristic philosophy and in the influence of Malthus upon his thinking. He believed that the important thing is to build a strong race.[4] Like others who believe in nurturing a strong race, he never faced the question, "Who is the strong man?" Reflection makes it obvious that strength is relative to conditions. One might say that Eskimos are strong because they are capable of conquering a bitterly hostile environment; but put them in a warm climate and they die like flies. There is no absolute strength or absolute weakness. In the tasks which civilization presents, the endowments of civilization add strength to man—despite the fallacious view of Nietzsche, who tends to view privation as a source of strength and the resort to brute animality as a mark of power. Not in privation but in the wealth of resources that civilization provides us is the foundation of human strength.

Holmes thinks he has refuted the common man's dislike for the enormous fortunes of the rich. He dismisses it by saying that the real question is not who owns the wealth of the country, but how the product is consumed.[5] This is a superficial and narrowly materialistic view. If this seems a harsh judgment on a titanic figure, we may quote the address of Oceanus to Saturn:

> Great Saturn, thou
> Hast sifted well the atom-universe;
> But . . . thou art the King,
> And only blind from sheer supremacy.[6]

Holmes ignores altogether the multiple and far-reaching effects of ownership. Ownership involves not only consumption of goods, but also power over the lives of people who are under the necessity of acquiring the goods that others legally own—so that he who owns property also has a qualified sovereignty over

---

4 "Ideals and Doubts," in *Collected Legal Papers*, pp. 303, 306.
5 "Economic Elements," in *Collected Legal Papers*, p. 279.
6 Keats, *Hyperion*.

those who need these goods. The accumulation of property is therefore equivalent to a concentration of power or sovereignty over the lives of those who need the goods owned by others.[7] The aggrandizement of economic power which Holmes defends is thus ultimately incompatible with political democracy.

Yet in all justice it must be said that although Holmes did not have the economic knowledge, he did have the intellectual power and the true liberal attitude that enabled him to rise above his hereditary class prejudices. Having devoted the years of his early manhood to the study of the history of the law, he came to admit freely that the future belonged to the man of statistics and economics. Having become conscious of his own limitations, he refused to do what his colleagues were doing, namely, using the judicial office to veto legislation that did not conform to their own idea of economic policy.

Justice Holmes used to contrast the specialist with the civilized man. The former, I take it, is the one who puts his best energies into some special work (e.g., Meredith in his novels), and leaves the commonplace residue for the rest of his life. Such men are not the best material for biography. The civilized man, however, develops great works as an enrichment and integration of his life. He makes you feel that the art of living is worth while. To have known Holmes was to have had a revelation of the possibilities of such human personality. His conversation and bearing were like rare music that lingers in one's memory. One is fortunate to hear some reverberating echo of it. It is the function of the great biographer to catch such echoes, and from conversations, letters, and scattered writings reconstruct some idea of the original integrated life. I think men with genius for biography will be richly rewarded if they turn to the life of Justice Holmes.

7 I have tried to indicate this more fully in my book *Law and the Social Order*, at pp. 41-67.

2. LOUIS D. BRANDEIS

All writing and especially reviews or criticisms are more or less unavowed personal confessions of faith. Perhaps it is well that we should, in general, try to cover up the limitations of our individual opinions by a decent pretense at impersonal objectivity. Respect for virtues that we do not possess may stimulate our efforts at their partial acquisition. But the reviewer who is expected and tempted to sit in judgment on books dealing with controversial human issues should rather be encouraged to speak in the first person singular and thus remind the reader and himself that what follows is not free from the partiality and fallibility to which all flesh is heir.

For nearly thirty years I have regarded Mr. Justice Brandeis not only as a great and good man whose distinguished public services have been both illuminating and inspiring, but also as coming near to the ideal of what a great judge should be, namely, one who combines broad human sympathies with thorough knowledge of all the relevant factors of the case before him. For this reason the contributors to this volume, especially Professors Hamilton and Frankfurter, seem to me to have rendered an important public service in calling attention to Justice Brandeis's unique technical competence as a lawyer. Not only has he by dint of liberal experience and special research mastered the social and economic incidence of the great cases that make the work of the United States Supreme Court of fateful significance, but he has done his work with all due regard to the most meticulous requirements of the continuous tradition known as the common law. This is a matter of tremendous importance today. It is needed to annihilate what is

Published in *The Harvard Law Review*, Vol. 47, p. 165 (Nov. 1933), as a book review of *Mr. Justice Brandeis*, a collection of essays by Charles E. Hughes, Max Lerner, Felix Frankfurter, Donald R. Richberg, Henry Wolf Biklé, and Walton H. Hamilton, edited by Felix Frankfurter, with an introduction by Oliver Wendell Holmes.

left of the argument that the individualistic *laissez faire* philosophy, which has been so disastrously read into the Fifth and Fourteenth Amendments, represents the eternal principles of the common law and not merely the personal opinion of elderly judges not too well informed about the meaning of the actual industrial and economic situation.

However, those who share Professor Frankfurter's belief, that the safety of our democracy is endangered when our courts block the world's present needs by an unrealistic philosophy, must regret that some contributors to this volume have exaggerated and even defended Justice Brandeis's own inability to free himself from the old-fashioned philosophy of free competition associated in his mind with a general fear of bigness in other fields than industry and finance. Great men have the defects of their qualities, and the very strength of Justice Brandeis's mind in concentrating on the case before him is naturally associated with an absence of what is generally called "the philosophic mind," the gift of clearly grasping ultimate issues, so beautifully exemplified by Justice Holmes. Having been brought up on the Continental liberalism of 1848,* which was also the liberalism of Jeffersonian democracy, Justice Brandeis naturally speaks in its individualistic terms. But his devotion to it is, in fact, not consistent and thoroughgoing. He has on various occasions, and especially in his dissent in the Oklahoma Ice Case,[1] given beautiful illustrations of how his sensitiveness to the actual demands of the situation makes him ready to sacrifice the dogma of free enterprise or competition to the need of communal regulation. But though the absence of an adequately coherent formulation of fundamentals is not a defect in a judge who has to decide the specific cases before him, it is a limitation on one's ability to guide or to give illumination to others on the way out of the morass of the difficulties in which we are

---

* I.e., the liberalism that existed in Germany before Bismarck revolutionized German thought and feeling by his tremendous military and diplomatic successes, which united the German people, opened the way to the development of big industry, and resulted in substituting the worship of power and efficiency for the old German *Gemütlichkeit*.

[1] New State Ice Co. v. Liebmann, 285 U.S. 262 (1932), Brandeis, *J.*, dissenting at 280.

sunk. Certainly, when our traditional economy has admittedly broken down, and its repeated crises continue to grow more serious, we need either a more cogent defense of the traditional individualism or else a clearer statement of how that individualism can be reconciled with the imperative need of a socially planned economy.

The most extreme defender of the old dogma that democracy can be maintained only by independent competitors in small business and not by employees of large corporations is, curiously enough, Mr. Richberg, now counsel for the NRA (pp. 131-32). According to Mr. Richberg's essay on "The Industrial Liberalism of Mr. Justice Brandeis," the issue must be sharply drawn between those who protest against bigness and those who believe that "bigness is the product of an irresistible force which, if not misdirected, could be harnessed and wisely directed in the service of mankind" (p. 129). Mr. Richberg is aware of the fact that "bigness" is conquering; but since he does not stop to ask why, he has no plan whereby its progress can be halted. The obvious fact, of course, is that the increased size of our industrial enterprises is the result of such factors as modern machinery, the integration of all parts of our country into one market, and the accumulation of the savings of the many made available through banks and insurance companies to finance the bonds and preferred stock of concentrated enterprises. The hope, therefore, of a return to a Jeffersonian state of free competition among small producers is as Utopian or Quixotic as a restoration of medieval knighthood. Nor is it really desirable. In a country in which mutual interdependence is so great, the industrial anarchy or warfare called competition is as wasteful and out of place as dueling. Surely, no one can seriously propose today that our farmers or businessmen extricate themselves from their sad plight by increased competition, or that our railways improve their position by breaking up into smaller and competing units. Mr. Richberg himself grants that competition should be regulated, but he quotes with approval as "the reckless superlative of passion and faith," " 'the right to be let alone—the most comprehensive of rights and the right most valued by civilized man' " (p. 137). To which the obvious reply is that to be let alone, when in need of the co-operation and help of others, is the worst calamity that can happen to any individual in human society. The hope that the growing concentration of industry and finance may stop is based on what Mr. Richberg calls the "cheerful" view of the "already demonstrated incapacity of human beings to administer wisely their superhuman organization." But if human beings cannot administer such big industrial or financial enterprises as the United States Steel Corporation or the Chase National Bank, what hope is there that they can administer the much larger and more complicated affairs of a nation of over one hundred and twenty million people and of hundreds of billions of wealth?

Mr. Lerner's essay on "The Social Thought of Mr. Justice Brandeis" is, despite obvious enthusiasm, remarkably objective and skillful in bringing different views together. In the end, however, I find it essentially vague on what Mr. Lerner himself regards as the fundamental issue: where does Justice Brandeis stand between those who believe that the old order of capitalistic economy and jurisprudence can and should be maintained substantially intact, and those who believe that its demonstrated evils are not mere excrescences but are inherent in it and cannot be removed without radical transformation? Mr. Lerner rightly points out that Justice Brandeis has adhered to the American tradition of individualism based on production for profit, yet he also claims him as an opponent of economic individualism. How, if at all, Mr. Lerner thinks he can reconcile these two statements is not clear. On one occasion Mr. Lerner attempts to justify Justice Brandeis's refusal to accept the validity of the issue between individualism and collectivism. He does this by maintaining, like Theodore Roosevelt, that some collectivities, trusts, or trade unions are good and some are bad. Quite so! But as to the test by which we are to make this important distinction, we are left completely in the dark. Ethical epithets like "good" or "bad" come well after social analysis but are hardly substitutes for it. I venture to add that no social analysis is adequate which either in the interests of optimism or because of "the contempt of a free and flexible mind for ideology and dogma" ignores the reality of the class struggle between workers and their employers.

In regard to the judicial function under the Constitution, Mr. Lerner holds that our case system is anti-absolutist and yet that Marshall's dictum about interpreting the Constitution rules out economic radicalism—that is, divesting capitalists of further increments of power. Neither assertion seems to me necessary. Case law can be extremely absolutistic—witness the Adair Case,[2] the Adkins Case,[3] or Coppage v. Kansas.[4] And through the same power by which our federal system has been largely changed in favor of capitalism—by limiting the power of Congress and of the states to experiment in social legislation—other judges can introduce different changes. Munn v. Illinois [5] might well offer a starting point.

Professor Frankfurter's contribution [6] is a skillful summary of Justice Brandeis's general views on the political and economic issues which under our peculiar system become questions of constitutional law. Not the least service that Professor Frankfurter has rendered lies in the way in which he has interspersed his own statement with sufficiently large extracts from Justice Brandeis's own writing, so that instead of somebody else's abstract report, we see the original mind in action. The result is impressive and must draw the admiration of all generous minds. But those who are realistically inclined and want to know the meaning of a formula before accepting or rejecting it will find little light as to what Professor Frankfurter thinks is *the* Constitution. He says that it has "ample resources within itself to meet the changing needs of successive generations" (p. 53). Does he mean by this that by the process of interpretation the judges can make what they will of it? Or are the resources of the Constitution for change to be found only in the special lacunae and ambiguities to which he refers? In any case, Professor Frankfurter's optimism does not deal adequately with the facts that on important issues those who, like Justices Brandeis and

2 Adair v. United States, 208 U.S. 525 (1923).
3 Adkins v. Children's Hospital, 261 U.S. 525 (1923).
4 236 U.S. 113 (1915).
5 94 U.S. 113 (1877).
6 "Mr. Justice Brandeis and the Constitution."

Holmes, see the need of adapting the Constitution to changing social conditions have been in the minority, and that there is no assurance of any change in this respect coming from the judiciary itself. Despite Justice Holmes's clear protest, the United States Supreme Court *has* read Herbert Spencer's individualism into the due-process clauses of the Fifth and Fourteenth Amendments, and has blocked social legislation such as the minimum wage law and others which Justice Brandeis and Professor Frankfurter have regarded as essential to make our law serve the needs of our national life. There are many thoughtful people today who think that the attitude of our courts in favor of free individual enterprise against necessary social regulation has, in no small measure, contributed to our present economic breakdown in which the wage of labor has fallen so far below the minimum of subsistence that it is no longer economically possible to employ our labor reserves to produce the things that our people so badly need. Certainly, candid minds must recognize that the ideas back of the NRA run counter to the dogmas or principles which have dominated our constitutional law, and Professor Frankfurter gives us no reason in history or logic for sharing his light-hearted optimism that when the new demands of our changing economic life clash with the old dogmas, the latter will give way through the force of the Constitution itself.

If we hold adequate knowledge to be the only safe basis of human decision (as does Professor Frankfurter), the power of courts to declare laws unconstitutional must be deemed the weakest part of our constitutional system. For of all branches of the government the courts have the least opportunity to be fully informed of all that is involved in the cases before them. No one today who wants to be adequately informed on a subject of vital importance would depend upon two briefs submitted by lawyers and a few hours' argument. Justice Brandeis's habit of making independent researches is one of those exceptional instances which illumine the rule. Nor has Justice Brandeis been infallibly right on economic issues. The famous Brandeis brief in Muller v. Oregon [7] contained appeals to decidedly questionable authorities. And, in his stand on the value of efficiency

[7] 208 U.S. 412 (1918).

engineering, he was not only oversanguine but succumbed to the popular illusion of our prevailing economic philosophy—to wit, that the mere production of things, regardless of the human effects, is a good. Mr. Lerner is certainly mistaken in his statement that labor had to confess error in its opposition to the program of the efficiency engineers. On the contrary, the Hoxie Report justified the stand of the labor unions; and even the leaders of the Taylor Society now practically admit as much. Certainly, increased mechanical productivity has not solved the difficulties of technologic unemployment.

These criticisms of a book that is a labor of love and piety may seem ungracious and even carping. They come, however, from one who believes not only that Justice Brandeis is big enough to be the object of an admiration that is discriminating, but also that the liberal tradition of 1776 and 1848 which he so gloriously represents will be strengthened if divorced from the antiquated and *a priori* economic individualism which he sometimes professes. Liberalism is older than modern capitalistic economics. It has its roots in the Hellenic spirit of free critical inquiry which laid the foundations of the sciences on which modern civilization rests. Only fanatical ignorance can deny the services of liberalism to all classes of people. It banished the Inquisition, persecution for heresy and witchcraft, and all kinds of cruelties which made life horrible. Even economically, while it has emphasized differences of wealth, it has brought to the meanest peasant and tenement dweller comforts which formerly monarchs could not enjoy. Why then has liberalism been steadily losing ground? Why are its characteristic institutions—representative government, toleration of religious and political differences, free thought and free discussion—so successfully attacked today from the right and from the left? The answer is to be found in the way liberals have clung to the economics of free competition, to the dogma of a pre-established harmony such that if everyone seeks individual profit the greatest good of all will be assured. This dogma was useful in destroying the older abuses of crown-granted privileges and monopolies. It satisfied, in a way, the needs of a predominantly agricultural people as in the United States during the nineteenth century. But it has led to unconscionable exploitation of men, women, and children in industry; and the opposition of liberals since Bright to needed factory legislation has alienated the laboring classes and strengthened the Tories in industrial countries like England and Germany. Thoughtful people today can no longer hope for salvation through economic warfare and anarchy. There is a general consensus that some social plan of production for the needs of a community, rather than for individual profit, is necessary if the routine of civilized life is to continue. The real question is: Shall the planning be done by some irresponsible dictatorship or by democratic representatives whose acts are subject to discussion and criticism?

This is the question which we must face if we are to stop the flood of fanaticism and barbarism which is already sweeping over parts of the world formerly cradles of enlightenment. And it is the supreme service of Justice Brandeis that he has unfalteringly held to the old ideal of liberal democracy, enlightenment, toleration, and respect for civil rights in which all that is valuable in civilized life is centered and for which we must fight valiantly today if we are not to lose the benefits that we have inherited from the liberal tradition.

Throughout his career Justic Brandeis has had something of the air of the Hebrew prophet about him, and many have had the impression that he is not very merciful or sympathetic to sinners or enemies of the law, in which category so many of us human beings occasionally fall. It is therefore well to learn from Justice Holmes that with the austerity that comes from high-mindedness there goes the gift of raising hope and inspiring strength. "In the moments of discouragement that we all pass through, he always has had the happy word that lifts up one's heart. It came from knowledge, experience, courage, and the high way in which he always has taken life." [8]

[8] Introduction by Justice Holmes, p. ix.

3. BENJAMIN NATHAN CARDOZO

A man's philosophy, his view of life, grows out of his own experience at the same time that it reveals his work.

Perhaps the most significant fact about Justice Cardozo's career is the way in which he achieved the almost unanimous reverence and affection of the whole nation. Extreme conservatives as well as the most advanced liberals urged his appointment to the Supreme Court for the vacancy occasioned by the retirement of Justice Holmes. Surely it is significant to ask how Benjamin Cardozo came to have this hold upon our thoughts and our imaginations. And it is heartening to reflect that there is only one explanation possible, and that is in terms of the sheer merit of his service to society. Benjamin Cardozo had no political connections or group pressure to back him. He had risen by sheer individual merit to the highest position in the judicial system of the Empire State and had set an example of what a great judge can do, not only in rendering justice in the individual cases before him, but in inspiring the bench and bar to a greater and more humane conception of their obligation to the community which they serve. He was not merely the chief judge of New York State; he was also the intellectual and spiritual leader of its whole legal profession.

What was it that made it possible for him to achieve this? We know of the great charm of his personality, his essential sympathy and kindliness, indeed his courtliness in the finest sense. We know, too, of his great learning and charm of cultivated expression. But behind all this and vivifying it was his humane outlook on life.

It is significant that Justice Cardozo was one of the few of our judges who, like the late Justice Holmes, thought it important to *have* a philosophy. In the forefront of humanity's most cherished heroes, among prophets, saints, philosophers, scientists,

Published, in major part, in *National Lawyers Guild Quarterly*, Vol. 1, p. 283 (September 1938).

poets, artists and inspiring national leaders, the number of lawyers does not loom large. Mankind as a whole cannot well live by bread alone, but needs sustaining and directing vision. It is hard for lawyers, bent on the affairs of the market place, to look up and see the heavens above, or to grasp entire the scheme of things in which they move. This is especially difficult in a country or epoch which, under the leadership of captains of industry and finance, worships a narrow practicality and acts as if theory could be safely ignored, if not despised. It requires, therefore, a high order of intellectual and moral energy for one who has been immersed almost all his life in the business of the law to avow and pursue an interest in its general backgrounds and ultimate outcome, following the maxim of the old Talmudic sages that he who would deal justly with the law must contemplate the eternal issues of life and death. It is because Cardozo tried to do this that he became not only a great judge, rendering justice in the individual cases before him, but also a highly beloved national figure, inspiring bench and bar to a higher and more humane conception of their duty to the community which they should serve.

The main features of Cardozo's philosophy, like those of any sound philosophy, are essentially simple, though it needs genius and energy to trace their implications and to carry them out consistently.

The first point is that law is not an isolated technique, of interest only to lawyers and to litigants, but that it is an essential part of the process of adjusting human relations in organized society.

The second point is that the law of a growing society cannot all be contained in established precedents or any written documents, important as are continuity with the past and loyalty to the recorded will of the people. In the law as a social process, the judges play a determining role, having the sovereign power of choice in their decisions. It was in this emphasis on the judicial process as selective and creative that Cardozo's thought centered.

The third point, the logical corollary to the foregoing, is that to meet his responsibility for making the law serve human needs the judge cannot rely on legal authorities alone, but must know

41

the actual facts of the life about him, the psychologic and economic factors that determine its manifestations, and must thus keep abreast of the best available knowledge which those engaged in various social studies, researches, or investigations can supply.

These three propositions are perhaps obvious, and they may even be said to have their roots in the old liberal faith which the founders of our Republic—men like Franklin, Jefferson and James Wilson—held with fervor. But it requires vision and heroic courage to maintain these views today against the inertia and passionate errors embodied in prevalent attitudes.

To the great majority of people, law is a special technique. It is something exclusively for lawyers and their clients. I remember a class in which a student complained that he didn't see the justice of a decision in a given case. The professor replied, "This is a class in law, not in justice." Now there is of course some measure of truth in this reply. It is unfortunately true that many laws are unjust and are none the less part of our law, to be observed and analyzed. But from the historic and moral point of view this is surely not the final answer. The law arises to meet social needs and can maintain itself in the long run only if it serves those needs both justly and to the general satisfaction of the community.

There have been great judges who have clearly understood and courageously served the just needs of society without impressing their views on their fellow judges, or often persuading losing counsel of the correctness of an adverse decision, or satisfying more than a bare majority of the community whose disputes they have decided. And it is even easier for a judge to satisfy prevailing public desires without embodying in his work the qualities of righteousness which will commend it to men of other times and places. It was the peculiar genius of Cardozo that he was able to achieve to a pre-eminent degree the combination of two great gifts. He pursued righteousness without being aloof or Olympian or zealously partisan towards the controversies of his day. And at the same time, without ever subordinating his high ideals to the pressing demands of popular opinion, he was able to give a sensitive ear and eloquent tongue to the percep-

tion and expression of the conflicting interests in almost every
case that came before him, so that few losing lawyers ever left
his court without feeling that their cause had been accorded a
fair and sympathetic hearing. Characteristic of Justice Cardozo's
penetrating and engaging sympathy was his remark to losing
counsel in a bitterly argued case—quoting the words of a judge
of the Confederacy: "Many a good cause has been gallantly
lost." The sensitivity and humility which made Justice Cardozo
so anxious to satisfy all the conflicting social interests represented in any given case made it possible for a gifted intellect
to formulate judicial decisions acceptable to all parties in an
extraordinary number of cases. Only thus, I think, can we explain the fact that the New York bar, consisting of lawyers who
had, in the main, lost as many cases as they had won before him,
loved and revered Judge Cardozo with so rare a unanimity.

It was this same conciliatory sympathy and catholic understanding that made it so difficult for Justice Cardozo's colleagues
on the bench to disagree with him or to fail to accord his views
the deepest respect on the rare occasions when they did disagree.
Thus he was able to influence the bench and bar to a far greater
degree than more brilliant or learned colleagues on the Supreme
Court. That the public at large appreciated the genuine liberality of Cardozo's mind is shown by the fact that no man was found
to object to his appointment to the supreme tribunal of the
nation.

The prevailing orthodoxy expressed some years ago by the
late Senator Root and still passing as authoritative insists that
the duty of the judge is simply to read and obey the statute or
the Constitution and that it is no part of his business to make or
change the law in any way. This assumes that the framers of a
law or constitution can foresee all possible future contingencies
and make definite provisions for meeting them, so that the judge
can be merely a logical automaton, a sort of phonograph repeating exactly what the law had definitely declared. But this is a
childish view which no student of law can maintain. The whole
common law has grown out of judicial decisions, and in our
constitutional law the meaning of such phrases as "due process,"

"equal protection of the laws," "interstate commerce," and the like is precisely that which the courts have assigned to them.

The fundamental fallacy in the "phonograph theory" of the judicial functions, against which Justice Cardozo's entire career was an eloquent protest, is the illogical view that general principles alone can determine individual decisions. Modern logic and modern science alike demonstrate the untenability of this conception. Established legal principles may supply guiding analogies, but the decision of any individual case depends on an understanding of the actual social conditions, and of the consequences of the decision, as well as on the judge's view as to which of these consequences are best or most important. Elevation to the bench does not make a man omniscient, and the obvious fiction that courts decide only points of law prevents us from giving them adequate facilities for investigation into the relevant facts of the case, and into the larger social consequences of their decisions. In our anxiety to make judges independent of the popular will we are making them independent of the knowledge necessary to make their work satisfactory.

The consequence of judicial recognition that the judges make law is the responsibility of making it in accordance with existing conditions. Now, for judges who are intelligent enough to recognize the inadequacy of their own training in economic and social studies, it is easy to take refuge in the thought, "We are judges of the law and have nothing to do with economic or social theories." But the refuge is illusory. Those who are not aware of theory assume as facts the theories of an older generation.

A great lawyer preparing a brief in the Consolidated Gas Case told his clerks not to quote any economists later than John Stuart Mill—the judges wouldn't have heard of them. The philosophy of Cardozo makes this position impossible. Not only is law connected with other phases of human life, but human life is changing and the content of certain abstract principles must change. The principles of economics formulated two generations ago can no longer be relied on today. They must be corrected by the best available knowledge. Absolute finality is not to be found in human affairs.

It was Justice Cardozo's essential humility which made it possible for him to recognize what many of his brethren on the bench found it intolerable to admit: that he as a judge had to rely not only on past judicial decisions but on developments in the various fields of social study. He was indeed criticized for quoting nonlegal authorities in some of his judicial opinions. But the sharp distinction between legal and nonlegal authorities is an arbitrary one which no serious philosophy of law can well maintain. History celebrates the occasion when thought is wedded to fact. That is the philosophy which has made modern science so fruitful in the field of technology, and that is the philosophy which makes possible the progress of the spirit and the life of society.

Cardozo's personal career is a tribute to the fact that the United States is still a country which offers opportunity for the development of a human vision that is not restricted to any one race or creed. The validity of this liberal ideal his life illustrates and his philosophy of law illumines. At a time when there is real danger of our reverting to the medieval or barbaric view that men are to be judged entirely by their tribal descent or by their conformity to a prevailing orthodoxy, we may all be justly proud that our country is still wise enough to take advantage of the highest service which human beings can render, by recognizing and giving opportunity to merit. But the career of Cardozo suggests that this pride is not enough, and that there rests upon us the obligation to preserve this heritage at a time when liberal ideals are ignored in practice and assailed in theory. We shall be conscious of this precious responsibility so long as we hold in our national memory the lives and teachings of America's great spiritual leaders, of whom Benjamin Nathan Cardozo is not the least.

4

EINSTEIN AND HIS WORLD

IT IS NATURAL for us to be interested in the views of great men on issues outside of the field in which they have achieved their distinction—in what Shakespeare, for instance, thought about Catholicism and Protestantism, or in what Goethe thought about the freedom of the press and the future of the working classes. Yet the example of the incomparable Newton, as well as of contemporaries like Millikan and Eddington, should warn us against assuming that those who achieve great things in physical science will necessarily display unusual wisdom in politics and religion. It is not merely that devotion to science leaves men little time to acquire comparable knowledge on these more complicated subjects. When Harvey suggested that Newton pay less attention to his theosophic and theologic speculations, the latter proudly rebuked him: "Sir, I have given these subjects prolonged study." But the result of this study, as seen in Newton's commentary on the Book of Daniel and on the Apocalypse, is a striking indication of how highly specialized is human genius.

The foregoing reflections should not lead us to deny or to diminish the inherent value of the book before us, which in fact contains a number of truly noble expressions of human feeling seasoned with shrewd wisdom. But the importance of the subjects discussed requires us to be especially on guard to judge the issues on their own merits. It is fair also to remember

Published in *The Menorah Journal,* Vol. 24, p. 107 (Spring 1936), as a review of Albert Einstein, *The World As I See It.*

that this volume was not prepared by Einstein himself as a reasoned exposition of his views. What we have before us is a collection of occasional writings of varied length and importance, some clearly not intended for publication. They have been gathered together by loving hands anxious to show us the man Einstein rather than the scientist. It is a pity that the editor was not always in a position to give us the dates or occasions of the various pieces. It would have made their content somewhat clearer. Be that as it may, the book is before the public as Einstein's and the views expressed therein deserve critical consideration for their own sake.

Despite the great variety of topics, the book is not devoid of all unity. Its unity is to be found in the way it reflects the intellectual temper of the author—a temper that may be characterized as idealistic in the currently accepted meaning of the term. Perhaps this is what we should expect of one who has devoted his life mainly to theoretic rather than experimental physics.

In the scientific section, we find popular expositions of the Flettner (Rotor) ship, of the meanderings of rivers, and, as may be expected, of the theory of relativity. The layman, however, must not expect to find the latter easier reading than Einstein's remarkable semipopular book on the subject. Only one who has sufficient mathematics to know what is meant by "the co-variance of equations in relation to Lorentz's transformation," and enough of the absolute calculus of Ricci and Levi-Civita to understand the (misprinted) formula on page 95, can really follow the exposition.

But the value of this section of the book lies not in any contribution to physics but rather in the glimpse which it offers us into Einstein's philosophy of science—a topic on which scientists are apt to follow nonscientific philosophers like Bacon and Mill, or at any rate to disagree as much as other philosophers do: witness the writings of Poincaré, Mach, and Planck. Einstein himself realizes this and wisely urges: "If you want to find out anything from the theoretical physicists about the methods they use—don't listen to their words, fix your attention on their deeds" (p. 30). Nor need this surprise us if we remember the specialization of human genius and that philosophers and scientists differ not only in their main interests but also in their tools. For while philosophers are interested in any specific field only for its contribution to a view of the world as a totality, for the scientist an integrated world view is at best only a driving force for the extension of accurate and demonstrative knowledge. The philosopher thus depends in the main on general conceptual analysis while the scientist must use more rigorous methods. Hence when physicists leave their mathematical equations and experimental operations they are apt to use concepts in the rather loose way that characterizes common discourse. Thus the technical philosopher can well object that Einstein has not developed a clear idea of causality to make good his distinction between physics and kinematics or theory of motion. The differential equations of modern physics, after all, only describe motion from point to point and do not involve causal reference any more than do integral equations.

The substance of philosophy, however, is in its main vision. And this Einstein gives us in his account of the ideas to which he held fast in working out the theory of relativity and in his illuminating sketch of the way in which Kepler arrived at the laws of planetary motion. This ought to be read by all those who think they are enlightened when they repeat Mill's foolish statement about Kepler's laws naturally following from Tycho Brahe's tables. Without abating an iota from the recognition that the laws or general assertions of science must be experimentally verifiable, Einstein rightly insists that science has not actually been built up by the process of induction or empirical generalization, which plays a necessary but subordinate role and often comes to a dead stop. Real progress, he insists, comes when one fortunately hits on some great unifying idea from which one can deduce consequences that can ultimately be brought into agreement (through elaborate mathematical processes) with observed and measurable phenomena.[1]

In the main Einstein stays in the Platonic tradition of Kepler,

[1] The statement on p. 48 that Kepler's laws were deduced from Tycho Brahe's observations is a slip into the loose popular language which fails to distinguish between deduction and abstraction. Einstein clearly recognizes that from no number of particular observations can we deduce a law, and

Galileo, and Newton: that "nature is the realization of the simplest conceivable mathematical ideas." As a follower of Mach, however, he is inclined at times to give a subjective interpretation to mathematical-physical theories and to refer to them as fictions. But how does it happen that these fictions turn out to be such powerful clues to the nature of the physical world? The reference to a pre-established harmony can hardly be taken as an explanation. There is, however, no mystery in the case if we regard physical axioms or principles as hypotheses (in plain language, guesses) concerning the nature of things, and mathematics as an accurate analysis of what is contained or involved in these hypotheses. If our guess happens to be true, its mathematical consequences will be in agreement with experience; if not, our mathematics will sooner or later show that our guess is not compatible with the world of empirical existence. Assuredly the mind is active or creative in the construction of physical theory, but when this construction is properly conducted it is found to be a process of exploration and discovery.

That there is an independent reality, which the physicist seeks to discover and understand rather than to create, is indeed the essence not only of Einstein's theory of science but of his theory of religion as well. While fully realizing the value of science as an aid in advancing the practical interests of the community, and also as a natural field of human activity wherein some can best exercise their intellectual energies, Einstein insists that the temple of science did not originate in the utilitarian way, and that it could not continue to exist if it were not for those to whom science has a religious value. It is a way of salvation, i.e., an escape from the life of purely personal concerns into a world of objective reality, revealed to thought as a vision—even if but a fragmentary glimpse—of the world as a whole. For though the rigorously accurate methods of physics enable us to grasp only a small and thin part of the cosmos, still, since all that truly exists contains physical elements, the physicist can feel that he

that the number of possible laws from which the actual observations can be deduced is theoretically endless. If we pick out any one of these laws in preference to others, it is on the ground of simplicity as well as compatibility with other known laws.

has some grasp of the totality, which grasp the progress of science can and does enlarge.

It is instructive to reflect on Einstein's position in the history of science. Hailed at first as a great revolutionary who overthrew the classical Newtonian system, we now see him rather as at heart a staunch representative of the classic tradition of the unity of nature—so poignantly expressed by Spinoza and Kant—trying, by introducing certain needed changes in the Newtonian system, to defend it against the purely statistical or probabilistic view which the younger revolutionaries are advancing.[2]

Now we may, as I for one do, share Einstein's conviction or faith that behind all the statistical variations there are ultimate invariant relations, and yet feel more of the difficulties in the way of our *ever* attaining a systematic account of nature in terms of simple laws. Nature, according to Fresnel, does not care about our mathematical difficulties; and one may well suspect that it contains a good deal of brute irrationality or lack of intelligible order. At any rate our descriptions of nature always have contained and probably always will contain an arbitrary element determined by human history rather than by the object studied.

This suggests certain reflections on a fundamental assumption of the theory of relativity. That theory is motivated by the idea that our system of co-ordinates is an arbitrary aid in our description, and that there is no reason for favoring the "inertial" system of co-ordinates over any other. This is part of the mathematical view of physics—that nature may be truly described from many points of view and that her true laws must be something common or invariant in all true descriptions. But we are in fact creatures of history, situated in a particular place and time; and *for us* all possible descriptions are not equally simple. Thus it is theoretically possible for one confined for life in a railroad car to take a set of co-ordinates fixed in his car, make true observations, and formulate true laws of nature to explain them. But

2 Indeed, followers of Mach may protest that Einstein goes back on the principle of relativity when he agrees with Newton that water in a rotating bucket revolves relative to space rather than with respect to axes fixed in the earth. This, however, ignores the fact that Einstein's "space" is a physical concept quite different from Newton's.

the task would be inhumanly complex. Indeed, according to general relativity, there is nothing inherently wrong about a Ptolemaic or geocentric description of nature; yet history shows that our modern physics could be formulated to include astronomy only when we learned to take our center of co-ordinates in the sun. Some sets of co-ordinates, then, are privileged because they give what are *for us* (creatures of time and place) the simplest expression of the laws of nature. The test of simplicity is itself conditioned by our inescapable human limitation.

Unduly monistic and rather *a priori* is the attempt to banish all "action at a distance." Contrary to Einstein's statement, common experience is quite familiar with action at a distance and finds the attraction of the magnet no more inconceivable than the attraction that food and other objects have for organic bodies. It is speculative science that tries to explain such phenomena by an intervening medium. Helpful though such efforts have often been, it is of importance to remember that Galileo and Newton were able to establish the foundations of scientific dynamics by deliberately turning their backs upon such speculations, and that the effort to do away entirely with empty space has failed from the days of Descartes to our own. Nor are the classic contradictions in the theory of the æther altogether eliminated in the modern theory of the "field" of an electron that is both a particle and a wave. We doubtless owe a great deal of advancement to this theory; but that it is a final and satisfactory expression of the nature of things seems unlikely. We have pushed back our difficulties, but we have not entirely got rid of them. In the general Scholium to his *Principia* Newton definitely refers to his own hypothesis of the æther, and his famous phrase *"hypotheses non fingo"* expresses his scientific self-restraint and rectitude, that such hypotheses have no place in experimental philosophy. This points to a limitation of experimental philosophy, though we have nothing better.

Einstein's identification of religion with cosmic emotion makes of it a highly individual, rather than a social, affair. On this point he makes several notable statements of ancient but ever fresh wisdom. The life of morality and devotion to the

interests of others, of our family, of our country, or of humanity at large, cannot exhaust the interests of a sensitive soul. We
have a cosmic consciousness in which we feel alone and yet at
one with something bigger than the whole human race. But
while this is undoubtedly a genuine experience, heroically expressed by Spinoza, and an element of which many religious
persons have shown themselves highly conscious, it seems to
fly in the face of history to call this the essence of religion. It
does not seem that those generally regarded as representative
of supreme religious genius, e.g., Moses, Isaiah, Jesus, Mohammed, and Buddha, attached very high importance to such cosmic emotion. For mankind as a whole all religions have been
inseparably intertwined with the anthropomorphic view of the
Deity as a father, friend, or potentate to whom men must do
service, pray, etc. Whoever, then, says that religious genius
"knows no dogma and no God conceived in man's image" (p.
264) says something that is historically not true in the commonly
accepted meaning of the words. He may well feel that the views
and experience of heretics like Spinoza have superior value.
But the dignity and value of such experience of cosmic emotion
does not depend on its being called religious. It seems to have
been felt by those who, like Lucretius and Shelley, frankly
called themselves, and were called by others, irreligious. The
current fashion of attaching an honorific value to the word
"religion" has caused it to be stretched so that it has no longer
any definite meaning.

Einstein's views on public issues, on pacifism, on the present
state of Europe and America, and on the present economic crisis,
are full of sound and penetrating insights. He foretold that if
France continued to arm, Germany could not be prevented
from sooner or later doing likewise. Einstein's pacifism is a
robust aggressive program. Yet when applied to the actual intolerable situation it does not seem to show a practical way out.
If we live on the borders of Germany today, what are we to do
in the face of the threat of German invasion? Shall we disarm
and thus invite German domination? At the time when Hitler
was crushing all resistance to his military dictatorship, Einstein
was reported to have said that if he were a Belgian he would

arm. Whether this be true or not, the practical question—what the Belgians are to do in the face of danger—is not adequately answered by any of Einstein's pacifist reflections in this book.

Like other opponents of military imperialism, Einstein is inclined to look upon the smaller European nations as on the right path. It is not cynicism but sober history which suggests that their present attitude is in part at least due to the fact that the path of military aggrandizement is no longer open to them. The records of Sweden, Holland, and Portugal are significant in this respect. In general it is important to remember that intolerance is not restricted to majorities (p. 160)—that minorities, when they get into power, do not hesitate to oppress others, as the history of Poles, Ukrainians, and others amply testifies.

Einstein is clearly aware that the present economic crisis is due to our system of production for profit rather than for use, to the fact that our tremendous increase of productive power is not actually followed by a corresponding increase in the purchasing power of the great masses of the people engaged in the production. But how are we to get rid of the regime of private profit when its traditions are hallowed by public morality, and when the press, our educational institutions, our courts, and the leaders of our public life are bent on defending the established system? Here again Einstein is the generous idealist in whose consciousness certain brute realities are not sufficiently emphatic.

A considerable part of this collection is devoted to Einstein's view of Judaism. The first point to note is that Einstein's knowledge of Jewish history, traditions, and background is very limited. According to his own testimony (p. 166), it was only when he returned to Germany in 1914 that he discovered for the first time that he was a Jew. His interest seems to have been aroused not only by his indignation at the horribly unjust discrimination against his people but also by his courageous sympathy with East-European Jews who, during the war and the post-war period, flocked to Germany, craving the assistance—alas, often in vain—of their fellow Jews. If at times he approaches the nationalist ideology of the Zionists, it is because he is repelled by those who lack self-respect and are ashamed of being Jews. In his heart he has not abandoned the classical liberal cosmopolitanism so nobly typified by Lessing, which regards civilization as dependent on our ability to overcome national and class egotism and to renounce the unlimited right of national self-determination.

As a scientist and as a humanist, Einstein naturally regards nationalism as a concession to a sad necessity. "If we did not have to live among intolerant people I should be the first to throw over all nationalism." Still, a certain chivalric devotion to his own oppressed people leads him to make assertions which empirical history does not justify—e.g., that the Jews are the oldest of living peoples. Also, when one says that love of knowledge for its own sake is a characteristic of the Jews, the obvious comment is that this is true of the Jews under certain conditions, just as it is eminently true of the Greeks; but it was certainly not true of the Jews generally in Old Testament and Talmudic times. Nor is it characteristic of all Jewish communities today. It is important to remember that the Jews are a widely scattered people and that we should not create them all in our own image.

These points are in themselves of minor significance; but when we come to deal with an historical question such as the Jewish tradition, we surely ought to exercise care.

The essence of the Jewish tradition, according to Einstein, is that it is "an affirmative attitude to the life of all creation" (p. 144). But not only may this be claimed to an equal or greater extent for the Hellenic and derivative European traditions, but any student of Jewish history can at once quote a long series of influential teachers of Israel, from the *Pirke Aboth* to our own day, to the effect that Judaism regards this world as but a corridor to the hereafter. Though the credal element naturally plays a lesser role in a nationalistic religion like Judaism, it is not true to say that it has no creed. (*Cf.* Schechter's *Aspects of Rabbinic Theology*, and especially the sixth essay in the first volume of his *Studies in Judaism*.) I do not understand why thoughtful people should regard the absence of a creed as a virtue in religion. How can people possibly unite in an intelligent way in any common enterprise unless they have some common belief?

One can readily challenge Einstein's repetition of the oft-quoted remark that in prophetic Judaism, and in the Christianity of Jesus purged of all subsequent teachings, we have something "capable of curing all the social ills of humanity" (p. 170). It seems to me obvious that, if this were true, humanity's ills would have been cured long ago. For these teachings and exhortations to follow them have been before us for some two thousand years. It has not been shown how Jesus' command to love our enemies, or the prophets' exhortation to feed the widow and the orphan, can solve our modern economic and international relations.

We may, in passing, also challenge the assertion of the "enviable spiritual equilibrium" of the German Jews before the Enlightenment (p. 155). Those who have actually lived under similar conditions do not want to return to them. It is tempting to put the Golden Age into the past, but sober history shows that every age regards its own troubles as the most serious. It would certainly be most unfortunate if the dicta of a man as enlightened as Einstein were used as an argument for a return to the spiritual ghetto of the days before Lessing and Mendelssohn. That is certainly not his intention. But in these days of adversity we must be on our guard against anything that would counsel despair in the process of enlightenment.

The foregoing may seem rather ungracious comments on the expression of faith of a truly noble spirit, detached, singularly free from worldliness, and yet ardently and with courageous intelligence devoted to human welfare. But it is precisely because I am heartily in sympathy with the essence of his liberal faith, and am convinced that there is no salvation in rejecting it, that I feel it is of the utmost importance for us to look carefully and realistically at the limitations of the old liberalism, as well as at the dangers in the romantic reaction against it which is at the heart of contemporary irrationalisms in politics, economics, religion, and general philosophy.

Einstein's great genius in science is well characterized by his tribute to Bohr: "His eye is immovably fixed on the underlying

principle" (p. 68). And while dealing with principles is futile unless one can master all the relevant details, there is a difference
in this respect between physical science and the interpretation of
social phenomena. In physical science we do not need to understand things in all their complex ramifications. When we are
interested in a certain defined phase of physical phenomena, we
can ignore everything else as irrelevant. That is why men of
genius in mathematics and theoretic physics seldom have a developed sense of history. Einstein is essentially a man who is at
his best in dealing with general fundamental problems, and
getting at the essence irrespective of what others have thought
about it. Like so many of the very young men who have revolutionized physics in our day, he has not been embarrassed by too
much learning about the past, or by what the Germans call the
literature of the subject.

But when we come to deal with social phenomena, not only
does the number of factors relevant to any inquiry become very
much larger, but we are seldom satisfied to understand merely
one abstract phase. We wish to change the total reality and
make it nearer to our hearts' desire, and to do this we need a
knowledge of all the relevant factors, past and future. History
is too fragmentary and contains too many irrelevancies to solve
our problems; but it contains, when pursued in a liberal spirit,
sufficient warning against hasty enterprises and partial solutions.

Doubtless, men of enterprise must to a certain extent be ruthless to those human habits which are the outcome of the past
and hinder a better future. Indeed, heroic leaders and great
religious teachers move mankind by their very partiality, by
their tremendous emphasis on some phase of human experience
to the complete ignoring of all other phases of life. But, in the
end, the faith which is to be effective must be organized in
some church, state, or social institution which, while it cramps
the faith of the founder, also provides the only way by which
it may be in part conserved.

Einstein's faith has the stirring and driving quality of all
truly spiritual leaders who are in the world but not of it. It
needs to be supplemented by a more realistic vision of the brute
actualities of our existence.

III

THE SUBSTANCE OF LIBERALISM

5

THE INTELLECTUAL BASIS
OF INDIVIDUALISM

IT IS, I think, unfortunate that critics of the modern doctrine of individualism have paid so little attention to its intellectual origins.

To the historian of ideas, the modern doctrine of individualism is the product of three great intellectual movements: the Reformation, modern philosophy (including psychology), and modern economic theory.

(1) *The Reformation.* On its material side the Protestant Reformation in England, France, and Germany was predominantly a movement on the part of the commercial interests who, with the national monarchs, fought against the Church, which as an international power sided against national kings and as a landed power fought with the landed nobles against the commercial interests. As to the religious content, the Protestants believed, first of all, in salvation by faith rather than by the instrumentality of the sacraments of the church. The church is conceived as the body of the faithful, the individual believers, rather than the hierarchy. Each individual soul comes into contact with God directly through faith. And this conception of the dignity of the individual soul continues throughout modern literature as well as theological and political thought. The Protestants themselves, to be sure, may have allowed very little

---

The major part of this paper was published in the *L.I.D.* (League for Industrial Democracy) *Monthly,* Vol. 10, No. 6, p. 3 (March 1932).

personal freedom in communities subject to their laws. The Calvinists at Geneva and the Puritans in New England believed in a thoroughly regulated commonwealth. Nevertheless, the lasting result of the Reformation was to enhance the value of the individual and to give him an independent status, the source of power and rights. I need not say anything against Protestant theology and the doctrine of salvation by faith. Few nowadays think that a complete and satisfactory social policy for present-day conditions can be deduced from the attitude expressed in Cain's question, "Am I my brother's keeper?" Besides, good Protestant theology is still expressed in Saint Paul's maxim, "We are all members of each other's bodies."

(2) *Modern Philosophy.* Modern philosophy since Descartes has been predominantly subjectivistic. It has been suggested that this developed as a compensation for the depressing effect of the Copernican discovery that the earth and the human scene on it are only an infinitesimal incident in the physical world. Idealism says in effect: "Lo! This whole physical world is only your private idea and possession. It all exists in your mind." This is perhaps a caricature. Nevertheless, it is of the essence of Leibniz, Kant, Hegel, and Schopenhauer, as well as of Locke, Berkeley, Hume, and Mill, to believe that individual consciousness is the ultimate reality. What is known as the Romantic movement in literature is a glorification of subjectivism. It shows itself in the theory of impressionistic literary criticism of Anatole France, according to which each mind is a cell into which nothing enters from another cell. It shows itself in the psychologic novel of the Russians and French—e.g., Goncharov's *Oblomov* and Proust's *A la recherche du temps perdu.*

The basis of modern individualism was perhaps most bluntly expressed by Jeremy Bentham. The good of life is happiness, which consists of pleasure. Each man knows best what pleases him and what does not. Therefore governments should not interfere in private transactions, since in such free transactions each man chooses that which pleases him most. Away, then, not only with the old usury laws, but (as his disciples among the manufacturers claimed) away with all attempts at factory legislation or at regulating the labor contract.

If the classical economics of Adam Smith and John Stuart Mill does not speak in theologic terms, the theologic values of individualism so permeated the intellectual atmosphere in which their books were composed that this influence is obvious. Even more obvious is the psychologic philosophy which analyzes motives of business transactions. There is also back of this the old Leibnizian and eighteenth-century optimism of a pre-established harmony, according to which every individual, pursuing his own selfish interests, is bound by help of God, Nature, or the Elementary Laws of Economics to endeavor to bring about the universal harmony. This metaphysical philosophy is no longer put in this form because it has clothed itself in terms of history and biology. Instead of saying, "This is the best of all possible worlds," it takes the form of a philosophy of progress— every change is for the better. History, according to this view, shows that if men are not perfect, they are at least indefinitely perfectible. The process of history is a process according to which we throw off the yoke of superstition, of fraudulent priests and tyrannous rulers. As men do that they become more enlightened; tyranny is replaced by freedom, and belief in dogma by enlightened reason. In the latter part of the nineteenth century, this belief in progress clothed itself in the biologic form of the doctrine of natural selection and the survival of the fittest. The old Providence which punished the wicked and rewarded the virtuous becomes a biologic law according to which the most fit survive and the unfit perish. On the basis of this biology, the Spencerian liberals opposed all intervention by the state in industry. On the basis of this supposed biologic law Nietzschean individualists oppose all forms of modern helpfulness to the unfortunate. Let the weak perish, for in that way the strong survive.

Against this glorification of individualism, the logic of actual events and the awakening of a critical scientific attitude have protested. The individualistic liberals thought that if once the restraints of monopoly were removed, if human enterprise were unshackled by the removal of restraints on commerce, the removal of vexatious taxation—*laissez faire, laissez passer*—then something like a rational world order, in which men could enjoy the fruits of their own labor, would come into being. Alas! When these individualistic liberals got their chance in England after 1832 and introduced their system, it brought frightful abuses with it. We need not recount the horrors of English labor history: the men, women, and children working semi-naked in the mines under most horrible conditions, the sweated industries, etc. Suffice it to say that despite the almost universal acceptance of the individualistic philosophy, England and other countries were compelled by the actual situation to restrain the so-called "free labor contract" and to regulate the conditions of labor so that the manhood, womanhood, and childhood of the nation might to some extent be preserved. The manufacturers and the professional economists protested against restraints on free contract, or against attempts to interfere with the supposed necessary laws of economics. But the facts clearly indicated that there is no free contract between the owner or owners of a large industrial enterprise and the individual workers.

Now, this practical bankruptcy of the individualistic philosophy in the actual economic system has led many people to review the intellectual arguments in favor of individualism and to discover their limitations. As to the philosophic argument, I can only point to the impressive rise of realism since the beginning of the twentieth century. Let me indicate briefly, however, the historical and biological frailties in the philosophical argument for individualism. The notion that history shows a continual progress and especially a progress in the liberation of the individual is amply refuted by many examples. Consider, for instance, the process whereby the free Russian peasantry of the sixteenth century lost their independence and became serfs by the end of the eighteenth. This is important. We must shake off the vile habit of thinking that the latest is always the best. Thus individualists argue against vicarious liability (which is collective responsibility through insurance) on the ground that this is a reversal of history. An intelligent appreciation of history, however, shows the recurrence of certain situations and therefore the appropriateness of similar remedial procedures. I need not say much about the doctrine of the survival of the fittest. It is a proposition that is meaningless in biology, as T. H. Huxley has pointed out, and it is confusing to introduce it into social policy.

(3) *Modern Economic Theory.* The argument most often urged in behalf of unrestrained competition, which is generally regarded as essential to modern capitalism, is that which urges that free competition makes for maximum productivity and therefore serves the interests of all. This theory involves three basic assumptions: (a) that the profit motive produces a maximum of productivity, (b) that maximum productivity is a proper social objective, and (c) that human energies are in fact dominated by the profit motive. No one of these assumptions can withstand rational scrutiny.

(a) The assumption that private profit leads to maximum productivity is not in accord with economic facts. Everybody has heard of fishermen who, when they make a big haul, dump a large part of their catch into the ocean lest the news of their great success depress the price. This is not exceptional. Publishers frequently find more profit in limited editions. And in general whenever monopoly considerations enter, this thesis fails in application.

On the other hand, the economic wastefulness of unrestrained capitalism is now generally recognized by capitalists themselves who have formed cartels and trusts. Unrestrained competition leads generally to unrestricted production. When too many things are produced, the costs of maintaining an adequate sales force to sell the unwanted surplus, as well as the cost of creating unnecessary plants and machinery, involve tragic economic waste.

Worse yet, there are many cases where it is more profitable to wreck an enterprise than to use it for productive purposes. The example of the Erie Railroad under the management of Jay Gould and his fellow-pirates, as described by Charles Francis Adams,[1] illustrates this. But this is by no means exceptional. The history of inventions shows how many labor-saving devices have their patents bought up and "frozen" because it is not

[1] *A Chapter of Erie.*

profitable to shift to the more economical process. The difference between productivity and profit is illustrated by a remark of Mr. Whitney, one of the most successful businessmen this country has ever seen, judging by the enormous fortune he accumulated. Speaking to Mr. Taylor, the efficiency engineer, he said, "Taylor, you don't know the first thing about business." Mr. Whitney was right. The first thing about business is to make profit, whereas Taylor was interested in increasing productivity. But the issue has deeper implications for a social philosophy. Why, we ask, have so many natural resources of the country been wasted? The answer is: Because the desire for immediate profit does not make for economy in the long run. Water power, timber resources, and other gifts of nature have been unconscionably squandered because the desire for immediate profit will not allow private owners to husband these resources for the benefit of posterity. This is typical of a large number of cases. It is more profitable to build a large number of cheap houses, the useful life of which terminates in a short time, than it is to build substantial houses that endure.

(b) There is a still more fundamental error that is involved in the classical position. Is material productivity always good? Obviously the answer to this question depends upon the cost of production. Now if the cost of production is measured not only in material goods but in human values, the case for material productivity becomes more than questionable. Consider, for instance, the production of phosphorous matches. Their production subjected the workers involved to a terrible disease popularly known as "phossy jaw." Very few people would vote for continuing the production of these matches simply because they were cheaper. The human cost was too great. This analysis can be indefinitely extended. Many things that can be produced at a saving of material cost can be obtained only with social consequences which no humane person will approve on reflection. In general, we may say that many things that can be produced economically from a material point of view are not worth producing from a broad social point of view.

This general principle is applied by all civilized people and many others in limiting the hours of labor. For of what use is it to increase material goods if thereby the opportunities for human enjoyment are diminished and human life itself is shortened?

(c) Finally, in accepting the classical doctrine that, by gratifying their selfish desire for profit, our captains of industry set in motion the productive forces that increase the supply of goods consumed by the masses, there is the assumption of the all-sufficiency of the motive power of individual profit. But strong though that motive undeniably is, it has many well-known limitations, which even the defenders of capitalism, such as Justice Holmes, occasionally recognize. The motive to obtain social esteem by distinguished service frequently runs counter to it and exceeds its potency. In general, what means anyone will choose for gaining the esteem of his fellow men depends upon general social conditions, in which the activities that receive social approval are, as a rule, more likely to prevail. Moreover, the motive power of individual profit may be strongest in individuals who lack the intellectual competence to overcome the technical difficulties in the way of increased production and distribution. And, conversely, individuals with great competence to solve technical problems of production and distribution may be more interested in their work than in its financial rewards.

Conclusions. Just now individualism is admittedly bankrupt throughout the world in the industrial field. In this country we have no national plan of how to overcome the obvious and simple stupidity of a system that has too much food and goods on the one hand, and want, bordering on starvation, on the other, without being able to bring the food from those who wish to sell it to those who need it. The economics of individualism, with its assumption of pre-established harmony, is as intellectually discredited as the belief in witchcraft. Yet I do not wish to conclude without saying that in my opinion the principle of individualism cannot and ought not ever to be completely eliminated. Nothing that has its roots so deep in human history can properly be supposed to be devoid of vitality. I think there is a good deal of foolish rhetoric in our popular sociologic theory which denies the reality of the individual. After all, we are born alone, we suffer alone, and we die alone.

If there were no individuals, there would be no society. Society is a unity of many, and the emphasis on the unity cannot deny the multiplicity. There are in all societies centrifugal and centripetal forces. Every living organism contains them both and there is no life without both. There are times when wisdom requires that we emphasize the centralizing, organizing forces. Such a time, I believe, is the present. But it is vitally important that we remember that the forces for individualization and decentralization are not only always with us, but are necessary to social health. It is extremely dangerous to throw everything upon the government, for the government consists of human beings and (except for the Pope, speaking *ex cathedra*) they are not infallible. Our only hope against the danger of radical errors on the part of central authorities is in individualism in the field of discussion. This means the utmost freedom of criticism of the government. Now, a government which has unlimited power over each individual, which directly controls his daily bread, does not readily allow criticism. Such criticism gums up the works, and governors have a desire to make things go.

How to combine the principle of collectivism with the principle of individualism is a problem that varies in different situations, at different times and places. In general, the principle of federalism, as applied to economics as well as politics, has sound instincts behind it. But the main point that interests me as a philosopher is this: Collectivism and individualism have been fighting faiths. Men have rallied behind them and have treated them as dogmas to be defended in their integrity for all times and places. A true philosophic or scientific attitude would look at these principles not as dogmas, but as working hypotheses. Life is a problem like painting a picture, rather than adding a sum of figures already put down. Our principles then are to be tried. We must have principles in order to have programs and to follow a given direction rather than get lost and wander aimlessly; but we must not follow a principle to destruction—that is the essence of fanaticism. The enlightened attitude in harmony with modern philosophy and science is to adopt one hypothesis and watch the facts of life to see whether they confirm our hypothesis. This experimental attitude toward life is helped by the realization that the hypothesis that guides us is not the only one, that there are alternative hypotheses possible which may have to be invoked when our principle is found to break down.

Theoretically, the two principles of collectivism and individualism supplement each other, and theoretically we may get at the same result by starting at individualism and making the proper correction in the interests of collectivism, or by starting with the principle of collectivism and making the necessary corrections for individualism. But in the practical realm, since we never complete our theoretic system, it makes a tremendously important difference from which end we start. Also, the emphasis as well as the individual notes makes the song. And so, for practical reasons, I think we must nowadays start with the collectivistic principle.

6

LIBERALISM AND IRRATIONALISM

IT IS OFTEN CHARGED that liberals or intellectuals are those whose convictions lack robust emotional vitality. But the plight in which American liberalism finds itself as a result of the cataclysmic events of recent years has brought forth the taunt from conservatives and radicals that liberals are also intellectually unresourceful. Candid liberals need not be at pains to deny this latter charge very strenuously. Liberalism is, in fact, a more difficult faith to maintain. It is rather easy for the conservative, supported as he is by basic human inertia and the

Published as an editorial in *The New Republic,* Vol. 30, p. 333 (May 17, 1922).

organic fear of the unknown or the untried, to maintain his position by merely demanding that the innovators should prove that their schemes will work better than those already in operation. In the uncertainty of human affairs such demonstration can seldom be complete.

This same uncertainty makes it also difficult to refute the radicals' faith that all the rooted evils in human life will be cured by some simple remedy, like the single tax, state or guild socialism, communism, or the anarchy called individualism. The liberal who has no *a priori* guaranteed principles of reform, but, like the student of physical science, uses principles as hypotheses to be constantly checked up by the facts of experience, has a more complicated task than that of merely maintaining his initial assumptions. He must view his own assumptions critically and be constantly modifying them to keep up with the revelations of actual life. If, like the radical, he starts with the conviction that human life and growth demand conscious change and the spirit of adventure, he cannot blind himself to the fatal dangers inherent in all such adventures. To liberate mankind from the mass of needless restraints and superstitions that is part of "the wisdom of the past" is not an affair of pronunciamento and simple magical formula. It demands varied and accurate knowledge, critical reflection, and a constant readiness to meet with the unexpected. The honest liberal must, therefore, frequently confess that life is baffling because it outstrips knowledge; whereas the faith of the radical or conservative, if held tenaciously enough, saves its devotees from the labor of constantly examining the factual evidence, and makes it unnecessary, even disloyal, to suspend judgment until further knowledge is attainable.

This circumstance explains why the liberal has the appearance of being irresolute and unresourceful. But far more important is the fact that it explains why in an impatient world liberals are constantly tempted to depart from their difficult path and either embrace some simple panacea or else solace themselves with a rather too easy skepticism. Indeed skepticism and credulity frequently go together, as in Professor Robinson's recent book,

The Mind in the Making,[1] which begins by rejecting the "findings of mankind" and then naïvely puts forth as "indisputable
historical facts" not only the incompletely verified hypotheses
of the newer social sciences but also old exploded views as to
the history of science. There can be no questioning the many
charms which this book possesses, not the least of which is its
cultivated urbanity. Professor Robinson shows himself therein
to be a true liberal not only by the fine scorn which he metes
out to the bigoted intolerances of the Luskers * but even more
so by his profession of faith in creative intelligence. But when
we come to ask for the method and content of this creative intelligence, Professor Robinson fails to give us anything positive
and substantial. He believes in a general way that human salvation depends on introducing the methods of physical science
into our social problems. But his acceptance of the fashionable
distrust of reason bars him from any careful analysis of what
constitutes the method and limits of physical science; and his
excessive haste to prove the conservative in the wrong leads him
to embrace the unhistorical notion that modern science began
when Bacon, Descartes, and Galileo resolved to escape from the
past (pp. 16, 154, 200). The fact, however, is undeniable that
the great founders of modern science, like Vesalius, Copernicus,
Harvey, and Kepler, were deeply learned in Greek science,
which was the indispensable basis of their work. Nor did Descartes and Galileo start with a new slate or *tabula rasa*. They
began rather with definite neo-Platonic theories—e.g., that the
book of nature is written in geometric terms. The contrary impression—that these men began by disregarding all previous
theories, determined to let the experimental facts tell their own
story—is due to the fact that literary historians do not find it
easy to read the original scientific works of the sixteenth and
seventeenth centuries, and are content to get their information
from popular accounts such as Descartes' *Discourse on Method*

[1] James Harvey Robinson, *The Mind in the Making* (1921).

* The Lusk Committee of the New York Legislature was the spiritual
precursor of the Dies Committee. It specialized in exposing liberal and
radical ideas in the schools and colleges. Its many-volumed report was
published in 1920.

or Bacon's *Novum Organum.* But Descartes' *Discourse* is misleading when detached from his *Geometry* and *Optics,* to which it was an introduction, and Bacon, despite his undoubted genius, has no more claim to be regarded as a founder of modern science than Theodore Roosevelt. Indeed, in respect to the Copernican astronomy, Bacon was rather the W. J. Bryan of his day.

The prevailing ideophobia or distrust of reason shows itself perhaps most characteristically in the way Professor Robinson's discovery of the importance of motives or "real" reasons leads him to belittle the process of rationalization or the finding of "good" logical reasons. Ordinary experience seems to indicate quite clearly that the reasons people give for their religious, political, economic, and legal policies do influence the development of these policies, and that the "good reasons" professed by our fathers yesterday are among the real reasons of the life of today. Is there any basis for the denial of all efficiency to the essentially human process of rationalization, except the half-baked metaphysical doctrine of determinism? This dogma is supposed to be proved by modern physical science, but reputable physicists are careful to disown it. Many today will probably sympathize with Professor Robinson's flippant contempt for metaphysics, a human enterprise which William James characterized as "but the obstinate effort to think clearly." But the most metaphysical of living philosophers, Bradley, long ago pointed out that if metaphysics is the assigning of bad reasons for that which we hold on instinct, the seeking for such reasons is itself an instinct, and one, we may add, that plays a leading role in the life of civilization. In any case some acquaintance with traditional philosophy might teach us caution in trying to *disprove* a fundamental human attitude like conservatism, by the fragments of the past we call history. For the selection of facts which constitutes our history is molded by our philosophy, and the conservative can thus select his facts and prove his case about as well as Professor Robinson. Indeed, at the basis of both Professor Robinson's position and that of the conservative there is the same disinclination to deal adequately with the specific instrumentalities by which any actual improvements in man's political or economic state can ever be brought about.

It must not be thought that all this is of purely academic interest. It is significant of the danger to true liberalism from the antirational modes which prevail among "intellectuals" today. The reaction against the follies of the old rationalism has led them to the opposite extreme of irrationalism. We must remember that the old liberalism which expressed itself in the Declaration of Independence and the French Declaration of the Rights of Man in 1789 was frankly rationalistic. By its faith in reason and rational principles it overthrew feudalism, introduced popular education, reformed the old atrocious criminal law, humanized the treatment of the sick in body and mind, liberated scientific research from the trammels of theology, and opened up new sources for the enjoyment of life. It came to grief because in its enthusiasm for reason it ignored the roots of humanity in brute animal nature. Its simple faith in the brotherhood of man ignored the voluminous emotions of nationalism, and its cherished belief that enlightenment would make free competition a universal blessing found itself foiled by the actual effects of private capitalistic concentration. This, however, means not that we must reject the older liberalism but that we must give it a firmer basis. For the discovery that the flowers of human life have their roots in the dark soil does not in any way deny the value and importance of sunlight. We seem to be living in a time when the worship of the Olympian gods of the air, the sky, and the sunlight is being replaced by the worship of the underground deities. But it is well to remember that it has always been of the very essence of liberal civilization that the organic or basic motives of man should be regulated and controlled by the light of reason.

7

CALVINISM WITHOUT THE GLORY
OF GOD

THROUGH THE STORMS of centuries the philosophy of Plato
has stood out as a beacon by the light of which all kinds
of mariners—mystics, skeptics, theologians, mathematicians, communists, eugenists—have steered their diverse courses. But men
are not as a rule satisfied with the light and the vision of beauty
which minds like Plato radiate in all directions. They must
claim exclusive ownership. Hence different schools and sects all
endeavor to annex Plato as one of their own. Mr. More tries to
make of Plato an orthodox Calvinistic moralist. I do not mean
to accuse Mr. More of willfulness. He has read Plato long and
carefully—more carefully than the hasty reader can well appreciate. But, as Xenophanes remarked twenty-five centuries ago,
men always make their gods in their own image, the Greeks
like Greeks, the Ethiopians like Ethiopians. Does not Milton
make the Lord argue like a theologic logician, of the school of
Peter Ramus? And does not Renan make Christ a sympathetic
but disillusioned romanticist?—while Tolstoi paints him as a
nonresisting Russian peasant. It is therefore quite natural that
Mr. More, apparently more interested in Calvinistic theology
than in Greek life and science, should represent Plato as a somewhat softened and more urbane Jonathan Edwards. No account,
however, of Plato can be historically accurate which considers
Plato's ethics entirely apart from any of the conditions of Greek

Published as a review of Paul Elmer More, *Platonism*, in *The New Republic*,
Vol. 16, p. 143 (August 31, 1918).

life, which considers Plato's theory of art, education, and politics as merely "subsidiary," which entirely rejects the light on Plato thrown by his great successors, and deliberately ignores Plato's relation to the mathematical philosophy of the Pythagoreans. Ancient tradition ascribes to Plato the motto inscribed over the portals of his Academy: "Let none ignorant of geometry enter here." Historical accuracy, to be sure, may be a secondary matter. The value of a man's view of life may be independent of the historical peg on which he hangs it, but surely it is a pity that an accomplished literary critic like Mr. More should fall a victim to the ruthless temper of philosophic controversy, and treat the dialogues of Plato not as works of art to be admired like the statuary of Praxiteles, but as clubs with which to hit the heads of contemporary philosophers who have a little more sympathy with the frail throbbing flesh that enters into our human nature.

Mr. More's own philosophy, which underlies his *Shelburne Essays* and comes to clearer light in this book, deserves greater attention than it has generally been accorded. It is true, as Mr. More with admirable courage admits, that the current of the day is against it. But it is still most powerfully entrenched. Its conception of morality is still taught in all our Sunday and week-day schools, and in almost all of our colleges. Its basic distrust of man's natural impulses still dominates our legal if not our theologic thought—since the framers of our national constitution of checks and balances were thoroughly imbued with Calvinism. If, then, this philosophy is losing ground among intellectual men, it is of some importance to know why. Mr. More himself does not suggest any adequate cause for this general falling away from grace; but the history of Calvinism in Europe, as well as in this country, makes it clear that its decay was due to the fact that it could not stand the light of that mode of thought which we call modern science, but which has its roots in ancient Greece. The spirit of free inquiry has no room for that reliance on and craving for "authority higher than reason" which is at the heart of Mr. More's whole effort.

Mr. More, it is true, begins by recognizing skepticism as one of the sources of philosophy. However, the manner in which he attempts to refute hedonism, his dislike of the term "probable," and the ready way in which he falls back on unproved dogmatic assertions ("spiritual affirmations") show how far Mr. More is from the robust skepticism of science. It is true, of course, that absolute suspension of all judgment is unattainable, that we are all forced by the demands of life to make some affirmation or choice. But this only proves that our knowledge is not always adequate for action, that life consists largely of hazardous leaps in the dark. Scientific honesty, however, makes us admit that where demonstrative knowledge ends only guessing begins. The fact that we *must* guess does not prove our guess true. Our brief lives are but momentary gleams between two eternities of total darkness, and we can gather but little as to the unknown and tempestuous seas of being wherein we find ourselves tossed. Only a little of the structure of our frail boats and something of the waters immediately about us are revealed by science. For the most part we must sail into the unknown without any absolute guarantee of safety. Mr. More has the right to stake his life on his own guess. He might, if he had chosen, have sought to show that in the light of history and science other boats are more likely to be shipwrecked than his own. But anyone who stands up and says, My spiritual affirmation is *the* truth because I have an "invincible assurance," shows a pathetic confusion between knowledge and guesswork. The resorting to epithets, the calling of our own guess "superrational intuition" and the guess of others piggish or "emanating from a plane below the reason," is a pitiable display of intellectual impotence, just as the poor pedagogue stamps and raises the voice of authority when he cannot give a satisfactory explanation. Even as a consolation these epithets are rather thin, since our opponents are always free to return the service in kind.

Though Mr. More is not an academic philosopher and writes with the easy grace and correctness characteristic of the courtly manner, the substance of his book is concerned with that most academic question, the rewards and penalties of the moral life. He will not question the view that the universe must be conceived like a Sunday school or penitentiary, where none of us would be "good" or moral unless we were promised some reward or threatened with punishment. Now there are few doctrines so intellectually dishonest as doctrines concerning the rewards and punishments of the moral life. They may be well-intentioned people who say that virtue always leads to success and vice to misery. But it is an obvious and monstrous falsehood in a world where we profit by the good deeds of our parents and where millions are suffering unutterable tortures because of the deeds of foreign potentates. That those who suffer must have been wicked, and that those who triumph must have been virtuous, is one of the most inhuman beliefs in history. As to the doctrine that the reward of virtue is to be found in a clear conscience or high satisfaction—that is an even more violent falsehood. The people who suffer most from their conscience are obviously the sensitive and high-minded, while self-approbation comes most easily to the complacent and fortune-favored Jack Horners. The doctrine that the reward of moral life is a *feeling* of satisfaction or happiness (pp. 74, 80, 89, 90, 116, etc.) is not only contrary to moral experience, but is intellectually sterile. The natural variation of individual feeling leaves us without any means whereby to tell what *is* the good or the moral. Indeed, though Mr. More constantly speaks of justice as the good, he never makes any attempt to tell us how to determine what is just. How can one possibly determine the justice of a labor dispute or the just claims of Ireland to self-government by means of conscience or one's feeling of happiness?

It is indeed a sad irony of fate to find in a book on Plato the subjectivist doctrine that the reward of the moral life is to be found in a feeling. Did not Plato write *The Republic* to show that the problem of morality or justice is not soluble unless we tackle it in terms of social organization? It seems a fact that modern subjectivistic or "conscience" theories of morality confine themselves to certain personal virtues and leave the larger questions of social morality either untouched or subject to external authority. But to do so is simply to perpetuate the prevailing standard based on past experience, ignorance, and prejudice. To make morality always synonymous with the mainte-

75

nance of the status quo is indeed to commit the great treason against the intellectual life and to make philosophy procuress to the lords of hell.

The nearest Mr. More comes to throwing light on the concrete problems of the moral life is in his insistence that all true moralists or Platonists say "No" to our natural impulses. Taken literally and absolutely, this is arrant nonsense. Moral life would be impossible without generous impulses. I suppose Mr. More simply wishes to insist on the eternal necessity of discipline and self-control. But even this, it seems to me, cannot be set up as the supreme good of life. The temptation of the flesh, like the instinct of the moth, may lead us straight into the flame; but it does not follow that it is worth while to struggle pitiably for the preservation of an existence devoid of all warmth and light. Discipline and self-control are undoubtedly great goods. Without self-restraint there can be no mastery, no worthy achievement. But to make self-control the end of life is as absurd as the position of those who would make good administration or the saving of money the end of government. People do not grow rich by mere saving, and self-control is not worth a farthing unless we build up a great self worth controlling. It is the merit of genuine philosophies that they paint for us some great object with which we can identify ourselves and thus make us worth while. Mr. More's negative song in a minor key does not do so.

Mr. More has written a serious book, hoping to touch the minds of a few of our generous college youth. In this I think there is little likelihood of his being very successful. The minds of youth cannot be stirred by eternal don'ts and warnings against the temptations of the flesh. Some great positive and generous faith, some great outlook on life, is necessary to arouse their energies. Historical Calvinism was effective, not because it preached restraints and supported them with the fear of hell, but because it gave men a vision of the glory of God. Mr. More's philosophy may not unfairly be called Calvinism without the glory of God. If the history of religion has any teaching, it is that the glory of God is not visible except to those who are profoundly moved by compassion for their fellow men.

76

This review of a scholarly and charmingly written book is probably somewhat unfair, perhaps grossly so; but if so it is not from any bias in favor of those against whom Mr. More is battling. I share Mr. More's distrust of vague beliefs in social service and "benumbing trust in mechanical progress," and above all I share his aversion for sentimental romanticism. But all of us have the defects of our qualities, and Mr. More's philosophy illustrates the danger of intellectual anemia which threatens all closet philosophers. We must, to be sure, get out of the tumult of the market place to gather our thoughts. But if we get up too high on the mountain or stay there too long, our thoughts lose the substance and the strength that come from immediate contact with the brute facts. The recovery of the Greek world, and of Plato in particular, meant to the modern world liberation from the medieval dogma that nature is sin and intellect the devil. This liberation, however, has never been completed. The rationalists wish us to recover reason, but they lose contact with nature. The romanticists wish us to recover nature, but alas, they lose contact with reason. The significance of modern science is that it is an organized attempt to keep reason wedded to the facts of nature. And no one can adequately interpret life or Plato without a sympathetic understanding of both reason and nature.

8

AN ETHICAL PHILOSOPHY OF LIFE

THE APPEARANCE of a book which formulates a distinct philosophy of life is a rare and noteworthy event. Recent philosophy, though loudly proclaiming its ambition to "make the world a better place to live in," has been singularly afraid of dealing with the fundamental question, What *is* good and what is *better?* Like the rest of the American public most of our philosophers seem to think it more important that a man should fix his attention on some incident in the current of events and "do" something about it, than that he should stop and inquire, Why? Where and whither this whole procession, and what is the good of it all? Doubtless a good deal of the older speculation on life and destiny was vain and insipid because of the theologic bias which made philosophers turn their backs on "the world" and prefer conventional piety to knowledge and fresh insight. But observations on the habits of the Australian Blackfellows and other "primitive" tribes, which form the staple of ultra-modern treatises on ethics, do not succeed in throwing more light on the vexed problems of social justice than did the older references to the lives of the saints. Professor Adler has shown us anew that it is possible to combine the insight of practical experience with the discipline of philosophic reflection, to mix with one's fellow citizens in the market place in such activities as tenement-house reform and child-labor committees, and yet retire at times to the mountain to pray and

Published as a review of Felix Adler, *An Ethical Philosophy of Life*, in *The New Republic*, Vol. 19, p. 254 (June 25, 1919).

survey one's work, the needs of the multitudes, and our cosmic background, with that time-conquering vision which is the essence of all genuine philosophy.

The great truth which Professor Adler sees with unsurpassed clarity and courage is the existence of humanly ineradicable evil, the inescapable frustration which results from our mortal finitude and makes the search for perfect happiness so pathetically vain. Neither in love nor in work, neither in society nor in solitude, neither in the arts nor in the sciences will the world of actuality permit us to attain perfection. The flowers of our hopes always wither and the fruits of our efforts are never free from the canker of disappointment. Professor Adler is too enlightened to share the orthodox belief that all the atrocious evil of life will be compensated in some "hereafter." He is too honest a thinker to take seriously the childish belief that by a few mechanical inventions or politico-economic changes we can create a heaven on earth where men will be happy forever afterwards. We know little of the conditions of our own happiness and much less as to what will make others happy. Certainly we have no guaranteed assurance that the blind forces of nature that crush man and brute, the just and the unjust, will permit the existence of the human race forever.

Despite the fact that modern popular philosophy blinks at these facts and calls anyone who insists on them pessimistic, there is nothing here to dampen courage or blunt the zest of life. An enlightened naturalist like Lucretius would say that the play of light on the waters is no less beautiful because our boat is likely to be wrecked by a storm. Moreover, the fearless understanding which is called philosophy, even if it cannot eliminate evil, can rob it of its terrors. But Professor Adler is not a naturalist. To him evil is transcended by becoming the occasion for the recognition of an eternal supersensible world of which all human beings are even now members. The arrows of misfortune thus become beams of spiritual light piercing the dark clouds of our mortal existence.

The arguments by which Professor Adler attempts to prove the reality of this supersensible universe seem to me entirely unconvincing—possibly because I cannot accept the Kantian metaphysics with its "reality-producing functions of the mind." To all attempted proofs that *my* mind created the world or the events in it, I instinctively rebel with considerable resentment. On purely logical grounds, however, it is quite clear that in his fundamental assumption as to the possibility of an "infinite totality" Professor Adler has failed to take account of the serious objections to this notion brought by Aristotle as well as by modern mathematical logicians. Nor would a logician regard the connections between Professor Adler's theoretical assumptions and his practical applications as at all necessary. One may grant, for instance (as I do), that we must always use the ideas of unity and plurality together without being thereby forced to admit that uniqueness as such is always ethically valuable; and one may admit the latter without granting that representation by industries is much of an improvement over our present parliamentary system. But it is not necessary to subscribe to the truth of a philosopher's metaphysical arguments to find his vision suggestive and illuminating—any more than it is necessary to believe in the geography of Homer or the astronomy of Dante. For genuine philosophic work, like genuine poetry, is an exercise of the imagination and as such frees us from the charnel house of petrified complacencies. Thus, though Professor Adler's starting point, and perhaps the influence of his vocation as an ethical preacher, lead him to adhere to the traditional legalistic conception of ethics, best represented by the Old Testament or the Stoics, the result of his experience and reflection is to undermine the traditional view of ethics as authoritatively fixed for all time and conditions and as ascetically contemptuous of human desires.

It is a grievous error to suppose, as many do, that the scientific spirit has already triumphed or replaced the theologic one in ethics. The life of science depends upon absolutely free inquiry, and the community generally does not expect and will not tolerate writers on ethics who will question the accepted views on property or marriage. Philosophers like Kant no less than the unreflecting multitude take it for granted that to seek for new ethical truths is preposterous or blasphemous, just as before the martyrdom of Bruno and Galileo men generally thought it outrageous audacity to seek for physical truths not already revealed by Aristotle or Galen. To be sure modern writers on ethics do sometimes speak as if they were embarking on a voyage of discovery, but people generally feel so strongly about the established beliefs that natural timidity makes our travelers really determined at the outset to arrive nowhere except where the innocuous virtues of respectability receive unquestioning homage. When men like Marx, Nietzsche, or Guyau announce new views on life they regard themselves as immoralists and the pious are taught to shudder at their names. Ethics thus becomes entrusted to the hands of pedagogues and professional preachers, retailers rather than producers of wisdom; and no one is surprised to find ethical treatises that are in the end nothing but more or less skillful apologies for the established order—whether it is Negro slavery in our own South, rotten boroughs in England, or the Prussian monarchy in Germany.

The root of this evil is the frantic certainty which men summon when they face the baffling issues of life. Experience amply shows that the intensity of this certainty is proportional not to the extent of our knowledge but rather to the fearfulness of our ignorance, which makes us cling desperately to old taboos. We really know less about the conduct of the whole of life than we do about limited and less complicated portions of it such as bridge-building. Yet no bridge builder would pretend to the awful certainty of the Hebrew prophet or law-giver who begins with "Thus saith the Lord." Such certainty cannot tolerate unbelievers, and, by crushing the doubts suggested by experience, it breeds the fanaticism which shuts the gates of mercy on mankind.

The critical spirit or mature skepticism which the Greek philosophers introduced into ethics, thus transforming morality into an exercise of wisdom instead of a timid observance of taboos and legalistic prohibitions, finds little express recognition in Professor Adler's philosophy. Possessed by the Kantian passion for absolute certitude where knowledge fails us, he cannot theoretically admit that life is largely a matter of hazard or taking chances, in which we have to learn by the method of trial and error. But his fundamental respect for human per-

sonality makes him instinctively eschew the method of authority, and he gives his teaching largely in the form of results of
his own experience. "Let others compare theirs with it." But
once the necessity of experience is admitted, it becomes impossible to maintain the traditional view that all ethical truth has
already been revealed. Hence Professor Adler rightly insists on
encouraging a certain "intrepidity of soul to venture forth on
voyages of discovery into unknown ethical regions, taking the
risks but bent upon the prize." This recognition of the element
of risk is of inestimable importance. It means that we must face
life without any absolute guarantees and rely instead on our
own courage. The risks of moral adventures are as grave as life
and death; yet without them there is no genuinely human life,
but only a slavish adherence to mechanically rigid rules which
choke the currents of ever-changing life. Rigorous and unqualified obedience to the accepted ethical rules is generally admired
as a virtue, but it really ought to be viewed as involving an
obtuse insensibility to the rich and subtle variety of human
relations. The rules of ethics certainly have no securer scientific
basis than the rules of hygiene have. Both sets are undoubtedly
useful as general maxims. But only quacks rely on such maxims
without further knowledge of the actual circumstances surrounding concrete cases. Hence, when traditional moralists like Kant
treat such rules as that against lying as absolute, never to be
broken even to defend an innocent life against a murderous
madman, they are guilty of contemptible insensitivity to the
multiplicity of human values. Professor Adler's position makes
such insensitivity unrespectable.

Perhaps the chief characteristic of traditional ethics is the
dogma that the highest good is equally attainable by everyone.
This necessarily makes the highest good independent of health,
food and raiment, congenial society, and all the joys and comforts for which men long but which largely depend upon the
accidents of birth and fortune. To be consistent the traditional
view must, therefore, adopt the Kantian view that nothing is
really good except the "good will." As we can never be sure
of the existence of this metaphysical "good will" in ourselves
or in others, ethics necessarily becomes a perfectly sterile doc-

trine, barren of any applications to the concrete issues of life. Professor Adler does not, it is true, totally break with this tradition. He clings to the violent assertion that "the best is within reach of all" (p. 102), and maintains a sharp dualism between spiritual and "merely" empirical goods. Thus personal attraction, mutual aid and comfort, taking counsel together, sympathy in joy and sorrow, may be valuable elements in friendship, but "they do not even touch the essential point" (p. 234). But, in the main, the importance which Professor Adler rightly attaches to the instrumentalities of life clearly suggests the need of a radical transformation of the traditional view according to which the business of life is the saving of one's soul in a universe which is a transcendental wage system designed to reward men according to their effort and sacrifices rather than their achievements. Professor Adler's conception of ethical life as an exercise of human energy provides a basis for a truly emancipating philosophy of conduct.

The radical and revolutionary character of Professor Adler's contribution to ethics is hidden by an intellectualistic psychology which is too rigid and clearly inadequate. I refer to his assertion that "we simply cannot act provisionally," and that we must have definitely formulated ideals before we can act at all. The procedure of the physical sciences which operate with provisional hypotheses is not exceptional but typical of all human effort that is open-minded and free from the delusion of finality. We doubtless must have an ideal to guide us in all our search and experiment, but our ideals are after all idealizations of our hearts' desire, and the progress of enlightenment shows itself nowhere better than in the change of our ideals.

The root and vital motive of ethical thought is the passion for the relief of human suffering. Discerning readers will surely not find Professor Adler himself lacking in this quality, but the book before us may leave the unfortunate impression that he regards metaphysical constructions as socially more potent for righteousness than natural human sympathy (cf. p. 49). No doubt Professor Adler is right in insisting that sympathy like any other empirical principle is often an unsafe guide. But history amply shows that all search, metaphysical no less than empirical, after absolutely infallible guides to human conduct has proved to be a chasing after the wind leading only to the overcrowded graveyard of human hopes. This lesson of history means not despair but the wisdom of living and working with the imperfect, and above all the necessity of assuaging that fierce moral fanaticism which so often makes life needlessly intolerable. Now more than ever we need the Greek counsel *Nothing in Excess,* or its equivalent *Live and Let Live.*

My own intense and perhaps partisan interest in the questions raised by Professor Adler has probably led me to do injustice to a book that is not only a distinct intellectual achievement but a great human document, compacting the experience and reflection of a singularly unified life and mind. The last chapter especially is one of rare impressiveness. But whenever I finish reading it I am tempted to turn to Anatole France's *Les Dieux ont soif* with the conviction that a complete ethics must include Epicurus as well as St. Augustine.

9

PHILOSOPHY IN WARTIME—AN APOLOGIA

DEAR FRIEND: Your letter gently but unmistakably intimates that I am a slacker, a slacker in peace as well as in war; that when the World War was raging bitterly I dawdled my time with subjects like symbolic logic, and that now when the issues of reconstructing a bleeding world demand the efforts of

Published in *The New Republic,* Vol. 21, p. 19 (December 3, 1919), under the title, "A Slacker's Apology," by Philonous.

all who care for the future of the human race, I am shirking my responsibility and wasting my time with Plato and Cicero. Your sweetly veiled charge is true, but I do not feel ashamed of it. On the contrary, when I look upon my professional colleagues who enlisted their philosophies in the war, who added their shrill voices to the roar of the cannons and their little drops of venom to the torrents of national hatreds, I feel that it is they who should write apologies for their course. For philosophers, I take it, are ordained as priests to keep alive the sacred fires on the altar of impartial truth, and I have but faithfully endeavored to keep my oath of office as well as the circumstances would permit. It is doubtless the height of the unheroic to worship truth in the bombproof shelter of harmless mathematics when men are giving their lives for democracy and for the public order which is the basis of civilization. But it would be sad if all the priests deserted their altars and became soldiers, if the Sermon on the Mount were utterly erased to give place to manuals of bayonet practice or instructions on the use of poison gas. What avails it to beat the enemy if the sacred fires which we are sworn to defend meanwhile languish and die for want of attendance?

Impartial Truth is a goddess whose worship is not without its difficulties even in a bombproof shelter behind the lines. She is hated by the great multitude of the impatient and despised by those superior persons who disdain her as old-fashioned. But as her sworn votary I cannot deny her. When the Germans sank the *Lusitania* I could not deny the women and children starved by the blockade. As a citizen I should have been glad, if conditions permitted, to volunteer for military service. But though I could conscript my body I could not conscript my mind. As a philosopher I could never assert that the war was a clear issue between the powers of light and the powers of darkness—or, as Bergson put it, between the mind or spirit on one side and brute matter on the other. I could never get myself to say that Japan had a better right to Shantung than Germany, or that it was better that Poles should oppress Russians and Germans than that the latter should be the oppressors. I could never believe that the world's iniquity would end the moment the Kaiser (or any other "boss") should be overthrown. Some there were who insisted that it was my duty to shout these doubts of mine from the roof tops. But I could not do this any more than I could shout them to the Germans across the barbed-wire entanglements. I believe in the division of labor. I am a priest or philosopher, not a soldier or propagandist. I yield to none in my admiration for the brave fellows who gave their all on the bloody fields of Flanders, but I have no respect for the bigots who cannot realize that "in my Father's house are many mansions," and that it would be a poor world if there were no diversity of function to suit the diversity of natural aptitudes. And when people begin to admonish me that if everyone did as I did, etc., I answer that humanity would probably perish from cold if everyone produced food, and would certainly starve if everyone made clothes or built houses. I admit the desperate need of men to defend the existence of our country, but I cannot ignore the need of men to maintain even in war the things that make the country worth defending. Purely theoretic studies seem to me to be of those fine flowers which relieve the drabness of our existence and help to make the human scene worth while.

I am aware, dear friend, that in my high valuation of purely theoretic pursuits I have the weight of contemporary authority against me. My fellow philosophers for the most part are too ready to assert that theoretic philosophy can justify itself only by its practical applications. But why the fundamental human desire to know the world is any less entitled to satisfaction than the desire for kodaks, automobiles, india-paper, or upholstered furniture, they do not tell us. Indeed, exactly what is practical, and what is the good of being practical at all, are just the kind of theoretic studies that they frantically refuse to undertake. I strongly suspect that in this they are influenced not only by the Puritanic aversion for the arts of free play, but also by the unenlightened prejudice that the bare necessities of life are more important than the "luxuries" which by giving life beauty and dignity make the struggle for it worth while to free men.

Our excessive specialization tends to make us blind to that which is outside our interests, and, hence, fiercely intolerant.

I have seen lumberjacks laugh to scorn an artist who was trying to fix on canvas some of the haunting beauty in the gloaming of the woods; and we have on public record the contempt of the aluminum manufacturers for those sentimentalists who want to preserve the scenic sublimity of Niagara Falls. It is just as natural for statesmen and journalists absorbed in the problems of the war and the League of Nations to scorn those who have other interests. But there are plenty of historic precedents to justify some skepticism as to the infallibility of the prevailing judgment on what is fundamentally important. Don't you now think the discovery of certain mathematical propositions by Archimedes to be more important than the siege and capture of Syracuse? They used to scorn Hegel for being concerned with his *Phenomenology* while the fate of Germany was being sealed at Jena almost at his very door. Yet history has shown the appearance of Hegel's unearthly book to have been of greater importance than the battle of Jena. The results of the latter were wiped out within seven years, while the results of Hegel's thought will for good or evil last for many years to come. When Darwin published his *Descent of Man* at the end of the Franco-Prussian War, the authoritative London *Times,* I think, took him severely to task! When the foundations of property and the established order are threatened by the fires of the Paris Commune, how can a patriotic gentleman concern himself with inquiries that are in no wise calculated to help or comfort those who have a stake in the country? Would anyone today defend that attitude?

If I had your persuasive talent, dear friend, and cared to exalt one human interest above others, I would contend that the really important issue before the American people today is not economic or political but moral and vital—the issue of Puritanism. It is the Puritanic feeling of responsibility which has blighted our art and philosophy and has made us as a people unskilled in the art of enjoying life. (No one who witnessed our victory celebrations will here ask for proof.) By making daily existence dreary and depressed it drove people to strong drink, and now it deprives people of their drink without inquiring into its cause or function. But I have no desire to brand as slackers those who will not enlist in the fight against Puritanism. What I wish to suggest is some modicum of doubt as to the complacent assumption that only by absorption in some contemporary social problem can the philosopher justify his existence. The great philosophers, like the great artists, scientists, and religious teachers, have all, in large measure, ignored their contemporary social problems. Aristotle, Leonardo da Vinci, Shakespeare, Newton, Buddha, Jesus of Nazareth, and others who have done so much to heighten the quality of human life have very little to say about the actual international, economic, and political readjustments which were as pressing in their day as in ours. The great service of Socrates to humanity was surely not in his somewhat superficial criticism of the Athenian electoral machinery of his day, but rather in developing certain intellectual methods, and suggesting to Plato certain doctrines as to the nature of the soul and ideas—doctrines which in spite of all their impracticality have served for over two thousand years to raise men above the groveling, clawing existence in which so much of our life is sunk. I know that Plato's otherworldliness is decidedly out of fashion. We believe nowadays that by progressive mechanical inventions and by some happy economico-political device we can bring about the reign of complete justice and happiness. Far be it from me to disparage this modern faith. As a great hope sanctified by the supposed evidence of "scientific" evolution, it is to many a real sustaining force in the presence of otherwise intolerable evil. But to fix all our hope on some temporal affair like the League of Nations is to leave us helpless when we come to the inevitable harvest of disappointment. We hold the benefits of civilization not in fee simple, to our heirs forever, but by knights' service. Much as we may leave to our successors, we can never manage it so that they shall be entirely free from toil, pain, and the agonies of death. Let us not, therefore, willfully impoverish their life by throwing away any of the things that have served as consolations to so many since the ancient days—among which are the writings of the divine Plato and even of the altogether unheroic Cicero, who so tragically illustrates the failure of scholars in politics.

IV

POLITICO-ECONOMIC ISSUES

POLITICO-ECONOMIC ISSUES

10

THE LEGEND OF MAGNA CHARTA

O^{N JUNE FIFTEENTH} will be commemorated the seven hun-
dredth anniversary of the signing of Magna Charta. If we
may judge from the past, the country will be regaled on that
occasion by stirring orations on the meaning of that "palladium
of our liberties" from orators who have neither the time nor
the historical learning to read that bulky medieval document
with understanding. In truth, the feudal incidents with which
it deals are not all clear even to expert historians, so that orators
find it more congenial and profitable to fall back on tradition,
and use the fact that Norman barons extorted certain conces-
sions from an Angevin king as a patriotic reason why we should
now be content with our own established order. The transformation of history for purposes of political controversy and
homiletics is, of course, an ancient process. But it would be
difficult to find anywhere a better illustration of the complete
triumph of political apologetics over historical accuracy than is
offered by the traditional account of the significance of Magna
Charta. Coke, whose undigested pedantry is the source of so
much legal omniscience, makes Magna Charta the source of
trial by jury and other fundamental popular rights; and Burke,
with a chivalric disregard of facts, maintains Magna Charta as
the source of effective representative government. There is absolutely nothing in or outside that document to support these
views. Though some details and technical terms may still be

Published as a *New Republic* editorial, Vol. 3, p. 136 (June 12, 1915).

matters of dispute among scholars, scientific historical research has shown beyond doubt that the granting of Magna Charta was in no sense the result of a popular movement, but was entirely due to a small group of powerful nobles bent on their own selfish interests. The people suffered as much from the French troops of the barons as from King John's army. Certainly the specific provisions of the charter were in the interests of the barons and bishops (lords temporal and spiritual). They offered almost nothing to the great mass of the people, who were then villeins, devoid of what we call civil and political rights. The oft-quoted clause 39, "No freeman shall be imprisoned, etc., save by the lawful judgment of his peers," did not guarantee jury trial. It did guarantee that no "peer of the realm" should be tried by the king's judges who were not themselves "peers," and that, similarly, clerics should be tried in their own court ("benefit of clergy"). In that respect there is some justice in Jenks's characterization of Magna Charta as "a reactionary document and a great nuisance and stumbling-block to the generation which came after it."

This truth does not, of course, altogether dispose of the importance of Magna Charta. Doubtless the tradition that Magna Charta did in some way protect the people's rights had great influence in English political development. Modern science, however, sees no reason why present-day political controversies should be fought with the fantastic weapons of legendary history.

11

SOCIALISM AND CAPITALISM

RECENT ECONOMIC CHANGES have increased the general interest in the issues between Communism or Socialism and what we have been used to call capitalism. In this discussion the assumptions common to both sides have not been sufficiently emphasized. Both sides believe, in fact, in a planned economy, in which science and technology are applied to production based on capital goods, tools, and machinery. In this sense both parties literally believe in capitalism, and their programs do and must have a good deal in common—more than is ordinarily recognized. They differ, to be sure, in their plans. According to the party of social capitalism, the planning is to be by the community or state, while according to the advocate of individualistic capitalism planning is to be by private individuals, who, under the illusion of self-seeking, are supposed to bring into existence economic harmonies established by God, Nature, or the eternal laws of economics. But history shows that planning of some sort is essential to all forms of capitalism—i.e., to all forms of society where the production of goods on a large scale for an anticipated demand depends on a stock of previously created goods.

It may clarify and vitalize the issue to call attention to the existence of another party, not so vocal just now but quite numerous, who do not believe in capitalism of either sort, who

The major part of this paper was delivered as a lecture before a Conference on Economic and Social Planning, March 10, 1932, sponsored by the Bureau of Personnel Administration.

are opposed to machinery in general, and who disparage all planning of an economic sort. Hence a philosopher, seeking to understand current controversies over planning, must begin by asking:

Why Plan at All?

The question may sound irresponsible. Is not the life of civilized man distinguished from that of the savage—nay, is not the life of man distinguished from that of the brute—by the fact that the former lives according to a reasonable plan rather than by fitful impulse? But the issue I raise cannot be thus brushed aside. A very high authority, in a book which after nineteen centuries is still a best-seller, has solemnly said: "Take therefore no thought for the morrow. . . . Sufficient unto the day is the evil thereof. . . . Consider the lilies of the field . . . they toil not, neither do they spin; yet . . . even Solomon in all his glory was not arrayed like one of these." Similar teachings are found in divers religions as different from each other as Buddhism, Islam, and orthodox Judaism.

Shall we dismiss this as a matter of religion to be believed only on Sunday but as something that has no application to everyday business? A large part of mankind does take this injunction seriously, and millions of men and women have lived by it. Nor is this confined to the Christian world. The Greek philosophers and the sages of the East have regarded preoccupation with monetary gain as far from being a virtue. And mankind at large to this day cherishes most not those who have made fortunes but the great religious teachers—Moses, Jesus, the Buddha; the great thinkers—Socrates, Plato, Aristotle, Kepler, Galileo, Spinoza, Kant, Newton, Darwin; the great artists— Homer, Phidias, Dante, Raphael, Shakespeare, Bach, and Beethoven, none of whom has directly contributed to our improved capitalistic economy.

Suppose we come in contact with a pious Mohammedan and find him dismissing many economic questions with the saying "Allah will provide." If any of us were to say to him, "That is why you do not progress or prosper," he might well reply, "Does the feverish anxiety that you call Progress and Prosperity bring your soul peace and salvation or what you call Happiness?" And he might add, "Has not your Son of Mary asked: 'For what is a man profited, if he shall gain the whole world, and lose his own soul'?"

Now, I do not wish to argue here for this religious view of life. I do not even wish to suggest that there is not some way of reconciling it with economic planning. But I think the hostility of so much of the world's thought to excessive pre-occupation with material economy should make us pause. May there not be some reason for our leading philosopher, William James, to refer to success as our "bitch goddess" and for others to refer to our preoccupation with pecuniary profits as a mania?

I do not myself agree with Gandhi or the followers of Rousseau or my friends of the unreconstructed South who are opposed to all machinery and industrialism. I do not believe that we can or should reverse the process of history and go back to the primitive. If we are to abolish machinery as such, why keep any tools at all—spades, shovels, needles, knives, or even the spinning wheel, which is certainly a machine? Yet the very existence of this protest against machinery should make us see the importance of the question, "Plan for what, or produce for what purpose?" Mere production of goods is not more rational than the miser's pursuit of money, or the maniac's accumulation of buttons. May not humanity be better off if we do not produce so many things that can be dispensed with? May not the enjoyment of life be advanced by limiting the production of goods that we could do without and cultivating rather the inner sources of peace and enjoyment? In any case, sanity requires that we be not satisfied with the test of material productivity but that we judge any human arrangement by the extent to which it ministers to ultimate human values. And this seems to me necessary in considering the issue between social and individual capitalism.

The Inadequacy of the Arguments Against Socialism

1. THE HISTORICAL ARGUMENT. This runs somewhat as follows: Individualistic economy is the outcome of the world's

experience. It has replaced the village-community type of economy because it has proved itself more economical. Individual ownership has led to improvement of land by more intensive cultivation.

This argument, however, is quite inconclusive. The forces that have led to individualism have in the last fifty years been successfully opposed by the forces of collectivism. Even in so-called private industry, large enterprise and elaborate machinery are made possible only by large combinations of men pooling their capital. In many cases, such as steel and oil, these combinations control a major part of national production in their fields. Why may not the community own the tractors, the railroads, the oil, the coal mines, the steel works, just as it owns the roads, canals, parks, schools, and post-office system? The economic functions of the central government have everywhere increased. History alone, therefore, cannot decide whether the individualistic or the collectivistic tendency is to be preferred.

2. THE PSYCHOLOGICAL ARGUMENT. We are frequently told that men will not produce unless they have an incentive, and that the most powerful of such incentives that experience has as yet shown is the profit motive. This argument, however, confuses what is true locally and temporarily with what must be true necessarily and in the future. Let us grant that under present conditions every business enterprise must either show a profit or sooner or later dissolve. The individual or company owners may continue to sink money into a losing business in the hope that future profits will compensate them. But if these hopes are not realized, the business cannot continue. There are, of course, those who are perfectly sincere when they talk of being in business for the service they can render. I have no doubt that there are those who really make sacrifices to carry on their business and to give employment, as they say, to those who have faithfully served them. But under our present conditions, a business enterprise must make a profit or become a charitable institution, drawing funds from those making profit elsewhere.

Despite the foregoing, we must regard the argument as to the necessity of the profit motive as psychologically most superficial.

The desire for profit is not an instinctive one. It arises only under certain conditions. And even under these conditions, men do not give their lives for profit as they do for love of religion, country, family, etc. In the church, in the army, in educational institutions, in social activity, other motives surely come into play in a more decisive manner.

Not only is much socially important work done without hope of profit, but profit frequently comes to those who only stand and wait. There are many forms of profit that are in no way due to the productivity of the one to whom these profits go. This is the case with speculative and monopoly profits and the unearned increment in land. Such profits may create investment funds, but their origin is parasitic. There are also cases where increased profit may result from lessened productivity; this we see when farmers are pressed to reduce the acreage of cultivation, or when the owners of oil wells agree to limit output.

The demand for profit, indeed, is frequently the worst enemy of productivity. A great deal of our national domain and natural resources have been wasted because the demand for immediate profits has forced an uneconomical and wasteful exploitation. Even in private business, boards of directors cannot always take a long-time view of the welfare of their business because stockholders demand immediate dividends and are not willing, as the citizens of a country are, that the profits should go to future generations. The brewers, for instance, might have saved their business from the impending confiscation of Prohibition if they had dissociated themselves from the saloons and the distillers. But such a reorganization would have postponed profits for a considerable time, and that was more than the shareholders were willing to stand for.

3. THE ECONOMIC ARGUMENT. The best version of this classical argument that I know of was stated by Justice Holmes: "We need to think things instead of words—to drop ownership, money, etc., and to think of the stream of products; of wheat and cloth and railway travel." How is enterprise to be initiated and by whom controlled? The answer, according to Justice Holmes, is that competition under private capitalism rewards that producer who has had the most accurate vision of what

the effective demand will be; in other words, the one who sees best what the community wants and produces these things most economically is the one whom our system rewards with increased power. And who is better qualified to direct the process of production?

This argument may have applied and may still apply under special conditions, but large industry today does not merely anticipate effective demand. Actually, by means of publicity, advertising, and standardization through monopoly, our captains of industry create and direct the effective demand. In the competition between financially powerful groups and smaller competitors, the former may prevail, not because of any superior wisdom, but through sheer financial power.

But the main weakness of this economic argument is that it ignores the fact that the process of competition, like that of natural selection, is a frightfully wasteful one. Of all the business enterprises started, only a small proportion survive over a year or two. Who bears the cost of all these unsuccessful experiments? Ultimately, it is borne by the community as a whole.

The waste of competition is an old and hackneyed story. Yet it is well to note that much of our present financial distress is directly due to it. Accumulation of profits creates funds which are not productively invested because idle capital cannot be too critical. Thus, we create new plants and machinery for peak production which is never attained, and large factories are thus idle and unproductive. We open coal mines and abandon them; or we build structures for the making of automobiles in excess of the number that the community can purchase—and then the workmen who build them lack food and shelter. The constant introduction and employment of machinery increases the total output, but reduces the labor staff and the relative amount of money that goes into wages, so that the purchasing power of the largest part of the community is relatively diminished.

Under our form of competition, also, too much of the monetary wealth of the country goes to advertisers and salesmen and to pay the cost of planless transportation, all of which could be eliminated by a rational plan of distribution. It was only under the pressure of the First World War that economy in sugar-shipping transportation was effected by an agreement according to which Cuba shipped its sugar to the United States, and Java to the Allies.

Finally, we come to the main consideration: Do we want to be productive, without inquiring what goods are worth producing and what cost in human labor and in human welfare is involved in producing these goods?

The defenders of private capitalism insist that under that system an enterprise will not continue unless its costs are less than the value of its products. But an enterprise may give rise to products that it does not sell, and shift to society (i.e., to other productive enterprises) costs that it does not pay. By-products of industry, such as uncompensated accidents and the ruined lives of child workers, may make an enterprise socially wasteful, although it continues to produce private profits. If an enterprise does not pay its employees a subsistence wage, this means that it is, from a social point of view, parasitic upon other enterprises.

Private business enterprises are naturally more unstable than those conducted by the state. Under private capitalism, there must necessarily be frequent dislocations of industry through the inability of private individuals or corporations to control general social or national changes which radically modify their supply of raw material or the markets in which they must sell. From this inherent instability of business there develops that terrible plague of modern life, the uncertainty of employment, an evil which private capitalism cannot possibly remove. For the individual employer does not feel responsible to the man who loses his job and cannot find another. And if the community does feel responsible in cases of actual lack of food, its powers to prevent unemployment under the ordinary workings of our prevailing economy are pitiably limited. It is this separation of responsibility from power that makes the chaos in which people, ready and eager to sell goods or services, can find no purchaser, while many others are in distress because they cannot purchase these necessary goods or services. To bring food from the farm to the city and manufactured articles from the

99

city to the farm is an elementary function that has actually broken down. We try to remedy it by charity, but that is a confession that our normal economy is not functioning and is incapable of preventing humiliating distress at a time when the country as a whole has an overabundance of wheat and other necessities.

It is said that the desire for profit makes private capital apply science or scientific management to discover new methods, and that this is in fact the way in which industry has become tremendously productive. In reply, it might well be urged that governments also use experts and men of science who go into the various bureaus of the government with at least as much enthusiasm, certainly, as they carry into private enterprise. But the most significant answer is that the efficiency engineers employed by private capital are subordinated to the profit motive of their employers. Modern scientific management tends, as Hoxie has pointed out,[1] "to the constant breakdown of the established crafts and craftsmanship and the constant elimination of skill in the sense of narrowing craft knowledge and workmanship. . . . It enables the employer constantly to lop off portions of the work from a certain class and thus constantly to create new classifications of workers with new conditions of work and pay." The effect of this is to mechanize the workman, to reduce his opportunity for skillful work, and to make him as easily replaced as a part of a machine. Under such conditions he can have little to say as to the conditions of the industry to which he gives the larger part of his life.

Under individual capitalism, where the employer is free to hire and fire, only the temporary efficiency of an individual is taken into account. It is not to the interest of the employer to ask, "At what speed should a man work between the ages of twenty and thirty so as to retain some efficiency after forty?" The employer does not feel responsible for what happens to the man who works so hard in his early years that he cannot do much after forty. But from the social point of view that is wasteful. Just as the reduction in the number of work hours

[1] *Scientific Management and Labor,* p. 129.

per week has been shown to be, in many cases, productive of a greater total output, so the reduction of speed may result in a greater output during the total life of an individual. But this is not something that an efficiency engineer working for a private employer can well undertake to study. In any case, the processes of speeding up production depend upon selecting younger people, and, as this is coupled with a tendency to make work mechanical and devoid of special skill, our workmen find themselves in middle life at the end of a blind alley and must depend therefore on casual employment or charity.

The fact is that "scientific management" is scientific only in small areas. The owner of a business is willing to use science to increase the productivity of his own plant, if increased productivity is profitable. But in its attitude toward large-scale economic problems, private capitalism goes back to a prescientific philosophy of divine natural harmonies, which may be summed up in the commandment: "Seek you each his individual profit and the Lord will provide general prosperity." This optimistic doctrine ignores the most basic of economic facts, namely, that under free competition one frequently makes slight profits by causing wholly disproportionate losses to competitors, employees, or the consuming public.

Another of the distressing effects of private capitalism that is not accounted for on corporate balance sheets is the great unhappiness that comes from unequal distribution of wealth. Envy of invidious distinctions is a primitive trait of mankind. A rational organization of society generally minimizes it by accustoming us to the standard of our own class. Generally speaking, in any ordered society that shows class divisions—as, for instance, in medieval Europe—it is considered immoral for the members of one class to try to imitate in dress or any other expenditure the manners of those of a higher class. Proust gives some charming illustrations of this; and I remember that in the town in Russia where I was brought up it was considered immoral for women of the working class to wear hats rather than kerchiefs, for the wearing of a hat was a pretension which no self-respecting workingman's wife would indulge in. In a capitalistic economy, however, there are no sharp distinctions of income, and everyone tries to increase his or her conspicuous expenditure in order to appear at least one rung higher in the social ladder. This is typified by young women of limited means who have to limit their food in order to buy silk stockings.

Another product of the unequal division of wealth is the constant temptation to crime which modern wealth offers. In all of our studies of crime we generally ignore this fundamental cause. But it is hopeless to find remedies for modern crime so long as we do not or cannot at least mitigate the intensity of the cause.

4. THE POLITICAL ARGUMENT. It is frequently urged that government control of industry is bound to be wasteful because the politicians who control the government have their ears to popular clamor or passion and do not give to affairs that considerate judgment which businessmen habitually do. Let us look at this argument not in a provincial but in a somewhat cosmopolitan way. The relative ability of different professional groups varies from time to time and from place to place. In China, until very recently, the businessmen were undoubtedly held in greater honor than the military class. The very opposite condition prevailed in Japan. In the United States, it is true that the greatest prizes and honors have, as a rule, gone to the successful captains of finance and industry, so that few of them have preferred public office. And yet, under President [Theodore] Roosevelt, a great impetus was given to men of ability to forsake private business for government service.

In general, as the business of the government becomes important, people honor those who serve them with distinction and more men of ability go into that service, just as men of ability today feel honored to serve the country as members of the judiciary, even though this involves, in many cases, great pecuniary loss. But is it true today that businessmen run their affairs more satisfactorily than politicians attend to theirs? Certainly, businessmen do not prove, as a rule, very successful as the heads of state or municipal governments, and that is a matter well worth serious reflection.

Why are honest municipal administrations so unpopular? Why are corrupt political machines returned to power by such overwhelming majorities after the people try a term or two of reform? It is easy to say that the people prefer corruption; but that does not get us anywhere. I think the trouble is with the reformers, in that they carry the businessman's idea into politics. They want an economical administration, which means saving the money of the taxpayer. But they forget that cities exist not to save money but to promote the good life. The businessman is too narrow in his conception of government, and people instinctively and, I think, rightly rebel against that conception. The businessman's training narrows his standards. He judges everything simply by the cash nexus. It is all very simple —much too simple. If your subordinate head of department shows a favorable balance at the end of the year, he is a good man; if not, you are sorry, and sooner or later he goes. But in government the test of whether a judge, a police officer, or a college professor is doing good work or not is not so readily settled. And so we often pick a man or woman as we pick a husband or wife, and let him or her have the job for life. Are our judges, or professors, our husbands and wives efficient? We do not determine their tenure of office by that consideration.

It is commonly urged and almost universally believed that government enterprise costs more because of graft. Is graft, however, unknown in private business? In fact, most political graft comes from the fact that businessmen want special favors and pay for them. But graft in business may be independent of politics. I know of a very large enterprise in which shares worth millions were given gratis to two individuals for the good and sufficient reason that it was feared that if their good will was not thus secured they would attack and hurt the business. On a small scale this would be called racketeering and graft. On a large scale it is high finance.

Let us, however, examine more closely the current complaint against graft in government. A municipal institution that I know has its own electric plant. One day one of its hustling young engineers made a thorough study of the situation and convinced his superiors that $26,000 of the city's money might be saved every year by abandoning the plant and buying the electricity from a private company. But at this suggestion the heads of the city government balked. The real reason, I suspect, was that a number of good party men would have lost their jobs as a result of the proposed change. Can there be a better example of a class of cases that make the blood of the municipal reformer boil with indignation? Can there be a clearer case of indefensible waste?

Yet, consider the families of at least four good party men working at this municipal electric plant. These men would lose their jobs, to which the reformers say, "Let them find jobs elsewhere. The city should not maintain an uneconomic venture merely for the sake of providing men with employment." In point of fact, however, the city does now engage men otherwise unemployed in order to keep their families from starvation. Why then discharge the men from the electric plant and then try to support them anyway, seeing that they are not likely to get other employment, or, if they do, will displace others who would be in a similar plight?

The United States Post Office service is generally run at a deficit. Suppose that a company undertook to render exactly the same service to the nation at the same charges and offered to pay the United States Government five million dollars a year or a percentage of its earnings. Would the people of the United States accept the offer? The chances are overwhelming that they would not. And why not? First, as a matter of pride: the sale of the Post Office would offend national honor in the same way as would the sale of our colonies to another nation. Without approving all the implications of this sense of national honor, I would suggest that in the case proposed it is based upon an imaginative participation in social control without which most of us should feel ourselves slaves. It is this sense of participation in social control which has given the Russian worker a new pride and, despite rigorous political restrictions, a new sense of freedom. These things are felt to be more important than the saving of money.

In 1912 a proposal was instituted to make the borough of the Bronx in New York City a separate county. The reformers with their businessman's bent for economy opposed the proposal because it would create new county officials at a cost of about

$700,000 a year. But was it not worth $700,000 to help decentralize the terrific congestion of New York City's traffic by creating a new local center in the Bronx so that people no longer need to go out of their neighborhood to record their deeds or transact other business requiring the aid of county officials? Again there is an intangible value that the businesslike reformers did not see, in the stimulus and satisfaction which this move gave to local pride. The desire for economy, like the desire for increased production, is normal in private business. But it becomes an irrational obsession when businessmen press it to the neglect of larger social interests which in the routine of private business seem sentimental.

The Limitations of Socialism

We have spoken of planning by the community or in the interests of the community. In point of fact, however, all planning must be done by individuals, and the government, no matter how chosen or how it comes into power, always consists of a differentiated group that has its own views which it will try with all its power to enforce. Professor Michels, in his book on the *Sociology of Political Parties,* has called attention to the inevitability of oligarchy or bureaucracy in all government, and he illustrated it in the organization of the German Social-Democratic Party before the First World War. The government in Russia calls itself a dictatorship of the proletariat; yet no one doubts that a good deal of the dictatorship came from men like Lenin, Trotsky, Lunacharsky, and others, who were not themselves workingmen or peasants. And if it is urged that these leaders obtained their power only by espousing the cause of the proletariat, the reply is obvious: that government is not merely a vessel whereby the great masses assert their will, but that the governors are themselves persons possessed of wills and of power, and that they naturally use that power to enforce their policies. Doubtless, the leaders of a Communist party may be, like Robespierre, personally incorruptible so far as monetary considerations are concerned (though this can hardly be claimed for all the subsidiary officials who are the tools on which government must depend). But the crucial fact is that those who govern in the name of the people or the workers, like those who govern in the name of God, are difficult to resist. Free thought, which must include some right to dissent and to express the ground of the dissent, finds as little toleration under Communism as under Fascism and Czarism. And here we have a danger whose gravity cannot be exaggerated. A government of limited powers, which cannot indoctrinate all its citizens with its dogmas and does not make all of its citizens directly dependent on it for their daily bread, cannot possibly be so dangerous to free thought and to all the achievements of art and science which depend on free thought. In view of the inherent uncertainty of all human arrangements, can we afford the risk of putting all our eggs into one basket and depending on one central government to exercise unlimited power? History does not show any example of genuine intellectual progress under a regime of absolute power. We must allow for variation and research, so that the existing good may not prevent the better from coming into being.

Concluding Reflections

In discussing the relative merits of individual and social capitalism as systems, we have taken the United States and Russia as types of these systems. But I do not wish to identify these logical types of economic system with the actual conditions which prevail either in the United States or in Russia. Theoretical types are useful in enabling us to analyze existing situations, but they must not be identified with the latter. To think of our present economy in this country as entirely private capitalism is to ignore the extent to which social capitalism actually prevails, both in the realm of government enterprise and in that of government limitation of the supposed absolute rights of private property owners. Theoretically it may be said that anyone who owns a share of Pennsylvania Railroad or United States Steel is an owner of the property. But in fact his ownership is so limited that, except for the shadowy right to vote for directors (if his stock has voting rights) and the right to receive some of the profits (if they are declared as dividends), he bears to the property practically the same relation as a stranger. For many purposes the law treats the officer of a public-service corporation as a public official rather than as a mere agent of stockholder-owners. The rights and duties of the owner of a city tenement house are now so fixed by law (in New York) that we may well look upon him as a quasi-public official.

In point of fact, no country that we know of is exclusively individualistic or collectivistic. No one in this country wants the government to give up its ownership of national parks, to go out of the postal business, or to cease to supply (free to the public) information of various sorts, such as weather reports. Certain enterprises are definitely national in all countries. On the other hand, no country, certainly not Russia, has a government which undertakes direct control over all economic activity. A great deal of private business in small industries still goes on in Russia, and it is extremely doubtful whether it can ever be eliminated. The issue between individualism and collectivism becomes therefore a question of how far one of these principles can be carried at the expense of the other, admitting that we can never completely eliminate one or the other. And this is instructive if we wish to understand the whole problem of social planning.

Principles of social aims and policy are frequently discussed as if they were eternal dogmas. There are those who regard *laissez faire* as an eternal principle of human freedom which is never to be violated with impunity. Others regard the principles of Communism as those of eternal justice, of the brotherhood of man, or of the necessary evolution of the system of production that has appeared in history. These attitudes are fighting attitudes. If we wish to go in a given direction we push with all our force against the enemy. But we might stumble if the enemy suddenly yielded. A philosophic analysis, however, that wishes to see the truth must recognize that social principles can never be proved beyond all reasonable doubt. They must be taken not as dogmas, but as provisional hypotheses, to be tried with as much intelligence and persistence as we can summon, but never without watching their consequences to see whether these hypotheses are really confirmed.

There are those among us who are always trying to reconcile conflicting principles and who, according to one wit, would like to unite Heaven and Hell by combining the good points of both. A sober consideration will show that we cannot so readily eliminate conflict and opposition. Nevertheless, I believe that some combination of the principles of individualism and collectivism is possible in a well-ordered society. We can combine these principles, however, only if we make certain necessary distinctions. Such a distinction, for instance, is that between a deficit and a surplus economy. As to the bare necessities of life, as to the fundamental needs of food, shelter, public peace and safety, collective planning is indispensable and is, in fact, making progress everywhere, though some of us prefer to call it by other names. Police protection, hospitals, and schools were all private enterprises at one time. The line between regulation and government ownership of railroads is becoming thinner and is at times quite unreal. On the other hand, the need for inventiveness, for increased production, will always call into operation the individualistic principle of rewards and penalties. These rewards and penalties may not be in terms of money or material goods; they may be in terms of honor. But no society can function without stimulating individual initiative by the prospects of special remuneration or honor and some effective deterrent for those who lag behind unduly in the social procession. We need not be frightened by the fear of forced labor. Under any form of society, men are actually forced to labor by the fear of starvation. And where there is no guarantee of the decencies of life, freedom and other legal rights are mockeries. But man cannot live by bread alone, and the exercise of free thought is essential to the dignity which makes life worth exercising.

All systems of economy that are to be compatible with man's continual adaptation to a changing world must employ both the principle of order and that of freedom. Social planning must provide for the general security and daily necessities, but also for feeding man's imagination as to future possibilities. It must put aside capital goods to continue to secure the continuity of our industrial life, but must also make provision for research into the ways in which our economic arrangement might better serve human needs. But, above all, we must not be so preoccupied with material production as to ignore the imaginative and other intangible needs of men. While art, science, and religion must have a certain freedom from government, the economic policies of any human government must make the free growth of these noneconomic activities possible.

BIBLIOGRAPHY

Oliver Wendell Holmes, *Collected Legal Papers,* 1921.

Bertrand and Dora Russell, *Prospects of Industrial Civilization,* 1923.

Harry F. Ward, *The Profit Motive: Is It Necessary to Modern Industrial Society?,* 1925.

W. Z. Ripley, *Main Street and Wall Street,* 1927.

Thorstein Veblen, *The Engineers and the Price System,* 1921.

Stuart Chase, *The Tragedy of Waste,* 1925.

Harry W. Laidler, *How America Lives,* 1931.

P. H. Douglas, "The Reality of Non-Commercial Incentives in Economic Life," in Tugwell, *The Trend of Economics,* 1924.

F. W. Taussig, *Inventors and Money Makers,* 1915.

John T. Flynn, *Graft in Business,* 1931.

M. R. Cohen, "Property and Sovereignty," *Cornell Law Quarterly,* 1927, Vol. 13, P. 8.

12

WHY I AM NOT A COMMUNIST

LIKE MANY OTHERS who are not Communists, I hold no brief for the injustices and stupidities of the present capitalist regime. Indeed, I have never ceased to be grateful for the illumination on historic and contemporary social issues which I found in studying Marx's *Das Kapital*. It prepared me to see that the present general breakdown of capitalist economy is not an unforeseeable accident but a consequence of the private ownership of the machinery of production, whereby the processes of industry are directed for the profit of individual capitalists rather than for the satisfaction of our common needs. The old optimistic but essentially anarchistic notion that the good of all will best be promoted by "rugged individualism," by each pursuing his own selfish economic gain, is a cruel superstition which no man possessed of both reason and a decent amount of human sympathy can maintain in the face of the hideous miseries of our present disorder. When good crops turn out to be calamitous to the farmers who toil to raise them, because the city workers cannot with their needed labor buy the cereals and cotton which they need for food and clothing, the bankruptcy of capitalism is as clear as anything in human affairs can be.

But while the foregoing or essentially similar criticism of the evils of capitalism is largely used by Communists, it is not peculiar to them. They share it not only with other Marxian socialists—whom, with self-defeating unfairness, they character-

Reprinted by permission of the *Modern Monthly*, April 1934.

ize as Fascists or social-fascists—but also with many liberal social reformers. For Marx himself freely borrowed his ideas from bourgeois historians as well as from Saint-Simon, Fourier, and their followers, whom he, with the characteristic human failing of borrowers, belittled as Utopians. (Note, for instance, how closely the *Communist Manifesto* follows Victor Considérant's *Principes du Socialisme, Manifeste de la Démocratie,* not only in ideas but also in their linguistic expression.) What distinguishes present-day Communists is not, therefore, their professed ultimate goal or their analysis of our economic ills, but their political remedy or program—to wit, the seizure of power by armed rebellion * and the setting up of a dictatorship by the leaders of the Communist Party. To be sure, this dictatorship is to be in the name of the *proletariat,* just as the fascist dictatorship is in the name of *the whole nation.* But such verbal tricks cannot hide the brute facts of tyrannical suppression necessarily involved in all dictatorship. For the wielders of dictatorial power are few, they are seldom if ever themselves toilers, and they can maintain their power only by ruthlessly suppressing all expression of popular dissatisfaction with their rule. And where there is no freedom of discussion, there is no freedom of thought.

This program of civil war, dictatorship, and the illiberal or fanatically intolerant spirit which war psychology always engenders may bring more miseries than those that the Communists seek to remove; and the arguments to prove that such war is desirable or inevitable seem to me patently inadequate.

Communists ignore the historic truth that civil wars are much more destructive of all that men hold dearest than are wars between nations; and all the arguments that they use against the latter, including the late "war to end war," are much more cogent against civil wars. Wars between nations are necessarily restricted in scope and do not prevent—to a limited extent they even stimulate—co-operation within a community. But civil wars necessarily dislocate all existing social organs and leave us with little social capital or machinery to rebuild a better society.

* Since this article was written armed intervention seems to have largely replaced armed rebellion as a technique for the seizure of power.

The hatreds which fratricidal wars develop are more persistent and destructive than those developed by wars that terminate in treaties or agreements.

Having lived under the tyranny of the Czar, I cannot and do not condemn all revolutions. But the success and benefits of any revolution depend on the extent to which—like the American Revolution of 1776, the French Revolution of 1789, and the anti-Czarist Revolution of March 1917—it approximates national unanimity in the co-operation of diverse classes. When armed uprisings have been undertaken by single oppressed classes, as in the revolt of the gladiators in Rome, the various peasant revolts in England, Germany, and Russia, the French Commune of 1871, or the Moscow uprising of 1905, they have left a deplorably monotonous record of bloody massacres and oppressive reaction. The idea that armed rebellion is the only or the always effective cure for social ills seems to me no better than the old superstition of medieval medicine that blood-letting is the only and the sovereign remedy for all bodily ills.

Communists may feel that the benefits of their Revolution of 1917 outweigh all the terrific hardships which the Russian people have suffered since then. But reasonable people in America will do well to demand better evidence than has yet been offered that they can improve their lot by blindly imitating Russia. Russian breadlines, and famine without breadlines, are certainly not *prima facie* improvements over American conditions. At best a revolution is a regrettable means to bring about greater human welfare. It always unleashes the forces that thrive in disorder, the brutal executions, imprisonments, and, what is even worse, the sordid spying that undermines all feeling of personal security. These forces, once let loose, are difficult to control and they tend to perpetuate themselves. If, therefore, human well-being, rather than mere destruction, is our aim, we must be as critically-minded in considering the consequences of armed revolution as in considering the evils of the existing regime.

One of the reasons that lead Communists to ignore the terrific destruction which armed rebellion must bring about is the conviction that "the revolution" is inevitable. In this they follow Marx, who, dominated by the Hegelian dialectic, regarded the victory of the proletariat over the bourgeoisie as inevitable,[1] so that all that human effort can hope to achieve is "to shorten and lessen the birth pangs" of the new order.[2] There is, however, very little scientific value in this dialectic argument, and many Communists are quite ready to soft-pedal it and admit that some human mistake or misstep might lead to the triumph of fascism. The truth is that the dialectic method which Marx inherited from Hegel and Schelling is an outgrowth of speculations carried on in theologic seminaries. The "system" of production takes the place of the councils or the mills of the gods. Such Oriental fatalism has little support in the spirit and method of modern science. Let us therefore leave the pretended dialectic proof and examine the contention on an historical basis.

Historically, the argument is put thus: When did any class give up its power without a bloody struggle? As in most rhetorical questions, the questioner does not stop for an answer, assuming that his ignorance is conclusive as to the facts. Now, it is not difficult to give instances of ruling classes giving up their sovereignty without armed resistance. The English landed aristocracy did it in the Reform Bill of 1832; and the Russian nobility did it in 1863 when they freed their serfs, though history showed clearly that in this way not only their political power but their very existence was doomed (for money income has never been so secure as direct revenue from the land, and life in cities reduced the absolute number of noble families). In our own country, the old seaboard aristocracy, which put over the United States Constitution and controlled the government up to the Jacksonian era, offered no armed resistance when the backwoods farmers outvoted them and removed church and property qualifications for office and for the franchise.

But it is not necessary to multiply such instances. It is more important to observe that history does not show that any *class* ever gained its enfranchisement through a bloody rebellion carried out by its own unaided efforts. When ruling classes are

[1] *Capital* (Tr. by Untermann, 1932), I, p. 837.
[2] *Ibid.*, pp. 14-15.

overthrown it is generally by a combination of groups that have risen to power only after a long process. For the parties to a rebellion cannot succeed unless they have more resources than the established regime. Thus the ascendancy of the French bourgeoisie was aided by the royal power which Richelieu and Colbert used in the seventeenth century to transform the landed barons into dependent courtiers. Even so, the French Revolution of 1789 would have been impossible without the co-operation of the peasantry, whose opposition to their ancient seigneurs was strengthened as the latter ceased to be independent rulers of the land. This is in a measure also true of the supposedly purely Communist Revolution in Russia. For in that revolution, too, the peasantry had a much greater share than is ordinarily assumed. After all, the amount of landed communal property (that of the crown, the church, etc.) which was changed by the peasants into individual ownership may have been greater than the amount of private property made communal by the Soviet regime. Even the system of collective farms is, after all, a return to the old *mir* system, using modern machinery. The success of the Russian Revolution was largely due to the landlords' agents who, in their endeavor to restore the rule of the landlords, threw the peasantry into the arms of the Bolshevists. Indeed, the strictly Marxian economics, with its ideology of surplus-value due to the ownership of the means of production, is inherently inapplicable to the case of the peasant who cultivates his own piece of ground.

Even more important, however, is it to note that no amount of repetition can make a truth of the dogma that the capitalist class alone rules this country and like the Almighty can do what it pleases. It would be folly to deny that, as individuals or as a class, capitalists have more than their proportionate share of influence in the government, and that they have exercised it unintelligently and with dire results. But it is equally absurd to maintain that they have governed or can govern without the co-operation of the farmers and the influential middle classes. None of our recent constitutional amendments—not the income-tax amendment, not the popular election of the United States Senators, not woman suffrage, neither prohibition nor its repeal—nor any other major bit of legislation can be said to have been imposed on our country in the interests of the capitalist class. The farmers, who despite mortgages still cling to the private ownership of their land, are actually the dominant political group even in industrial states like New York, Pennsylvania, and Illinois.

The Communist division of mankind into workingmen and capitalists suffers from the fallacy of simplism. Our social structure and effective class divisions are much more complicated. As the productivity of machinery increases, the middle classes increase rather than decrease. Hence a program based entirely on the supposed exclusive interests of the proletariat has no reasonable prospect. Any real threat of an armed uprising will only strengthen the reactionaries, who are not less intelligent than the Communist leaders, understand just as well how to reach and influence our people, and have more ample means for organization. If our working classes find it difficult to learn what their true interests are and do not know how to control their representatives in the government and in the trade unions, there is little prospect that they will be able to control things better during a rebellion or during the ensuing dictatorship.

If the history of the past is any guide at all, it indicates that real improvements in the future will come like the improvements of the past—namely, through co-operation among different groups, each of which is wise enough to see the necessity of compromising with those with whom we have to live together and whom we cannot or do not wish to exterminate.

I know that this notion of compromise or of taking counsel as the least wasteful way of adjusting differences is regarded as hopelessly antiquated and bourgeois, but I do not believe that the ideas of so-called Utopian socialists have really been refuted by those who arrogate the epithet "scientific" to themselves. The Communists seem to me to be much more Utopian and quite unscientific in their claims that the working class alone can by its own efforts completely transform our social order.

I do not have very high expectations from the efforts of sentimental benevolence. Yet I cannot help noticing that the leaders of the Communists and of other revolutionary labor movements

—Engels, Marx, Lassalle, Luxemburg, Liebknecht, Lenin, and Trotsky—have not been drawn to it by economic solidarity. They were not workingmen nor even all of workingmen's families. They were driven to their role by human sympathy. Sympathy with the sufferings of our fellow men is a human motive that cannot be read out of history. It has exerted tremendous social pressure. Without it you cannot explain the course of nineteenth-century factory legislation, the freeing of serfs and slaves, or the elimination of the grosser forms of human exploitation. Though some who regard themselves as followers of Karl Marx are constantly denouncing reformers who believe in piecemeal improvement and hope rather that things will get worse so as to drive people into a revolution, Marx himself did not always take that view. Very wisely he attached great importance to English factory legislation which restricted the number of hours per working day, for he realized that every little bit that strengthens the workers strengthens their resistance to exploitation. Those who are most oppressed and depressed, the inhabitants of the slums, do not revolt—they have not energy enough to think of it. When, therefore, Mr. Strachey and others criticize the socialists for not bringing about the millennium when they get into power, I am not at all impressed. I do not believe that the socialists or the Labor Party in England have been free from shameful error. But neither have the Communists, or any other human group, been free from it. Trite though it sounds, it is nevertheless true that no human arrangement can bring about perfection on earth. And while the illusion of omniscience may offer great consolation, it brings endless inhumanity when it leads us to shut the gates of mercy. Real as are our human conflicts, our fundamental identity of interest in the face of hostile nature seems to me worthy of more serious attention than the Communists have been willing to accord it.

If liberalism were dead, I should still maintain that it deserved to live, that it had not been condemned in the court of human reason, but lynched outside of it by the passionate and uncompromisingly ruthless war spirit, common to Communists and Fascists. But I do not believe that liberalism is dead, even though it is under eclipse. There still seems to me enough reason left to which to appeal against reckless fanaticism.

It is pure fanaticism to belittle the gains that have come to mankind from the spirit of free inquiry, free discussion, and accommodation. No human individual or group of individuals can claim omniscience. Hence society can only suffer serious loss when one group suppresses the opinions and criticisms of all others. In purely abstract questions compromise may often be a sign of confusion. One cannot really believe inconsistent principles at the same time. But in the absence of perfect or even adequate knowledge in regard to human affairs and their future, we must adopt an experimental attitude and treat principles not as eternal dogmas, but as hypotheses, to be tried to the extent that they indicate the general direction of solution to specific issues. But as the scientist must be ever ready to modify his own hypothesis or to recognize wherein a contrary hypothesis has merits or deserves preference, so in practical affairs we must be prepared to learn from those who differ with us, and to recognize that however contradictory diverse views may appear in discourse they may not be so in their practical applications.

Thus, the principles of Communism and individualism may be held like theologic dogmas, eternally true and on no occasion ever to be contaminated one by the other. But in fact, when Communists get into power they do not differ so much from others. No one ever wished to make everything communal property. Nor does anyone in his senses believe that any individual will ever with impunity be permitted to use his "property" in an antisocial way when the rest of the community is aroused thereby. In actual life, the question how far Communism shall be pushed depends more upon specific analyses of actual situations—that is, upon factual knowledge. There can be no doubt that individualism à la Herbert Hoover has led millions to destruction. Nevertheless, we must not forget that a Communist regime will, after all, be run by individuals who will exercise a tremendous amount of power, no less than do our captains of industry or finance today. There is no real advantage in assuming that under Communism the laboring classes will be omniscient. We know perfectly well how labor leaders like John

Lewis keep their power by bureaucratic rather than democratic methods. May it not be that the Stalins also keep their power by bureaucratic rather than democratic methods?

Indeed the ruthless suppression of dissent within the Communist Party in Russia and the systematic glorification of the national heroes and military objectives of Czarist days suggest that the Bolshevik Revolution was not so complete a break with the Russian past as most of its friends and enemies assumed in earlier days. In any event we have witnessed in the history of the Communist movement since 1917 a dramatic demonstration of the way in which the glorification of power—first as a means of destroying a ruling class, then as a means of defending a beleaguered state from surrounding enemies, and finally as a means of extending Communism to neighboring lands—comes imperceptibly to displace the ends or objectives which once formed the core of Communist thought. Thus, one by one, the worst features of capitalist society and imperialism, against which Communism cut its eye teeth in protest—extreme inequality in wages, speed-up of workers, secret diplomacy, and armed intervention as a technique of international intercourse—have been taken over by the Soviet Union, with only a set of thin verbal distinctions to distinguish the "good" techniques of Communism from the corresponding "bad" techniques used by capitalism. As is always the case, the glorification of power dulls the sense of righteousness to which any movement for bettering the basic conditions of human living must appeal.

The Communist criticism of liberalism seems to me altogether baseless and worthless. One would suppose from it that liberalism is a peculiar excrescence of capitalism. This is, however, not true. The essence of liberalism—freedom of thought and inquiry, freedom of discussion and criticism—is not the invention of the capitalist system. It is rather the mother of Greek and modern science, without which our present industrial order and the labor movement would be impossible. The plea that the denial of freedom is a temporary necessity is advanced by all militarists. It ignores the fact that, when suppression becomes a habit, it is not readily abandoned. Thus, when the Christian Church after its alliance with the Roman Empire began the policy of "com-

pelling them to enter," it kept up the habit of intolerant persecution for many centuries. Those who believe that many of the
finer fruits of civilization were thereby choked should be careful about strengthening the forces of intolerance.

When the Communists tell me that I must choose between
their dictatorship and Fascism, I feel that I am offered the
choice between being shot and being hanged. It would be suicide for liberal civilization to accept this as exhausting the field
of human possibility. I prefer to hope that the present wave of
irrationalism and of fanatical intolerance will recede and that
the great human energy which manifests itself in free thought
will not perish. Often before, it has emerged after being
swamped by passionate superstitions. There is no reason to feel
that it may not do so again.

13

MINIMIZING SOCIAL CONFLICTS

THROUGHOUT THE AGES the great religious teachers, prophets,
and saints have preached the grace of universal peace and
the folly of human strife, and men of good will have persistently
sought for remedial or preventive measures against our destruc-
tively pugnacious inclinations. Yet the intensely bitter conflicts
raging today in international affairs, and in our class warfare
on economic, religious, racial, and political grounds, all make
the long-hoped-for day seem as far off as ever. One is thus
tempted to yield to despair and let the waves of fanatical hatred
spread and engulf all the hard-earned gains of recent centuries.

Reprinted from *The Annals of the American Academy of Political and Social Science*, Vol. 203, p. 114 (May 1939).

But "if hopes were dupes, fears may be liars." Certainly, thoughtful people who have had the benefit of a humanistic or scientific education are in duty bound to avoid hasty judgment on such vital questions and to examine the issues in a fearlessly critical spirit.

The analogy of progress in the field of medicine suggests that before prescribing remedies for social ills, we should study the causes behind the symptoms and consider whether or not proposed remedies may produce more harm than the diseases against which they are directed. This involves for us the prior questions: Is social conflict always an evil, and to what extent is it at all possible to get rid of it?

Is Conflict Good or Evil?

From the days of Heraclitus to those of Nietzsche and the neo-Darwinians, not to mention the perennial apologists or glorifiers of war, we have had with us the preachers of the doctrine that strife is the father of all things, or at any rate of all things heroic; and modern psychology seems to reinforce the lesson of biology and history that the combative impulses are deep-rooted and pervasive, so that it is foolish to expect them to be eradicated from human life. In view of this age-long conflict of opinion, it is easy to take either side and to find supporting considerations. What is more difficult but much more worth while is to exercise discrimination and to try to discover under what conditions and to what extent conflict is an evil and how far that evil may be minimized if not eliminated.

It would obviously carry us far afield to go into an exhaustive consideration as to what is the proper principle or criterion to enable us to discriminate between ultimate good and evil; but no one doubts that some of the results of social conflict are worse than others, and though there are differences of opinion in specific instances, experience shows that at least in moments of regret we recognize that some of our judgments have been mistaken.

Now, in point of fact, few if any actually condemn all forms of social conflict. Combat in the field of sports, contests in various forms of games, and friendly rivalry or competition in the arts are generally approved. The combative impulse in human nature may thus find an expression which is compatible with the general conditions of humane civilization. Indeed, without it we should not have active life, but stagnation and death; for if there is any evil in human life to be eliminated, we must oppose those who fight every effort at improvement, and the struggle against them thus becomes as imperative as the struggle against the ills of nature. It is easy to give long lists of devastating conflicts such as those which destroyed Greek, Roman, and Saracen civilization, which drenched Europe in blood in the sixteenth and seventeenth centuries, and which threaten to destroy all that we hold dearest in present Western civilization. But in the same way we can show that all these goods were obtained by prolonged combat in which heroes and martyrs had to sacrifice their lives. Social conflict, then, is not, as such, either good or bad. The goodness or badness of its results depends upon whether they further or hinder certain accepted ends of civilization.

But can destructive conflicts be eliminated? The widespread negative answer to this question is itself one of the principal obstacles to remedial effort.

A narrow and antiquated conception of science still supports the view that all human thought is a necessary and inevitable outcome of purely material or economic conditions, and that no knowledge or reflection can change the "iron laws" that govern the historic process. While an *argumentum ad hominem* is not logically conclusive, we may well note in passing that the apostles of complete historic determinism also preach revolutionary effort and recognize the powerfully misleading effects of Fascist or Nazi propaganda. But it is not necessary for our purpose to refute the metaphysics of determinism, for a consistent determinism cannot deny that if effort is a fact in the world, other factors will be influenced by it; or, as Justice Holmes put it, effort is one of the ways through which the inevitable comes to pass. Nor can there be any question that men's efforts are not independent of their convictions. The clear grasp of truth and the removal of error cannot but have some effect on the character of social conflict. In any case, elementary re-flection shows that while human effort is limited in its effective-ness, and there are forces too powerful for conscious human striving to overcome, it is not true that all forms of social con-flict are so inevitable that nothing can be done to mitigate their pernicious effects.

Social conflicts are, of course, inevitable where two groups desire the same necessities which only one can procure. If an invading horde wants to deprive us of the land necessary to support our life, there is bound to be a war to the finish, just as in the animal world under similar conditions. There is, however, a wide variation possible as to what men may con-sider necessary and as to what they should desire under given conditions. And one of the functions of human intelligence is to devise ways whereby conflict is minimized, if not altogether avoided. Thus, if peoples who are starving wish to come into our country to take advantage of our superior resources, we may exclude them by force. A more civilized and humane ar-rangement which intelligence makes possible is to exchange some of our surplus food in return for certain goods or services which they are in a position to render us.

Race Antagonism

Just now, however, those who preach and promote race an-tagonism insist that it is instinctive, ineradicable, and even necessary from the point of view of social hygiene.

Ignoring all the pseudo-scientific arguments in regard to the latter point, a distinction must still be made. It is doubtless true that some forms of race prejudice have had an almost con-tinuous existence for centuries. Thus, there has hardly been a time since the Crusades when expressions of anti-Semitism were entirely absent in Germany, and one may safely predict that it will be a long time before the dogma of inherent Negro in-feriority will be entirely eliminated in our own southern states. But it is well to realize that social antagonisms are not biolog-ically innate, but are acquired by tradition. The way white chil-dren play with blacks or become attached to their black "mammies" shows that they are no more born with a loathing for the black race than with a corresponding love or admiration for every member of the white race. There is in all of us a natural shrinking from the unfamiliar, but normally we get over it, just as the horse gets over his fright at first sight of an automobile.

The persistence of what is called race friction is often due to nothing more than resentment against certain individuals who do not treat us properly. Thus we are told by a competent observer [1] that the hatred of Orientals for Europeans is due to the position of the latter as economic exploiters. "It is the hatred of the underdog for the powerful animal which stands growling beside him." The fact that race friction develops only when the number of aliens is relatively large shows that it is influenced by the conditions of social life. Race theories are indeed not only a modern invention to explain such group conflicts, but also a means for fomenting them.

Predisposition to Conflict

But though political and other forms of cultural intolerance of dissent are obviously the results of tradition, direct teaching, deliberate incitement, and group contagion, they are in a sense inevitable if we do not know how to control their causes. The preachers of war and group hatred could never be effective if the powder of group irritation and fear of the unknown were not there ready to be fired and exploded.

The charm of simple explanations makes us look for some single, all-important cause for any one social conflict; but a sound psychology must not neglect the predisposition to group conflict due to the cumulative irritations produced by many petty differences in manners and customs as regards speech, gestures, dress, and ways of behaving on different occasions. Most of our life is regulated by the conventions of our group which have no rational justification except that "it isn't done," and when someone does it we are disagreeably shocked. We may be tolerant of, and even amused by, the foreigner's mispro-

[1] L. B. Putnam Weale, *The Conflict of Colour* (1910).

nunciations or peculiar intonation when he is alone in our midst and we patronize him. But when we are not sustained by this feeling of superiority, such differences affect us unpleasantly. In civilized life we are constantly taught to ignore the peccadillos of others. But the irritation is there, and the accumulation of it supplies the powder which can, by skillful manipulation of group fear, be exploded into a violent outburst of xenophobia, or hatred for everything alien.

Another way of looking at the same phenomenon is to recognize that not only does common experience in a group develop pride in the group and its ways, but also such pride prevents us from becoming familiar with and understanding the ways of some other group, especially any group that is in some way our rival. Thus, even the educated inhabitants of a city or members of a college or a profession can readily be led to applaud any fling at some rival city, college, or profession.

The existence of these conflicts, however, surely does not mean that we cannot minimize their destructive effects. Religious differences, for instance, need not develop into bloody religious wars and persecutions. We now know of countries where religious differences exist without such cruel results. There are, indeed, some who maintain that the regime of religious toleration has become possible only because we have lost the primal intensity of religious conviction. But even the Catholic Church, which systematically rejects the doctrine of toleration, does not feel called upon to suppress all who differ with it. It often allowed Jews and Saracens to live within its territories. In general, religious differences alone do not always bring about bloody conflict. Politico-economic motives enter very often. Thus, the zeal of the Inquisition to burn heretics was not uninfluenced by the fact that it acquired at least part of the property of the condemned.

This is not to assert that economic motives alone are responsible for religious persecution and conflict. For the most part, churches, like other bodies, persecute the dissenter when they fear that his example will endanger their safety. Those who are confident that their views will prevail in the forum of free and open exchange of ideas or practices do not need to resort to violent means. Hopeful trust makes for peace, just as suspicious fear makes for war.

The foregoing considerations should be borne in mind in dealing with the various methods of minimizing group conflicts.

The Method of Suppression

In that delightful classic, *1066 and All That*,[2] there is a brief but profoundly philosophic account of the conflict between the African Zulus and the British Empire. It runs as follows: "Cause of the war, Zulus. Result, extermination of the Zulus." Certainly, one of the most ancient ways and still a most effective way of minimizing any group friction is to get rid of the cause by exterminating those who differ with us. The persistence of international and civil wars shows that, no matter how much we may dislike open brutality, no alternative to war has as yet proved to be always available or satisfactory. Recent historians, to be sure, have cast doubt on the old view, assumed for instance in the Bible, that when states are formed by conquest the invaders kill off all the natives and take their place. But there is enough evidence to show that not only conquests but the establishment and maintenance of any orderly state generally involves the extermination of some of the recalcitrant opposition. The Anglo-Saxons, for instance, may not have killed all the natives when they conquered Albion; but within the areas where they established their kingdoms, the British population was wiped out as a distinct group. Nor did the Christian descendants of these Anglo-Saxons establish themselves in the major part of North America by peaceful fusion with the aboriginal Indians. The authority of Holy Writ,[3] as well as the example of the enlightened Athenians, justifies the procedure of killing off at least all the males.

There is a tradition, which has grown up during the dominance of the liberal ideology, that suppression is always ineffective and that in the end it defeats itself. This, however, is not always true. Of course, all human arrangements succumb to the

---

[2] By Sellar and Yeatman (1921).
[3] Deuteronomy, 7:1-2; 20:17; Numbers 31:17.

attrition of time. But taken over a limited period, which is generally as far as human prevision can go, suppression has often achieved its goal. Paganism was suppressed in Christian lands, and so were various forms of heresy. Spain got rid of Protestants as well as of Jews and Moors, and France achieved unity by suppressing the Huguenots. The ruthless eradication of the Paris Communards by the Versailles troops of Thiers, of the Socialists in Finland by the counterrevolutionaries, and of all liberal and dissident parties by the Bolshevik, Fascist, and Nazi governments, are a few of the examples that can be cited of the successful achievement of unity by deliberate and systematic suppression.

However, total suppression by complete extermination or expulsion of any considerable number of people is generally so costly in life, wealth, and our normal or customary routine that it is rather exceptional; and national unity is more often sought by so oppressing and depressing an opposing group that it loses the power of revolt. This may be effected by law and by other means more subtle than brute force. Thus, while formerly rebellions were suppressed by hanging the rebel leaders, we now achieve that result more effectively [4] by inviting them to dinner. But these and other ways by which opposition is paralyzed do not prevent resentment from smoldering and sometimes breaking out into blindly destructive revolt.

Far more costly to any community are the general brutality and the cynical demoralization which result from these methods. From the point of view of liberal civilization, national, religious, or cultural solidarity that involves such unanimity as is produced in an army by rigorous military discipline is itself an evil. Even where group differences result in regrettable friction and conflict, the cost of eliminating such friction may be too high. The free and open expression of group differences is a necessary stimulus to prevent the evil of stagnation.

[4] L. T. Hobhouse, *Democracy and Reaction.*

Altruism

Those who are impressed by the evil of social conflicts have frequently adopted the view that we can get rid of such conflicts by following the command to love our neighbors as ourselves. There can be no doubt that, when men are stimulated by sympathy or intelligent regard for the welfare of their fellow men, the ugly phases of social conflicts recede; and it would be folly to insist that the preaching of brotherly love through the ages has had no effect whatsoever. But to rely upon this as a complete solution, and not to inquire as to when such teachings are applicable, is a form of irresponsible sentimentality. One may well maintain that the commandment to love our neighbors as ourselves was surely not given to the complacent ones, to those who love themselves much but not too wisely. We cannot in fact love the ugliness or vicious meanness in our neighbor, though we may sympathetically understand the causes that make him that way.

Love is a "grand" word that carries a rich afflatus with it; but for the solution of social problems we cannot dispense with the requisite critical intelligence. Turning the other cheek to the brute who assaults you seldom stops his offensive conduct. In the field of international relations we have recently had some very vivid illustrations of the ineffectiveness of thus yielding to aggressors. In this field it is not feasible even to follow the example of the conscientious Quaker who when slapped by an irate neighbor turned the other cheek and then knocked his opponent down with a well-aimed blow.

In this connection it is well to recognize and do justice to what might be called the rights of natural aversion. In the village or open country you cannot ignore your neighbor. If you do not go to church, he will call on you to inquire the reason. If you do not agree with his views on morals or politics, the difference may become a serious hindrance in your daily routine. In the city you are more free from unwelcome intimacy. You can associate with those who are more sympathetic to your ways or views. This separation of private from public life makes possible free civic co-operation on the part of people of diverse temperaments and points of view. Civil liberty is thus possible in a city without violence to personal inclinations. But there is a price that we pay for this freedom. Associating only with those who are congenial to us breeds a stultifying narrowness and blindness to the world about us. We gradually lose in this way the stimulus and enlargement of vision which come when we·are forced to deal with somebody who does not share our peculiar whimseys, prejudices, or intellectual limitations. No harm seems to result from excluding certain people from our clubs or social life or from neighborly courtesies. But such exclusion is likely to result in educational and economic discrimination and thus to create on the one hand a pariah class, and on the other hand a narrow-minded and hardhearted group blinded by false pride.

This brings us to the doctrine of toleration. Those who think that they have the absolute truth can find no justification for tolerating contrary and therefore erroneous views. It is as hard for the Catholic to admit that Unitarians are Christians as it is for the latter to believe that Hindu polytheists can be enlightened. Even those who believe in religious tolerance seldom accept the full consequence of their position. Thus, this country would not tolerate the polygamy of the Church of Jesus Christ of Latter-day Saints. We persecute Jehovah's Witnesses, who will bow only to the Lord and not to any man-made object such as the flag; and we penalize Jews and Seventh-Day Adventists, who believe in the Biblical command to rest on the Seventh Day. But the Father of all mankind seems always to have tolerated a diversity of views among His children; and from the point of view of pure intelligence, it does not appear that any group has a better proof than any other that the Lord has appointed it His executioner on earth. In any case, it does not seem blasphemous even to the most dogmatic of churches to leave the punishment of some sins to God or His providence.

Sophists have contended that the principle of tolerance is self-defeating, since it gives freedom to those intolerant ones who would overthrow it. This, however, is a fallacy. Tolerance does not mean anarchy, i.e., letting anyone do what he pleases. It is anarchy that defeats itself, since freedom of action for anyone is impossible unless there are rules restricting the freedom of others to interfere. To assure real freedom we must have enforceable regulations. Hence those who wish to overthrow a liberal regime and introduce intolerant oppression can be consistently resisted. As long as they are preaching their doctrine in the forum of popular discussion, they can and must be met in that arena. It is only when they try to carry their doctrines into overt acts that they have to be suppressed by the machinery of law and order. But we must be on guard against the fallacy of those who urge us to fight fire with fire and suppress Fascism or Nazism with their own lawless and brutal methods. If it is an evil to lose our liberty in a war, it is much worse to sacrifice it ourselves on the altar of fear. The fact that liberty is in danger does not justify us in stifling it ourselves.

Adjustment to Fixed Forms

To those who are not misled by absolutistic phrases, and are willing to prefer the better when the best is unattainable, a great deal can be said for the method of adjustment whereby the rights of each group are so delimited that conflict is reduced because irritating contact is minimized. On the lowest plane this means the caste system, whereby each group moves within its own sphere and the boundaries between it and others are protected by the whole community. The same principle operates in the segregation of the sexes. In general, it has been a dominant principle in all societies with a fixed economy. The ethics of this type of social philosophy is expressed in the phrase "My station and its duties." Traditional forms channelize life and thus save us from the distracting burden of having to think and decide at every step. By accepting these channels one finds the happiness of those who are satisfied with their lot.

This attitude is so repugnant to the current ideology of liberalism that it is necessary to exercise one's historical imagination to realize that order, rather than progress, is for most people the prime requisite. Where, for instance, son is expected to succeed father without intermediate war, the principle that a career should be open to talent seems anarchic. Human expectations must to some extent be met in all societies, and it is impossible to do so without some fixed order. The difference between our modern progressive society and the medieval fixed one is therefore only one of degree or circumstance. It is only in our current ideology that the contrast is made absolute.

Yet there can be no doubt that the emphasis on fixed order frequently results in pernicious restraints against growing and vital movement. The caste system prevents the most effective cooperation for the common good; for without sufficient contact, diverse groups naturally breed and develop "instinctive" repulsions.

The Caste System

A modified form of the caste system, seldom if ever recognized as such, is the system of quotas for diverse ethnic or political groups. In many communities there is a tacit understanding among the different elements that certain offices or certain proportions of them should go to certain groups. In student organizations certain offices are regularly allocated to certain fraternities. In New York City, Tammany Hall seems committed to the proposition that the District Attorney should be a Protestant and that a certain proportion of the judges of the State Supreme Court should be Jews.

There can be no question that this arrangement promotes a certain peaceful stability among groups that might otherwise be in conflict. The principle, however, for such quotas is in open conflict with the principle that is commonly professed, namely, that the man best qualified to fill a position should be the one chosen. There is little reason to believe that all abilities are homogeneously distributed in the different groups. On the contrary, there is a good deal of evidence to indicate that for historical reasons, the Norwegians send more than their proportionate share of able men into the maritime occupations, the Scots into the civil service and engineering fields, the Irish into the police and fire departments of our larger municipalities, and the Jews into law and medicine. To ignore this and restrict any group to any fixed quota is thus to deprive the community of the best obtainable service.

Some medical schools, for instance, have recently been assuming that since the Jews constitute only about 5 percent of our total population, the number of Jewish doctors should be so limited. But quite apart from certain statistical considerations (such as that professional classes are predominantly drawn from the urban population where the Jews constitute a much larger proportion), there is no evidence that they are incapable of producing more than 5 percent of the ablest doctors. And it is precisely because the principle of quotas offends the American faith in deciding each case of educational opportunity purely on the principle of individual merit, that our medical schools dare not openly confess their restrictive policies.

As a rule, ethnic and geographic groupings have little relevancy to the ability of experts, such as priests, teachers, judges, or generals; and to choose these on the basis of race, religion, or political affiliation is rightly regarded as socially reprehensible. But regional and group pride often prevails against the best interests of the entire people.

Integration

Group friction and conflict are generally mitigated when people realize their common interests, especially in the face of a common enemy. One of the intellectual weaknesses of the Marxian dogma of the class conflict is its neglect of the fact that the existence of such conflict cannot deny that we also have common interests. An epidemic, an earthquake, a fire or a flood, indeed any touch of nature, makes the whole world kin.

The actual experience of mankind seems to indicate that class conflicts recede in importance when national feelings are aroused. Thus the conflict between German or French employees and their respective employers pales when a conflict between the two nations is threatening. A common religion, such as Judaism or Catholicism, may unite workmen and capitalists in defense of their common rights and honor. The history of imperialism or of the growth of larger political units cannot be explained except by taking into account the fact that such unions generally minimize the amount of conflict between the groups thus united. The Persian, Greek, and Roman Empires, like the British Empire today, maintained themselves not so much by virtue of the superior force of the conqueror as by the service rendered in giving peoples the peace that enabled them to pursue their daily occupations in security. But the penchant for uniformity and the intolerance of local and other differences create friction which sooner or later disturbs the peace and makes imperialism an evil.

If human beings could be persuaded that the common enemies of humanity are disease, poverty, ignorance, and superstition, many of the differences that cause conflicts would be minimized; but the inability of men to take a long-range view and to subordinate what seem immediate group or national advantages to the greater common good prevents the realization of the ancient ideal of peace through a world federation. In general, spiritual forces such as art and science develop enthusiasm for common interests that transcend those peculiar to any group. People are united by common traditions, especially those of common suffering or heroic achievements. But the limitation of these, the inability to appreciate the history and ideals of others, prevents the elimination of unnecessary conflict.

In this connection it is well to note how social conflicts are minimized when different groups find a common leadership. The principle of vicarious glory, according to which the poorest individual participates vicariously in the heroic achievements of a common but exalted leader, is one of the most important bases of government and organized social life; for in following such leaders men sink their differences, though sometimes, alas, also their independent judgment. Yet life would be unbearable for most of us if we could not participate in any glory other than that of our own limited achievements.

On the other hand, one of the causes that intensify social conflict is the unreflecting glorification or even sanctification of common interests which we should be ashamed to confess as our individual motives. Thus, if two of us are drowning and there is a log in sight sufficiently strong to support only one of us, neither of us, usually, will feel guilty if he swims ahead and gets that log; but he would hardly feel any moral superiority in his achievement, any more than the man who by proper speed and adroitness obtains the last seat in a crowded subway car. But when a nation succeeds in taking away a market from another, there is associated with it a feeling of sacred patriotism. All national egoism seems to be sacred. Though vengefulness is not generally regarded as a great virtue, cruel reprisals are viewed as a national duty. Cruelty to helpless children is generally regarded as one of the greatest abominations. Yet probably few of the hundreds of millions of readers of the Psalm, "By the rivers of Babylon," have felt any indignation at its concluding barbaric curse against Edom: "Happy shall he be, that taketh and dasheth thy little ones against the rocks."

The sanctification of group selfishness manifests itself also in regard to the relations of economic classes within a society. In our individual capacity we may want to get things as cheap as possible, but we do not generally mount to high moral indignation when our nurse or teacher wants an increase in salary in order to make a decent living. We are, however, apt to grow indignant at policemen or subway workers who demand a decent scale of wages, if it involves an increase of taxation or of the fare. Yet by calling ourselves "the public" we do not really acquire any right to demand that others should sacrifice themselves for our economic advantage.

A narrow conception of integration is illustrated in the conception of Americanization as the utter abandonment of any loyalty to foreign cultural traditions on the part of the foreign-born. Those who preach this do not realize how it would impoverish America if our immigrants did not contribute from their own tradition to the common stock of American civilization. Our political parties seeking to attract the votes of the foreign-born do much more to Americanize them by giving their representatives a place in our political life.

The Way of Understanding

If, as indicated before, the principal predisposition to group hatred and conflict is ignorance and fear, it would seem that education should be the principal means for minimizing its evil. Unfortunately, however, the term "education" is ambiguous. Most often it denotes academic schooling, and recent history shows that, by and large, the privileged class that has had the benefit of academic training is as subject to class bias and prejudice as are others. It is true, however, that while knowledge of the actual life of those opposed to us may not eliminate all conflict, it can, if it leads to sympathetic understanding, remove frantic fear and fanatical hatred. Real education in this respect comes only if our social imagination is stimulated to overcome the natural inclination to hold that nothing alien can be human. When I was a boy, the mere reading of the New Testament was regarded by my people as a mortal and unpardonable sin, just as the reading of Marx's *Das Kapital* would be to a member of the D.A.R.; but my attitude changed when I became acquainted with the actual contents of the Gospels. How many modern heresy-hunters would be so intense in their hatred if they had any acquaintance with the literature which they wish to burn or banish from the earth? Such acquaintance might not remove the opposition, but it would make it more discriminating.

We may dislike the general squalor among the poor Italians, but this repugnance is bound to melt somewhat when we keep in mind their great contribution to the arts and see their beautiful weaving and the gardens that they manage to place wherever there is a bit of soil. We may think of all Scotsmen as dour and cheese-paring; but what sweetness in the poetry of Burns and Lady Nairne! To Americans who know the Chinese only as laundrymen, the latter seem dull almost to a subhuman extent; but our respect rises when we become familiar with the long history of Chinese civilization. The repulsive characteristics of the Jews have become a legend; but no one who really knows their literature can remain untouched by their intense spiritual life, by their devotion to art, literature, and science, and by their ardor for social betterment. When we do not know a people, it is easy to picture them entirely according to a conventional, preconceived pattern. When we know a few, we are likely to make hasty generalizations. But more adequate knowledge is bound to cure us of the popular illusion that all the members of a group in any way foreign to us are all of one mold.

If the feeling of injustice is what gives momentum to much strife, it would seem that the practice of justice would be the most effective way of minimizing such conflict. But it is not easy for diverse groups to see eye to eye as to what is justice in any given case. Every group strives for what it calls its rights, which to others appear nothing but selfish interests. So enlightened and moralistic a people as the English seems not to have been impressed by the outrageous injustice of its forcing China to buy India-grown opium. But in the long run, intimate knowledge and sympathetic understanding are bound to minimize such cruelties.

Chivalry

While war or conflict cannot be entirely eliminated, it is possible to substitute humane or chivalric methods for those of savagery. The atrocities of the First World War shocked us so much that it seems ironic to draw a distinction between civilized and uncivilized warfare. But without saying anything in defense of modern methods of bombing defenseless men, women, and children, there is still a difference between a war of extermination and a war in which we are aware that sooner or later we shall have to make peace with our opponents and live with them.

In the intellectual realm, chivalry or courtesy means the general disposition to admit that our opponent may be sincere and perhaps even right, even though we are quite convinced that we are on the side of truth. In the end, there is no way in which people can live together decently unless each individual or group realizes that the whole of truth and virtue is not exclusively in its possession. This is a hard lesson to learn, but without it there can be no humane civilization.

These principles are as applicable to the modern problem of the refugee as to the early religious conflicts. If a way out is to be found, the eventual path must lead along the way of understanding.

14

THE SYMBOLS OF GOVERNMENT

PROFESSOR ARNOLD HAS DISCOVERED the old but still important truth that men actually live by ideals and principles, by faith in ancient formulae, dramatic myths, and accustomed ritual; and that not only will they refuse to abandon these for the sake of progress or practical convenience, but that they will defend them at the cost of life itself. One might learn this from the classical theologians who, despite their quaint supernaturalism, were not devoid of shrewd human insight. One might also learn it from classical jurists such as Dernburg, Jhering, Holmes, or Tourtoulon. Professor Arnold seems, however, to have come at it through ultramodern psychoanalysis—whose adherents, like the followers of Mohammed, are inclined to regard the ages prior to the advent of their prophet as those of utter darkness. At any rate our genial author, having some gifts as a clever satirist, uses his discovery mainly to bring out the absurdity of the conventional views of our legal and political order. By means of a brilliant series of striking examples of the great disparity between the professed principles and the actual functioning of our governmental institutions, a picture is drawn of our legal and political thought as a Don Quixote pursuing noble

Published as a review of Thurman Arnold, *The Symbols of Government*, in the *Illinois Law Review*, Vol. 31, p. 411 (November 1936).

ideals that in no way help in the process of adjustment to the actualities of terrestrial life. Professor Arnold is not altogether insensitive to the great truth of art and religion, to wit, that ideals and principles enable us to live in what would otherwise be an intolerably chaotic world. He even realizes at times that his realistic colleagues, the Sancho Panzas of jurisprudence, fail to see all that there is to be seen in this world of ours. But in at least nine of his ten chapters he is above all a critic; and when in the last chapter he comes to state his own positive ideal of what should be, he feels bound to characterize this part of his work as "speculative." The critical part he thinks is objective and scientific (p. 259).

Though the world has not placed the satirists in the forefront of its intellectual heroes where are found poets, artists, moral and religious teachers, philosophers, and great theoretical scientists, there can be little doubt of their indispensable service in disinfecting us from the deadly virus of cant—pious noble phrases about ideals which serve only to cover up ancient confusion and iniquity. And Professor Arnold certainly makes some telling points along this line with a deftness that will disarm orthodox heresy-hunters.

From this point of view *The Symbols of Government* is a stimulating and brilliant book, full of acute and liberating observations which deserve to be widely disseminated. Particularly apt are his observations on our professed fear of "bureaucracy" and the need of "freedom" for business. One would wish that it should be read and taken to heart by all who make a fetish of our Constitution and who with mechanical piety continue to believe the fiction (characterized long ago by Austin as childish) that judges have nothing to do with making the law what it is and that they shuffle off all human fallibility and partisan bias when they mount the bench. One who has for a quarter of a century been trying to make some of Professor Arnold's points in paler and more abstract terms is naturally tempted to dwell on this phase of the book. But Professor Arnold does not want to be regarded merely as one who attacks error with satire. He has written what he believes to be a contribution to scientific anthropology, and due respect for such effort requires that it be judged by rigorously scientific standards.

Now though Professor Arnold admires natural science he has not had before him models of its rigorous procedure. He has relied rather on secondary or popular accounts of it which are inaccurate and misleading. It is even worse than that. Failing to discriminate between science as the search for truth, and its application to the art of healing, especially the insane, and believing that the discussions of psychology in our popular journals are objective, he has naturally fallen for the contemporary, popular, but loose and confused antirationalism which is really hostile to all genuine science. Let me add, in all sincerity, that next to the pure scientist who maintains our rational logical standards, I, like De Morgan's friend, most admire the man who sets out to break them down. For to be concerned with logical issues shows a wise interest in something more enduring than the passing show. No one can deny that the logical views of Plato, Bacon, Mill, Hegel, and Keynes, even when erroneous, have aroused a more enduring interest than their views on the political situation of their day. In any case, at a time when so many of our legal doctrines have shown themselves to be intellectually and morally bankrupt, rational and practical considerations unite in urging that any reformation or reconstruction should proceed on the basis of sober and logically probative evidence and not on clever plausibilities. Even though Goethe said it, it is well to remember that it is relatively easy to make brilliant observations if we do not feel responsible for their accuracy. Accuracy requires that our statements be loaded with qualifications. This is inimical to popular appeal but essential to scientific progress.

Satirists from the days of Juvenal, Voltaire, and our own Veblen have, like other human beings, had their own sentimental weaknesses which have made them believe things no less illusory than those they have attacked. And this, alas, is a pity because by an easy *argumentum ad hominem* their own position is rendered ridiculous, and the elements of truth in it rendered ineffective. Professor Arnold's sentimental weakness is his naïve faith in the popular myth that science consists in observing the facts and ignoring theories. This subjects him to the moralist's illusion that it is only obstinacy in human nature that has throughout the ages prevented mankind from observing the social facts around us and thus from building up a science of human affairs comparable in effectiveness to our knowledge of physical nature.

If, however, we follow the progress of some actual scientific research, it becomes obvious that without some guiding principle, idea, or theory as hypothesis, we cannot even determine what facts to look for. Nor is it at all true that we can always find and recognize the truth or the facts by mere observation. If that were the case, the progress of science would be a much simpler affair than it is, and anyone could manage it. Actually, however, scientific research involves very difficult and elaborate methods for eliminating what seem to be facts to the ordinary observer. Professor Arnold's idea, therefore, of beginning with an examination and synthesis of all the facts and details (p. 30), without any theoretic assumptions or rational logical apparatus, is not only utopian but tends toward blind dogmatism. For it makes us observe as facts many things that are not so—for instance, that regard or respect for law enforcement is greater in America than in England (p. 169), or that "the original notion of respect for law which is above the king was invented as a justification for revolt against constituted authority acting in an arbitrary way" (p. 156). Theories are points of view or perspectives for seeing things in their connections. They are, as Chauncey Wright pointed out, the true eyes of the scientist, wherewith to anticipate and discover things hitherto invisible.

Of course, theories have a certain emotional grip which makes us sometimes cling to them despite evidence to the contrary. But do we not with equal obstinacy cling to our opinions on matters of fact? Two points must be noted with regard to this. In the first place, in science as in other human enterprises we cannot well dispense with tenacity. For what seems to be evidence contrary to our theory, may, on careful re-examination, turn out to be rather a needed verification and extension of it. This has been recently illustrated in the history of Einstein's relativity theory.

The second and more important point, however, is that in actual scientific procedure an hypothesis is abandoned only when some other hypothesis is shown to be more in agreement with all of our previous knowledge as well as with new observations. The way to a real knowledge of the facts, therefore, is not by avoiding theories or anticipations of nature but by systematically multiplying the latter so that we may develop many points of view and thus overcome the tendency toward too much confidence in any one. That is why the logical or mathematical technique of physics, chemistry, general biology, and other theoretic sciences has been so fruitful in enabling us to discover hitherto unknown facts.

Professor Arnold claims that his approach is anthropologic. But history shows that the numerous observations by travelers and missionaries could not build up a scientific anthropology— that the latter became possible only with the development of rational method in the critical and systematic examination of abstract categories and such theories as social evolution.

That the progress of social science is not aided by the dogmatic distrust of theory is clearly illustrated when courts declare that they have nothing to do with theoretic economics and then proceed to repeat ancient and questionable economic assumptions which they happen not to have questioned, just as Professor Arnold happens never to have questioned the popular theory of the nature of scientific method.

The foregoing reflections help us to see more clearly the real cause of the relative backwardness of social science. No doubt many fail to observe the real facts in regard to human affairs because they are more interested in maintaining their preconceived theories. But let us remember that this human motive also affects men working in physical science, as illustrated in the struggles over non-Euclidean geometry, Copernican astronomy, modern geology, transformist or evolutionary biology, and more recently in the opposition to non-Newtonian mechanics. The relative backwardness of the social sciences cannot therefore be entirely due to the devotion to theory, but is at least in large part due to the inherent complexity of social facts. Social facts depend upon many factors, including physical and biologic ones. Hence it is intrinsically more difficult in the social field to formulate relations in accurately stated laws than to do so in physics. Our power to manipulate formulae or equations wanes when the number of independent variables increases. When we come to social affairs the number of qualifications necessary to make a proposition true is generally more than we can manage. Also, since we cannot generally subject human beings to experimental conditions as we do hydrogen gas or fruit flies, we cannot always isolate any one factor and study its specific influence.

Professor Arnold makes a great point of the fact that natural science is concerned with the present, while social science is occupied mainly with the past. This sounds plausible, but it is not entirely or strictly true. Not only historical geology and biology but astronomy and other physical sciences are vitally concerned with the records of the past. It is obvious that if every physicist started anew in ignorance of what others had done before him there could never be the cumulative growth of knowledge. This is not to deny that attention to past thought plays a greater role in social than in physical science. But that is to be expected if we recall that ideas are social forces (i.e., part of the very subject matter of social science), and some views advanced by certain influential thinkers are certainly a less negligible part of the human than of the cosmic scene. Also, as different masters of social studies have lived at different times and under different social customs and institutions, their observations give us diverse points of view which would not ordinarily occur to us. Thus, Professor Arnold's treatment of respect for law would, I think, have been greatly improved if he had paid more attention to Aristotle's view that it depends largely on our vital preference for the customary. The chapter on Jurisprudence would, I am sure, have been more substantial and less flippant if the work of great jurists like Bentham, Jhering, Holmes, Demogue, Esmein, and Kelsen were not so cavalierly ignored. A similar neglect of the more substantial writers on economics prevents Professor Arnold's treatment of the subject from being adequate or satisfactory. The same failure to make necessary discriminations which leads him to blame theory as such for the defects of the doctrine of *laissez faire* makes him attribute to economics generally the attitude of those who, confusing the descriptive with the normative point of view, regard observed tendencies or approximate uniformities as moral and political imperatives. The criticism is obviously valid against those guilty of the confusion. But his analysis of the sources of the confusion lacks necessary clarity and precision. For Professor Arnold himself is, because of the realistic mis-interpretation of the method of natural science, quite confused as to the distinction between existential and normative consid-erations, between problems as to what exists and problems as to what is desirable or what ought to be, irrespective of whether it is or is not as yet in existence. Some, like Professor Kelsen, have perhaps overemphasized this difference; but to ignore their arguments, as Professor Arnold and his realistic colleagues such as Professors Moore and Robinson do, in no way strengthens the position of the latter; and when, under such circumstances, Professor Arnold blithely speaks of the "irrefutable logic" of the realists (pp. 32, 33, 37) he is only exemplifying the supposed wisdom of the ostrich.

By ignoring the differences between the normative and the existential and by failing to note certain differences between social and physical science, he scores a seemingly easy victory over President Hutchins's contention that the mere accumula-tion of facts will not get us anywhere in dealing with the law. But clear thinking that gets beyond false analogies shows the latter contention to be essentially sound. In dealing practically with the law we have to evaluate conflicting ends or diverse views as to what should prevail, and, while knowledge of cer-tain facts may be *necessary* for the solution of such problems, such knowledge alone cannot in the nature of things be *suffi-cient;* we need also assumptions as to what is good or desirable. The fact that banks do certain things or that juries are some-times bribed does not prove that such practice is or should be the law. Similarly, a study of biologic facts may enable us to determine whether a diet of buttermilk will prolong life in a case of Bright's disease, but it cannot settle for any of us the question whether we should wish to live on such a diet or prefer Bright's disease.

Though he admits that men do care more for the vital satisfaction of maintaining certain ideals than for obtaining ordinary practical effectiveness, Professor Arnold seems to assume that this is an irrational attitude and produces more harm than good. But how can he prove that assumption unless he has a moral code or theory of his own as to what is good and what is harmful? If he does not want us to accept his theory of the good on his mere authority, he needs to give us some rational ground for it. His own evidence clearly indicates that as a matter of fact few are willing to abandon principles or ideals for what Professor Arnold regards as the *summum bonum,* namely, a world governed like a lunatic asylum (pp. 232, 233, 239). May one not express a doubt whether Professor Arnold has observed the government of lunatic asylums very closely?

Like some other "realists" who ignore the problems of ethics, of the final evaluation of our human interests, he still clings naively to the popular American worship of efficiency and to the pseudo-moralistic view that what has no practical application cannot be real science. Yet some of the most developed parts of mathematics, physics, and biology have never had any practical applications and there is no evidence that they ever will. Professor Arnold might, of course, by an arbitrary definition identify science and its practical application. But from this he is debarred by his insistence that the scientific observer is detached. Obviously the engineer constructing a motor-boat or the physician curing a fever is not so detached an observer as the pathologist or morphologist.

In criticizing the actual functioning of our legal system, Professor Arnold cannot help expressing his view of what the law ought to be—despite the supposed realistic proof that this ought not to be done. But in view of the actual conflict of interests which has to be adjusted somehow by the law—so long as we are not in a state of civil war or anarchy—we really cannot ignore the questions whether (1) the decision in any given case is in conformity with the general expectation based on the prevailing legal traditions, and (2) whether this tradition conforms to our

present ideas of justice. To the extent, therefore, that any decision is influenced by these considerations there is a law that
is not derived from, but rather determines, the individual
decision.

The notion that there is no such a thing as a case wrongly
decided will not work—and the realists cannot consistently maintain it. Calling the principles by which any given decision is to
be judged "a brooding omnipresence in the sky" will not disprove their applicability. It only proves the philosophic poverty
of those who have to resort to pejorative epithets as their argument.

"Principles," Professor Arnold tells us, "have been obstacles
and not aids." "This struggle to formulate ideals and principles
which are sound, systematic and consistent, leads only to the
building of Utopias on the part of reformers and the defense of
abuses on the part of conservatives." The "chief obstacle" in the
path of discovery is "rational thinking" (pp. 4-5), and "principles, once formulated into a logical system, and accepted, seem
to paralyze action in the actual arena of human affairs" (p. 5).
"Legal and economic thinkers can never discover new techniques
in government" (p. 6). Now it does not require much historical
knowledge or acquaintance with what is going on today to pile
up long lists of examples to show that not all ideals, principles,
or theories obstruct the process of government or its reformation. Indeed, was there ever a substantial reform in government
or social practice—such as the introduction of religious toleration, the extension of the suffrage, free education, more humane
treatment of debtors, the abolition of torture and of witch-burn-
ing, the freeing of slaves, or the liberation of women—which had
not previously been a matter of principle and theory? The belief
in the *truth* of the theories of natural rights and social progress
has certainly had practical effects in the legal and political
realm, just as Professor Arnold's writing of his book has been
influenced by his belief in the truth of what he has written. Indeed, when he leaves off his satiric criticism and formulates his
own theory or philosophy of politics, he explicitly admits that
those who view "ideals and principles as escapes from reality
are pursuing a half truth" (p. 251)—which means, of course, a

half-falsehood. Scientific progress clearly depends on eliminating every possible element of detectable error.

The contradiction between the assertion that principles paralyze action and the equally positive assertion that they are greater drives to action than practical convenience, so that efficiency belongs more to the fanatic who rigorously follows his principles to the bitter end, might be resolved by arguing that while principles are effective drives, they cease to be so when logically or theoretically elaborated. In answer to this, numerous examples to the contrary might be adduced from the history of the Catholic Church or of the Socialist movement. But waiving this, it is well to note that it is characteristic of the irrationalist temper to trust impressionistic observations and not take sufficient pains to arrive at consistency. In the practical realm this nominalism or distrust of system shows itself in an impatience with considerations of permanent and integrating interest when these conflict with temporary ones. A good many of Professor Arnold's criticisms are expressive of this temper, which, though it deserves attention as a persistent human trait, is essentially anarchic and can never support any kind of order, legal or otherwise. It is safe to assume that as long as there is human society there will be some more or less enforced order leading to some inconvenience, and criticisms based on the anarchistic motive will remain futile in immediate practical effect, though an indispensable challenge to prevent the cake of custom from becoming too hardened.

According to Professor Arnold's contentions, rational thought is always compelled to retire into an unintelligible and abstract literature in order to reconcile finally the conflicting ideals which it must represent (p. 70). Stated thus baldly, this is an unwarranted and untenable assertion. Any attempt to adduce evidence for it would obviously be rational and thus defeat it. I confess I do not know what induces people to make such absurd statements. My guess is that, not having any clear idea of what is meant by "rational thought," they identify it with the effort of monistic idealists who try to reduce everything to some one principle and thus do violence to the diversity of things and forces in our actual world. But it is not the business of rational thought to deny the element of diversity or to insist on more unity in our world than can actually be found in it. It is, however, the business of science or organized rational thought to be constantly seeking for more connection between diverse things than meets the eye of the one who observes nature without any penetrating idea or theory.

The foregoing observation will enable us to find an element of truth in another dogma of irrationalism, *viz.*, that no human individual or institution can possibly follow any consistent or systematic set of principles (p. 8). Because of the incompleteness of our knowledge of a world of conflicting forces, there is bound to be a diversity of conflicting ideals and theories, and the discovery of new facts compels the rational thinker to re-examine the adequacy of his previous generalizations. Absolute consistency can therefore never be the permanent possession of one whose knowledge is growing in time. But the ideal of it is necessary to give direction to our effort, just as the ideal of beauty is necessary to give direction to our aesthetic efforts. Science is above all an organized effort to eliminate as much inconsistency from our view of the world as our knowledge will permit. And the extent of our achievements in any practical field depends in the main on the extent to which we follow a coherent plan. The one who has no consistent idea of what he wants to bring about will hardly succeed in achieving anything.

The method of observation that Professor Arnold follows pretends not to consider the truth or falsity of the principles or theories considered. The pretense of having done that, however, is one that it is almost impossible to sustain. Under the guise of showing the psychological origin and motives of certain doctrines, there is often a good deal of intimation that therefore these doctrines are false. Taken seriously, such an argument, based on a confusion between the truth of a proposition and the motives of the one who professes it, is of course an old fallacy. Rhetorically effective, but of dubious value scientifically, is thus the parallel between jurisprudence and theology which, whether intended or not, will be generally taken as an argument against the truth of the former. But as such, it is simply an appeal to the antitheologic prejudice. To a really detached or scientific

146

observer, the question would remain open whether this parallel does not indicate rather some shrewd insight on the part of both theologians and jurists—which in no way implies that such insight is always used in a good cause. Also, for those who care for factual historical truth it should be added that it is entirely false to assert that the church "stopped the scientific experiments of Galileo" (p. 253). Galileo's difficulties with the church had nothing to do with his experiments. They developed, apart from purely personal causes, out of his refusal to yield to the request that he treat the Copernican hypothesis as an hypothesis, which in the light of modern relativity was not an unreasonable request. There seem to be as many myths about Galileo as about any of the saints.

I have discussed the irrationalism of Professor Arnold at perhaps inordinate length and have given it an emphasis which it may not have in his own mind. But to one interested in the progress of jurisprudence that is the critical point which will decide whether the realistic movement is to become journalistic and rhetorical or soberly scientific. The heart of the realistic movement is sound when it rejects the hitherto prevailing method of beginning with supposedly self-evident legal principles, deducing their consequences, and then concluding that the latter are necessarily true. But the attitude of those who because of this abuse reject all logic or rationality, is as silly as it would be to rebel against sharp knives or machines that sometimes cause injury. It is the part of wisdom to master tools which could not be useful if there were no possibility of their being harmful. And indeed the cure for the traditional abuses of logic has been worked out not by the romantic rebels, but by those engaged in the patient analysis of logic itself. Reckless or intransigent irrationalism is bound in the end to saw off any branch of knowledge on which it may temporarily rest.

Rationality in thought and conduct is a continuous and arduous process which we find irksome in our weaker romantic moments when we lazily imagine that we can attain our heart's desire without rational effort, just as we might imagine that we could swim more freely if there were no water to resist us. The rational organization of science or life by human beings always involves artificial restraints on the primitive Adam of natural spontaneity. But spontaneity without order means disintegration and death. The demands of life therefore are certain to compel the romantic rebels to set up rules of their own if they ever succeed in overthrowing the classical tyrants. The new rules may turn out to be better than the old ones. But human inertia, or, if you like, the aversion for death and destruction, will always challenge the rebels to show that they have something better to offer than the poor rules which happen to exist. That challenge should be gladly met, even though to do this requires more sustained labor than that involved in mere criticism or in the wholesale rejection of the old.

15

THE INDUSTRIAL DISCIPLINE AND THE GOVERNMENTAL ARTS

IN HIS PREVIOUS WRITINGS Professor Tugwell showed himself to be of the younger school of economists who, under the influence of recent pragmatic philosophy, view their field less as a department of pure or theoretic science than as a way of guiding practical life by bringing the light of intelligence to bear upon it. Insisting on the experimental and inductive study of the facts—especially American facts—he favored the ethical emphasis in economics but without any critical examination of the ultimate ends or justification of economic activities. Theories such as Professor Hamilton's concerning wages were

Published as a review of Rexford Tugwell, "The Industrial Discipline and the Governmental Arts," in *Columbia Law Review*, Vol. 33, p. 1273 (1933).

to be tested by whether they worked, but nothing was said as to the test of satisfactory working in a society in which there are sharply conflicting opinions on this point. In the present volume there is a more mature appreciation of the importance of general philosophy in integrating our facts and clarifying our values. We need to grasp and define the essentials in order to master the flux: "Some hypothesis concerning the nature of industry is necessary to any generalization about men's relations to it" (p. 22), and, "The sources of our values are made sterile by a lack of philosophy" (p. 3).

It was in Russia that Professor Tugwell had the illuminating experience of beginning to doubt his own previously unquestioned first principle, which he, like other modernists, had naïvely accepted from the classical economists, to wit, that greater productivity is always a good. A poor ignorant Russian peasant challenged this by preferring the less productive but humanly more congenial way of his ancestors.

This led Professor Tugwell to an appreciation of the wisdom of his teacher, Simon N. Patten, in seeing that life can become cheap through the increase of cheap goods, and to the even more ancient wisdom that life cannot be significant without such human values as faith in something customary and the feeling of being part of a larger whole. A greater abundance of commodities made possible by machinery may indeed enrich life by eliminating drudgery. But this consummation has been prevented by the spirit of acquiescence, by the empirical attitude of living for the needs of the moment. The latter is encouraged by the false philosophy of *laissez faire,* which assumes that if each will pursue his own economic profit, the good of all will be assured by an eternally pre-established economic harmony.

It is from this point of view, not always clearly articulated in his own mind, that Professor Tugwell analyzes our contemporary industrial system with a view to indicating the forces which, if properly directed, may bring about a more desirable social order. The latter inquiry, to be sure, is not avowedly carried on as such but is pursued in the guise of a speculation as to the probable future. But this concession to the fashionable positivism, or behaviorism, which deems it more "scientific" to discuss what *will be* (as if the future were ever certain) instead of what we *want to be,* is not likely to mislead anyone.

With all due allowance for the legitimate role of individual enterprise, Professor Tugwell clearly rejects the notion of economic salvation through the warfare known as competition. The day of Theodore Roosevelt's "trust-busting" or Wilson's "new freedom" for the small *entrepreneur* is definitely put behind us. Not so clearly or emphatically does he reject the individual-profit motive as sufficient to produce the goods that society needs—though there is a general recognition that the system based on that motive has definitely broken down. Despite our boast of efficiency and unsurpassed natural resources, our highest prosperity has never eliminated overwork, unemployment, dire poverty, and heavy industrial accidents. Nor has it provided security for young and old. Indeed, Professor Tugwell thinks that the traditional high standard of living in America has affected only businessmen and skilled laborers. As the cause of this paradoxical situation he vaguely refers to some group friction; but in general he recognizes that while production for profit may be technically efficient it is socially wasteful. It leads to the production of unnecessary machinery and capital goods and to wasteful advertising and forced sales. "It is doubtful whether nine-tenths of our sales effort and expense serves any good social purpose" (p. 180). Under the system of production for profit the workers cannot buy all the things that they have produced, and this leads to periodic breakdown of markets, with consequent unemployment in a vicious cycle.

Despite this general point of view, there are curious relapses into the older way of economists, amounting, at times, to flat contradiction. Thus (p. 55) Professor Tugwell blames labor for not accepting the argument of the old economists that a saving anywhere will necessarily benefit everyone. But (p. 98) he characterizes this theoretic argument as in fact not true: "There is no assurance that a higher social income will go to the workers at all." An even more striking example of this reversion to an older point of view is the statement (p. 107) that "Organized labor bitterly but fruitlessly opposed Taylorism and all its implications in spite of its universally admitted advantages. . . .

They fought it tooth and nail for twenty years before capitulation was made to the inevitable." This is simply not true as a statement of fact. Labor did not capitulate at all. On the contrary, the Hoxie report justified labor's opposition, and even the leaders of the Taylor Society now admit that their original program contained serious error. But quite apart from this, Professor Tugwell's own premises should lead him to regard Taylor and his followers as fanatics, madly pursuing increased productivity of commodities regardless of its human effects. Not only was Taylor himself opposed to trade unions, but his bonus system would have speeded up labor in a way to exhaust men in a few years—mechanical wisdom, but human foolishness. Moreover, if the value of human life be greater than that of increased supply of many things now manufactured, the substitution of unskilled for skilled labor is a serious social loss according to Professor Tugwell's own appreciation of the value of interest in one's work. Even from the point of view of the narrowest economics, it is poor wisdom to increase the efficiency of our machinery if thereby a glut and unemployment result. These contradictions are not altogether accidental. They are connected, it seems to me, with Professor Tugwell's inability to shake himself free from the old optimistic view of inevitable progress. While he is preaching the need of taking control of things and remolding them nearer to our hearts' desire, he occasionally falls back into the old attitude that whatever happens to our industrial system is for the best. "We proceed by trial and error to a better situation" (p. 95). "We move, uncertainly it is true, but also nevertheless perceptibly, toward a more closely articulated system into which devices for planning will grow without any of the revolutionary changes which are usually visualized by those who abhor such a proposal" (p. 101). He admits that machines can now produce goods at a cheaper cost than that at which human workers can be supported, and this means that the unskilled will become more and more of a load on society. Yet he dismisses this rather lightly: it will not stop our industrial advance.

I cannot help feeling that this light-hearted trust in evolution is partly at least due to a real unfamiliarity with the ups and downs of history, as well as to a disinclination towards taking its many tragedies seriously. Certainly, Professor Tugwell is rather unfortunate in his one reference to political history, which he pictures as a growing tendency "to diffuse the administration of public services among various private organizations" (p. 181). While this is true in a few cases, the general tendency has been rather the other way since the Industrial Revolution. The State has taken on all sorts of new functions, such as charity, education, the promotion of agricultural and industrial experiments, and the like.

Professor Tugwell's general view of economic history leaves him no doubt that our competitive system has broken down, that it cannot achieve sufficient stability to assure anyone in it continuous employment. We need a radical transformation. "The worker must press for revision—he must refuse to be a machine . . . and he must fit himself for the really human task of managing natural materials and forces" (p. 97). How is this to be attained? Not, we are assured, by the present methods pursued by labor. "Simple bargaining for higher wages and shorter hours achieves immediate relief; but at best it gains relief only. It can never create a new workers' world" (p. 62). We need drastic reconstruction. On the other hand, we must accept the present state of affairs and build on it for a more desirable future. It is easy to dynamite an industrial system but it requires a long and rigid discipline to bring something better into existence (pp. 62-64).

Professor Tugwell does not give much attention to the difficulties in the way of realizing his general program. Such a program clearly involves regulating prices as well as wages and production, and this means limiting profits. Obviously, this will be resisted by businessmen and by other leaders of our public life who depend on profits, and by the courts and others that are still wedded to the old ideals as to the beneficent workings of individual ownership of the means of production. Still, the point is aptly made that what is not now practical will not become practical if its possibility is not considered and discussed, and also (1) that we are today led, in the main, by businessmen who are not well qualified for the job; (2) that their argument that government must keep out of business is untenable; and (3) that our courts' attachment to the old economic theory makes us "the most backward among all industrial countries."

(1) No one can well deny that today many of our national policies result from private decisions of bankers who claim that they are merely bankers and nothing else. The result is power without responsibility and economic activity directed to individual profit rather than vital social needs. Why do Americans tolerate this government of our economic life by irresponsible, short-sighted, and self-interested leaders? Professor Tugwell answers: because we fear the red tape and a certain lack of flexibility and freedom in political control. Ought not one to add also historic habit or social inertia?

(2) No one really believes that government should consistently keep out of business—least of all the businessmen who are always demanding more and more government aid in the form of tariffs, ship subsidies, aid to bankers, protection for foreign investments, and the like. Professor Tugwell does well to call attention to the obvious fact that people generally blame the government for depressions and are for it during periods of prosperity. Government, then, is generally assumed to be a controlling influence. In any case, if it is held responsible, it must have power. If the power to regulate is the power to destroy, why may it not also be the power to provide? Certainly, a government must either control or be controlled by the "supertrust outside of political form (which may swamp the State in the backwash of its progress)" (p. 19).

(3) In discussing the opposition of our courts to any legislation not in consonance with the old economic theories, the point is well made that if the diminution of old privileges is a taking of property, the keeping of those privileges involves the taking of property from others. But we (i.e., the conservatives) "happen to be more shocked when the government does it for the public benefit than when businesses do it for their own benefit" (p. 192).

Professor Tugwell makes the usual assumption that the letter of our Constitution hinders progress. It is time that this should cease to be current among intelligent people. There is nothing in the Constitution itself to justify this view. It is only since the last decades of the nineteenth century that our judges have so interpreted the due-process clauses in the Fifth and Four-teenth Amendments in favor of theoretical competition and against actual social control and protection. This, however, was clearly an innovation undreamed of by the "people" when the Fourteenth Amendment was adopted. In England, up to the eighteenth century and in our own colonies, the government normally controlled the price of wages, food, and the like—only it was done in the interest of the employers. A different set of judges can well adopt an altogether different interpretation —though that is not likely so long as our judges are selected from elderly lawyers. Nor is there any justification for Profes-sor Tugwell's assumption that it is the function of the courts to be conservative. Why may not judges be as progressive as educators, physicians, or engineers, on whom also the safety of society depends? Religion also is frequently said to be a con-servative function. Yet the greatest figures in it are those who reveal new truths.

Professor Tugwell's central hope is for a time when labor, as mechanical drudgery, can be completely eliminated. This is obviously a far distant and literally unattainable ideal. Even if machines needed no human attendance, they could not repro-duce or create themselves. Some amount of routine labor will therefore always be necessary, especially in the temperate zone and for people who wish to live in cities. Hence, an adequate solution of the social-economic problem must face the question how the necessary labor should be performed without dehuman-izing men by getting them into the mechanical rhythm of the machine with which they have to work. A certain amount of compulsion will always be required, so long as human beings are imperfect. And yet no life is possible without a certain amount of joy in our work. Absolute freedom and leisure would be deadly. We should not then know what to do with ourselves. The solution of this problem is one that is usually assigned to the philosophy of the fine arts and play or recreational activi-ties. Though all absolute distinctions between the fine and the industrial arts generally break down, we can say that communal compulsion must generally be applied to the production of the necessities which should be distributed so that all are guaranteed a minimum of subsistence or else mercifully put out of existence. But as to the arts of leisure, freedom and individual self-expression must receive the maximum encouragement. For, alas, we are all imitative herd animals, and free variation is necessary for growth. I venture to think that no one will in the future write on the industrial discipline and the governmental arts without touching on this essential phase of human life.

Neither can I help noticing, in conclusion, that this book says nothing about international trade relations—surely an important factor in the workings of our economic system. Nor does Professor Tugwell refer to the population problem—which seems to me like planning a dinner without taking into account the number of guests who are likely to come.

16

DEMOCRACY INSPECTED

Men have always been more willing to fight for their gods than to look at them too closely. This is certainly true of the modern god, Democracy. No modern subject, probably, has brought forth so much lyric liturgy and acrimonious debate devoid of illumination. In this country, at least, people are so intensely *for* anything covered by the word democratic that it is as difficult to get a clear analysis of what democracy really means as it is to get a fair statement of the case against Germany from a German professor. The reason is precisely the same in both cases. The cause of democracy, or of our country

Published as a review of Robert Michels, *Political Parties,* in *The New Republic,* Vol. 8, p. 303 (October 21, 1916).

in peril, is so dear to us that genuine doubt—the condition of all scientific inquiry—appears as impious treason. Nearly all the books have been written as briefs for the democratic cause, having no room for any misgivings as to its complete adequacy. No one, it would seem, can make a real scientific contribution to a debatable subject like politics unless his love of truth, of playing the scientific game fairly according to the rules, is stronger than his preference for one or the other outcome of his investigation. Professor Michels's book, like Graham Wallas's *Human Nature in Politics,* is one of the very few books in this field that can be said genuinely to aim at a scientific rather than an apologetic treatment of the subject. This does not mean that Professor Michels has succeeded in suppressing his own bias. He certainly has not. But the fact that the book consciously aims at scientific rectitude gives it a distinction which can be accorded to very few books on politics in recent years. All the more the pity, however, that the author's conception of scientific method leaves so much to be desired.

Professor Michels, like all positivistic sociologists, bases his conception of scientific method on the tradition that nature is ruled by hard, eternal, immutable laws. Now a philosopher might here interpose that physicists themselves do not always take this view of the matter, and that men like Mach and Whetham believe the mechanical mythology to be as unfounded as the animistic one. But plain, ordinary experience is sufficient to show that the human nature which enters politics is very complex, and that all sorts of opposing assertions are in part true of it. Hence, all easy sweeping generalizations can only generate opposing ones which are just as plausible, and can only help to prolong the interminable disputes between different schools. "Man by nature hates restraint and loves freedom," assume the anarchists of all schools, and conclude (quite logically) that all government rests on violence and fraud. But it is just as true to say that even apart from all craving for a human object to worship, most men dislike the burden of having to take the initiative and really would rather take orders than stand the trouble of originating them. Whether it is a social club, a prayer meeting, a philanthropic or stock company, the majority are only too glad to find one or a few willing to undertake the burden of active management. "Men are fundamentally interested only in the results of government, and not in its machinery," say the conservatives, and conclude that the interest attached to external democratic machinery like popular elections, etc., is superficial. But it is just as true to say that equality is one of the ends desired for its own sake. Jealousy, as anyone who has watched children knows, is a fundamental trait of human nature; and many are the men and women who would forgo having one more vote or dress if this would mean someone else's having two more. "In politics," say those abreast of the latest philosophy, "wisdom means that we should take account of the *élan vital,* the urge within us towards new forms of life." "In politics," say those who boast of being sober-minded, "we should above all respect man's supreme desire for orderly routine, fixed habits which economize effort." "You cannot change human nature," says one, with a feeling of having plumbed all the depths of wisdom. "Human nature, like other nature, is constantly changing," says another, with a feeling of being in possession of the final revelation. Clearly, until the strength of all the conflicting tendencies can be definitely measured and numerically expressed, political generalizations will continue to move in the twilight of opinion rather than in the full daylight of science.

The difficulty of attaining certainty has led some to the hasty skeptical conclusion that all political discussions are sketches on the sand. This ignores the fact that some opinions may be much better founded than others. Professor Michels's book, though it fails in its claim to establish immutable laws, makes, by virtue of its large use of appropriate material, a substantial contribution as to the foundations of the oligarchic tendency inherent in all democratic movements. The thing has been done before, but only in an argumentative way by those unfriendly to democracy. Professor Michels is a democrat, but one of the free spirits who refuse to admit that the practical necessity of making a choice imposes any duty of blinding ourselves to the inevitable defects of the lesser of two or more evils.

The basis of the inevitable oligarchic tendency Professor Michels finds to be due primarily to the need of organization, which makes technical leadership indispensable. This is reinforced by the eagerness with which the multitude fall into the attitude of hero worship and unquestioning obedience, and the natural tendency of the leaders to identify their own interests as leaders with those of the party itself. Any movement or party that consists of a part of the people can succeed only if it is effectively organized, so that through perfect co-ordination it may dominate the larger and less organized body. But organization and administration depend upon special knowledge and ability, which grow more and more technical as the party develops, so that the great majority of the party become increasingly incapable of intelligently deciding for themselves the problems of party management. The statement that the elected leaders represent their followers is but a euphemism to hide the fact that the great majority have lost the power. The majority does not know—and, as the referendum frequently shows, it often does not care—what the leaders do. The need for party discipline also leads to ever greater power being lodged in the leaders, until they control the election machinery, the party press, and, as guardians of party orthodoxy, its whole intellectual activity. Moreover, the more experienced the leader grows, the more indispensable he becomes, until his threat of resignation becomes a powerful club to beat a dissenting majority into line. In addition to the ineradicable tendency to hero worship, to elevate to party leadership anyone who has acquired any distinction, e.g., as a professor, the element of gratitude enters as a potent element. "Neither the money in our money boxes, nor the words in our mouths, nor the wine in our cellars, nor the wives in our beds, will be safe from him. He will always be saying to us, 'I delivered you from the Genoese. I am the victor of Alis Campo.'" The situation is aggravated by the fact that, as the party leaders and officials become more and more absorbed in their technical job, they increasingly lose contact with the point of view of their followers. It is vain to contend that the leaders decide only questions of management and that the rank and file decide the fundamental aims. The interest of the party organization often proves stronger than the fundamental aim for which it is organized. Thus the German Socialist party, organized as a revolutionary labor party, is forced by its desire to succeed to become more and more legitimate, until it sacrifices its fundamental principles of internationalism and antimilitarism. To increase its vote it must attract the vote of farmers, clerks, and the like; and thus it tends to abandon the Marxian program based exclusively on the struggle between the workingmen and their employers.

Within recent years people have begun to recognize this inescapable tendency of the elected representatives to exploit the workers, and syndicalism, or industrial unionism, has been proposed as a remedy. But strikes, like wars, need chiefs. The men cannot win if each fights for himself; and in time of violence and passion, the control which the workers can exercise over their leaders is even less than that which in time of peace they can exercise over their political representatives. We are thus left with the melancholy conclusion that no popular movement can effect a permanent change. Its success can only mean the creation of a new governing class. The only check on the inevitable growth of oligarchy—and it is a very limited one—Professor Michels finds in the spirit which makes people demand of their officials, Why do you say or do so and so?

The extraordinary wealth of illustrations with which this thesis is worked out leaves the reader with little doubt that the author is dealing with a real tendency. But the scientifically minded will withhold their assent until someone works out, more thoroughly than Professor Michels has done, the counteracting forces which prevent the oligarchic tendency from developing beyond a certain point. No multitude of illustrations can prove a given tendency to be a necessary law. Indeed, frequently the multitude of illustrations only hides the inherent improbability of an assumption such as that the interest of a part of the people can never coincide with that of the whole (p. 389). Surely the interest of those engaged in scientific research is not always opposed to that of the community. Michels's whole psychology is thoroughly atomistic or individualistic. He entirely leaves out of account the group consciousness which makes the individual think lightly of his own separate interests. Not only in times of war will one give up for his country his substance, life or limb, and those dearest to him; even in times of peace the individual in poverty will be sustained by the consciousness of being a member of the richest, most powerful, most glorious country. One of the easiest ways in which the great majority can achieve glory or that exaltation of their selves which is one of our most primal instincts is vicariously through the glory achieved by the leaders of the group with which they are identified. The humblest peasant can thrill with pride that one born in *his* district was the first to win the Nobel Prize, and the colorless respectable college student or graduate will feel elated because a member of *his* fraternity broke certain records; and in the same way the elevation of the Socialist or labor leaders serves to feed the self-importance of the mass of followers. *"Our* Bebel is the greatest orator in the Reichstag." *"Our* Jaurès has written the most brilliant book on philosophy." This principle of vicarious glory also shows the shallowness of the belief which Michels shares with others, that it makes no difference to the multitude whether they are oppressed by an hereditary Bourbon or by a Bonaparte elected by their own votes. The consciousness of having voted to put a great chief into office is not to be belittled by those interested in the actual scale of human values.

To many critical minds the unquestioning faith in panaceas is one of the most pathetic features of human history. Always men pin their hope of universal salvation on some cause. Freedom of conscience and worship, the spread of secular education or of popular learning, universal suffrage and the removal of political privilege, Socialism or economic equality—all these arouse grand aspirations which quicken the energies of men. But as soon as they become embodied in actual life their charm vanishes, and they leave tracks of despair and new additions to the overcrowded graveyard of human hopes. But despair and sorrow cannot be permanent, and always new waves of hope arise to shatter themselves in turn against the sands of actuality. This spectacle is disheartening only to those who believe, as do the writers of fairy tales, in some divine consummation to be followed by a dead level of "happiness forever afterwards." To those who value life and activity even more than results, these periodic waves of enthusiasm are among the glories that redeem human life. Who knows but that the whole universe, with its rhythmic seasons of growth and decay, travails in similar pulses of hope and despair?

17

FREEDOM: ITS MEANING

O F THE FORTY-ONE EMINENT MEN who have in this volume expressed their views on what freedom means to them, one is a mathematician, three are physicists, five are biologists, one is a former college president, two are literary men, two are anthropologists, five are economists or political scientists, two are historians, one is a professor of jurisprudence, and one is a former judge. The other eighteen are, or have been, professors of philosophy. Whatever the editorial instructions may have been, there was obviously no collaboration among the contributors. No one except Professor H. W. Schneider seems to have had any regard for what anyone else has written for this volume. The papers are grouped into five divisions: (1) Freedom Invades History; (2) Freedom for the Mind; (3) Freedom in the Body Politic; (4) Cultural Patterns for Freedom; (5) The Essence of Freedom. But these headings seem to have had little influence on the content of the contributions. Indeed, they are ignored by Professor Schneider who, under the heading "Epi-

---

Published as a review of *Freedom: Its Meaning,* a symposium edited by Ruth Nanda Anshen, in *The Harvard Law Review,* Vol. 54, p 1424 (June 1941).

logue: The Liberties of Man," writes a sort of critical summary of all the other papers.

As was to be expected from such a large number of writers in a volume of over a quarter of a million words, we have here a great variety of suggestive ideas which it would be difficult to summarize within the length of an ordinary review. But every such miscellany naturally contains a great deal of overlapping, and a good many dry pages which do not help to make the whole book easy reading.

As the term "freedom" like "liberty" has an honorific connotation, some of the writers indulge in high lyric notes which strengthen our faith and our abhorrence of those who differ from us. Others see the necessity for greater discrimination and clarity, and make a number of useful distinctions as to the meaning of freedom. Only a few devote sufficient attention to the evils of freedom which make most men run away from it or restrain it by legal and other social penalties. Croce and others here assume that freedom is only for people "who are neither wicked nor criminal nor insane, nor inexperienced and immature." But what proportion of any modern people is completely free from desire to break the law, has no taint of madness, or is entirely mature and experienced? Moreover, very few of us care to be really free or independent of our fellow men and women. Most men gladly sell their freedom for security, for bread and work. None are so miserable as those who are wholly free or loose in the world and none so happy as those who have given up their freedom and gladly enslaved themselves to some leader, beloved person, or sacred cause. Only when we realize the extent to which freedom of choice is felt as a heavy burden by most people can we understand what makes possible the organization of industry, government, or other social institutions, what makes religions of resignation so pervasive and powerful, what makes Islam, Calvinism, and other forms of fatalism or determinism sweep over mankind like wildfire over dry grass.

It is natural for those of us who have been brought up in the liberal tradition to be passionately aroused by the extinction of freedom in Europe and the spreading danger to our own country. But any effective resistance on our part is impossible without an understanding of the motives which make men abandon the liberty acquired after ages of toil, and especially that which makes men follow enthusiastically some dictator after a painful revolution against previous despotism—after the French Revolution of 1789, or the Russian Revolution of 1917, or the German of 1918. We shall not understand if we cling to the assumption that men always crave freedom and that only the devil or some wicked man brings about its eclipse.

To protect certain kinds of freedom and suppress other kinds is one of the principal functions of a legal system, and so the reader interested in this phase of the subject will naturally turn to the contributions of Professor Corwin and Justice Brandeis. It should be noted that Justice Brandeis has not written anything expressly for this volume, but has (presumably) permitted the reprinting of his address on "True Americanism" delivered in 1915, and Professor Corwin has for the most part here restated his article in *The Harvard Law Review* on "The 'Higher Law' Background of American Constitutional Law." [1]

Professor Corwin begins by drawing a clear distinction between civil liberty, "which one enjoys because of the restraints which the government imposes on one's fellows," and constitutional liberty, which is liberty against government itself, implemented in America by judicial review, especially against acts of the legislature. Tracing the antecedents of the doctrine of our Bill of Rights, Professor Corwin points out that the framers of the American Constitution originally looked not to courts, but rather to legislatures, as, using Madison's language, "the safest guardian both of public good and private rights." But "with the State legislatures pretty generally under the control of the debtor class, the proprietarian interest and its professional spokesman speedily developed the theory that only the judicial branch could authoritatively declare the meaning of the standing law and hence of the Constitution" (p. 98). This was strengthened after the Civil War by the *laissez faire* philosophy typified by Herbert Spencer. The courts then reduced the

[1] *The Harvard Law Review,* Vol. 42, pp. 149, 365 (1928-29).

power of legislatures under the Fourteenth Amendment and became, in the language of Justice Miller, "a perpetual censor upon all state legislation." The great fallacy of this ideology, according to Professor Corwin, was the assumption that the power against which free men need to be protected is only political and not economic. "An utterly jejune conception of Natural Rights" defied the teaching of modern psychology as to the fundamental needs of human nature and ignored the facts of human interdependence and the tremendous power of wealth to control the conduct of a large number of persons. Professor Corwin concludes that since the Jones & Laughlin Case,[2] upholding the constitutionality of the National Labor Relations Board, the United States Supreme Court has abandoned its position as a "super legislature touching economic and industrial relations" and has entered a period of greater regard for civil rights.

In the light of the foregoing analysis, Professor Corwin's concluding argument for the retention of the judicial review or power to upset the laws passed by legislature and executive is not very convincing. He ignores the danger from which we barely escaped in the Gold Clause Cases,[3] of a small number of judges upsetting in a time of crisis the deliberate judgment of both houses of Congress and the Executive, on the basis of nothing better than hearing two lawyers argue for several hours and reading briefs that are based on the utterly false conventional theory that the court decides only on matters of law and not on the great factual issues at the basis of national policy.

Under the heading, "True Americanism," Justice Brandeis defends two of our traditional ideals: "the American standard of living" and "inclusive brotherhood." The first, which depends upon everyone's receiving a reasonable income, regularity of employment, healthy working conditions, and hours of labor short enough to allow some leisure, is essential for democracy because "men are not free if dependent industrially upon the arbitrary will of another. Industrial liberty on the

[2] NLRB v. Jones & Laughlin Steel Co., 301 U.S. 1 (1937).
[3] Norman v. Baltimore & O. R.R., 294 U.S. 240 (1935); Nortz v. United States, 294 U.S. 317 (1935); Perry v. United States, 294 U.S. 330 (1935).

part of the worker cannot, therefore, exist if there be overween-
ing industrial power. Some curb must be placed upon capitalistic combination. Nor will even this curb be effective unless the
workers co-operate, as in trade unions. Control and co-operation
are both essential to industrial liberty" (pp. 351-52).

The second ideal, which Justice Brandeis regards as even
more distinctively American, is "the principles of equality of
nationalities as well as equality of individuals." America "recognizes racial equality as an essential of human liberty and true
brotherhood and on this basis it has given like welcome to all
the peoples of Europe" (p. 353).

Now while the American people may still profess the principle that all men are equal before the law, they did not before
the Civil War regard the Negro race as the equal of the white,
nor have they since then treated Asiatics as the equivalent of
Europeans. Our present immigration laws were passed to favor
immigrants from northern and western Europe. Some of us
may regard this as an abandonment of the traditional American
liberalism embodied in the Declaration of Independence and
a weakening of the faith which successive waves of immigrants
have strengthened. But it is well to note that the abandonment
of this second ideal has been largely based, in the public mind,
on the need of maintaining the first, the American standard of
living. While there may be some difference of opinion as to
the justice of this policy, there can be little doubt of the fact
that the opening of our doors to all the distressed people of
Asia and other parts of the world would lower our standard of
living, at least immediately, unless we simultaneously insisted
upon measures, such as wage and hour laws, which would prevent the lowering of that standard.

In connection with the question of nationalism, Bertrand
Russell's article suggests that the ideal of complete independence for every nation is essentially as anarchistic as would be
the complete independence of every individual. And it is well
to note that the anarchy of international relations, which results
in war and militarization, thus leads to the suppression of liberty
within nations. It is surprising as well as regrettable that there
is so little reference anywhere in this volume to federalism (as

opposed to nationalism) as a method of organizing as much freedom as is compatible with the actual interdependence of human groups.

Father Ryan raises the old question of natural inalienable rights. Obviously the word *right* is here used in its moral sense. But in a heterogeneous society, under changing conditions, differences of opinion arise as to what should be included and what should be excluded from the domain of inalienable rights. Who shall decide? Father Ryan would doubtless say that it should be his church, since it has divine authority to settle all questions of morals. But a society that does not accept the authority of the Catholic hierarchy in matters of legislation will naturally resort to the machinery of the state. Doubtless the state may, and often does, decide unjustly. But the remedy against that is either Socratic disobedience or open revolution (if all its dangers are taken into account). That the state is necessarily more unjust than any other human agency has not as yet been proved.

If we leave the theme of absolute rights (of which logically there cannot be a multiplicity, since if two clash, one at least must cease to be absolute), the problem becomes one of choosing that combination of liberties and restrictions which will be sufficiently acceptable to be generally obeyed. On this point some very pertinent observations are made by Professor J. M. Clark. He points out the inadequacy of the usual formula that everyone should be free so long as he does not interfere with the equal liberty of others. Literally, that is compatible with a strong man using a bludgeon on the street corner if he is willing to take a chance that others should do likewise. And one might add that this principle does not tell us when two heterogeneous rights are equal, as when my right to tell the truth is equaled or exceeded by my right to peace of mind, or to carry on business as usual. Professor Clark also notes the importance of considering the range of our choice when the action of choice determines our subsequent role as when one chooses a career, a ruler, or representative, etc. His essay concludes with some interesting, if not altogether conclusive, points in regard to *laissez faire*, Socialism, and the New Deal economy. He considers to what extent the first allows people to have money and yet refrain from using it for productive purposes, and to what extent a socialistic democracy would allow freedom to the individual consumer and the pioneer experimenter who is inclined to be a nonconformist.

In restricting this review to the foregoing points, no attempt has been made to do justice to the rich content of the whole volume. But to these the table of contents and the concluding essay of Professor Schneider are sufficient guides.

18

ECONOMIC PIETIES

THERE are several excellent essays in this volume and it may be ungracious to find fault with a book for what it does not deal with. But it is surely worthy of note that a book concerned with the effects of the war shows no indication that the war has produced any radical change in the current mode of American business economic thought—the same vigor and acuteness in dealing with particular ways and means and the same disinclination to deal with vital aims and purposes, which have made our economic discussions such artificial and inhuman affairs.

In the first part of the book we have indeed an eloquent essay on "The American of Tomorrow" which shows that the former Chairman of the Progressive party can still speak the language which thrilled so many in the campaign of 1912. We

Published in *The New Republic*, Vol. 18, p. 155 (March 1, 1919), as a review of *American Problems of Reconstruction,* a symposium edited by Elisha M. Friedman.

should be inspired "not by the spell of the setting of yester's sun but by the vision of the dawn of a new day." But if Mr. Perkins himself has the vision he has not communicated it in this essay. He says that men are being bound closer together and that collectivism is bound to replace individualism. But what in terms of concrete human experience all this means to Mr. Perkins is shown in the following: "The man of exceptional ability, of more than ordinary talent, will hereafter work for his rewards, for his honors, not in one direction but in two, first and foremost in some public work accomplished and second in wealth acquired."

Though a good deal of the book is devoted to international commerce—indeed the bulk of the book is devoted to questions that are primarily financial—there is nothing said about reconstruction in international relations. To the layman it might seem that while before the war * we regarded international commerce as a purely private affair between individual merchants, the war has forced all the nations to see that their very national existence depends on the exchange of food, raw materials, and manufactures. But the writers in this book do not seem to be troubled by any question of the equitable distribution of the world's supply of raw material. The keynote is struck by Mr. O. P. Austin who insists that "world trade currents cannot be radically changed by even the greatest of wars or the commercial regulation which may follow." Parenthetically Mr. Austin makes the startling assertion that the war has grown out of commercial ambition; and in a paper on foreign investments, Mr. Sisson, of the Guaranty Trust Company, warns us that foreign investments in the future must not lead to territorial aggression. But how that is to be avoided in the future which has taken place in the past we are not told. In general the writers are entirely opposed to an economic war after a military war, but are all averse to tackling the problem of tariff and free trade.

In regard to internal policy the various writers are disinclined to come to real grips with the vexed question of public

* I.e., the First World War.

control in industry. There is agreement, in the main, that under government direction during the war great economies have been effected. Despite the withdrawal of men into war and into the making of munitions, our output of food, raw materials, and even our manufacturing facilities have been increased. Production has been speeded up, waste eliminated, and by the stimulating of research vast possibilities for the future have been opened. But the articles on the railroad and the shipping problems tamely repeat the traditional and conventional arguments in favor of private ownership with a mild admixture of government control. It is doubtless unsound to argue that what can be done by the government in time of war can also be effected in time of peace. But is it so certain that zest and enthusiasm for human welfare cannot possibly be aroused in time of peace?

In the chapter on capital, labor, and the state, we come nearest to a serious effort to deal with fundamental changes. Mr. Wehle thinks that the war has weakened the position of capital and has strengthened the position of labor. When "profiteer" became a term of reproach, the natural alliance between the big interests got broken up. Manufacturers, raw-material men, bankers, and railroad men lost their solidarity and began blaming each other for the high prices. On the other hand, labor has received greater government recognition than ever before. The need for increased production to pay the national debt and to satisfy other demands must lead the government to continue to be vitally interested in those factors which make for industrial stabilization. To the extent, therefore, that the tendencies obtaining during the war will continue, industry will be democratized and decasualized—democratized by giving labor a voice in determining working conditions, and decasualized by making the employment relation more permanent. The great outstanding fact in the wage system, according to Mr. Wehle, is the insecurity of the laborer—the fact that he may be fired at any time for any or no reason. This is the fundamental basis of labor's antagonism. By making the labor group a legal partner in industry and giving it a share of the increased product, the productivity of labor would be greatly increased. This together with the government's regulation of the supply of raw material will also turn out to the advantage of manufacturers by eliminating elements of risk and interruption.

There can be no doubt that giving to labor a greater share in determining labor conditions and a greater share of the product would mean a radical transformation of our wage system. The complete humanization of labor, however, calls for more factors than Mr. Wehle mentions and much more than American employers and their supporters are ready to grant. Intelligent men, however, must recognize more and more that the solvency of a nation depends on its power to produce, and that the present wage system is frightfully wasteful—huge losses being due to preventable accidents, disease, overstrain, undernourishment and forced idleness, and indifferent or hostile workmanship.

While all questions as to the future must remain somewhat uncertain, one thing seems beyond doubt, and that is that after the war we shall have to raise more taxes. The manner in which the burden of these taxes will be distributed will be decisive for our future welfare. Whether we decide to carry the public debt as England has in the past or to pay it as Professor Seligman advocates, there will in any case be a huge interest on the public debt and if the world is to be made safe for democracy there must be increased expenditures for social legislation. How shall the revenue be raised? It is good to see Professor Seligman press the point that taxes should be paid by those who are able to do so, by those who enjoy privileges. This means not only an increase in the income tax, making the scale of progression steeper, but that we shall, like England and Italy, draw the distinction between earned and unearned income and go in heavily for a graduated inheritance tax.

That government intervention in the financing of industry will be necessary to prevent the burden of the higher interest rate from bearing too heavily upon those least able to bear it, is the natural conclusion from Professor Kemmerer's long paper on the rate of interest.

The only paper in the whole collection dealing with politics is the one by Dr. Cleveland, the former Director of the Bureau of Municipal Research, and is entitled, "Can Democracy Be

Efficient?" Dr. Cleveland contends that our political machinery has been inefficient because it has had no competition. Politically we have lived in the illusion of "that time-worn, dog-eared philosophy known as *laissez faire.*" The war, he thinks, has broken that illusion by showing the need for efficient co-operation. Efficient government means strong centralized leadership instead of our traditional division of authority, and also a highly trained staff of specialists. Such government can be democratic by making it responsible and responsive to public control. Dr. Cleveland thinks this can be brought about in this country by making the Cabinet responsible to Congress, which can be effected by simply changing the rules of Congress so as to give priority to executive measures, and requiring Cabinet members to appear personally before the House and explain and defend their measures. Under those conditions a refusal by Congress to pass such a measure would force the President either to amend the measure or to change the Cabinet.

Doubtless an executive budget and closer co-operation between the Cabinet and Congress would make for more efficient government; but Dr. Cleveland's entire scheme illustrates how easy it is to devise efficiency schemes if you only ignore inconvenient facts. The inconvenient fact in this case is the President of the United States who, being also elected by the people, will never consent to yield to Congress on all occasions and thus become an ornamental figurehead like the King of England or the President of the French Republic. Indeed, if Dr. Cleveland were to study French politics of the few years previous to the election of Poincaré, he would see that the subordination of cabinets to Congress is not without its serious drawbacks. Dr. Cleveland, however, is wise in insisting that specialists or experts must be subordinated to public control. The danger of government by experts is briefly and wisely put by Secretary Lane in his introduction to this book.

Volumes of symposia, collected essays, and other vaudeville performances are notoriously uneven and devoid of genuine unity. Men generally do not give so much careful attention to works of this sort as they do to systematic books of their own. It is easy enough for an editor to map out a field and to obtain the promise of a number of notable men to treat the various topics assigned to them, but it is very difficult to make them do it, especially if they are distinguished citizens over whom the editor has not even the power that a periodical editor has over his contributors. Efficient editing is impossible where there is no power of rejection, omission, and revision. This was impossible in the volume before us not only because the contributors included bankers and trust magnates—men like Schwab and Vanderlip—but largely because the editor had no very definite views of his own other than the prevailing pieties, which he has with labored harmlessness made clear in the two introductory essays of his own. While the contributors have taken rather lightly the request to tell us what are the temporary and what the permanent effects of the war, and what should be our national economic policy, they have brought forth a good deal of valuable information on more or less relevant industrial and financial problems. There is for instance a highly interesting article by Professor Fisher on stabilizing the value of the dollar which calls to our attention the profoundly unscientific character of our currency. One cannot help wondering how little progress our science of physics would have made if its units of measurement were as variable as are the units of economic value. The reader will also find in this volume a clear survey of the mineral resources of our country by the Director of the U. S. Geological Survey and an illuminating and persuasive article on free ports by Professor Clapp; also an interesting article by Senator Owen on the international rate of exchange.

This chaste and impersonal book does not say a word about woman in industry.

V

LAW AND JUSTICE

19

CONSTITUTIONAL AND NATURAL RIGHTS IN 1789 AND SINCE

ALL PEOPLES have pious fictions and sacrosanct expressions which make free thought and honest speech seem improper. This is true even among people noted for their progress in science and technology. Thus Japanese engineers or military commanders must always speak of their successful achievements as due to the virtue of the Emperor, and our sober British cousin must attribute everything to the pleasure of His Majesty, the King. The King is always pleased to sign the appropriation bills, though he would lose his job if he did not. And woe to the Chancellor of the Exchequer who should wish to allude to the latter fact realistically! Can it be that we too in the United States have such fictions? Men who dare to call the Emperor naked when he has no clothes have been pointing out that time-honored national dogmas in regard to our constitutional system are full of logical fallacies and historical errors. It is therefore the business of scholars or those engaged in weighing evidence to examine these issues critically, regardless of the fact that for doing so they may be called unpatriotic by ignorant men in popularly influential positions.

The Constitution and the Will of the People

It has become customary to assert that our constitutional law is the solemn will of the people expressed in the written Con-

Published in *National Lawyers Guild Quarterly*, Vol. 1, p. 92 (1938).

stitution, and that the judges have nothing to do with making or modifying it. Like phonographs, they merely repeat what the law says, or, if intelligence be attributed to them, they are engaged in drawing the logically necessary consequences of its plain meaning. Hence, if the people are dissatisfied with the results, the only proper procedure is to change the Constitution. This, if we stop to think, is an amazingly unbelievable contention. Unless we claim that the people who adopted the Constitution in 1789 had supernatural foresight, we cannot reasonably maintain that they then foresaw all our present conditions and made complete provision for all possible contingencies. If then, our constitutional law does change from time to time or adapts itself to new conditions, it must be that the process of interpreting the Constitution is really a form of legislation or constitution-making. It is not the man who writes a law or those who vote for it, but the one who has the last word in its interpretation, who determines its final meaning. And this is, in fact, admitted by conservatives who speak of Chief Justice Marshall's making or molding the Constitution. As one of our most conservative papers once put it, the Supreme Court is a continuous constitutional convention; only, it should be added, the results of its vote do not have to be ratified by the people.

As the recognition of the latter fact, however, goes contrary to the democratic doctrine that the Constitution is the will of the people, the fiction is maintained that all that the judge does in deciding whether a statute is constitutional or not is, as Justice Roberts put it, to read the statute and the Constitution and see whether they square or conflict.[1]

But, if the matter were as simple as that, why should there be so much difference of opinion as to what is and what is not constitutional? If the meaning of the Constitution is clear, why should Taney differ from Story and Marshall, Bradley from Chase, Field from Waite, or Brandeis and Holmes from Butler and McReynolds? In point of fact, no historian can deny the fact that in the making of our constitutional law there generally

[1] United States v. Butler, 297 U.S. 1, 62 (1936). *Cf.* Beard, "The Act of Constitutional Interpretation," *National Lawyers Guild Quarterly*, Vol. I, pp. 9, 13 (1937).

enters the personal opinion of the judge as to what is desirable
or undesirable legislation. And this is inevitable, since the words
of the Constitution themselves cannot decide every issue. We
can see this when we go through the actual body of decisions as
to what is interstate commerce, what is due process of law, or
what is included in the police power (the last is not even mentioned in the Constitution). To say, for instance, that the people of 1789 intended to give Congress power to prohibit lottery
tickets [2] but not to regulate insurance policies,[3] has no support
in any words of the Constitution and runs counter to all that
we know of the mores of the eighteenth century when lotteries
were the foundation of charitable institutions and insurance
underwriting was recognized as a form of gambling. Nor is there
any justification in the Constitution itself for the contention
that Congress may tax state banknotes [4] or oleomargarine [5] out
of existence but not the products of child labor,[6] that Congress
may order railroads to introduce certain coupling devices [7] but
may not prohibit them from posting notices threatening to discharge men for joining trade unions.[8] A thousand instances of
such subtle distinctions can be readily enumerated. And if anyone should say that these distinctions *were* foreseen and were
intended by the people who adopted the Constitution, the historian of human beliefs might well see in it an illustration of
the doctrine *credo quia absurdum*. Let us take some constitutional provisions adopted nearer to our own time. What historian will maintain that, when the people voted for the Fourteenth Amendment after the Civil War, they intended to give

[2] Lottery Case, 188 U.S. 321 (1903).

[3] Nutting v. Massachusetts, 183 U.S. 556 (1902).

[4] Veazie Nat. Bank v. Fenno, 8 Wall. 533 (U.S. 1869).

[5] McCray v. United States, 195 U.S. 27 (1904).

[6] Bailey v. Drexel Furniture Co., 259 U.S. 20 (1922).

[7] Southern Ry. v. United States, 222 U.S. 20 (1911).

[8] Adair v. United States, 208 U.S. 161 (1908), may perhaps be said to have
been overruled by Supreme Court decisions upholding the Railway Labor
Act and the National Labor Relations Act. Texas and New Orleans R.R. v.
Brotherhood of Railway Clerks, 281 U.S. 548 (1930); National Labor Relations
Board v. Jones & Laughlin Steel Corp., 301 U.S. 1 (1937). But the ruling in
the Adair Case was for years the constitutional law of the United States,
and was followed by Coppage v. Kansas, 236 U.S. 1 (1915), and other decisions.

the Negro so few rights and to deprive white laborers of so much legislative protection as the courts have interpreted that amendment to convey? No historian will venture to deny that in the history of the common law and English legislation the phrase "due process" always referred to procedure, that "liberty" meant freedom from bodily imprisonment, and that "property" did not before 1886 include the right to make contracts without any governmental regulations. The present extended meanings of these phrases are inventions of the courts whereby they have assumed wide and almost boundless power not granted by the people who adopted the Fifth or the Fourteenth Amendment. Did the people who voted to give Congress the right to tax incomes from *whatever source derived* really *not* intend what these words explicitly say, but *did* intend rather to create a privileged class who pay no federal tax on their income, because it is derived from state bonds or the bonds of municipalities? When the amendment was up before the legislature of New York, Governor Hughes, later Chief Justice, contended that this would give the Federal Government the power to tax state bonds and that this would destroy the financial power of the states. Economists, such as Professor Seligman, produced ample evidence to deny that this would be the effect of a general income tax. But lawyers attach more importance to an irresponsible dictum of Marshall than to demonstrable facts.

Possibly the clearest instance of the logical and historical absurdity of a decision declaring an act of Congress unconstitutional was the case of Marbury v. Madison,[9] which lawyers have, for over a century, worshiped with blind piety. The section of the Judicature Act of 1789 which Marshall declared unconstitutional had been drawn up by Ellsworth, his predecessor as Chief Justice, and by others who a short time before had been the very members of the constitutional convention that had drafted its judicial provisions. It was signed by George Washington, who had presided over the deliberations of that Convention. Fourteen years later, John Marshall by implication ac-

[9] 1 Cranch 137 (U.S. 1803).

cused his predecessor on the bench, the members of Congress such as James Madison, the Father of the Constitution, and President Washington, of either not understanding the Constitution (which some of them had drawn up), or else willfully disregarding it. It should certainly require a good deal of evidence to prove such a contention. If, however, we examine the exact wording of the Constitution, we find that Marshall's contention is based upon an interpretation which is logically quite unnecessary, and which follows only if we allow him to interpolate a word which the Constitution does not contain. Marshall argues that when the Constitution (in Art. III, Sec. 2) says that the Supreme Court shall have appellate jurisdiction, this means that it shall have appellate jurisdiction *only,* and hence that Congress cannot *add* original jurisdiction in certain *mandamus* proceedings. His assumption that this is the only possible interpretation is demonstrably false. The granting of the appellate power by the Constitution certainly *can* mean that Congress may not take it away; it does not necessarily exclude the possibility of an addition. Indeed, as Professor Freund has shown, the principle of Marbury v. Madison has been disregarded by the Supreme Court itself in the cognate case of foreign consuls in which the grant of original jurisdiction to the court did not prevent it from accepting also appellate jurisdiction.[10] To a secular historian it is obvious that John Marshall was motivated by the fear of impeachment if he granted the *mandamus* or dared to declare the Republican Judiciary Repeal Act of 1802 unconstitutional.[11] Having thus refused aid to his fellow Federalists ousted from offices created for them by a "lame duck" Congress, he resorted to a line of sophistical dicta to get even with his political enemy, as indeed he did also in the Aaron Burr case. In his letter to his colleague Chase, Marshall offered to abandon judicial supremacy in the interpretation of the Constitution in return for security against impeach-

[10] Freund, *Standards of American Legislation* (1917), p. 277.
[11] We have it on the authority of Beveridge that Marshall to the end of his life believed that the Judiciary Repeal Act of 1802 was unconstitutional. See Beveridge, *Life of Marshall* (1919), Vol. 3, p. 122.

ment.[12] Yet these obvious facts are ignored and Marshall has become a supposed model of rigorously logical thought to what is regarded as a learned profession.

The dogma that judicial decisions follow logically from the provisions of the Constitution involves the unbelievable psychological assertion that when men mount the judicial bench they become, unlike all other human beings, altogether free from personal or class bias or the prejudices of their limited education and experience. History, however, indicates that their actual decisions do depend upon their personal, social, and economic opinions. For the issues that come before them are largely of that character. Who really doubts that, if the personnel of the court were to change, its decisions would be different? Certainly not those who objected to the confirmation either of Brandeis and Black or of Hughes and Parker. The fact is that the most important issues that come before the court are not questions of well-settled law but concern issues of public policy about which well-informed and well-disposed people differ, because we do not know enough of the manifold consequences of a given enactment and we do not all agree as to what are the most desirable results. In fact, no really knows how the Supreme Court will rule except on the basis of the past views of the individual judges. But even in this respect the law is uncertain, since we cannot tell whether a judge voting in a minority in one case will in the next similar case vote with the majority on the principle of *stare decisis* or maintain his own opinion as to the true meaning of the Constitution. There are precedents for both positions.

When, therefore, judges say that the Court will not declare a statute unconstitutional unless it is obviously unreasonable to hold differently, they assert that not only a majority of both houses and the President but even some of their colleagues are devoid of reason in entertaining a contrary interpretation. One

12 ". . . I think the modern doctrine of impeachment should yield to an appellate jurisdiction in the legislature. A reversal of those legal opinions deemed unsound by the legislature would certainly better comport with the mildness of our character than a removal of the Judge who has rendered them unknowing of his fault." Letter of John Marshall to Justice Chase, Jan. 23, 1804. *Ibid.*, p. 177.

wonders, then, whether not only their sense of reason but also their sense of humor and even of courtesy is not somewhat esoteric.

The Constitution as Eternal Reason

When forced to abandon the pretension that constitutional law is the expressed will of the people, its proponents contend that it is the expression of eternal reason or justice, or at any rate of the principles of Magna Charta and Anglo-Saxon liberty. But not only the differences of opinion among individual judges, but the changed attitude of the court at different times in regard to the constitutionality of such provisions as a national income tax, statutes regulating hours of labor, and the like, show that not everything that the court decides is dictated by eternal reason or eternal justice, but that the changeable human —all too human—element plays its part.

As to the contention that our constitutional law, especially the interpretation of the Bill of Rights, goes back to Magna Charta and to the principles of Anglo-Saxon freedom, that is even more readily disposed of. By actual count (witness Domesday Book) the vast majority of Anglo-Saxons were serfs; and Magna Charta was a feudal document by which Norman barons tried to control an Angevin king. It did not prevent Yorkist, Tudor, or Stuart tyranny. Our constitutional system of judicial control is not only foreign to the English tradition but is definitely distrusted by liberal England. I refer to the notable speech by Premier Asquith when it was suggested that a Bill of Rights be put into the Irish Home Rule Bill. This, he pointed out to the satisfaction of the House of Commons and to the British liberal public, would make judges the final arbiters of legislation and so make law as uncertain as it is in the United States.[13]

[13] I have discussed this point at greater length in *Law and the Social Order* (1933), pp. 152-53. Premier Asquith's views were generally supported by editorial comments: "All administration would be checked in the American fashion while laws were tossed from court to court for years in a vain effort to ascertain whether or not they need be enforced. The trouble with the constitution of the United States . . . is that nobody has ever been able to find out what it means." *London Chronicle*, cited *ibid.*, p. 153. "Judges are not trained for that kind of function and no man who knows the history

I take it that it is not necessary to go over the work of Professor Plucknett in demolishing the myth which Coke wished to create that the judges of England could set aside acts of Parliament as contrary to natural right. A few careless dicta repeated by Hobart and Holt cannot establish a rule of law. There is certainly not a single authenticated case [14] of an English judge declaring an act of Parliament void as contrary to Magna Charta or to any natural right; nor for that matter is there, so far as I know, any authenticated case of any colonial judge doing this to an act of a colonial legislature.[15]

The Power of Judicial Review

Did the people who adopted the Federal Constitution definitely intend that the courts should have the power to void as unconstitutional not only acts of state legislatures but also acts of Congress approved by the President? The arguments for the affirmative are (1) that it is expressly granted in the Constitution, and (2) that it was generally understood that the courts would exercise that power.

(1) The first argument seems to me altogether devoid of merit. The Constitution does say that the laws and treaties of the United States, as the supreme law of the land, shall be so recognized in the state courts. It does not say that, when judges give a different interpretation of the Constitution from that which the Congress and the Executive maintain, the latter are bound to yield to the former. John Marshall's argument from the fact that the judges take an oath to enforce the Constitution can readily be turned against him. For the members of Congress and the President also take the oath and they do not, when they swear to obey the Constitution, add any provision limiting it to the *way interpreted by the courts*. Oaths are presumably insti-

of the exercise of this function by American judges but will agree that it would erect one of the most galling of all possible tyrannies." *London News,* cited *ibid.*

14 Even Dr. Bonham's case, 8 Coke 113 (1609), assuming that it was an actual case, did not involve declaring a statute of Parliament unconstitutional.

15 See Boudin, *Government by Judiciary* (1932), Vol. 1, app. B.

tuted to bind the conscience of the individual who swears, not to bind him to the dictates of somebody else's conscience. Of course, there would be no government if three independent organs each followed a different interpretation of the supreme law of the land. But that is a consequence of the absurd theory of a complete separation of powers. The custom—and this is all that it can be properly called—according to which Congress and the President tacitly agree to abide by the interpretation of the Court, is a practical accommodation or adjustment conditioned by historical circumstances and not at all a necessary consequence of the wording of the Constitution.

The basic assumption underlying Marshall's and the usual argument on this point is that the interpretation of law is exclusively a judicial function and that therefore the final decision belongs to the Court. But this is entirely baseless. Congress in legislating and the President in executing a law must interpret the relevant provisions of the Constitution; and in the Oregon Telephone Case [16] the Supreme Court has admitted that the interpretation of at least one provision of the United States Constitution, namely the meaning of "republican form of government," must be left to Congress and the Executive, even though every part of the Constitution is the law of the land. Nor can there be any historical support found for the view that at the end of the eighteenth century it was anywhere a generally recognized doctrine that the interpretation of laws was exclusively a judicial function. Blackstone, who was regarded as an unquestionable legal authority when our Constitution was framed, not only explicitly recognized the right of Parliament to interpret the laws, but clearly indicated its supremacy. There is undoubtedly an ancient and widespread view that Parliament could not legislate against natural or moral law, and the colonists based their Declaration of Independence on it. But nowhere, except in the United States after John Marshall, was the doctrine established that judges were the only safe guardians of natural or moral law, and even with us the term "natural rights" was abandoned, and the same result obtained by stretching such

[16] Pacific States Tel. Co. v. Oregon, 223 U.S. 118 (1912).

terms as "due process," "property," "liberty," and the implied limitations on all "free" government.

(2) I do not wish to deny that there were some people who previous to the adoption of the Constitution did suppose that the courts would have the power to declare acts of Congress unconstitutional. The later papers of *The Federalist* say so explicitly.[17] But history shows that this was by no means generally understood or taken for granted, and the extent of this power was certainly not indicated with any clarity. Madison and even Marshall made contradictory statements on this point.[18]

It is an elementary precaution of historical research not to attribute hastily to a former generation a clarity or emphasis which is ours today. Extensive reading of contemporaneous literature in regard to the proposed federal constitution shows that this matter of judicial supremacy did not loom large in the consciousness of the great majority of the people. They were much more concerned with such practical political arrangements as the power of Congress to designate the localities where elections should take place. This, they thought, might give Congress the power practically to disenfranchise certain groups—a fear which practice has not shown to be justified.

[17] See, for example, Hamilton's argument in *The Federalist,* No. lxxviii.

[18] "The legislative authority of any country can only be restrained by its own municipal constitution: This is a principle that springs from the very nature of society; and the judicial authority can have no right to question the validity of a law, unless such a jurisdiction is expressly given by the constitution. It is not necessary to enquire, how the judicial authority should act, if the Legislature were evidently to violate any of the laws of God; but property is the creature of civil society, and subject, in all respects, to the disposition and control of civil institutions." *Per* Marshall, *arguendo,* in Ware v. Hylton, 3 Dall. 199 (U.S. 1796), cited in 1 Boudin, *op. cit. supra* (note 15), p. 187. *Cf.* Marshall's views in Marbury v. Madison, 1 Cranch 137 (U.S. 1803) and, again, his views in his letter to Justice Chase, *supra* note 12. If Madison agreed with Hamilton's argument in *The Federalist* (*supra* note 17), he took a quite different view when he wrote in 1788, commenting on a draft of the Virginia constitution: "In the state constitutions and indeed in the federal one also, no provision is made for the case of a disagreement in expounding them [the laws], and as the courts are generally the last making the decision, it results to them, by refusing or not refusing to execute a law, to stamp it with its final character. This makes the Judiciary Department paramount in fact to the Legislature, which was never intended and can never be proper." Quoted in 1 Boudin, *ibid.,* pp. 90-91.

It might be well to suggest that in 1789 the courts were not generally considered as important as they are today. This is seen in the action of John Jay in resigning as Chief Justice. The question whether the courts could declare laws of Congress unconstitutional seemed then as remote and academic as does to the ordinary citizen today the question whether the courts can declare a treaty of the United States unconstitutional. Doubtless most lawyers, moved by the force of analogy, will answer this in the affirmative. But we do not see organizations formed to protect our liberties and our lives by strengthening the prestige of the courts against the treaty-making power of the President and the Senate.

It is hardly necessary to answer Marshall's argument that the judicial veto is an inevitable consequence of our Constitution being a written one. There are plenty of written constitutions where this power does not exist. (It did not exist in the French constitution, written before Marshall made this contention.) Nor is it necessary to consider in detail the argument that this power is necessary for a federal system. The Swiss constitution is a perfect example of a federal system without the judiciary having such power. The late Justice Holmes said: "I do not think the United States would come to an end if we lost our power to declare an Act of Congress void. I do think the Union would be imperiled if we could not make that declaration as to the laws of the several states." [19]

I see no force in this latter argument. It assumes that the issues on which the courts declare state acts unconstitutional are purely legal and can therefore be settled only by a court of law. That this is actually not the case is most convincingly indicated by the comment of Justice Holmes himself: "As the decisions now stand, I see hardly any limit but the sky to the invalidating of those rights [constitutional rights of the states] if they happen to strike a majority of this court as for any reason undesirable." [20] Actually, our courts have, by their decisions, largely destroyed the virtue of a federal system, namely, the power of the states to experiment in the field of social legislation.

[19] Holmes, *Collected Legal Papers* (1921), pp. 295-96.
[20] Holmes, J., dissenting, in Baldwin v. Missouri, 281 U.S. 586, 595 (1930).

There are historians like Professor Beard who would probably subscribe to all of the foregoing yet still seem to insist on maintaining this unique power of judges. They are afraid, as Professor Beard puts it, of the sadism of Congress. But I venture to assert when we consider the long roll of judicial decisions such as the Dred Scott Case,[21] the Lochner Case,[22] the Adair Case,[23] the child labor cases,[24] the Coppage Case,[25] the minimum wage cases up to 1937,[26] the voiding of Congressional legislation to protect the Negroes against lynching [27] and deprivation of civil rights,[28] or the public against being gouged by ticket scalpers,[29] fraudulent bakers,[30] and conscienceless employment agencies,[31] the sadism of the courts will far outweigh that of Congress even though esthetically the procedure of the courts is more refined. But this is a question which need not be pressed here. I have tried to indicate that there has grown up in the United States a body of beliefs as to the Constitution and the courts contrary to the evidence of logic and history. And what I wish to do in the remaining part of this article is to indicate the lines along which an adequate explanation of the origin and growth of these errors must move.

The Economic Interpretation of Constitutional Rights

The explanation that appeals today most extensively to the younger generation of historians is the economic interpretation

[21] Scott v. Sanford, 19 How. 393 (U.S. 1857).

[22] Lochner v. New York, 198 U.S. 45 (1905).

[23] Adair v. United States, 208 U.S. 161 (1908).

[24] Hammer v. Dagenhart, 247 U.S. 251 (1918); Bailey v. Drexel Furniture Co., 259 U.S. 20 (1922).

[25] Coppage v. Kansas, 236 U.S. 1 (1915).

[26] Adkins v. Children's Hospital, 261 U.S. 525 (1923), Murphy v. Sardell, 269 U.S. 530 (1925); Donham v. West-Nelson Mfg. Co., 273 U.S. 657 (1927); Morehead v. New York ex. rel. Tipaldo, 298 U.S. 587 (1936).

[27] United States v. Harris, 106 U.S. 629 (1883); Hodges v. United States, 203 U.S. 1 (1906).

[28] Civil Rights Cases, 109 U.S. 3 (1883).

[29] Tyson v. Banton, 273 U.S. 418 (1927).

[30] Burns Baking Co. v. Bryan, 264 U.S. 504 (1924).

[31] Ribnik v. McBride, 277 U.S. 350 (1928).

advanced by Professor Beard; [32] and I have no desire to reject its main findings. It seems to me unquestionable that the forces which made for the adoption of the Constitution came from the commercial interests and the seaboard aristocracy, that it was the Federalist party of "the rich and the well-born" which first exalted the judiciary and intrenched itself in it when it was defeated in the election of 1800, and that to our own day it is, in the main, the propertied interests which have sought to build it up as a restraint on popular legislation. So long as the last word on all of our affairs comes from judges sufficiently old, according to Justice Holmes, to distrust all new ideas at sight, the forms of democratic political action can be tolerated. I think, however, that the economic interpretation is too simple and does not go far enough. It is too simple in not assigning sufficient importance to intellectual and sentimental factors, and it does not go far enough on the economic side, in its inadequate appreciation of the role of the farmer or small property owner in the development of the American ideology.

I submit that those who talk of the capitalist class as the absolute rulers of this country are the victims of a mythology. Not only were the agricultural elements in the majority in the United States to the end of the nineteenth century, but they still dominate our political life through the gerrymanders which enable them to control even the most industrial states, such as New York, Pennsylvania, Illinois, and Rhode Island. Now political nihilism—the view that that government is best which governs least, the view that sees no harm if a legislative enactment is struck down by the courts—generally fits the conditions of a sparsely settled country, where each locality and indeed sometimes each family must look after itself and cannot wait for regulations from a seat of government far away. This rural mentality has dominated our judiciary.

[32] *An Economic Interpretation of the Constitution of the United States* (1913).

The Ideology of Constitutional Rights

But in its origin, the apotheosis of the Constitution and the judiciary is not simply a matter of class interests. In dealing with the origin and growth of an ideology we must not leave out of account the purely intellectual factor. The modes of thought to which we become habituated, especially in our youth, resist all change no matter how extensively economic facts and interests diverge from them. Unanalyzed habits of thought are the most stubborn of facts.

What, then, were the ideologic conditions which led to our glorification of the Constitution and the courts to an extent unknown in any other country? Professor J. B. Thayer suggested that the analogy for the power of our courts to declare statutes unconstitutional was set by the British Privy Council in declaring void some of our colonial legislation on the ground that these acts contravened the powers granted in the charter.[33] This sounds plausible and has found wide acceptance. But while it perhaps may be an element in the situation it is certainly far from being the whole story. The Privy Council was not passing on the acts of a co-ordinate branch of the government. Moreover, the acts of the Privy Council were certainly widely resented by our people, and could not have become a convincing precedent to the great mass of Americans. In point of fact, a careful examination of all the early arguments in favor of judicial restraints on legislative powers reveals hardly any references to such English precedents. It is rather to political theorists and jurists such as Grotius (through Rutherforth), Montesquieu, and Vattel that the appeal is made. We must remember that in the eighteenth century the legal profession in this country was not technically so far developed as it is today,[34] that many of our early judges were laymen, and that the tradition of deciding cases in accordance with the common interpretation of the law of God and authorities on natural law was

[33] See Thayer, "The Origin and Scope of the American Doctrine of Constitutional Law," in *Legal Essays* (1908), pp. 1, 3.

[34] See Reinsch, "The English Common Law in the Early American Colonies," in *Select Essays in Anglo-American Legal History*, Vol. 1, p. 367.

quite extensive. It is amazing to see how many books on natural law formed the equipment even of our most technically trained lawyers.

Now the eighteenth century was a period of classical education, and the one thing that every gentleman learned besides his Cicero was Euclid's geometry, in which everything seemed to follow from a few self-evident principles. This made plausible the analogous idea of a simple code of nature containing self-evident principles of natural right from which the solution of all possible problems as to just law could be rigorously deduced. It is well to remember that in the eighteenth century this did not sound so unreal or legally anarchic as it does today. There was then much more consensus among leading writers as to what were the specific dictates of natural law—possible because social conditions then were more stable. Before the rise of modern romantic nationalism the community of the Christian Latin Empire had not been completely broken up among the learned. The Bible and the classics, including Roman jurists, reigned as final and unquestioned authorities, and the writers on natural law most often read and cited showed, despite minor differences, a fair degree of agreement. *That,* then, is the background from which we must start. It is well, however, to note that in its conception of natural law the philosophy of the Enlightenment marked a distinct departure from the scholastic doctrine. In the latter, self-evident principles were conservative, because limited by the authority of Scriptures as interpreted by the Church. Grotius, in discarding supernatural authority for natural rights, opened the way for revolutionary notions.

What is self-evident to any human being is largely determined by the ideas to which he is accustomed. Hence in medieval thought custom is the dominant and determinant element in ethical, political, and economic issues. Thus the right price or the just wage reduces itself to the customary one, to the one that is usually expected; and medieval constitutional rights, as in England, were those arising from *consuetudo*. Now the philosophy of the Enlightenment not only rejected the authority of the Church but summoned customary law before the bar of reason. Thus instead of being conservative it became a revolutionary philosophy used by the commercial interests in their struggle for emancipation from feudal restraints on manufacture and free commerce (*laissez faire, laissez passer*). The rights of the governors are like any others that arise from contract—not general, but specific, and given in consideration for a promised protection of life and property, especially property.

The results of the French Revolution brought about a reaction against this absolute right to revolution. Not only Burke but the apostle of bourgeois philosophy, Jeremy Bentham, gave voice to this reaction. Jefferson, however, in this country for some time maintained the revolutionary philosophy. "The tree of liberty must be refreshed from time to time with the blood of patriots and tyrants," [35] and the people's remedy against the abuse of government is not in the courts but in the right of revolution. And this in principle was maintained by such an ardent Federalist as James Wilson.[36] Indeed, the Constitution itself was a revolutionary or illegal setting aside of the provision which required unanimous consent for any change in the Articles of Confederation.

In Europe, the view that that government is best which governs least was crushed by the growth of industry, city life, and the demands of nationalism, philanthropy, and socialism for

[35] "And what country can preserve its liberties, if their rulers are not warned from time to time, that their people preserve the spirit of resistance? Let these take arms. . . . The tree of liberty must be refreshed from time to time with the blood of patriots and tyrants. It is its natural manure." Thomas Jefferson, Letter to Stephens Smith, *Letters of Jefferson* (Ford ed., 1897), Vol. 4, p. 467.
"I hold it that a little rebellion now and then is a good thing, and as necessary in the political world as storms in the physical." Letter to James Madison, *ibid.*, p. 362.

[36] ". . . a revolution principle certainly is, and certainly should be taught as a principle of the constitution of the United States, and of every State in the Union." *Works of James Wilson* (Andrews ed., 1896), Vol. 1, p. 18. "In many parts of the world, indeed, the idea of revolution in government is, by a mournful and indissoluble association, connected with the idea of wars, and of all the calamities attendant on wars. But joyful experience teaches us, in the United States, to view them in a very different and much more agreeable light—to consider them only as progressive steps in improving the knowledge of government, and increasing the happiness of society and mankind." *Ibid.*, pp. 343-44.

state action. These weakened the faith in salvation through economic anarchy or unregulated competition. The unconscionable exploitation of men, women and children by the new industrial order offended not only humanitarian sentiment but also the natural interests of the military and landed classes, so that state interference, in the form of factory legislation and social insurance, became part of the Tory program. And this could not be the case in a free land economy such as existed in the United States during the nineteenth century when home rule and federalism rather than centralized nationalism prevailed.

In Europe the rapid growth of natural science and later the progress of mathematics diminished the general confidence in self-evident principles, so that today no logicians or geometers hold that axioms guarantee their own truth. Even, therefore, if legal reasoning were always strictly deductive and impersonal (which is not the case), the conclusions could be attacked by questioning their premises. Not so in this country. Education in this country was largely under clerical influence up to the end of the nineteenth century. Nearly all of our colleges were denominational in origin and few college presidents were not clergymen. Generally the college president was also professor of philosophy. The dominant philosophy throughout the nineteenth century here was Scottish intuitionism, in which every dogma was elevated into an eternal intuition of the human mind. It was in this climate of opinion that the various doctrines as to the nature of constitutional law spread and took root—not uninfluenced, of course, by the fact that it lifted issues out of the forum of politics, where the votes of the majority could decide, into the forum of law where those who could hire the ablest lawyers had a distinct advantage, especially since lawyers for the government generally looked for a career in private practice after leaving government service.

Sentiment, Symbol, and Direction

In the foregoing I have left out what is psychologically the most important element, namely, sentiment and the need for some objects of worship to strengthen the authority of government. We see it in England in the mystic devotion to the Crown, especially when the occupant is colorless or lacks distinctive personal traits. In other countries it is the army, the nobility, the emperor, or some other symbol of national unity which calls forth the most intense devotion so that men are willing to throw away their lives for its glory. In the United States we have no crown, no hereditary nobility, no standing army, no national church, nor even the convincing consciousness that we are a distinct race. The Constitution and the courts that guard it therefore become the symbol of our uniqueness and of our superiority over other nations that know not the blessings of liberty, security, and prosperity.

Since Plato there have never been absent those who believe that the great mass of the people are unreasoning beasts that must be controlled by inoculating them with myths or fictions (unfeeling skeptics call them pious frauds.) I do not wish to discuss here the advantage of controlling the will of a democratic majority by the judgment of a few elderly gentlemen who are removed from popular clamor. But it is curious to note that it is those Americans who are at heart distrustful of democracy who speak of the courts as standing between us and dictatorship, and yet their arguments are precisely those which the adherents of Hitler and Mussolini use against the frailty of democratically representative or elective government. This is a question of political philosophy beyond the range of this article. If, however, there are any principles of political science which enlightened experience makes clear, they are (1) that the worst form of government is that which separates power from responsibility, and (2) that the weakest government is that which has relatively little access to the sources of information. And does not the fiction that the courts only follow the words of the Constitution in fact relieve them of the responsibility for the fatal results of their decisions? And is it not also true that this fiction that the courts decide only questions of law prevents us from organizing the courts so that they could have the opportunity of making adequate investigation into the actual facts on which they have to pass? Do we want our judges to be not only irresponsible to any earthly power, but also independent of adequate knowledge of the social consequences of their decisions?

20

THE SACCO-VANZETTI CASE
REWEIGHED

NO CRIMINAL CASE since the Dreyfus affair has stirred the world so much as that of Sacco and Vanzetti. The conviction of Mooney was a clearer instance of the miscarriage of justice; the trial judge himself is now convinced that it was brought about by deliberate perjury. But if William James be trusted, insensibility to abstract justice is characteristic of the American people; and those who disapprove of Mooney's career in the labor movement can say, as they do: "He is a bad man, and ought to be in jail, even if not guilty of the particular outrage of which he was convicted. The State of California did enough for him by commuting the death sentence to life imprisonment." Not so in regard to Sacco and Vanzetti. They are now dead, and in life were either cold-blooded, mercenary murderers or else, as their letters reveal them, singularly high-minded, if unpractical, idealists. Their guilt or innocence is thus a matter of intense faith to millions who have never examined the record of the case. Nor is the latter task an easy one. Very few have the time and the disposition to go through six volumes of detailed testimony, motions, arguments, and technical judicial decisions, in

Published in *The Nation*, Vol. 133, p. 702 (December 23, 1931), as a review of Osmond K. Fraenkel, *The Sacco-Vanzetti Case*.

order to arrive at an independent opinion on a case which was legally terminated four years ago.

And yet the question whether Massachusetts did or did not, in a state of hysteria, execute two innocent men, is of the utmost importance to those who care at all for actual justice.

One of Voltaire's chief claims to fame was that he fought for years to prove that an old man, Calas, was broken at the wheel only because he was a Protestant in a Catholic community. And numerous other brave and enlightened Frenchmen fought hard to prove that Dreyfus was convicted only because he was a Jew. What shall we think of those Americans who contend that Sacco and Vanzetti were cruelly done to death because they were dissenting foreigners? Our conservatives, like the French clericals and militarists, preach the duty of blind, unquestioning faith in Massachusetts and in the infallibility of her officials. But that is inconsistent with the mentality of free men, and really subversive of all the traditional ideals of Americanism. It is the claim of our conservatives that our courts are bulwarks of justice against popular hysteria. Was that true in this particular case? Only a careful study of the evidence will enable us to give an honest answer one way or the other. And for this purpose Mr. Fraenkel's book is most helpful. It is indeed a great public service to give us in one volume a remarkably clear account of the legal history of the case and a transparently fair analysis of its principal issues. I do not know of any book on a public question that exceeds its scrupulous honesty in handling all the available evidence. The essentials of the case are put before us in the first two hundred pages illumined by apt extracts from the record. This includes an appendix on the Bridgewater case, in which Vanzetti was condemned for an attempted hold-up. Mr. Fraenkel deals quite objectively with the evidence (he mentions without comment, for example, an identification of Vanzetti as having "run like a foreigner"). He is rightly critical and cautious about accepting the subsequent confession of Silva (printed in the *Outlook*) which exonerated Vanzetti. But Mr. Fraenkel admits that "Silva's knowledge of the case was great and that the opportunities for collecting such knowledge after the event were very slight." It might be added that Silva was hardly of the type that could or would make a study of the official record.

In the second part of the book we have the analysis of all the points advanced to prove Sacco and Vanzetti guilty of the Braintree murder and a similar treatment of the chief countercontentions of the defense:

1. The first point relates to the identification of the accused as having been at or near the scene of the crime. I think that after reading what Mr. Fraenkel has written no fair-minded man will deny that the government witnesses had little chance to observe the actual murderers. Nor were the identifications made under the safeguards that common sense and sound police practice dictate. Some of the witnesses, like Lotta Packard, offered obviously absurd testimony in order to get into the case. None of the witnesses for the prosecution was positive all the time. The only government witness who claimed to have seen the actual shooting was not only contradicted by other witnesses, but he told a quite different story to both sides before the trial. On the other hand, not only witnesses for the defense but even a government witness positively denied that Sacco and Vanzetti were the men involved. Mr. Gould, who admittedly had the best opportunity of all to get a full view of the murderers, was never given a chance to testify. But so strong was his subsequent affidavit to the effect that Sacco and Vanzetti could not have been the men he saw, and so weak did the government's case seem in retrospect in 1924, that Judge Thayer was forced to say that the verdict did not rest on the identification of the accused men by eyewitnesses.

2. It was argued that one of the fatal bullets had been fired through the pistol carried by Sacco. There was little evidence for this and the district attorney himself did not at first take much stock in it. But later he and the judge "put it over" on the jury by perverting the intent of Captain Proctor's testimony. The latter's subsequent affidavit clearly pointed this out, but, alas, in vain.

3. During the trial it was also contended that a cap found on the scene of the murder was Sacco's. But the evidence for it was so insufficient and so contradicted by most reliable testi-

mony that the Lowell committee dismissed it as trifling. Yet in arguing against a new trial, the district attorney contended that the cap was sufficient basis for conviction.

4. It was also urged that the gun found on Vanzetti at the time of his arrest belonged to one of the victims of the crime. It is on the face of it inherently improbable that anyone who planned a crime so carefully as to prepare peculiar tacks to interfere with pursuing cars should for weeks after the act carry the evidence of the crime about his person. In fact, the real evidence on this point was so flimsy that both district attorney and judge had to misrepresent it to impress the jury.

5. Judge Thayer himself, especially in his subsequent defense of the conviction, insisted on the consciousness of guilt which Sacco and Vanzetti had shown at the time of their arrest. This of course is readily explained by the fact that they were afraid that because of their radicalism they would be maltreated like their friend Salsedo. It cannot be denied that not only the lies that both Sacco and Vanzetti told to the district attorney, but also those that some of their friends told on the witness stand, profoundly prejudiced judge and jury against them. But here we must note that people such as the Italians, Russians, and others who have lived under oppressive governments get into the fixed habit of not telling the truth to government officials, just as patriotic soldiers avoid telling the truth to their enemy captors.

For the defense, Mr. Fraenkel considers, in the first place, the alibis of both Sacco and Vanzetti. Sacco's testimony that he was in Boston on the day of the murder is not only corroborated by others, but his own recognition of a fellow-passenger on the train from Boston is clearly incompatible with his presence that day at Braintree.

To get around this point Governor Fuller distorted the testimony, and President Lowell acted as a partisan seeking to vindicate the prosecution. When President Lowell thought he had secured evidence to discredit one of the supports of Sacco's alibi he exclaimed, "There goes your strong alibi." But when it turned out that Sacco's witnesses were right on the particular point at issue, he ignored the matter.

The innocence of Sacco and Vanzetti becomes reasonably certain when we consider the strong cumulative evidence that the murder was committed by the Morelli gang as confessed by one of its members, Madeiros. There was obstinate fanaticism in the way this phase of the case was passed over by Judge Thayer and the Lowell committee. The crime was clearly the work of professional or experienced bandits who had studied all the phases of their job, such as when the money would be carried, when their own car should arrive and get away, and how to elude pursuing cars. Will a skilled laborer like Sacco, with a growing family, a garden, and a savings-bank account, suddenly take a day off from work to join professional bandits in such a desperate enterprise? No part of the money was in fact ever traced to Sacco or Vanzetti. And the Morelli gang not only had the requisite motive and experience to commit the robbery but were in funds right after it.

In view of the fact that no other court really passed on the question of Judge Thayer's prejudice, it is important to consider his own intemperate expressions to Professor Richardson and others. Can anyone who gloated so at what he did "to those anarchist bastards" be rationally considered free from prejudice? Yet Judge Thayer not only presided at both trials and passed on the new evidence offered by the defendants, but was also the judge of his own fairness. No wonder that so many of our law-school teachers, including Judge Hinton, an authority on the law of evidence with judicial experience of his own, publicly and emphatically declared that Sacco and Vanzetti did not have a fair trial.

Mr. Fraenkel has had to restrict his task to the purely legal side of the case. He does, however, refer to the general anti-Red panic of the time as a significant circumstance. If so, would it not have been relevant to make more of the letters that Sacco and Vanzetti wrote from prison? Surely such letters throw some light on the character of their writers. If I were to accuse an archbishop or college president of having picked my pocket, it would surely be reasonable to demand more evidence than that which would be sufficient to convict one who had shown a more ready disposition for that sort of enterprise. For that reason I think all those who wish to avail themselves of the best evidence on this case should also read *The Letters of Sacco and Vanzetti*, edited by Gardner Jackson and Marion Frankfurter.

It is to be hoped that someone will write a careful history of the human side of the whole case, of all that went on behind the scene and caused the various changes of public, newspaper, and official opinion. But no one will have to write again concerning the trial and the evidence. Mr. Fraenkel has done it so as to leave nothing more to be desired.

21

A SCANDALOUS DENIAL OF JUSTICE: THE BERTRAND RUSSELL CASE

Nullius liber homo capiatur . . . aut aliquo modo distruatur
. . . nisi per legale judicium parium. . . .
—Magna Charta, Sec. 39.

THE LEGAL SYSTEMS of all modern civilized people recognize the fallibility of judges of first instance, and therefore make provision for appeal and review. And our judicial statistics show that in a high proportion of cases the rulings of the first court have in fact been declared erroneous. The denial of the right of appeal is, therefore, a denial of justice. Such a denial is all the more grievous if it is due to pressure from a political or hierarchical source interfering with the due course of judicial proceedings.

In a number of famous instances, such as the Dreyfus case,

Published in the symposium volume *The Bertrand Russell Case*, edited by John Dewey and Horace Kallen (1940).

enlightened public conscience was properly outraged by the fact that the accused did not receive a fair trial. For on the fairness of judicial procedure depends that security against baseless charges which is indispensable for dignified civilized life. But in the case of Bertrand Russell an internationally honored teacher, scholar, and philosopher was foully condemned, branded as a criminal, and ignominiously deprived of his position as a professor by a proceeding which had not the barest resemblance to a trial.

The reader will find in *The Harvard Law Review* of May 1940 a brief but incisive legal critique of the irregularity of Judge McGeehan's procedure and the absurdity of the unprecedented doctrines on which his decision rested. But it does not require much legal learning to see that the most elementary requisite of just judicial procedure is violated when a man is condemned without being given a chance to be heard, to confront his accusers, and to offer evidence in refutation of their disingenuous charges.[1] If ever there was a case that called for

[1] One does not expect perfect candor or a nice regard for truth in lawyers' briefs, and it is therefore not surprising to find the counsel for the complainant denying the public fact that Russell had been a teacher for most of his life, in England and China as well as in the United States. But one is taken aback to find gentlemen who are members of the Board of Higher Education telling the Appellate Division that "the post of Professor of Philosophy at City College is a brand-new position. It never existed previously and was never held by any prior incumbent. Indeed, the Department of Philosophy itself is a new department created by the Board in 1940." The fact—which any reader can verify—is that the Department of Philosophy has existed at the City College almost from its beginning. In my own lifetime Professors Newcomb, McNulty, Overstreet, and myself were officially designated as professors of philosophy. Can this have been unknown to Mr. Tuttle, who has been a member of the Board for more than thirty years and for a long time chairman of the Administrative Committee of the City College? It is rather the Department of Psychology, an offshoot of that of Philosophy, that was first established in 1940. And it was the post of Professor of Psychology, to which Dr. Murphy was appointed, that was then created. Russell was to fill the chair left vacant by Professor Overstreet's retirement. Acting President Mead in recommending Russell also mentioned the position still unfilled since my own retirement as professor of philosophy early in 1938.

It is also, I confess, hard to believe in the sincerity of these gentlemen's concern about Russell's acquiring permanent tenure after a year's service, when they knew that the whole term of Russell's service could not, because of the legal age limit, be more than a year and a half. Strange, how men

the review for which higher courts are instituted, this was surely one. Yet such review was effectively prevented by a barrage of dubious technicalities. That such a thing can happen in a great American city is an ominous indication of how precarious are the constitutional rights of "due process" which are often supposed to go back to Magna Charta.

Let us look at the main facts of the record.

Bertrand Russell was, on the recommendation of its Philosophy Department and of its Acting President, regularly appointed Professor of Philosophy at the City College and thereupon resigned his previous professorship at the University of California in Los Angeles. Soon thereafter a public clamor was raised by Bishop Manning (supported by various noneducational bodies) that Russell's appointment should be rescinded—i.e., in plain English, that he should be dismissed because of his views on religion and morals. Against this proposal Russell's fellow-teachers of philosophy throughout the country, and all the educational authorities of the institutions with which Russell had been connected, publicly protested and endorsed his qualifications. The Board of Higher Education then voted to stand by its original appointment.

The next day a complaint was brought in Judge McGeehan's court in Manhattan in the name of a Mrs. Kay of Brooklyn, asking that Russell's appointment be declared illegal because he was not a citizen and not a man of moral character. No evidence was brought to sustain the latter charge except the submission of several volumes of Russell's writings, published some years ago. The Corporation Counsel appeared on behalf of the Board of Higher Education (through an assistant, Mr. Bucci) and contended that the complaint should be dismissed. Mr. Bucci properly offered no evidence in refutation of the complaint, since proper judicial procedure required that the court first rule on his motion to dismiss the complaint as a legally insufficient cause of action. Within two days Judge McGeehan announced his decision disqualifying Russell in language which clearly showed the heat of a biased or partisan pleader eager to

zealous for public morality will so often be disdainful of honest truth in their arguments.

convict, rather than the careful judgment of a responsible judge who has, in conformity with the duty of his office, conscientiously considered the rights of both sides of the case. There were also a number of statements in his written opinions which are simply not true. Thus he said that "the Court had witnesses [note the plural] produced in court." The record shows this statement to be categorically false. No witnesses appeared in court. Mrs. Kay merely swore that she was the petitioner, on the judge's assurance to the Corporation Counsel that this was merely "so that her name will appear in the record." No one claimed that Mrs. Kay was a competent witness to testify as to Professor Russell's fitness for the position of professor. Nor can we accept as true the statement of the judge that the respondent "informed the Court that he would not serve an answer." Mr. Bucci denied it in a sworn affidavit which was never challenged. This was confirmed by a sworn affidavit by Mr. Fraenkel, who at no time was given a chance to produce evidence refuting the scurrilous and defamatory statements in the complaint and in the judge's written opinion. Judge McGeehan's reference to the proceedings as a trial has no support in fact or law. He pronounced judgment on Russell on the supposed ground of having read some of his books, but without asking Russell whether the views which he (the judge) read into these books were really there and if so whether Russell still adhered to those views.

Let us now consider the three alleged legal grounds for declaring Russell's appointment illegal.

The first point was that an alien may not teach in a New York college. The statute invoked clearly refers to public schools, which are directed to hold Arbor Day and other exercises that no one supposes to be obligatory in a college. It provides that teachers shall be graduates of normal schools and hold licenses, which no college professor is ever required to do. Even in the public schools the law allows an alien to teach if he declares his intention to become a citizen. Professor Russell had at least ten months in which to do so before qualifying for the active performance of his duties. Judge McGeehan tried to disregard this clear provision of the law by the arbitrary guess that the Federal courts would bar Russell from citizenship. If there were any real basis for this guess, the opponents of Russell would surely have tried to have him deported on the ground that a person of moral turpitude was not qualified to enter this country. But Judge McGeehan's mind was obviously not on the law. He himself declared that he would be writing for the legislature as well as the Court of Appeals, and it is not unfair to suspect that he also had in mind the daily newspapers. This is shown by his final appeal to a narrow local prejudice in the argument that "other universities and colleges both public and private seem to be able to find American citizens to employ." As an argument this is clearly worthless in law as well as in logic. Any implication that our institutions of higher learning do not employ foreign scholars is patently false. Long lists can readily be compiled of foreign teachers in municipal and state institutions as well as in private Catholic, Protestant, and Jewish colleges. In New York City not only the city colleges, New York and Columbia Universities, but the institution which Judge McGeehan himself attended, have gladly availed themselves of the opportunity when a distinguished foreign scholar was available. This has long been considered an honored practice in New York as in other states. The laws of the United States have recognized its national advantage and have exempted such foreign teachers from the usual immigration quotas. To deprive our students of the best available teachers would obviously be to impoverish our country intellectually. Only petty ward politicians, ignorant of the essentially international character of all science and philosophy that seeks the truth, can ignore this. In any case, we surely have an issue here that should not be settled by the arbitrary whim of a judge of first instance who gave barely two days to the hearing of the case and to the writing of his opinion. Surely this should receive the careful consideration of the highest appellate courts.

The second ground on which Russell's appointment was declared illegal was even more unprecedented and revolutionary in its implication. It is that a professor in any public college in New York State must take a civil service examination (by whom?). This is a view so contrary to the experience of our institutions of higher learning that it is hard to believe that anyone in the smallest degree acquainted with the practices of modern colleges can in good faith maintain it. If this ground of the decision in the Russell case were sound law, every one of the professors in every one of our state-supported colleges would have to be dismissed and every member of the Boards of Trustees of Higher Education be penalized for the illegal appointments. Also, the Commissioner of Education of the State of New York would have to be punished for permitting so many to teach in violation of the law. The truth is that not even all the teachers in the public schools of New York State outside of two large cities are required to take examinations at all. The law clearly provides that examinations shall be held only when practicable, and the educational authorities in touch with actual conditions have never found examinations practicable in the appointment of professors in institutions of higher learning. Yet Judge McGeehan blandly asserts that the assumption by the Board of Higher Education that competitive examinations were impracticable was "unwarranted, arbitrary, and capricious." One might with more justice apply these epithets to the judge's own decision.

The third ground of the decision is of fateful significance not only to the independence of our educational system but for the general conception of the judicial function. That an individual judge may, on the basis of reading a number of passages in a scholar's works, set up his own judgment as to whether the author is fit for a professorship in a college, and venture to overrule the faculty and the educational authorities to whom such determination is expressly delegated by law and who have had more opportunity to study and competently to interpret these works, is a strange and ominous legal doctrine. Judges are not supposed to be endowed with superhuman wisdom or omniscience in all matters. They are therefore generally restricted to passing only on the question: What has the law provided? Hence it has always been regarded as a sound and established legal principle that, where discretion is expressly conferred on administrative officials, no judge may interfere by simply setting up his own judgment as to the wisdom of what an administrative body did. He may act only if there can be no reasonable doubt that the administrators have gone beyond the power granted them. That this cannot possibly be so here is evidenced by the fact that almost all qualified educational authorities who expressed themselves in the case, including hundreds of American teachers of philosophy, regarded Professor Russell as eminently fit and urged the Board of Higher Education not to revoke his appointment.

The Western Philosophical Association, after the decision in the Russell Case was announced, unanimously adopted a resolution which in effect insisted that teachers of philosophy (as of other subjects) should be selected on the advice of those competent in their special field and not by judges after listening to arguments of lawyers. (What distinguished scholar will want to accept a professorship if thereby he subjects himself to having his name besmirched in a litigation in which he has not even a chance to appear in court to clear himself?) And Chancellor Chase of New York University won the reluctant approval even of the *New York Times* (which had been rather hostile to Russell) when he urged that, no matter how much one may disagree with Russell's views, the question whether a judge may overrule educational authority in passing on the fitness of a teacher (on the basis of the latter's *opinions*) had not been properly settled and needed to be reviewed by the higher courts.

The statement that the appointment of Professor Russell "is in effect establishing a chair of indecency" is a rather scurrilous way of referring to the several hundred eminent teachers of philosophy who endorsed his appointment to the Universities of Chicago and California and to Harvard, where he had served as professor of philosophy to the expressed satisfaction of students, fellow-teachers, and educational administrators. One had a right to expect that a court of law pronouncing judgment as to the possible influence of a certain teacher would take into account the testimony of actual pupils as distinguished as Dr. Marjorie Nicolson, Dean of Smith College (where Russell had lectured) and president of the national association of the United Chapters of Phi Beta Kappa. Dr. Nicolson had been a pupil of Bertrand Russell at the British Institute of Philosophical

Studies and wrote that both in a large popular course and in a small seminar "Mr. Russell never introduced into his discussions of philosophy any of the controversial questions which his opponents have raised. . . . Mr. Russell is first and foremost a philosopher, and in his teaching he always remembers that. I should have had no way of knowing Mr. Russell's opinions on marriage, divorce, theism, or atheism, had they not been given an exaggerated form in the newspapers."

Judge McGeehan condemned Russell as an immoral person because of his divorce record in England. This record was known to the authorities of the many colleges, including those for women and the co-educational ones, where Russell was invited to teach and gave a course of lectures. In a country where many leaders of our public life have been divorced, can it be said as a matter of law that teachers who have gone through such marital difficulties must be dismissed? [2] Many, perhaps a majority, of our people regard George Eliot as one of the noblest women of the nineteenth century, though she lived in what was legally an adulterous relation with George Henry Lewes.

It is not necessary to point out to any literate audience how forced and utterly unwarranted is the misinterpretation of Russell's writings adduced in justification of the monstrous charge that Russell's appointment would endanger the health and morals of New York through his inciting young people to masturbation or to the crimes of homosexuality and abduction. But the tolerance and even favorable comment which Judge McGeehan's rhetorical opinion received in parts of our public press show how urgent it is that those who know anything about the history and importance of freedom of thought should keep the public informed as to the necessity of the distinction between incitement to crime and the free expression of philo-

[2] In this connection it is curious to note that while Judge McGeehan was District Attorney of Bronx County a large number of divorces were there granted on legally sufficient evidence of adultery. But though adultery is a crime in New York State, District Attorney McGeehan never prosecuted a single one of the parties whose guilt was thus officially recorded.

One is reminded of the story of the lady who congratulated Dr. Johnson on having left out all obscene words from his dictionary. "Madam," said the honest Doctor, "I am sorry you looked for them."

sophic doubt as to the adequacy of our traditional or conventional morality. In defending society against crime we must
not suppress the questioning mind, which has been the basis
not only of democratic but of all liberal civilization, as distinguished from societies of robots that act either from habit or
according to what others tell them.

Judge McGeehan himself publicly expressed his expectation
that his decision would be appealed and reviewed by the higher
courts. What prevented the important issue which he raised
from receiving due consideration from any of our higher courts?
The first obstacle was the technical ruling (unfortunately sustained by our Court of Appeals) that Mr. Russell could not be
made a party in a suit in which his reputation and his position
as a teacher were at stake. This is marvelously strange when
we consider the interest of Mrs. Kay in the suit. None of her
children could possibly have been able to take any of Russell's
courses at the City College. In the first place they lived in
Brooklyn, and if they went to college at all they would naturally
go to Brooklyn College rather than tó the City College, which
is in upper Manhattan. In the second place her daughters could
not be admitted to the City College, which in its regular classes
does not admit women. And in the third place, as Russell would
have to retire in 1942 because of the age limit, none of her
children could possibly have managed to qualify for admission
in Russell's classes. If she was really interested in keeping her
children from contact with Russell's ideas she should have applied for an order restraining publishers from publishing Russell's books, booksellers from selling them, and public libraries
from circulating them; for in fact Russell has had far more
popular influence through his writings than through his classes,
which have always been highly technical. I think it is important
to bear in mind the fictitious character of Mrs. Kay's interest
which the courts were so eager to protect that they refused to
let Mr. Russell answer her complaint. The reason given was
that she was suing the Board of Higher Education and should
not, therefore, be compelled to litigate with Professor Russell,
though in fact she was trying to deprive him of the right to
pursue his calling, on which he and his children depended for

their living. If this is law, then surely, in the language of Dickens, "the law is a ass."

An honest friend of the venerable doctrine of "due process" might have expected that it would operate against depriving a man of his property and reputation without ever giving him a chance to be heard. But such expectation would also have shown serious innocence as to the forces behind the scenes in this case.

Very significant is the part played in this unsavory case by the Corporation Counsel of New York City. At first he appeared (through his assistant, Mr. Bucci) as counsel for the Board of Higher Education and contended that there was no justification in law for the removal of Professor Russell from the position to which he had been appointed. But after Judge McGeehan's decision he not only refused to vindicate the law by appealing the case but actively and effectively opposed the effort of the Board to do so.

What reason did he give for this radical change of attitude? Clearly not that the judge's written opinion convinced him that the office of the Corporation Counsel had been mistaken as to the law in the case. On the contrary, in his letter to the Board of Higher Education he quite definitely intimated that Judge McGeehan's decision was not in conformity with the law. The reason alleged for his "advice" was a rather thinly veiled opinion that the higher courts could not in this case be trusted to decide the issues involved on their merits. He therefore urged the Board to obey a decision unwarranted by the law and break a contract entered into in good faith by both parties, thereby committing a serious injustice against Professor Russell, who had resigned his previous position in California in reliance on the honor and official action of the Board of Higher Education in New York City.

It is, frankly, hard to believe that an honorable legal official of a great municipality could thus be willing to participate in a grossly dishonorable (if not illegal) procedure, if he were not under some pressure not referred to in his letter to the Board. And indeed there is some evidence of intervention by the Mayor, who gave the identical advice to the Board. Two incidents point in this direction. The first is the haste of the Mayor in putting into the city budget a provision that no part of the money of the Board of Higher Education should be used to pay Russell's salary. This was an unprecedented move of no real legal force, for if anything is established in the Education Law of New York it is the complete freedom of a school board to control expenditures within its own budget. Certainly the Mayor and the Board of Estimate have no right to interfere in the appointment of a professor in our city colleges, nor have they the right to bring about the removal of anyone who has been appointed. The action of the Mayor was just "a play to the gallery" for political reasons, as was the action of the City Council.

The second indication is the Mayor's subsequent action in publicly directing the Corporation Counsel not to appeal a case where the Board of Education was involved. Now a city, like any other client, may instruct its counsel not to appeal a case if such appeal will not serve its best interests. But where an agency such as a Board of Education has by law been granted certain powers, with which the Mayor cannot interfere, then his preventing an appeal hamstrings by indirection that which he may not directly control. No Mayor will openly tell the Board of Higher Education to appoint Professor X or to dismiss Professor Y. Yet to prevent the college from using its funds to pay a given teacher is to all intents and purposes compelling it to discharge that teacher. The Mayor has not been provided with facilities, and the law certainly gives him no power, to deal thus with the employees of our educational institutions. But whatever the influence of the Mayor, there is no doubt that an effective judicial review of the issues raised by Judge Mc-Geehan's decision was prevented (1) by the Corporation Counsel's refusal to appeal from an order the granting of which he had opposed on good legal grounds, and (2) by the Appellate Division's sustaining his power to prohibit the Board of Higher Education from appearing in court through any other lawyer. This extraordinary situation, by which an administrative body is prevented from defending in court the legality of the acts within its province, was sustained by the Appellate Division in an argument which, to say the least, begs the whole question. That court said: "There is no duty resting upon the Board to engage the services of Russell." But since this court refused to consider the merits of the contention that Russell's original appointment was illegal, the *prima facie* contract between the Board and Professor Russell could not be thus set aside. Even an Appellate Division cannot abrogate a contract while at the same time it refuses to consider the question of its legality.

Despite all technicalities, no one can deny the obvious fact that by a solemn official act the Board appointed Professor Russell and that he in reliance thereon gave up another position. In the minds of all honorable men, therefore, the Board of Higher Education incurred a contractual obligation to disregard which would be disgraceful to the fair name of any city.

Even more important is the larger significance of the unlimited power thus given to the Corporation Counsel. For by preventing the Board of Higher Education from appearing in court to defend what it regards as the proper interpretation of its duties, the Corporation Counsel thus becomes not its legal servant but its master, and this subjects it to all sorts of abuses without its having any legal recourse. The cherished independence of the educational system of New York from political interference, which has been built up through the years and has been recognized by the highest courts,[3] is thus completely destroyed. This is an ominous and sinister situation. The office of the Corporation Counsel is instituted so that the city and its various departments may have adequate legal advice and have their rights defended in the courts. The Corporation Counsel is a lawyer. He may advise his clients that they have a bad case in law, or perhaps even that they are likely to lose a good case because of his suspicion that the judges of last resort are prejudiced and will not decide according to the law. It may even be argued that he has a right to express his opinion that the Board of Higher Education would be wasting the city's money in

[3] "If there be one public policy well established in this State it is that public education shall be beyond control by municipalities and politics."—Chief Judge Crane in Matter of Divisich v. Marshall, 281 N. Y. 170, 22 N.E. (2) 327 (1939).

litigating a given case. But this was not the situation in the Russell case, where the members of the Board of Higher Education, anxious to deal honorably with Professor Russell and to carry to the Court of Appeals the grave issues involved, generously agreed to pay for counsel at their own personal expense. Certainly there is no sound reason of public policy why the Corporation Counsel should be able, by his own arbitrary opinion, to prevent important issues from receiving the full consideration for which our courts are instituted.

VI

LITERATURE AND LITERARY CRITICISM

22

FORCES IN AMERICAN CRITICISM

THE PAST TWO DECADES have witnessed both a notable increase of interest in the history of American literature and a considerable insurgence against the traditional ideas which have long prevailed with regard to it. Under the influence of what may be broadly called the Anti-Puritan and the Marxian points of view, the rebels have protested either (1) against the "Puritanic," "genteel," or "Victorian" subordination of literature to conventional morality or (2) against treating literature apart from the economic, political, and social conditions under which people actually live. The slogan that literature should express "life" has been used so much by both groups that it has obscured the fact that the differences between them are in some respects greater than that which separates the second group from their supposed common enemy. Indeed, the Marxian group might well be called neo-Puritanic, since they are hostile to the idea of literature for the sake of enjoyment (no matter how refined) and insist that it must be judged not by purely esthetic or artistic considerations but by the writer's conformity to the proper doctrine, which must now be politico-economic rather than, as formerly, politico-theological.

The Marxian view of literary criticism is put forward with considerable vigor in Bernard Smith's *Forces in American Criticism*. And though Mr. Smith joins some Freudians in the notion

The substance of this essay appeared as a review of Bernard Smith, *Forces in American Criticism: a Study in the History of American Literary Thought*, in the *Journal of the History of Ideas*, Vol. 1, p. 241 (April 1940).

that the salvation of literature is to be found in greater freedom in dealing with sex, the main force of this book is directed against impressionists, expressionists, esthetes, and hedonists, as fundamentally undemocratic. It opposes Socialism to Bohemianism.

While neither in originality of thought nor in scholarly research does this history of American literary thought claim to be a major contribution, it represents the views of a spreading group and it touches on many ideas that are certainly in urgent need of more critical examination.

What is literature? What is the function of literary criticism? What are the requisites of a scientific history of literary thought? Some answers to these questions are involved in any history of American literary criticism.

I

Previous to the appearance of Parrington's vivid and stirring *Main Currents in American Thought,* which has strongly influenced Mr. Smith, the word "literature" had a fairly definite meaning among English-speaking people. It was generally synonymous with *belles lettres,* and did not at all extend to all the writings that specialists, according to Germanic use, refer to as the "literature" of a subject. It included poetry, novels, dramas, essays, biographies, and those histories which could be regarded as works of art. It excluded official records, statistical or scientific reports, political, economic, or theological books or pamphlets, unless they were written with a certain elevation of style that made them worth reading apart from one's agreement or disagreement with the views expressed in them. One does not have to accept Dante's Catholic philosophy to recognize with the atheistic Shelley that the *Paradiso* is great literature, whereas it still hardly occurs to anyone to maintain that every sound or correct manual on mathematics, astronomy, physics, chemistry, physiology, or law is necessarily a work of literature. Parrington, however, was not only a professor of literature but even more an ardent devotee of Jeffersonian democracy; and so he wrote a book whose title and subtitle indicated two distinct interests which, despite his great literary gifts, he did not fully integrate. As a history of American thought it is obviously inadequate, failing to do full justice to the course not only of religious, scientific, and philosophic but also of political and economic theory. And as a history of literature it is too much concerned with politics and too little with the appreciation of poetry, or the art of the novel or of the drama. The vigorous vitality that made Parrington's a great work despite its obvious limitations has not, however, been inherited by his disciples. Thus Mr. Smith fails to make up his mind consistently as to whether literature, like other fine arts, demands both special aptitudes and cultivation for its adequate appreciation as well as for its production, or whether the esthetic point of view is to be utterly condemned as that of a privileged minority class. Thus he asserts that it is "in a small but intensely alive community" that "literature is created and assimilated" (p. 366), and he admits that the mass of the common people are at times even hostile to art and consider its enjoyment by the educated a vice (pp. 3 and 70). The masses, therefore, have to be educated by poetry and literature generally (p. 118), to be guided "away from grossness and cupidity towards spiritual grace" (p. 149). On the other hand, we have the rejection of the view that delight in literature may be an end in itself; and the quest for beauty in literature is condemned as "aloofness from common life," as "indifference to the fate of the community," as "involving a sense of superiority to the passions and ideals of the mass of men" (p. 359). The literary artist must be responsible to the electorate and be the conscience of society (p. 112). He should spread the democratic gospel (p. 184) on a materialist rather than religious basis (p. 112).

Carried to its logical conclusion, this would lead to the view that any proletarian novel, or for that matter any democratic pamphlet, is greater literature than the poetry of Homer, Spenser, Shakespeare, Goethe, or Keats. But Mr. Smith has not the courage of his confusion, and does not deny the literary merit of Shakespeare, who certainly shows contempt for the lower classes whether they worship Caesar or rebel against the King of England. Indeed, we have the admission that some

Tory critics have a finer ear for poetry than some democratic ones. In the main Mr. Smith's standards are those set forth by G. B. Shaw, in claiming that his plays, because they contained more social ideas of contemporary interest, were for that reason superior to Shakespeare's. This, however, ignores the distinction between the intrinsic and the extrinsic values of literature. Ordinary social-problem plays such as Shaw's at best contain intimations as to how the general happiness might be increased, and they therefore lose their interest when conditions change, while great literature is in itself a permanent source of intense and ennobling enjoyment.

This brings us to the popular confusion between the idea that literature *does* express "life" and the view that it *should* do so. Marxian determinists often seem to be arguing that all literary or any other cultural activity of any period inevitably expresses the socio-economic life which conditions it, but also, that writers frequently fail to do this, and that those who exemplify such failure should be condemned as bad. But even apart from this, there is undoubtedly a widespread confusion in the use of the word "life" in this connection. Like so many other terms that have been used for honorific purposes, its denotation is extremely vague. In the strict sense of the word every writer except those who restrict themselves to inanimate nature deals with life. But obviously those who so eloquently insist that literature should deal with life do not use the word in its literal sense. What they really demand is that it should be concerned with the kind of life in which they happen to be interested. Men like Parrington are interested in Hamilton's reports on manufactures and the method of financing the United States, as an expression of his class bias. But a vast number of others are more interested in such matters as his affair with Mrs. Reynolds or his duel with Aaron Burr. Since none of us can be equally interested in all phases of life, an expression of one's consistent preference is legitimate, provided it does not set itself up as the only valid one, to be enforced on everybody. And here the democratic test of contemporary popular suffrage has no authority. The multitude votes for Longfellow or Ella Wheeler Wilcox or Harold Bell Wright rather than for Walt Whitman or Thoreau, and critics like Mr. Smith feel in no way bound thereby.

II

What then is the proper function of criticism? The currently popular notion shared by Mr. Smith condemns the criticism of the eighteenth and early nineteenth century as didactic and moralistic. He maintains that it was the aristocratic character of society that led to the conception of the critic as a censor, enforcing the proper moral and social standards on all who ventured to make their writings public. But he does not deny that the genuine critic must have both a widely varied and keen sensitiveness in the perception of what constitutes esthetic or literary merit (pp. 358, 379). We must distinguish between criticism and pedagogy (p. 284), or, as Lowell said a century ago, between singing and preaching. On the other hand, social-democratic views lead our author to assert also the direct opposite (e.g., pp. 219, 345). The ideal critic is a guide who influences social and political affairs, one "by whom we wish to be taught" (p. 219), who instructs the artist how his work should affect society (pp. 365-66). Mr. Smith is confident of the critic's ability to do this, to pass judgment on the *truth* of any writer's metaphysical, economic, political, or social-historical views, because he has not the least doubt that by accepting Marxism the critic becomes a scientist (p. 386). To recognize the class-factor in culture is to achieve the highest merit that a critic can have (p. 301). But even if we were to grant that social-economic truth is the supreme test of great literature, it would not follow that we must accept Marxism as the final word of science. One may be a good literary critic and yet doubt whether Marx's theory of exchange value fits the facts of economics. One may even hold that history has stubbornly refused to live up to the prediction of Marx and Engels as to the elimination of the middle class or as to other inevitabilities which follow from materialistic Hegelianism. But it is not necessary to argue this. Mr. Smith himself at times recognizes that there are values permanent for all classes (p. 291), and that no matter how much society changes no class can (or should) throw away all the experience of the past (p. 286). Indeed, if social and economic changes wiped out all previous conditions, it would be impossible to explain how ancient literature could still be read and enjoyed. But to cap the climax we have the quotation from Marx himself that certain periods of highest development of art "stand in no direct connection with the general development of society, nor with the material basis and the skeleton structure of its organization" (p. 288).

Due consideration of this statement of Marx should lead to a recognition of the truth that the critic does well to concentrate on the content of the work of art before him and make explicit the significance implicit in it, so as to promote thereby a fuller and better appreciation of it, rather than to indulge in speculations (always more or less dubious) as to how the author came to write as he did.

III

During the nineteenth century the view became generally popular, and it is still current among some historians of literature, that belief in determinism is enough to make one "scientific." On the assumption that virtues and vices—presumably including literary ones—are "natural products like sugar and vitriol," Taine tried to derive and thus explain all English literature from the factors of race, climate, and "the epoch." Mr. Smith is not so certain about climatic influence and hardly refers to race at all. But he stresses the bias of the ruling economic class of the time, as the determining cause at least of literary criticism, if not of poetry and fiction. The main point is the assumption of a "modern fool-proof historical inquiry and explanation" (p. 262), that if we know a certain (small) number of social "forces," we can deduce or predict the form that literature will at any time take. This amounts to eliminating personal genius or, if you like, personal variation as a factor in literary history. Now we may well admit that to refer to the "genius" of any writer is at best but to point to some of his characteristics, not to explain their origin. But if any writer has distinctive individual traits it is well not to begin by denying

218

their existence; and it is also necessary to recognize the strictly logical principle that laws alone can never be sufficient to "explain" any individual phenomenon. That which is common to a number of writers at a given period in any country cannot possibly account for the more important things in which they differ, such as that which distinguishes Emerson from other New England Transcendentalists, or Poe from the other critics who wrote at the same time and who may have grown up under similar social conditions. A striking example of the disregard of this actuality is shown in Mr. Smith's overconfident rejection of the suggestion that personal temperament prevented Henry Adams from entertaining the Marxian point of view. The "scientific view" requires that this be explained only in terms of class bias. Now, it happens to be the fact that Henry's brother Brooks, belonging to the same social class and environment, did entertain the Marxian point of view as regards the development of law and other social phenomena. Indeed, did not Marx, Lassalle, Lenin, and other revolutionary thinkers overcome the bias of the class into which they were born? Jefferson and Marshall were relatives who came from the same class—but how different their points of view! Any writer may be behind or ahead of his time.

The truth is that positivists generally have a very confused and inadequate view as to the kind of determinism required in scientific procedure in history or any other field. Scientific statements take the form of abstract laws asserting that certain classes of events or characters are connected with certain others according to relatively simple relations. This means that we must reject the view that everything is directly dependent on everything else. For there would be no point in saying that A depends on B if it were equally true that it depends on everything else in the same way. It is, therefore, not sufficient to assert that there must be a relation between the forms of literary expression and the kinds of economic systems. To prove that a direct causal relation prevails between the two surely requires more evidence than mere sequence or even correlation—though very little of the latter has actually been shown, and the specific instances of noncorrelation are many and conspicuous. In any case, it seems, *prima facie,* far more plausible to suppose that what we call literary ability or genius is the resultant of so many factors that no one of them, and no small number of them, will carry us very far as a sufficient explanation. It is curious that a Marxian and a materialist should deny physiologic causes of, or predispositions to, the melancholy temperament (p. 187). Another such fundamental omission is the purely mental factor of imitation. We find, in fact, that literary fashions in this country, despite our War of Independence and differences of economic conditions, have followed in the main British and foreign patterns. Indeed, did not our predominantly agricultural West, according to Mr. Smith's own testimony, imitate the literary models of mercantile and capitalistically developed New England?

To challenge the assumption of direct causal relation (i.e., that one is the necessary and sufficient condition of the other) is not to deny all connection whatsoever. But such connection may be indirect and complicated rather than direct and simple. It is highly improbable that any two Americans taken at random are absolutely unrelated (i.e., have no common ancestor), if we take into account the thousands of generations in the course of human existence. But it does not follow that they are brothers or even first cousins. There is surely a connection between flowers and the soil in which they grow. But different flowers grow in the same soil, and the same kind of flower may grow in different soils.

It seems plausible to assume that certain social conditions will have some influence in determining what forms of literature shall become fashionable and thus be the objects of imitation. But that is quite different from being able to explain adequately why Simms and Poe, or Lowell and Emerson, came to write as they did. The phenomena of selection do not explain the causes of variation. It is also well to remember that to determine which modes or fashions did prevail—e.g., to what extent Transcendentalism was typical or exerted any general influence (p. 230)— is a historical and statistical inquiry, and not to be disposed of by mere impressions.

Any sound history of literary criticism that can claim to be scientific or scholarly must necessarily conform to the general canons of history which distinguish it from mere speculation. It is not, therefore, sufficient to assume plausible principles and to deduce from them what must have happened. We must be careful to examine critically whether there is sufficient evidence that these things did happen. And here most Marxians are too devoted to their dogma to give a sufficient welcome to the truly critical spirit. They approach American history from the point of view of their leader's analysis of capitalistic production, whereas our country was up to the end of the nineteenth century predominantly agricultural and, because of the large supply of free or cheap land, without a landlord class, except for a time in the South. In their preoccupation with economics these literary historians leave out the most obvious intellectual influences that shaped the development of American criticism, such as the traditions in our schools and colleges. The Scottish philosophy, for instance, was taught during the nineteenth century in nearly all of our colleges and thus influenced various phases of American thought. Kames's *Elements of Criticism* appeared in this country in more than seventy editions, and Blair's and Campbell's *Rhetorics* were used in almost all of our high schools. Hence, though economic conditions in America and Scotland were different, the canons of literary criticism were for a long time much the same. Again, the increase not only in absolute number but also in the relative proportion of high school and college graduates in our population has certainly had its effects on the standards of literary writing and criticism —probably more than any revolt against a parasitical aristocracy.

Mr. Smith follows the fashion set by Parrington and others of dividing the literature of our country into three periods: (1) the colonial and early national period, which he calls provincial and sometimes characterizes as classic, (2) the romantic period, and (3) the present realistic one. This raises the questions: What precisely do the terms "classicism," "romanticism," and "realism" denote? Is there sufficient evidence that these represent three chronologically successive periods? And finally, is there sufficient evidence to show that changes from one to another period are the result of economic causes? In discussing any of these questions it is well to keep in mind that great figures in literature—Emerson, for example—have been claimed by classicists and romanticists as well as by realists. And Emerson felt free to criticize each of these schools; there was, in fact, in him something of them all.

Let us in the first place consider Mr. Smith's conception of romantic criticism. Among the romantics he includes the Transcendentalists, Prescott, Poe and a few Southern writers; and it is rather hard to see what is common to all of them. He equates the romantic with the revolutionary attitude. It is the dream of the disinherited (p. 68) and is grounded in disappointment and anticipation. But was there ever a society in which men and women did not experience anticipation and disappointment? The fact seems to be that romances and romantic plays were read by the ladies and gentlemen in the French and English courts, while leaders of the romantic movement such as Burke and Friedrich Schlegel were definitely counterrevolutionary. And which of the romantics in the United States represented the lower classes? Certainly not those Mr. Smith mentions. Prescott and the Transcendentalists belonged to the class that had dominated New England thought in the previous two centuries. Moreover, American eighteenth-century novels were certainly romantic, if that means ecstatic reference to the beauties of nature, the simple life, the humble people, and the truths of the spirit (p. 28). And when Mr. Smith asserts that the time, place, and circumstances explain these romanticists so well that little reference need be made to their cultural borrowings, he overlooks the fact that every phase of what he regards as the American romantic movement had its antecedents in England. Emerson's Neoplatonism, for instance, can be directly traced back to Cudworth and the Cambridge Platonists. And in considering romantic literary criticism it is well to remember that Coleridge's *Biographia Literaria* was published in the United States in the same year as in England and was as frequently reprinted here.

Turning to realism we find that its distinctive trait, according to Mr. Smith, consists in dealing with the observable human scene (p. 182), and this he interprets in materialistic terms.

Identifying science with materialism, he argues that realistic criticism must reject any considerations of the artist's aim (p. 283). But our author is too devoted to the democratic faith to carry out any such attitude consistently and he does not hesitate to praise writers for their benevolent aspirations.

We may well raise the question whether literary "idealism" and "realism," in the commonly accepted sense, are in fact mutually exclusive, whether they cannot exist not only at the same time in different writers, but even in the same work. No work of art can fail to exercise a certain amount of selection and idealization of its material. Certainly it is difficult to see how any tests of realism which Mr. Smith uses can exclude an eighteenth-century novel such as Defoe's *Moll Flanders* or Fielding's *Tom Jones*. (The morality of the latter is as wholesomely anti-Puritanic as any civilized modern could wish.) But we may waive this point. Let us assume that the realistic novel of the type of Dreiser's *An American Tragedy* is a brand-new phenomenon. Is it to be explained by the rise to power of a new economic class? Curiously enough a similar phenomenon in Russia is expressly admitted to be due not to any economic change but to imitation. And certainly there is no evidence of the rise of any new economic class to power in America to explain the vogue of novels such as Mr. Dreiser's, or even the kind of criticism that Mr. Smith stands for. There is, to be sure, in our country today a much wider group of readers, but Mr. Smith does unusual violence to the facts when he contends that the average reader, meaning, I suppose, the most numerous class, prefers realism in fiction (p. 134). Most of the fiction in our popular journals, such as *The Saturday Evening Post,* or the novels most in demand in our public and private circulating libraries, are distinctly romantic in the sense that they deal with an imaginative realm to which men and women like to resort to escape the drabness of their daily routine. Mr. Smith and other moralists may contend that people ought not to do that, but there can be no denial that not only is this the actual preference but in some measure it always has been. Sherwood Anderson, generally regarded as a realist, has expressed it by saying: "The life of reality is confused, disorderly, almost always without apparent purpose, whereas in the artist's imaginative life there is purpose. There is determination to give the tale, the song, the painting, form—to make it true and real to the theme, not to life." "Realism, in so far as the word means reality to life, is always bad art—although it may possibly be very good journalism." For we must remember that human interest in a work of art depends not upon its photographic accuracy but upon many types of psychological effect on the mind of the reader.

It is interesting to note Mr. Smith's rejection of Frank Norris's own characterization of himself as a romantic. Norris quite definitely identified the romantic with that which is peculiar or special as opposed to the common, with the invisible as opposed to what is obvious. Thus, not the peaceable citizens of the West who are in the majority, but the local adventurers, the cowboys, miners, and the like, are his deliberate choice. This, of course, is in line with the historic revolt of romanticism against the classic preoccupation with the universal elements in humanity. Mr. Smith justifies his characterization of Norris as a realist because the latter "sees more significance in reality than in any imaginary world," even though the reality is not the life of the common people. But is there no imagination in Norris's pictures? Norris certainly rejected Mr. Smith's test of literary reality, "the life of ordinary or recognizable men and women rather than unique or precious individuals" (p. 147).

Mr. Smith says very little about classicism. In the main he uses that term to denote the type of literature and criticism represented by Dryden, Pope, Addison, and Dr. Johnson, and he condemns the imitation of it in our colonial and early national literature as un-American. But literary nationalism not only is inconsistent with the emphasis on democracy and the class-struggle but ignores the fact that this Augustan literature besides showing French influence also, like most modern writing, inherited the classic tradition from Greece and Rome. Until recently in America as well as in other countries, educated men had read Cicero and Horace, as well as Euclid; and this was true not only of the landed or mercantile aristocracy but also (in our country) of the sons of farmers and other youth of humble origin who worked their way through college. The truth is that the rise of the modern national state and even of the vernacular literatures did not completely destroy the cultural community of the West as embodied in Christianity and Hellenistic learning. Humanistic culture has never been purely nationalistic, any more than science has. To preach the sloughing-off of borrowed cultural traits would mean that the French should discard their language of the last fifteen centuries and go back to Celtic dialects.

In this connection it is worth while to note the close relation between romanticism and nationalism. In America, of course, the latter had its obvious beginning in our War of Independence, in natural pride and resentment against English assumption of superiority. This is clearly seen in the literature of the Revolutionary War and in the period immediately following, especially in the writings of Freneau and Joel Barlow. But later nationalism is also a revolt against the classic tradition of reason and humanity that we inherit from Greek and Roman civilization. Emerson in his protest against aping the past, in his insistence that we too are men and must express our own life, gave encouragement to this nationalism. Whitman asserted it more stridently in his early writings, never tiring of contrasting American democracy with effete Europe. In Mark Twain's *Innocents Abroad* and other writings this often borders on the glorification of Philistinism. Against this shutting off America from the sources of universal culture, Lowell protested. Can't we in America appreciate Dante and Cervantes? The best part of world literature can be translated. It is true that there are things in the world about us which the Greeks and English did not know or treat of, but to be truly human does not mean to exclude what others have achieved. We should not ape English critics and approve everything they do, but neither should we approve everything because it is American. The romantic idea places emphasis upon local color, but Shakespeare can take his scenes in Greece, Rome, Italy or in the Never-Never Land as well as in Merry England. The great figures of literature, such as Job, Ulysses, Aeneas, King Arthur, Hamlet, Faust, Don Quixote, interest us not because they are national but because they are human. The emphasis on nationalism in literature, on local color to the exclusion of fundamental universal human traits, is in the end but a glorified provincialism.

In this connection, it would be highly praiseworthy if those who speak of the "genteel" tradition would vouchsafe some clearer indication of what they mean by that fashionable term. Mr. Smith speaks of it at times as if it began in 1815 as the reaction of a hereditary aristocracy against the business community (p. 41). But at other times he identifies it with the attitude of the middle class (p. 52) or with that of the mercantile group. The latter, however, came into power even before the Revolution, and was as strong in Philadelphia, Charleston, and New York, as in Boston, though the literary developments in these several centers were quite different. In any case, if we think of the "genteel" tradition as aristocratic, we are surprised to find the sentence: "genteel he was . . . nevertheless he was receptive to continental literature" (p. 268). Interest in continental literature was, certainly until recent days, confined to our upper classes.

On the other hand, so far as we have any indications of the specific traits ascribed to the genteel tradition in literary criticism, they are found in the colonial period as well as today. The obvious truth, indeed, is that the points of view of individual critics do not always represent the economic class from which they come. And Mr. Smith himself, who contends in the main that Marxism expresses the outlook upon life of the lower classes (p. 286), is forced to admit that most American workingmen are bourgeois in outlook (p. 287).

It would not be fair to say that this book represents the strongest case that can be made for economic determinism in literature. The adherent of the latter view may well reject Mr. Smith's assumption that criticism is more directly representative of or responsive to the general conditions of life than is fiction. They may point to the patent fact that those who read novels far outnumber those who read literary criticism, and those who write the latter have been a more narrowly select class. It is also possible for those who believe in the social-economic interpretation of literature to pay closer attention to the actual history of the United States and to make more effective use of it. A Marxian need not follow Mr. Smith in ignoring the history of Carthage, Athens, and Venice as well as of modern England, or in asserting that "the traditions of a mercantile community are incompatible with empire" (p. 266). But the outstanding fact remains that the diverse attitudes of literary critics do not correspond to successive forms of economic organization; and the case is obviously even weaker if we consider the divisions between rival contemporaneous schools. For no economic differences in origin or status separate the Neo-humanists from such writers as Spingarn, Mencken, and their followers. It is not good scientific method to reduce a wide range of very complicated and highly individualized phenomena to too simple a pattern.

23

IMPRESSIONISM AND AUTHORITY IN LITERARY CRITICISM

THE CRAVING for order and stability in human affairs naturally expresses itself in the field of criticism by emphasis on rules, standards, and authority. Poets or creative spirits in literature may be men of the feverish or unstable temperament popularly known as the "artistic"; but critics have hitherto been for the most part pedagogues, men who preferred to occupy positions where they could live sheltered lives. Hence while scholars may discover in the literary criticism of the past an occasional antinomian or anarchic note, the presence of a whole school boldly

Published in *The New Republic*, Vol. 28, p. 252 (October 26, 1921).

emphasizing that attitude is a phenomenon characteristic of the present age. It may be due to the large number of people who find an easy if not lucrative occupation in passing quick rather than deliberate judgment on the literature of the day; or it may be due, as M. Brunetière suggested, to the leadership of men like Anatole France who are themselves primarily artists and who in their criticism simply play or experiment with ideas. But in any case it is a significant and distinctively contemporary phenomenon.

Like other widespread *isms,* impressionism has its definite creed. Its leader, Anatole France, has formulated it thus: There can be no such thing as objective criticism, for the critic can only give his own impressions, or narrate the adventures of his soul among masterpieces. It is easy to see that the dogmas that "we are shut up in our own personality as in a perpetual prison" and that "we can never come out of ourselves" are but naïve repetitions of our fashionable Berkeleyan subjective idealism, viz., that we can never know anything but our own impressions. This has a certain verbal plausibility so long as we entertain the dubious image of knowledge as a sort of material thing encased in the cranial cavity. But without stopping to rehearse the numerous philosophic fallacies involved in this view, common sense can be satisfied by simply denying the assertion that "we can never come out of ourselves." Whenever we learn something or express ourselves in any way we do come out of ourselves. Language and other social institutions are all visible denials of the claim that each of us is forever locked up in his separate cell and held in a state of incommunicado. Is not the admission that there are authors who have written books, and that the critic has a soul which can meet with adventures in reading these books—is not this fatal to the subjectivist dogma? With characteristic geniality Anatole France admits that if we had the courage and followed his doctrine consistently we should have to be silent. But such austere and inhuman courage is, in fact, far from his temper. He passes many acute and discriminating judgments on diverse books and some of these judgments are very vigorous condemnations.

All this was pointed out by M. Brunetière more than twenty-five years ago in an essay on Impressionist Criticism which it has proved easier to ignore than to answer. M. Brunetière also seems to me eminently just in allowing for the half truth that makes the impressionist's professed credo so plausible. He admits that our judgment of a literary work depends in part on what we bring to it; but this surely does not deny the existence of something in the work which evokes our judgment, something put there by the author who had certain aims and used more or less appropriate means to attain these ends.

The world, however, does well to ignore the intellectual weakness of the dogmas by which impressionism has sought to justify its practice, for this practice does not really depend on nor grow out of dogmatic skepticism or nihilism—certainly no more so than M. Brunetière's practice really grows out of his appeal to evolutionist biology to justify the distinction between higher and lower forms. Not being professional philosophers the impressionists have just grabbed at the first available ambient idea as a reason or defense for refusing to depart from a cause to which they are impelled by much profounder and less easily formulated motives. Certainly there can be no doubt as to the admirable character of much of their actual achievement in literary criticism. It is even possible to maintain that the leader of this school, Anatole France, is generally more just, more learned and truly catholic, and more penetrating in his literary judgments than is the admirable leader of the classical authoritarian school, M. Brunetière himself. Thus, M. Brunetière, like his American imitators, is so passionate in his dislike of the unconventional Rousseau that he cuts himself off from the possibility of really explaining why Rousseau was able to stir so profoundly, not only the multitude of his and subsequent generations, but also such a typically unromantic philosopher as Kant. Conservatives may refuse to admit that there was profound justice in Rousseau's bitter arraignment of a social order that, despite elaborate cultivation and nice conventions, rested on such galling iniquity that the storm of 1789 toppled it over completely and no effort of the reaction after 1815 could restore it. But surely arguments for interpreting Rousseau's disagreeable nervous instability as insanity cannot deny the patent fact that he clearly saw the causes of a revolution where learned historical scholars like Gibbon could see only order and stability. Contrast with this the justice of Anatole France to the aristocrats of the old regime. He sees them not as mere symbols of social parasitism—which he could truly do if he were only a partisan of the left—but as men and women, somewhat naïvely pompous, but possessed of true nobility which enabled them to walk to the scaffold maintaining their essential human dignity.

M. Brunetière suggests that the admirable character of the literary criticism of the impressionist school is due to the fact that men like Anatole France and Lemaître were trained in the old classical school. It would be unwise to doubt that sound perceptions and just judgments are more likely to come with than without cultivation. But surely classical training itself will not guarantee against the blindness which comes from a narrow adherence to preconceived principles. A remarkable illustration of this is to be found in the last book of the most accomplished and cultivated of our American classicists—Mr. Paul Elmer More. His admiration for the older Oxford dons makes him lose all sense of proportion in ridiculously extolling obscure and complacent worthies of rather dubious self-control at table. At the same time he cannot forgive John Morley because the latter, though sensitive to the graces of aristocratic society, nevertheless honestly tries to remove the social iniquities which these graces adorn and by which they are supported.

I do not for a moment wish to maintain that the authoritarian school has not given us criticism of the greatest value; nor would I deny that in this country, especially, impressionism is sometimes but a cheap and thin veneer for obvious ignorance, indolence, and incoherence. Indeed, any attempt to weigh and pronounce judgment on the relative values of the actual contributions of these two schools is entirely beyond my competence. What I wish to suggest is that the difference between impressionism and authoritarianism does not grow out of the reasons professed by the two, but rests rather on a ground more akin to that which separates modern inductive science from the classical *a priori* procedures. In opposition to the traditional distinction (which identifies impressionism with romanticism) we may note that nothing can be more classical than the judgments of Anatole France and Lemaître on authors like Zola and Ohnet; and nothing can be more typically romantic and subjective than the way Messrs. Babbitt, More, and Sherman think they can ignore the relentless march of the methods of the natural sciences by burying their heads in the sands of their own arbitrary intuitions, or, like Mrs. Partington, try to sweep back the incoming tide with the frail pedagogic broom of authority.

The root of classic authoritarianism seems to me the horror of diversity and the craving above all for the peace and security of a prim and closed world where all our cherished possessions will be forever undisturbed. The root of impressionism is the horror of premature and cramping unity and the craving above all for the factual truth and fullness of life. Nisard, whose history of French literature is still the high-water mark of clear and courageous classicism, has put the case in a nutshell by identifying classicism with the predominance of discipline over liberty—discipline is the dominant end and not merely a necessary means in the service of freedom. There can be no doubt that most people fear freedom and gladly set up authorities to avoid the disagreeable business of having to decide for themselves. "What is the correct dress for a boy of eight at a children's afternoon party?" writes an anxious mother to a daily newspaper, and the answer of this freely chosen authority brings genuine relief to the one governed by it. Anatole France comes nearest to expressing the fundamental motive of impressionism when he defends his admiration for both Lamartine and Leconte de Lisle by saying: "It seems to me that one has less chance of going entirely wrong in one's admiration when one admires things that are very different." In a world where the multitude of conflicting authorities and standards is bewildering and where there is hardly a first principle which has not led its devotees to the most irrational violence and heartless cruelty, it seems safer to trust to the immediate deliverance of our perception of fact. After all what, in the last resort, is the basis of any authority if not in something that we can perceive or apprehend? The perception of the past must, of course, be considered, and to cultivate the ultramodern virtue of a completely open mind to which everything is possible is a feat which only the insane achieve. But in a rapidly changing world we are most likely to err grievously if we systematically distrust our own perceptions in favor of principles supposed to be derived from the perceptions of our ancestors.

This skepticism toward principles and trust in the facts of our own experience explains why Sainte-Beuve is the fountainhead both of impressionism and of the type of criticism which calls itself scientific—I mean the criticism of Taine, Hennequin, Ricardou, and their imitators in American universities. To the minds of many unbiased observers the latter school has made very little contribution to a right understanding of literature, and I think it is so largely because it has been more in love with the traditional *theory* of induction than with the facts of literature. This is shown in Taine's clinging to such abstractions as race, climate, and epoch, which are hopelessly thin as explanations of literary masterpieces. But who can deny that light can be thrown on the meaning of literary creations by the intensive study of the actual social and psychologic conditions under which they were produced? Certainly Sainte-Beuve made a notable beginning in this direction. In a complex and changing world the impressionist's distrust of hard and fast principles generally leads to greater justice towards conflicting claims, while the classicist-authoritarian by elevating his bias into an eternal and unalterable principle is apt to abandon the discrimination which is the essence of critical judgment. The authoritarian is always denouncing arbitrariness and willfulness, but his refusal to consider the doubtful character of his own first principles—which others do doubt—shows more truly his motives and weakness.

One who approaches the subject from this point of view is tempted to say that the authoritarian suffers from the fear due to deficient vitality while the impressionist suffers from a vitality that is untamed. I think, however, that a great American philosopher, Charles S. Peirce, has given us a means for a more just and instructive, if less epigrammatic, analysis. Over forty years ago he published a series of articles in the *Popular Science Monthly* entitled "Illustrations of the Logic of Science." The second of these articles proved to be the basis of the philosophy now called pragmatism, but the first article, on The Fixation of Belief, is more significant for our present purpose. All men, Peirce assumes, desire a certain stability in their ideas. But there are two main roads by which this can be attained. The first is the method of iteration and authority. It is the method by which most people attain nearly all the beliefs they have. In a homogeneous community it works almost unconsciously through imitation—we imitate the beliefs of the community in which we are born as we imitate its language and dress. One brought up in a Mohammedan village where everyone recites the famous formula five times a day is not likely to be disturbed by any doubts as to whether Mohammed *is* the true prophet. But the moment he comes into contact with others, doubt is bound, sooner or later, to penetrate the armor of unquestioning repetition. The first reaction of communities to such doubt is to try to exterminate it by repression, varying from hard glances and ostracism to the burning of the doubter. But these methods of the Bastille, the Inquisition, and the fires of Smithfield cannot succeed while the cause of the doubt, the actual diversity of belief in the world, remains. It is the Greeks who discovered a method of attaining a progressive rather than a fixed stability of ideas by welcoming all possible doubt and dispensing with all authority. It is the method of science, as illustrated in Euclid's geometry. But the mathematicians of the nineteenth century have improved and extended this method by dispensing with any appeal to axioms as self-evident principles and showing that all material principles are but hypotheses—guesses in common language—to be justified by their consequences in the factual realm. With this the intellectual basis of the old authoritarianism is forever destroyed.

24

DANTE AS A MORAL TEACHER

EXCEPT for those who believe that they can enjoy a poem without knowing what it means, the first requisite of an honest and intelligent discussion of Dante should be a frank recognition of the fundamental difference between his view of the world and that which is distinctively modern. Dante lives in a closed world, limited in time and space, and authoritatively mapped out for all time by Aristotle and the Christian Fathers. Man—meaning Christendom inhabiting the Mediterranean basin —is the center of this universe. Around man's abode all the stars revolve in eternal and perfect circles. The plan of this universe is so well revealed that there are not and there cannot be in it vistas of essentially new truth or of new possibilities of achievement. It is a world in which the beginnings of human history are not lost in the dim past, nor is its future particularly perplexing. The number of generations from Adam to Christ is definitely known and the number of generations from Christ to the final day of judgment is also limited. Heaven and hell have a strictly limited capacity. The mystic rose of heaven was half filled by the Hebrew saints who lived before Christ, and it would be relatively easy to figure out the maximum number that hell can possibly contain after the resurrection when the sinners' earthly bodies will all be located there.

This aspect of Dante's fundamental belief is not popular today. His expositors and commentators try to avoid it by two suggestions, first, that Dante does not mean to be taken literally,

Published in *The New Republic*, Vol. 28, p. 181 (October 12, 1921).

and second, that Dante's moral and spiritual ideas are independent of his view of the physical universe. Both of these suggestions are flagrantly false.

That Dante meant to be understood in an allegoric *as well as in a literal sense,* his dedicatory letter to Can Grande, and passages in the *Inferno,* in the *Purgatory,* and in the *Convito* explicitly affirm. When commentators then go on to assert that the punishments in the *Inferno* represent only the mental condition of the sinners in the act of sinning, they are grossly unfair to Dante and to his readers. To say that Dante did not believe in the actual and eternal post-mortem suffering of the damned is to accuse him unjustly of heresy and willful preaching of what the Church had expressly condemned; but, worse yet, it makes nonsense of the references to creation, the day of judgment, the resurrection, and other ideas which are the warp and woof of the whole *Divine Comedy.* It is doubtless true that many of the punishments in the *Inferno* may be viewed as symbolizing the inner state of the sinner. This is clear in the case of the hypocrites who drag themselves around in heavy armor gilded on the outside but leaden inside. It is even more subtly true in his picture of illicit love—Paolo and Francesca locked in each other's arms and driven by the wind of passion in a sunless air deprived of all other human ties which enrich true love. But it is absurd to pretend that the punishment of heretics like Farinata or schismatics like Mohammed describes *their* state of mind. In the case of Capaneus we are explicitly told that though his continuing to defy Jove would be in itself sufficient punishment, he nevertheless receives also the outer punishment meted out to the violent. The fact is that all the punishments in Dante's *Inferno,* though seldom devoid of a certain horrible appropriateness, are essentially vindictive in their nature. Retributive punishment is the essential of medieval justice, just as the law and duty of vengeance was an essential part of its code of honor. God's honor, like that of the medieval knight or more primitive Corsican, would be tarnished if He did not take vengeance against those who willfully or unwillfully insult Him, and the medieval view of law and justice required that the magnitude of one's vengeance should be commensurate with one's power.

Similarly does a careful reading of Dante reveal the absurdity of the frequent suggestion that we can reject the medieval view of nature and yet keep the moral and spiritual ideas based upon it. Dante's very distinction between the morally higher and lower is bound up with his geocentric astronomy. That Dante's moral views cannot be ours is obvious when we reflect that he places in Hell not only innocent children, but noble characters like Plato, Socrates, and Farinata, while high in Heaven are placed an oppressive and polygamous despot like Solomon, a simpleton like Adam, and a savagely persecuting bishop of dubious morality like Folquo. But perhaps the most instructive case is that of Ulysses, who would be condemned to Hell by Dante not only for his stratagem at Troy, but also for inducing others to join him in his "eagerness to win experience of the world" and to venture beyond the geographic limits set for mankind, viz., the Strait of Gibraltar. In Dante's perfectly created world there is no need for intellectual exploration or moral adventure. The whole of necessary wisdom has been revealed and the rightly diligent can acquire it. We who live in a limitless world not especially created for us, where conditions are changing and the future most uncertain, must seek new wisdom, not only as to the physical world, but as to man's nature, possibilities, and tasks; and the medieval morality of fixed order and obedience to authority must become a subordinate part of the morality of changing or growing life.

To those whose vision of the world has been widened as a result of modern exploration and science, Dante's morality is essentially negative. His supreme good, the beatific vision of the "Love that moves the stars," is generally unattainable in this life and comes only to a chosen few as a matter of grace. It has little sympathy with the earthly joys and sorrows that fill our life here. Though called Love, Hell is forever in the center of it. The Inquisition, or the burning of heretics, is its true earthly symbol—as Spanish Catholics like Unamuno insist to this day. To the great multitude it offers no positive plan of life beyond "Fear God and avoid evil (or sin)."

It is doubtless true that the dangers that surround human life are so many that without the prerational organic fear which makes us shrink from the unfamiliar we should all soon perish. But without the spirit of daring and adventure this fear would paralyze all life. Hence wherever life is expanding, the morality of fear with its eternal prohibitions or taboos must be actually disregarded.

This explains why Dante's political theory is so utterly barren. He has no conception of the multitudinous forces within the community that intelligent direction can harmonize into a brighter and fuller life. Order, according to him, must be imposed by an emperor from without. The silly and pedantic arguments by which Dante tries, on the basis of childish myths in Livy and Virgil, to prove that this emperor can be no other than the Holy Roman Emperor, then represented by a Hohenstaufen, is not merely indicative of his times. It is also indicative of Dante's complete other-worldliness and lack of any civic and political vision. Despite their atrocious factionalism, the growing cities of Italy showed wisdom in rejecting these claims of the Empire; for in the oriental despotism of Frederick II they had a visible example of what imperial order and authority actually brought.

It was not only in politics that Dante, like other prophets, was behind the day and generation that he denounced. His scholastic learning made him totally blind to the significant movements of his own times, to the growing industry and commerce, to the opening up of intercourse with other peoples, of which his older contemporary and countryman, Marco Polo, was such a notable representative. This is important if we remember that the merchant adventurers, like the early Greek merchants, were but the pioneers of the navigators, explorers, great scientific investigators, and mechanical inventors who followed them.

The widening of our view of the world by science is intimately connected with a change of emotional attitude to sin and punishment. In Dante's time it was possible to view all nature as following harmonious, eternal laws against which man and the Devil were the only rebels. Modern biologic study, however, leads us to think of man's actions as in general due to causes or circumstances similar to those that influence other organisms; and the maladaptations which disfigure human life and render it so tragic are but extensions of the maladaptations of which all organic life is full. The earthquakes and plagues that sweep away plants and animals as well as human beings are just as natural as the paths of the stars, which we now know to be neither perfect circles nor eternal, but subject to the unpredictable flux of generation and decay which has been called cosmic weather. Hence we are not afraid today to admit greater kinship and sympathy with purely animal life and suffering.

The conviction is certainly widespread today that, great and important as are our differences in disposition and achievement, we are all of the same human clay, subject to the same instinctive impulses and weaknesses or diseases of the flesh. Certainly the idea that some men are all perfect and deserve eternal blessedness, while others are all wickedness and deserve eternal damnation, cannot be justified in the forum of enlightened human experience. If sanctification, crucifixion, and resurrection are to have any meanings in that forum, they must refer to something which all of us undergo in diverse ways in our daily toil. The ease with which, in moments of complacency, or when judgment is beclouded by resentment, we attribute the brutish passions and inhuman frauds of others to an unnatural prompting of the Devil, cannot maintain itself after honest knowledge and sober judgment. We become more grave when knowledge and imagination enable us to realize in some degree what would have happened to us if we had been similarly circumstanced.

There are those who with light and irresponsible rhetoric berate our times as too soft and sentimental because we do not insist on sufficient severity in our punishments, or because we regard some crimes as diseases. But actual history shows the frightful futility of the unutterable cruelty that was formerly meted out indiscriminately to the criminal, the insane, and the sick—all suspected of being inspired or possessed by devils. We may be sure that reaction against this wasteful cruelty has not as yet gone far enough. But it is encouraging to hear the words of a kindly Dominican Father: "My Faith requires me to be-

lieve in the existence of Hell, but not that anyone is there."
This may not express the dominant attitude of his church, but
it certainly represents a marked modern tendency. At any rate,
few nowadays can read with enjoyment the horrible punishment meted out in Dante's *Inferno* to a thoroughly honest,
gifted, and devoted soul like Piero delle Vigne because in his
high-mindedness he could not bear to live amid undeserved dis-
grace and cruel suffering. The whole idea that God created men
and women knowing that they will sin and thus subject themselves to eternal torture is odious today; and when Dante says
that Hell was founded by Eternal Love we feel that the cruelty
of his life and the violence of his times poisoned his conception
of love as well as deprived him of an indispensable support for
moral sanity, to wit—the gift of laughter. The idea of an eternity of suffering is horrible enough, but to glorify it and call
it, as Dante does, "supreme wisdom and primal love" makes us
ashamed of the human nature that is capable of entertaining
such horrible perversity and disloyalty to our natural sympathy.

This rejection of Dante's claim as a moral teacher, like the
rejection of exaggerated claims for the magnitude of his learning, does not deny his obvious greatness as a poet—though
Dante himself and the men of his generation down to Petrarch
emphatically subordinated his poetry to his moral philosophy.
Dante undoubtedly manifests to a supreme degree the distinctive gifts of the poet, heightened imaginative vision and divine
music of language. In his workmanship, too, he shows both intense titanic energy and a perfection of form that is classic and
definitive. But this is clearly due not to his medieval views but
to the passionate vitality and intensity of his nature. Doubtless
the acceptance of any philosophy or "ordered scheme of things
entire" gives a certain integrated unity to the material of the
poet's experience and makes for profound simplicity and dignity on a truly grand scale. But we must not exaggerate the
consistency of the medieval world view or of Dante's representation of it. Omitting the hardly successful reconciliation of the
dogmas of free-will, grace, and predestination, we may note that
in the passages which in modern times are taken as typical of
Dante at his best—e.g., the incident of Paolo and Francesca or

of Ugolino—Dante distinctly breaks through his medieval faith
and generously draws our pity, though such pity according to
his own assertion shows lack of faith in the justice of God's
judgment on the wicked. Dante also rises above his medieval
faith by endowing some of his sinners with superb human dignity. Thus the picture of Farinata holding all Hell in contempt,
of the indefeasible nobility of Brunetto Latini and Aldobrandi,
or of the heroic appeal of Ulysses, is hardly consistent with the
orthodox hatred of the sinner. It is rather typical of the dawn-
ing Renaissance of which Dante, despite his medieval creed,
may be regarded as a glorious example. The naive way in which
his pride of ancestry and of poetic achievement breaks through
his pious humility is most instructive in this respect.

Moreover, though the modern liberal cannot without self-
stultification accept Dante's medieval faith, he cannot afford to
ignore its wonderful strength. Through long and dark ages, it
preserved—even if it cramped—the essentials of humanity
within its hard and forbidding shell. While the morality of
order, authority, and repression cannot be for us the supreme
law, it will always continue to represent an essential part of
the truth. No great achievement is possible without the renunciation and self-mastery which is the result of long and arduous
training. This is perhaps the first lesson that the young and
unenlightened have to learn, though the bondage of authority,
alas, often leaves men too weak for the life of freedom. Then,
too, we must reckon with the unripe wisdom of modern moralists who emphasize the struggle, "upward and onward," but
have not the courage to accept frankly the natural goals of enjoyment and the satisfaction of the heart's desire. Discouraged
by such an outlook, men naturally abandon the struggle and
prefer to live in a closed, unventilated, medieval world. "Lead
Thou me on, I do not ask to see" is the expression of a profoundly natural human weakness. We may be sure, therefore,
that Dante will long continue to be a favorite of those who
value above all the passive virtues of submission. In all respects,
indeed, he is the poet of order and measure. Despite the strain
on the limits of good taste in some of the horrors of the *Inferno*
and expressions of personal rancor in the highest heaven, Dante

is par excellence the poet of civilized life, courtliness, and polished manners. He has a real contempt for the ways of unculti-
vated country folk and cares not for the wild and rugged in
nature any more than for the untamed desires of the human
heart. Like other city-bred men he has an eye only for the peaceful in nature. The turbulence of wind, rain, and snow, the
evanescent play of clouds, the surge of the sea, and the massive
grandeur of woods and mountains do not solicit him as much
as the formal gardening of flowers and the steady play of light.
He is not even intrigued by the white marble hills of Carrara.

Though Dante's poetry will thus for ages continue to be
among humanity's most cherished possessions, his negative and
other-worldly morality will continue to make the *Divine
Comedy* more alien to the modern spirit than the more distant but more human world of Homer. The peace and order
which we demand of modern morality and ultimately of modern poetry—the two cannot be forever sharply separated—are
the peace and order that nourish an ever-growing harmonious
human life on this earth, which, despite its limited possibilities,
supplies the material for the heart's desire.

25

HEINE

IT WAS NOT to be expected that any of our newspapers should
notice that, in the midst of the war, a new edition of Heine
was completed in Germany. Yet to those who care for discriminate judgment this was an event of greater significance than

Published, under the pen-name Philonous, as a review of Heine's *Sämtliche
Werke,* in *The New Republic,* Vol. 20, p. 15 (November 26, 1919).

many that were made the object of special cablegrams. For it is only by noticing facts of this sort that we can correct the tendency to conventionalize and oversimplify our picture of the typical German, forgetting that nations are at least as complicated as the individuals who compose them. Doubtless rigid discipline, unquestioning obedience to official authority, and a ruthless pursuit of ends at the expense of finer susceptibilities are outstanding characteristics of Imperial Germany. But the German people read and sing Heine even in wartime, and that is a capital fact which all sweeping judgments as to German national characteristics should take into account.

In all literary history it is difficult to find a parallel to the official, well-organized, and persistent effort to read Heine out of German literature. Since the Kaiser himself and Treitschke set the fashion, all the tame and collared professors of German literature have vied not only in the denunciation of Heine's unpatriotic attitude to his native land, but in frantic efforts to blacken his character and disparage his literary genius. It is generally easy to revile the victim of misfortune, and the charges which have been thus accumulated against Heine are many and grievous. His failure to maintain his financial independence certainly made him unheroic. His hypersensitiveness to the lures of the flesh is certainly offensive to those whose imaginative sympathy is more piously limited. A morbidly nervous constitution and a life full of physical suffering made him naturally petulant and lacking in that self-control which is the essence of human dignity. In his impatience with solemn mummeries he was undoubtedly guilty of Rabelaisian sallies that are out of accord with the standards of modern polite society. Yet none of this is the real basis of the officially cultivated hatred against Heine. Other and more honored Germans have been guilty of similar sins. Did not Goethe himself keep aloof from the patriotic national struggle and openly express his admiration for Napoleon? And does the story of Goethe's egoistic private life compare favorably with the epic of Heine's touching tenderness to his mother, sister, and wife? Against the charge that Heine had little sympathy and understanding of Germany, his *Deutschland* is a crushing refutation. Heine's vital insight into the past of Germany was shown in his judgments on Luther, Kant, and Hegel, and his penetrating vision into its future by his estimate of Karl Marx, Lassalle, and Wagner, when these were young and unknown. It was this penetrating vision which enabled him prophetically to forewarn France and Europe against the Germany of 1870 and 1914 as well as against the horrors of Communism, against the Kantians "who will ravage without mercy and not only with sword and ax through the soil of all European life."

What irritates official nationalistic Germany most, and drives it to paroxysms of impotent rage, is just the fact that Heine, a cosmopolitan Jew, a fervent admirer of France and hater of Prussia, is, after all, the real national poet of Germany. For more of the classic national songs of Germany have been embodied in Heine's lyrics than in those of any other poet, not excepting Goethe. The hardheaded Bismarck, realizing more than lesser followers the limitations of military and bureaucratic power, opposed the anti-Heine campaign and advised the policy of nationalizing him as had been done in the case of cosmopolitans like Lessing, Kant, and Goethe. But the intellectual suppleness of the man of blood and iron is impossible to a brood of pedants bound by pseudo-learning about Aryan, Teutonic, and Semitic races. That a Jew exiled in France should bring the German language to the degree of perfection that Heine undoubtedly did in his prose, as well as in his exquisite and incomparable lyrics, is perpetually irritating to those who have not learned that the vision of beauty, like love and hunger, can be the expression of our common humanity, rather than of a mythical national soul.

But it is not only the lackeys of militant nationalism who feel it their duty to depreciate Heine. The pharisees of the left and the courtiers of King Demos are no less displeased at one who, though willing to fight for popular freedom, could still speak of the "unwashed multitude" and scorn a state of universal equality. The fanatics to whom all life is a clear issue between the powers of darkness and of light cannot readily forgive the detached poet who will not subordinate the free artist to the militant revolutionist.

But though no party, school, or sect can claim Heine as a faithful follower, he was undoubtedly right in regarding himself as a loyal soldier in the great war for the liberation of humanity. As a poet he was always the faithful worshiper of the beauty and love of life, freed from false shame and the misery of needless chains; and as a satirist he always used his keen wit to pierce the hollowness of canonized superstition and to heap eternal ridicule on the slavish spirit that supports the clumsy violence and pious frauds of authority.

It is the fashion nowadays to belittle the work of the emancipator. To build up any positive faith is held to be nobler than to destroy obstacles no matter how harmful. But though it may be better to cultivate health than to cure disease, it does not follow that the physical trainer is always superior to the surgeon or physician. But the fact is that the great destroyers of shams are always men of simple faith who are compelled in order to cultivate the fields of life to remove the stones of obstruction. Thus Voltaire believed naïvely in the saving character of the experimental philosophy of Locke and Newton, Mark Twain in the beneficial omnipotence of public schools, and Bernard Shaw has a most touching faith that salvation is at hand if we but remove the romantic veneer with which we generally cover the nakedness of things. The spirit of Heine is more profoundly disillusioned, but steeped in a profounder faith in freedom and love of life because not disposed to ignore the mysterious cruelties of nature. During a life that was almost a continuous grappling with pain, he always kept his indomitably youthful spirit, continuing in the service of poetry and playing with life, love and destiny even on his mattress grave. "Dieu me pardonnera! C'est son métier."

It would be vain to claim for Heine a place among the world's foremost masters. His keenly sensitive spirit reflected the conflicting currents of his time, but he lacked the robust strength to master them. Romanticist and realist, rationalist and mystic, lover and satirist, he expressed in exquisite melody and weird magical word-pictures the joys, sorrows, and poignant doubts that perplex the modern suffering spirit. "Ah, dear reader, if you would complain of discordancy, let your complaint be that the world is rent in pieces. . . . Through this heart went the great rifts of the world, and hence I know that the high gods have given me grace above many others and have counted me worthy of the poet's martyrdom."

VII

HISTORICAL PERSPECTIVES

26

PARRINGTON'S AMERICA

THIS THIRD VOLUME of Professor Parrington's *Main Currents in American Thought* brings to an incomplete close one of the major contributions to the understanding of American life, conceived and written, withal, in the truly grand manner. Though the author's tragically sudden death occurred before he could quite finish his task, he carried it far enough to put the critical reader in a fair position to judge the adequacy of its fundamental ideas.

The rich and illuminating insight of this book makes it instructive to note a certain vagueness in Parrington's own mind as to the precise character of his task.

Despite the subtitle, "An Interpretation of American Literature," it is inept to view it as a history of literature, even if modeled on Taine's classic work. If six times as much space is devoted to the financial manipulations of Jay Cooke as to the life and work of Henry James, it is because the author *is* throughout primarily concerned rather with the economic and political life of America. Not that Parrington as a professor of English was uninterested or even devoid of special gifts in the field of literary analysis and appreciation. He could in a short paragraph put his finger on the characteristic strength and weakness of an author like Hergesheimer; and in his treatment of Sinclair Lewis and Cabell he revealed not only the heart of

Published as a review of V. L. Parrington, *The Beginnings of Critical Realism in America (1860-1920)*, in *The New Republic*, Vol. 65, p. 303 (January 28, 1931).

what they have to say but the characteristic manner in which they achieve their results. But more than a teacher of literature Parrington was a Western progressive, with a genuine faith in the old Jeffersonian agrarian democracy. In his effort to show how our geographic expansion and capitalistic economy modified our basic and formative traditions, he gives scant attention to the history of the American heart, taste, or imagination. It would perhaps be carrying irony too far to say that in his neglect of the artistic, the playful, and the purely hedonic aspect of literature—he says practically nothing about the theater, or the literature of the other arts—he is a spiritual descendant of the Puritans. But in any case, though he dares not omit the great masters in the art of letters, literature to him becomes at times synonymous with any printed expression of opinions, whether in textbooks on economics, pamphlets, or newspaper editorials, on the controversial issues of politics and public finance.

There is doubtless some advantage in this wider and more realistic perspective. It is certainly refreshing to find that instead of the usual complacent repetition of the old New England pieties, figures like Howells, Hamlin Garland, and Willa Cather are discussed in terms of the frontier, the capitalistic system, the New England Brahmin oligarchy, the plight of the farmer and the city workman. And if it is rather startling to find De Leon, Debs, and Victor Berger in the plan of a history of literature, it is certainly good to be told that Brahmin darlings like Thomas Bailey Aldrich had narrow social vision, and that respectables like Hay and Godkin were snobs and no better than demagogues. But unless we are to accept unhesitatingly the deterministic dogma in blind faith, we may well doubt whether every branch of literature is thus explained and clarified. Are there not certain moods and emotions which men and women have experienced throughout the ages? And is there not a somewhat mysterious thing called individual genius involved in so expressing these moods and emotions as to constitute great literature which survives the changes of climes as well as of fashions? Many who do not know anything about the economic conditions of America in the days of Walt Whitman or Mark Twain are stirred by their work, even as some of us may be by *The Song of Songs* or *The Arabian Nights*. Grant all that Parrington says about Aldrich, Hay, and Godkin, still *The Story of a Bad Boy*, "Little Breeches," or "Jim Bludso" (which Parrington does not mention) will continue to charm many readers, while even those who admired the editorials of Godkin will not think of rereading them. Do we not have a real difference here between literature and the mere written expression of opinion? Precisely because the book reveals Parrington as such a vital personality, delicate in perception and felicitous in expression as well as robust of faith in the better possibilities of human life, there is real danger in a conception of literature so hazy as to allow the utilitarian to crowd out the artistic or to let that which is useful merely as a means suppress that which is delightful in itself as the heart's desire. Public issues are of undoubted importance, but serious students must not forget that great literature is concerned also with those vital realities of our inner personal life and those enrapturing superpersonal cosmic vistas compared with which the issues of public life are pale and relatively inconsequential.

Professor Parrington's politico-economic progressiveness not only befogs his conception of literature but also prevents him from fully realizing what is involved in any attempt to write of the main currents of thought of any period. For one thing, he did not sufficiently inform himself to do justice to the history of American thought in religion, science, art, education, or even law.

Nothing at all is said (or was planned to be said) in this volume on American religious thought, or even on the social and economic significance and effects of our organized religious movements. (The references to religious thought in the earlier volume, e.g., in the chapter on Jonathan Edwards, were regrettably deficient in point of historical scholarship.)

Though like other progressives he insists that science has radically modified American thought, he shows scant knowledge about how and when this took place. In referring to the undoubted influence of Spencer, Parrington exaggerates the scientific attainments and influence of Fiske and underestimates the practical effectiveness of men like Youmans of the *Popular Science Monthly*. Parrington indeed shows little real appreciation of the continuity of our native scientific traditions from the days of Franklin (whose scientific work is passed over in complete silence in the first volume) to those of Bowditch, Joseph Henry, Benjamin Peirce, Pickering, Willard Gibbs, and Simon Newcomb, not to mention more recent names. Certainly it is not knowledge of science or of its American history, but rather a conventional fable, that speaks of "the changing mental attitude that resulted from familiarity[?] with scientific methods, the shift from deductive reasoning to inductive investigation . . . and the slow drift from metaphysical idealism to scientific materialism" (pp. 191-92). Nor is there one iota of evidence that since 1870 natural science has favored collectivism any more than individualism.

Can we talk of the main currents of American political thought and ignore altogether the prevailing theory of law professed by judges and lawyers and by the academic tradition? If not, the legal opinions of Supreme Court Justices like Waite, Field, or S. F. Miller, or of legal writers like O. W. Holmes, T. M. Cooley, and Langdell, are far more important than most of the political writers who, like Woolsey, came to Parrington's notice. It is a great mistake to regard the American lawyers as a merely professional group. They have supplied not only the legislators and administrators of our country, but, as a most vocal class, they have also supplied the bulk of our public eloquence, the importance and influence of which is not to be lightly disregarded by the historian.

When we come to recent times, we must allow for diversity of opinion as to the relative importance of different writers. But surely no one who wishes to portray the main current of American thought can say that U'Ren is more important or significant than Lester Ward, or that Randolph Bourne or Walter Weyl was more influential than John Dewey. Do these instances represent inevitable human slips in judgment, or are they part of Parrington's bias against thinkers who try to get at fundamentals? I am not sure that the latter suggestion is just to Parrington. But I think it is generally true of our progressive brethren of the democratic faith; they are impatient with those who do not keep in step with the rapid but futile gyrations of the crowd.

The impartiality necessary to distinguish history from propaganda is very difficult of attainment and, in its perfect form, beyond human reach. It is therefore good for the historian to confess his bias, and this our author does with admirable candor. But such candor is not an adequate substitute for historical competence. For all his preoccupation with economics, Professor Parrington did not, alas, always take the trouble to inform himself on his subject matter; and some of his references, e.g., to David A. Wells as "a scholar deservedly distinguished as an economist," or to Bastiat as a left-wing economist like Proudhon or Louis Blanc (p. 139), are simply ridiculous. But this is perhaps a minor matter compared with the common tendency to indulge in fanciful *a priori* schematism and to group facts according to some striking epithet rather than any real factual connection. (This, ironically enough, is most often true of those who, like our author, are skeptical of metaphysics or general philosophy.) It is a pretty conceit to characterize the colonial attitude as Calvinistic pessimism, the first half of the nineteenth century as romantic optimism, and the latter part of that century as mechanistic pessimism. But sober history will not bear it out. Nor can Walt Whitman be adequately summarized as "the afterglow of the Enlightenment," or Mark Twain as the "backwash of the frontier." Such epithets are engaging and frequently suggestive; but almost always do they hide from us the complexity of the actual. Parrington's fondness for *a priori* schemas certainly led him to exaggerate the influence of the French Enlightenment. The liberalism of Jefferson and even of Tom Paine was predominantly British in origin, derived from Locke and the eighteenth-century deists (whose real strength in colonial America our author did not fully appreciate). *A priori* schemas also prevent our author from dealing adequately or even justly with American sociology, the social settlements, and the uplift movement.

A notably generous and at times incisive thinker, Professor Parrington is not often a close reasoner. Thus, he speaks of the election of 1896 as the final and definite defeat of the American agrarians, betrayed into an alliance with the Democratic party. This is a superficial and misleading judgment. The main demand of the agrarian movement, for cheap money, was certainly met in the ensuing era of higher prices (and though this came to pass mainly through purely economic causes, the aid to the farmers through irrigation works and the service of the various scientific bureaus of the Department of Agriculture in the Roosevelt regime helped to increase farm products and make them more marketable). Nor did the political demands of the Populists fail. The initiative, referendum, and recall did get into the government machinery of our Western states, and parcel post and postal-savings banks became part of our federal government service. In time, also, came popular elections of United States Senators and a graduated income tax. Indeed, none of the constitutional amendments or major pieces of legislation of the last generation, with the possible exception of the Federal Reserve Act, can be said to be purely capitalistic in origin. The manufacturing interests were able to defeat the proposed child-labor amendment only when they succeeded in getting the farmers to join them.

It is well to insist on the reality of rural influence. It is still dominant even in industrial states like New York, Pennsylvania, and Illinois, which have their capitals in relatively small towns. The facts are squarely against the myth that the country is ruled by the capitalist class alone. The bankers had nothing to gain from our last tariff legislation, and their desire for greater participation in European affairs has been balked by rural opposition.

Similarly it is not true that it was the capitalist interests alone which designed the constitutional restraints to thwart democracy and to give lawyers and judges the power to protect the interests of the propertied classes against those of the general public. Jeffersonian Democrats even more than Hamiltonian Federalists desired restraint on the power of the government. It was part of their faith in the *laissez faire* philosophy. And in our own day the rural attitude provides a good deal of the backbone of the judicial veto on welfare legislation for the city worker. The opposition between city and farm workers can well be seen in their respective votes for Governor Smith in 1928.

There are two good reasons for dwelling on the limitations of this book:

In the first place, those who share Parrington's faith in the traditional American liberalism (or, if you please, eighteenth-century Jeffersonian democracy) must be on guard against hurting a good cause by hazy inconsistencies and other obvious weaknesses in its defense. It would be somewhat unfair to call Professor Parrington an intellectual Senator Borah. He is so much more alert and free from middle-class complacency and conventional taboos. Indeed, to an amazing degree for an American writer, he realizes the havoc wrought by preoccupation with moral judgments when understanding is what is required. Yet, like Western insurgent leaders, he is not free from a characteristic insularity and subjection to provincial sentiments which often prevent him from thinking things through in a thoroughly cosmopolitan manner.

But in the second place, this is a book whose faults must be pointed out with some emphasis precisely because its merits are so obvious on every page that the sympathetic reader is likely to be carried away by enthusiasm and to lose his critical caution. But I cannot close without repeating my homage to the extraordinary wealth of illuminating insight and to the remarkable verve and felicity of expression which make this a rarely delightful book. I must resist the temptation to illustrate by quotations, but will refer the reader to the section entitled "Figures of Earth," confident that no one who reads it will lightly put the rest of the book aside.

Altogether this is a work to be put beside De Tocqueville's great classic. It is immeasurably superior to the turgid superficialities of Bryce.

27

AMERICA: DREAM, EPIC, AND REALITY

As a nonacademic historian, James Truslow Adams writes not for the classroom or for his professional brethren, but for the general public that reads only when intrigued by an author's substance or manner. The often illuminating insight of his *The Founding of New England,* and the genuinely high tone of his book on *The Adams Family* have made it possible to think of him in connection with the great American galaxy of nonprofessional historians from Bancroft, Prescott, Motley, and Parkman to Lea and H. O. Taylor. But it is doubtful whether, in writing the book before us, Mr. Adams has had that tradition in mind. He seems to have aimed at journalistic fluency more than at substantial depth, at producing a good best seller rather than a classic.

It is of course refreshing to find historical events and figures described in the language of living men rather than in the stilted phrases of conventionalized pedagogues. Freedom of language makes for freedom of judgment. One who is not afraid to speak of "the stark and damnable injustice of the present regime" can see how the large mill-owners have dictated the policy of the United States and how patriotic American employers try to prevent the union of labor by stirring up hatred between its different sections, black and white, native and foreign-born. Not being connected with any college or university,

Published as a review of James Truslow Adams, *The Epic of America,* in *The New Republic,* Vol. 69, p. 274 (January 20, 1932).

Mr. Adams does not have to fear offending any money barons who are the angels or benefactors of our educational institutions. He knows from personal experience that some of them have "the souls of pushcart peddlers." Now for myself I am inclined to protest that I have known at least two pushcart peddlers with great souls: one of them translated Sophocles into modern Greek and the other wrote a wonderfully penetrating and sympathetic essay on Gray's "Elegy." But it is well to have a popular history written by one who knows that ours is a business civilization and that its leaders do not form a superior class in character, intelligence, or culture. A history for adults should deal with reality rather than with edifying myths.

But the journalistic manner has obvious limitations. Sensational or snappy chapter headings do not of themselves produce insight, nor is that end attained by melodramatic juxtaposition of things that are not inherently connected, such as the sinking of the *Titanic* and the outbreak of the World War. No gain but a lapse from the high tone of seriousness comes from attributing the old New England preoccupation with hell-fire to the severity of its winters.

Far more critical is the fact that in his desire to attract the reader Mr. Adams has not brooded long enough on his main theme. He has undertaken to write a prose epic. What is the great achievement that he thus intended to celebrate? It is not the physical conquest of a great continent amidst fearful hardships. For that, according to Mr. Adams, has resulted in the worship of a narrow practicality at the cost of refinement of spirit, and even in the degradation of religion. When Mr. Adams formulates the object of his epic, he identifies it with the popularly persistent dream of a better world for the common man. But does that mean simply greater political and economic opportunity? Mr. Adams himself does not show any great enthusiasm for these. Democracy dilutes the content of education and is hostile to genuine distinction and liberality; and the eager exploitation of our economic opportunities has led to the worship of money-making as in itself a virtue. This in turn has led to the neglect of the fine arts which ennoble the enjoyment of life. It has prevented us from cultivating dignified leisure, and has driven us instead to gossip and to preoccupation with other people's personal morals. Indeed, the intense struggle for economic opportunities has even contributed, according to Mr. Adams, to our national lawlessness.

An epic of human aspiration should make real to us those efforts that remain significant despite frustrating fates. A realization of this would have led Mr. Adams to give more attention to the traditional American liberalism which survived the Spanish War in the form of the Anti-Imperialist League and which, as the progressive movement, was submerged but not eradicated by the World War and the Harding-Coolidge prosperity.

Mr. Adams's tendency to ignore the imponderables makes his history rather flat when he comes to recent years. There is, for instance, no adequate account of the tragedy of the collapse of Wilsonian idealism, a collapse which really began when, in order "to win the War," he allowed liberal opinion to be repressed, so that he was without support in a crisis when the reactionaries got the chance to turn against him.

Mr. Adams has aimed to tell the story of the American people rather than that of its political, military, diplomatic, social, and economic strands. But obviously there is no American life without these factors. Hence the question for the historian is always that of their relative importance. Mr. Adams has chosen practically to ignore the role of religion and idealistic effort and to say almost nothing about literature and art. This deprives his book of outlook and color, and results, in the main, in a rather conventional political history with an economic setting. But the strictly economic issues themselves are rather vaguely conceived. The specific ways in which our distinctive free-land economy interacted with and molded the other factors of our national life are not concretely shown. Some of his judgments on recent events, such as the "achievements" of the Clayton Act, are rather naïve, to say the least.

Though on the whole realistic, Mr. Adams often falls into traditional sentimentality, as in his reference to the freedom of the Anglo-Saxons in the German forests—an exploded early-Victorian legend. And he quite naïvely speaks of the *Mayflower* Pact as something possible only to Englishmen of that period, whereas that procedure was rather common to trading companies originating in Italy, as the term "ballot" indicates. On the other hand, he admits that in some respects the Puritans who came here were made of weaker metal than those who stayed home to fight it out with the Stuarts. In speaking of the Constitution he freely recognizes that it was a compromise and that it required "adroit management and even political chicanery" to force its adoption, yet he is entirely conventional in regard to its merits and to its weaknesses, such as the breakdown of the electoral system and the failure to define states' rights or the status of slavery is such a way as to avoid civil war.

Mr. Adams's judgment of persons is generally sound but devoid of distinction. Thus his high appreciation of Washington is certainly just. But there is no adequate clue to the sterling qualities that made Washington able to carry on where men more brilliant but with less character would have failed.

The intellectual content of any history is largely determined by its author's sense of historical causation. In this respect Mr. Adams is generally sensible, but devoid of incisiveness. Why, for instance, did the South lose influence in the two decades before the Civil War? The suggestion that this was due to its adopting an attitude of defense is clearly inadequate. It was on the defensive because it was losing in population and wealth relative to the industrial North and the rapidly growing West. And the decline of its intellectual prestige was connected with the bankruptcy of its older landed aristocracy (typified in the distress of Jefferson, Madison, and Monroe) when new land, cheaper and more fertile, was opened for the cultivation of cotton.

History is generally assumed to be of value because it explains how we have become what we are; and this, Mr. Adams assures us, has been one of his primary aims. But here also his harvest is uneven. The principal traits which, according to him, distinguish Americans are optimism, aggressiveness and self-assertion, and a certain unteachableness. Following the fruitful idea of Professor F. J. Turner,[1] he explains all these in terms of the conditions of open frontier life. Men who went out to

[1] *The Frontier in American History* (1920).

make their homes in the wilderness or on the edge of it necessarily put away the past and lived for the future. They had to rely on their own individual efforts or perish. Where each man had to do all things there was little respect for the expert, especially in public life. But all this, while true, will not get us far enough. Why, for instance, has the American woman enjoyed relatively greater freedom of motion than her European sister? Mr. Adams's explanation in terms of border life, even if it were convincing, would not explain what has made that freedom persist in our older Eastern cities.

Less monistic and *simpliste* is Mr. Adams's effort to trace the causes of our national addiction to lawlessness. While he contends that colonial America was rather free from crimes of violence, he recognizes that it is foolish to put the blame on the foreign-born. The first roots of this lawlessness are traced to the general colonial habit of disobeying ruinous laws made in England for the exploitation of the colonies. But the outbreak of lawless violence after 1830 is not adequately explained by the three causes which Mr. Adams mentions: viz., our system of education, our theory of popular sovereignty, and our excessive worship of business enterprise, so that all sorts of corruption are condoned as leading to the development of the country. Doubtless the conditions of a newly settled region like California favor violence before the orderly process of government becomes customary. But why should the highest homicide rate today be found in the old South? There are obviously many more factors involved in this problem than Mr. Adams has recognized.

Mr. Adams is a competent historian who writes with good sense and, what is even rarer, with liberal detachment from narrow orthodoxy or heterodoxy. But he is at times careless and it cannot be said that he has set himself unusually high standards. The most impressive lesson which at least one reader carries away from the book is the extraordinary difficulty in the way of a general history of the United States in one volume for intelligent people. Publishers will doubtless continue to call for one to satisfy the popular demand for "outlines." But genuine enlightenment requires first a more critical and discriminatory consideration of what it is that is of primary significance in American life.

28

LIBERALISM AND THE RUSSIAN MIND

A MERICANS are generally impressed by the insistently violent notes of Russian life, by the marked weakness, if not absence, of the spirit of tolerance, moderation, and compromise which goes to make up our traditional liberalism. In politics this shows itself in the preponderance of the extremist parties, Czarists and revolutionists, and the almost negligible role of the parties we should call liberal, such as the Constitutional-Democrats. Within the monarchist and Socialist parties themselves the extremists again preponderate. In other countries, the Socialists who believe in immediate and complete revolution (Spartacists or Communists) are in the minority; in Russia they are the majority. A similar temper prevails among the monarchists. The revolution of 1905 failed because the Socialists insisted on the immediate carrying into effect of their whole program, without any compromise with the "bourgeois" parties that helped to bring about the revolution; and the failure of the monarchists to get back into power, despite the generous aid of the Allies, was similarly due to their refusal to give up an iota of their old prerogatives, as illustrated in their insistence that the landlords' agents administer things in the old ways in all the territories conquered for them by Kolchak, Denikin, et al.

Published in *The Survey*, Vol. 49, p. 731 (March 1, 1923).

This absence of the spirit of accommodation or compromise doomed the coalition government under the liberal Prince Lvov, despite the frantic enthusiasm with which it was almost universally greeted when it succeeded to the rule of Czar Nicholas.

The same absence of middle-ground positions is seen also in the religious life. There is practically no liberal Christianity in Russia. With the possible exception of a few recently formed groups, men either accept the whole of Byzantine Christianity with all its antiquated supernatural apparatus, or they are thorough positivists or nihilists, completely denying all the values or claims of religion and treating it all as one mass of superstition.

Anyone acquainted with Russian life and literature can add an indefinite number of parallel illustrations. Of no other literature does it seem equally true that its characters are preponderantly either inactive dreamers who rise to heights only through their suffering, or else active types that are rather hard and forbidding—thus producing a total impression of taking little delight in human achievement.

It is tempting, especially in view of certain parallels in Polish history, to explain all this by racial traits, in terms of the Slavic mind or soul. But, after all, we know nothing of racial endowments except what people actually manifest in their lives; and to translate these manifestations into racial traits is no more an explanation than the traditional attempt to explain the effects of opium by a dormitive principle. Nay, what is worse, we are misled by the unity of the word Russian as by the word German, French, etc., into the complacent acceptance of a distinct communal mind having all the properties of a single individual. This communal animism is one of the major difficulties in the way of mutual understanding between different peoples. A stranger may, after a brief visit—or even without one—confidently describe the typical American. But those who know better are those who are aware of the diversity of types in America. The Russian people are even more heterogeneous than the people of the United States.

The denial of explanatory value to a fixed racial soul or mind need not, however, prevent our noting the peculiar ways or manner in which Russian mental life manifests itself, or from noting how these peculiarities are connected with the conditions under which Russian life has to operate. Now, the outstanding fact about Russian mental life is that Russia has only in comparatively late times entered into intellectual commerce with Europe. Russia never had direct connection with the Rome which provided the basis of medieval and modern Europe. It received its Christianity from medieval Byzantium, and was soon cut off even from that dim source of enlightenment by the Tatar invasion and domination, which submerged some promising beginnings in southern Russia. If there be any truth in the attempt to explain the hard intolerance of the Spanish people by their long fight to recover the independence of their country from Mohammedan rule, it must be much more so in the case of Russians whose heathen Tatar rulers had very little of the superior culture of the Saracens.

In any case, Russia came into direct contact with Western Europe, by way of the Baltic, only in the time of Peter the Great. The introduction of European civilization was forced from above by despotic rulers chiefly for military and political reasons. Its remarkably recent character is shown by the fact that the first regular high school in Russia was opened in 1726 and the University of Moscow in 1775. Not only the teachers but most of the pupils of these early schools were Germans who came into Russia with the reigning German dynasty and with the annexation of the Baltic provinces. It is also well to remember that European civilization of the eighteenth century was in its outer expression molded by the courts of Louis XIV and XV; and the liberalism of Voltaire and of the Encyclopedists imported into Russia by Catherine II did not prevent that remarkably licentious woman from increasing the oppression of her people to the point of causing actual rebellion. All of this was certainly calculated not to make European civilization very attractive to the great masses of the Russian people.

But even the religious liberalism of the eighteenth century was smothered as a result of the reaction against the French Revolution and the Napoleonic invasion. For the next century the government was in the hands of avowed and fanatical reactionaries, except for a few years after the humiliating defeat in the Crimea when the vacillating Alexander II freed the serfs and coquetted with some liberal ideas. The term "progress" was officially banished, and Nicholas I expressed the Romanov attitude most intimately when he referred to a university as a wolf's den. This hostility to intellectual enlightenment—a combination of religious fanaticism and politico-economic stand-pattism —made it possible for the Czar to be ruled during the World War by an unscrupulous and disreputable monk, Rasputin.

As Russia was almost entirely an agricultural country, the opportunities of culture and civilization were open mainly to the landlords; and it is in the main from this class and its humanitarian motives that the early attempts at liberation came. Because of the paternal and despotic character of the government all such effort was necessarily regarded as revolutionary. Only in the later years of the nineteenth century was industry on a large scale introduced, and even then a large number of the workmen were peasants who left their villages only for certain seasons and whose earnings belonged legally to their undivided family.

With this background in mind it is not hard to understand Russian political inexperience. The autocracy never tolerated co-operation or even the expression of opinion by the public in governmental affairs. Men had either to accept everything ordained by the government or else be revolutionaries; and as revolutionary parties were necessarily secret in their organization, they were also absolutist in their government. A revolutionary party cannot exist at all except where people trust their leaders implicitly. In either case government could not be based on free discussion.

When against this background we reflect how long the English and American people have been used to parliamentary and local self-government, and how even with their experience they have been unable to settle several issues without resort to arms, the absurdity of expecting the Russian people to settle all the fundamental issues by our own processes of parliamentary government becomes unmistakably clear. The spirit of tolerance and accommodation has never been acquired by pious resolution, but only by a long and painful process of experience; and it can function only when a certain minimum of the essential decencies of life is no longer at issue. When one reflects how readily conservatives in England and the United States, as well as in Germany and Italy, have rushed to illegal violence to fight radicals, the Russian situation ceases to be anomalous.

This simple reference to the historical background of Russian life will also explain the characteristics of the Russian attitude in religion, philosophy, and literature.

As Russian education has up to very recently been restricted to the upper classes, it is natural for the masses to hold on to their primitive orthodoxy—an orthodoxy supported by the force of the central government, whose interests were antagonistic to the conditions of free religious life. We must, however, remember that though the Russian church has not yet experienced anything like the Protestant Reformation with its assertion of the freedom of conscience, it was the Russian church itself that was partly reformed by Peter the Great, and the schism formed thereby was due to the fact that millions of Russians were not prepared to take that very small step in the direction of religious enlightenment.

A significant characteristic of Russian mental life is the scantiness of its attention to technical philosophy. Russians have made notable contributions in the positive sciences—witness Mendeleief in chemistry, Pavlov in physiology, and Lobachevsky in geometry. Yet they have made no contribution of first-rate importance in philosophy. (Soloviev, the foremost name in Russian philosophy, is a mystic seer.) This seems to indicate that the Russian is still interested either in concrete issues of sociology or in mystic religious speculation but not in abstract questions of scientific method. Masaryk, in his admirable book on *The Spirit of Russia,* has remarked this and has attributed it to the fact that the problem of the nature of knowledge, which has agitated the human mind since Hume and Kant, has —for reasons not clearly indicated—failed to influence Russia.

However, the whole history of science and philosophy makes it quite clear that the critical or skeptical spirit which makes us distrust tempting generalizations, or seemingly self-evident truths, comes only with long cultivation of science. Just before the war there were several indications of a developing Russian interest in philosophy, notably the work of Loskii.

Similar considerations will enable us to see in proper perspective the violence of Russian literature as typified by Dostoievsky, Gorky, and Andreyev. Russian literature has been for the most part the expression of a small class oppressed by the rigors of nature as well as by the hopelessness of the social task of Russian life. Its agonized consciousness leaves little room for the Hellenic serenity which can see life steadily and see it whole. Yet does not the art of Turgeniev give us the same type of elevation and mastery as does Sophocles? It is now not typically Russian—but one can with equal truth say that Shakespeare is European rather than typically English.

29

THE SIGNIFICANCE OF NAPOLEON

AGAINST THE PROTESTS of the Socialists, France is celebrating the centenary of the death of Napoleon. In this, as in many other cases, all the arguments of liberal rationalism seem clearly on one side, but the deeper instinctive admirations of men are to the contrary. It seems almost impossible to resist the obvious reflection that this is not a propitious time for France to remind the world that the most ruthless imperialist of modern times, the one to whom we are so largely indebted for the terrible burden of standing armies, was not of German origin. Moreover, it cannot be denied that the progress of historical studies has

The substance of this paper appeared in *The New Republic*, Vol. 26, p. 311 (May 11, 1921).

been seriously minimizing the value of Napoleon's achievements. It is not merely that in the light of scientific history Napoleon's campaigns are of little importance compared with the perfection of the steam-engine by Watt and the introduction of vaccination by Jenner. It is to facts like the latter that we must go if we are to understand the real basis of the remarkable increase in the population of Europe in the latter half of the eighteenth century, and of the material and social changes caused thereby.

But even from the point of view of conventional military and political history, Napoleon was a failure, and the sum of all his conquests a dead loss to France, from which she has not recovered. The positive political achievements which he and his apologists esteemed highest, viz., the administrative and the educational system of France and the Code Napoléon, all of which have been widely copied and have survived many revolutions, are now the objects of increasing disparagement. Even the most thoroughgoing nationalists are beginning to recognize the need of decentralization and of loosening the rule of the bureaucratic administrative system which is the heritage of Napoleon. Admirable as is the French national educational system in many respects, few today defend its appalling uniformity expressed in the legend that the Minister of Public Instruction can look at his watch and tell what verb is being conjugated at that time in all the schools of France. The Napoleonic Civil Code, also, has few defenders against those who are pointing out that in its subordination of the wife to the husband, in its mechanical individualism and distrust of voluntary associations, and in its inadequate provision for the protection of the working classes, it has always been woefully antiquated.

Moreover, the institutions that Napoleon most abominated—parliamentary government, free press, and the profession of idealistic or humanistic sentiment and philosophy—have made most progress in the century since his death. Napoleon's own later program of liberal imperialism, which his supposed martyrdom at St. Helena and the atrocious stupidity of the reactionary Holy Alliance turned into a gospel of hope for the many, proved a broken reed. And when France relied on it, she suffered the terrible ignominy of 1870.

Yet, despite all this, and despite the long list of personal defects and coarseness of character, the vast majority of men do and will long continue to regard Napoleon Bonaparte as one of the greatest figures in human history. When sober historians of diverse faith such as the contributors to the *Cambridge Modern History* come to write of the nineteenth century, the figure of Napoleon stands out pre-eminent above all his contemporaries. For good or for ill his direct or indirect influence is a decisive factor in the struggles for liberalism and nationalism in Germany, Holland, Belgium, Russia, Poland, Jugoslavia, Greece, Italy, Spain, and Spanish America. It is vain to urge that the abolition of serfdom and of hereditary class privileges, the emancipation of the Jews, the introduction of civil equality, and the toleration of religious diversity, were all bound to come even without Napoleon.

The fact is that it was his titanic energy that broke the fetters of medievalism which cramped the growth of a Europe beginning to find fresh life through new sciences and new industries based on them. A plain commoner, he made princes look ridiculous in the art supposed to be peculiarly their own, the art of war. Thereafter, the commonest peasant had no need to feel any fatal inferiority to kings and hereditary nobles. The bounds of his possibilities had been widened in the mind of the ordinary mortal, and what greater service can be rendered to the sons of men? After all, what has maintained the human race on this globe, despite all calamities of nature and the tragic failings of man, if not elemental human energy and faith in new possibilities? In both of these respects, Napoleon was a marvelous revelation, and unsophisticated mankind will long continue to accord him its naïve admiration.

It is unfortunate that the great and beneficent achievements of the arts and sciences are not so readily visible to the untutored imagination as are the glories of war. But it would be equally unfortunate if the craving for glorious achievement were wiped out of human nature in the interest of the thrift and prudence in which the French are also supposed to excel.

Those who become enlightened as to the savage waste of war need not ignore the splendid gifts of mind and body which are used or wasted to produce successful military campaigns. Thorough mental discipline, unflinching honesty in looking facts in the face, continuous inventiveness, quick decision, and prompt execution—who makes all these qualities so visible to men as Napoleon? Who else has shown such marvelous capacity of mind and body, such amazing memory and physical endurance, and the inexhaustible patience which can master all the details of an enterprise and leave nothing to chance? Only obstinate folly or ignorance can deny supreme genius—though in an evil direction—to the man who won such marvelous victories and accomplished so many things previously thought impossible. It is well to remember that when finally his natural faculties began to decay and he was overthrown, it was only by those who were his pupils and even former aides.

It is well to demand that achievement be beneficent in its results. But we must also remember that all great achievement—altogether apart from the character of the results—is the triumph of mind over circumstance and therefore in itself a great human good. That is why men naturally admire Hannibal though the success of his cause might have been calamitous to the progress of civilization. That is also why, despite all his pettiness and his horrible disregard for life, millions worshiped Napoleon, and gave their lives enthusiastically for the "Little Corporal," and why the generations will continue to admire his achievements as they will continue to admire the heroes of Plutarch's *Lives*.

VIII

EDUCATION

30

EDUCATION AND THE CHANGING
SOCIAL ORDER

PROBABLY no single word carries more prestige among us than *education*. It is not only on our lips—it has its roots deep in our hearts. Nowhere else in the world does the universal disinclination to pay taxes yield more readily to the Open Sesame of any word than does the heart of America yield to the word *education*. From the poorest hamlet or village to the largest metropolis, people gladly tax themselves to provide elaborate buildings for school purposes, and almost all of our states have provision for state universities, which, considering the limited available funds of the more sparsely settled of our states, are most generously provided with laboratory equipment and other necessary facilities. American parents are most anxious to provide their children with the best possible opportunities for their physical and moral development, and many a poor workman or farmer, or even his widow, struggles hard to earn enough to send the boy or girl to college. For that is the principal source of high and honorable positions for their offspring and just pride for themselves.

All this is emphatically true of the external side, i.e., in respect to the buildings, physical equipment and other accessories of the business of education; but we are as a people in a state of chaos and confusion in regard to the aims, purposes, and methods of education. A comparison of the typical European conception of education with that which prevails in America would bring this out: In Europe—whether we take France, England, or Germany—liberal education has been regarded as a privilege of the upper or wealthier classes, and the ideal of the educated man is that of one who is disciplined by thorough training in the humanities, which have their roots in aristocratic Greece or patrician Rome. With us the democratic tradition assumes the inherent right of every child to receive the best possible education, and the confusion results in the main from the attempt to make the traditional humanistic straining— which is essentially aristocratic—fit the practical needs of a democratic people.

The roots of this confusion appear even more clearly at a lower level of education in the fact that American parents, especially those who regard themselves as liberal or progressive, fear to hamper the development of their children through frustration or suppression that would prevent the development of the full personality or individuality, and yet are even more fearful of the possibility of their children's developing such individuality or personality as to make them unpopular with their fellows. That, it is generally assumed, would prevent their getting on in the world. Such confusion calls for a critical analysis of the ideas of nature and society.

Taking the word *natural* as excluding the artificial or the tamed—i.e., wild as opposed to cultivated—the word *nature* seems to be incompatible with any process of education, for education necessarily involves some kind of cultivation essential to the taming of the wild impulses of any natural being. No parent would be so cruel as to allow his child to grow up not to avoid fire or any of the dangers which threaten his life or limb; and all precautions against such dangers involve some amount of training or discipline which necessitates a certain degree of constraint upon natural inclination.

Rousseau's plan for the education of Émile according to nature—i.e., by teaching him the natural consequences of his acts—is possible only if Émile has a tutor all to himself who controls his environment, and contrives such arrangements as will prevent Émile from suffering fatal consequences. Worse yet: Rousseau's plan, if adapted to Émile and Sophie, as described by Rousseau himself in the second part of his *Émile,* leads to their inability to adjust themselves to any social order, so that at the end they are completely dependent on their tutor because they have not been trained to live by themselves. It is unfortunate that people who read *Émile* do not go on to read the second part, which describes the mess into which Émile and Sophie involve themselves because their education was altogether natural and in no wise social.

Now if we regard human nature as containing the social element—viewing as natural the requirement of living together with one's fellows—we have to take account of the nature of society. Rousseau assumes that human nature is altogether good as it comes from the Creator, that all impulses no matter how wild which are natural and not artificial must be good, that all artificial societal arrangements are evil in their consequences, and that society necessarily corrupts human nature. Unfortunately, human experience provides many examples to support this view. The artificialities of society are proverbial. We need not give any long list of them. The cruelties of dressing children as very young gentlemen or ladies and requiring them to behave as such are relatively minor forms of traditional social cruelty. But let us press our inquiry deeper: The idea of preparing children for the society in which they are to live involves the ethical assumption that such society is *good* in its effects; or at any rate that to adjust the child to his society is a good. But not every social order is the best for the young as well as the old; and we are thus driven to inquire: What is a good social order? For, unless we face that question honestly and fearlessly, we are in danger of perpetuating an unjust social order through the very process of education.

It may be a most unpromising task to seek the form of the most perfect society, but, if we are more modest and recognize that absolute perfection is humanly unattainable, we may limit the scope of our inquiry somewhat. Tennyson, in reflecting on the passing of the order of knighthood around King Arthur, says:

> "The old order changeth, yielding place to new,
> And God fulfills himself in many ways,
> Lest one good custom should corrupt the world."

In, other words, no social order can be ultimately good unless it makes improvement possible. It may be objected that we cannot tell what improvement is unless we know what is the ultimate good; but such objection is altogether *a priori* and does not recognize the empirical fact that, even without knowledge of what is the ultimate good, it is possible to recognize which of two practical alternatives is the better. To prefer the better constitutes the essence of wisdom. This is the heart of the liberal attitude to education as well as to all other activities.

Perhaps our difficulty in adapting the classical tradition in education to the demands of a democratic society is accentuated by our failure to distinguish clearly the different levels of education. Our educational institutions, especially our colleges, suffer from confusing the different functions of elementary and higher education. Our so-called high schools limit themselves to little more than elementary instruction, and even our colleges do little more than give the students access to the world's past learning. The instruction in our colleges, even those that call themselves universities, is mostly what the European calls secondary education—i.e., giving the students access to the world's past learning—but does little to prepare him to entertain independent views of his own, or even to understand what changes in the world's body of learning have taken place in more recent times.

To be sure, in America, as in the rest of the world, there has been a marked movement to modernize education—to free it from the fetters of the Old World system, which, since the Middle Ages, has been profoundly other-worldly, addicted to writing treatises *de contemptu mundi*. In line with this reaction there has been emphasis on modern studies, especially in the natural and social sciences, but the hopes which this movement aroused at first have not been fulfilled, and teachers of the natural and social sciences have lost a good deal of their enthusiasm after seeing the results of the new studies. Certainly the public in general feels disappointed with the results.

For one thing, the reaction against the teaching of Latin has gone too far. To be sure, the old teaching of Latin and Greek was hopelessly inadequate in its results. After years of studying Latin, boys could not master the subject enough to acquire any considerable proficiency in it, and the total result seemed to be a waste of time; but the traditional values of studying Latin cannot be altogether denied. After all, a knowledge of Latin grammar opens the gates to an understanding of the traditional element in modern culture—even to an understanding of modern English grammar, which has been unduly influenced by Latin; and students of languages and literature are handicapped by ignorance of Latin. Even students of science and medicine find advantage in the knowledge of Latin; and wise parents who do not want to see their children handicapped still insist on the study of Latin.

More important is the failure of modern studies to live up to the promise and hopes which educational reformers at first offered. The teaching of science has not noticeably increased the general level of understanding. The teaching of social science has turned out to be a way of promoting glibness and free expression of personal opinions. Probably all this is due to the fact that the newer studies have not been well taught. But, whatever the cause, the general feeling prevails that the earlier hopes which were aroused have not been fulfilled.

But I do not wish to extol the continental classical conception of education above the democratic American ideal. The democratic ideal in education is inherently more difficult to put into practice. But, as Spinoza has remarked: All things excellent are as difficult as they are rare.

Perhaps the shortcomings of the old continental idea were best expressed by Mr. Dooley: "I don't care what ye larn thim so long as 'tis onpleasant to them." ("The Education of the Young.") Taken literally, this delight in cruelty to the young is the essence of sadism. But in a more liberal sense, the overcoming of intellectual difficulties is necessary to the growth of intellectual power, just as the overcoming of physical difficulties is necessary to the development of physical strength.

From this point of view it is not impossible to combine the classical idea of discipline in education with the democratic ideal that education should provide the best opportunities for all members of society, provided we recognize the inherent diversities of temperaments and native abilities and aptitudes.

31

THE NEED FOR A MODERN UNIVERSITY

LORD BRYCE somewhere sententiously remarks that all the great institutions that enjoy the respect of mankind have their roots deep in the past. Our universities as highly respectable institutions are no exception to this rule. They originated in the Middle Ages and still bear clear traces of their origin. For the very strength which enables a deeply rooted institution to weather all kinds of storms necessarily hinders its free mobility. Now it must not be forgotten that our medieval universities were founded not for laymen but for monks and clerics whose business was primarily not with worldly affairs but with the eternal hereafter. We must also keep in mind that the students of the medieval universities were boys or very young men, and that the sum of human knowledge which could be imparted to them was definitely limited to a few well-known texts. In spite of the splendid progress which many of our universities have made, these medieval features are still controlling, especially in this country. Thus, in our popular discussions as to academic freedom it is generally taken for granted that the universities exist to give instruction to the young whose tender minds must

Published, under the pen-name Philonous, in *The New Republic*, Vol. 17, p. 130 (November 30, 1918).

not be brought into contact with disturbing doubts. Let the reader turn back to the newspaper comments on Professor Charles A. Beard's resignation from Columbia, and he will notice that not one of these perceives any distinction between universities and schools for the young, between scholarly research and the repetition of what pass as established truths. The medieval conception of a definite and fixed fund of human knowledge underlies the view that every citizen respectable enough to become a trustee knows all that ought and all that ought not to be taught.

The subservience of all studies to theologic dogmas has survived in this country longer than anywhere else, and we think it perfectly proper for a university to be committed in advance, openly or semi-openly, to sectarian teaching. We take it as a matter of course when supremely able men like John Fiske or C. S. Peirce are debarred from teaching because they are not free from theologic heterodoxy, or are not of unimpeachable outer conformity to the conventional moral code. I do not mean to raise here the issue as to whether parents have a right to bring up their children so that the latter will never hear anyone question, in deed or word, the theologic or social beliefs of their parents. But surely humanity's need for new knowledge in all matters is so pressing that it is most foolish not to make adequate provision for an army of intellectual pioneers. Nobody, of course, likes to see his cherished beliefs questioned, and we are all convinced that the safety of the universe depends on the maintenance of what are to us established truths. But unless we adopt the Mohammedan or medieval view that the sum of all truth is limited and has already been revealed, and that therefore all genuine inquiry is pernicious, we must leave those engaged in research absolutely free to question all things and to publish the results of their inquiry. The keen destructive criticism which one's professional colleagues are always ready and most willing to accord to any new views is a sufficiently powerful force against the too hasty spread of new errors.

It is true that many of our universities profess to be solicitous about promoting research, and two or three of them have even made provision for research professorships. But it cannot be denied that the present conception and organization of our universities is profoundly antagonistic to free research. It is not merely that the control of our universities by propertied interests makes a free and radical inquiry into social affairs a risky business for any professor. Far more serious is the fact that the public at large does not think it the professor's business to inquire into anything. He is to teach what he is told to, whether at a state or at a private university. When President Lowell * recently pointed out the importance of freedom in academic teaching, he was taken to task by a conscientious legalist who pointed out that our universities are endowed institutions, endowed to teach certain things only. More than any other country, we have replaced the ancient idea of a university as a society of scholars with the legal idea of so much property administered by trustees. We think it not at all contrary to public interest that the university should be bound—by someone who has made a fortune in oil or on the stock exchange—to teach forever the virtue of protective tariffs, the historical philosophy of law, or the validity of nonepiscopal ordination. Though our so-called private universities are liberally supported by the public through remission of taxes and in other ways, they remain in law and in public opinion entirely private corporations with the right to hire and fire professors at pleasure.

Undoubtedly the trustees of our American universities are, as a class, public-spirited citizens who with the best intentions are trying to promote the public good. But they are businessmen and not men of learning; and when they try to manage educational matters the result cannot be better than if successful scholars were entrusted with the supreme responsibility for the private business of the trustees. It is natural for trustees to carry into the administration of universities the same ideas which they have employed in their industrial and commercial enterprises. One example may serve as a typical illustration. When President Loree of the Delaware & Hudson Railroad became a trustee of Rutgers College, he found that a certain high percentage of the freshmen were marked deficient. He objected that, if so high a percentage of locomotives were found

* A. Lawrence Lowell, President of Harvard University.

deficient, he would fire the employee responsible. At any rate, there can be no doubt that our universities are actually run as degree factories. To standardize the degree business, there has been developed an elaborate machinery of standard courses, hours, marks, and credit points, together with a complicated administrative machinery for compelling attendance at lectures which could not be given if attendance were not compulsory. As the prizes of the teaching profession, the honors and high salaries of deanships and presidencies, are awarded for administrative ability, they serve as constant and insidious bait to lure ambitious professors from the field of scholarly research. So large a part of a professor's time is occupied with administrative matters that one of the greatest of our American scholars, George Foot Moore, has proclaimed the view that the only kind of academic freedom that is really important is freedom from committee meetings; and one of the foremost of America's contributors to the progress of science, Theobald Smith, has been quoted to the effect that no one can carry on research here except by stealth.

If the discovery of new truth is a real social need, it seems necessary for a modern university to dissociate itself from the school business of communicating to young or immature minds that which is already known, and to concentrate its efforts on the extension of the fund of human knowledge. A modern university, therefore, should have nothing to do with degrees, courses, and students. This does not necessarily mean that it will not teach. One who assists in a laboratory research or an industrial survey generally learns more than the professional student who takes courses and lectures. The various faculties of the French universities with their closely connected scientific academies in effect approach this modern ideal very closely. But even in France before the war too many men wasted their time preparing courses of lectures when they could more profitably have engaged in important research. The lecture system at the universities is, after all, but a survival from the days prior to the invention of the printing press. The universities are loath to reconcile themselves fully to this modern invention, and more than ninety percent of our university lectures contain nothing that is not already accessible to the literate. The enterprising college president who would venture to introduce the phonograph into the classroom could cut his operating expenses over seventy-five percent. There are doubtless many to whom lecturing is a stimulus in the process of research, but regular class lectures are as a rule inimical to those qualities which make effective investigators. Lecturing unconsciously begets an easy omniscience and satisfaction with apparent or rhetorical truths, which is a serious danger to real research. No man, no matter how critically-minded, can stand up before a class and refrain from saying more than he knows. The demand on the part of adolescent minds for indubitable and definitive answers to all questions is so overwhelming that no one can completely escape its insistence.

These considerations are not conceived in a spirit unfriendly to our present universities. On the contrary, a careful study of history shows that the great progress of our universities has always taken place after other institutions showed the way and compelled imitation. Thus the universities introduced Greek and humanistic studies only after the way had been shown by groups like the Florentine Academy. For the introduction of science teaching, likewise, the universities are indebted not to their own initiative but to the efforts of the men who founded the Lincean Academy, the Royal Society of London, and similar scientific societies. Nearly all the great founders of modern science in the sixteenth and seventeenth centuries were men outside of the universities. Outside of the universities also developed our modern literatures; and the introduction of the vernacular instead of Latin as the language of instruction has been perhaps the most important vitalizing factor in our university life. For, so long as men lectured in Latin, they were learned men even if they had nothing special to say. The old situation, however, has in a measure been revived by the introduction of technical terminology, as in psychology and sociology, and by the fashion of lecturing on the history of a subject to hide the absence of original insight.

In recent times several research institutions have been established devoted in the main to the extension of physical science.

A modern university could be established by adding to such institutions provision for research in the social sciences, the activity in which our present universities are weakest. But it would be a serious mistake to make it too dependent on private endowment, however much that may be necessary in the preliminary stage. A modern university may be built up as an organized exchange by those actually engaged in various types of research. In all kinds of modern activities, in industrial and commercial institutions as well as in the various forms of public service, men are required to devote themselves to various specific researches. An organized exchange of those engaged in physical, social, and purely theoretic investigations would be a sound nucleus for a genuinely modern university.

32

THE PRESTIGE OF IDEAS IN AMERICA

THAT THE PRESTIGE of purely intellectual work is very low among us can hardly be doubted. In no other country is the word *intellectual* so often used as a term of derision and opprobrium. This is true not only in our backward, rural, and Southern regions where under the influence of poverty, ignorance, and fundamentalism intellectual enlightenment is genuinely feared. It is also true in our supposedly more advanced Eastern states.

The same trait which makes American business heap its main rewards on the promoter and the salesman rather than on the producer makes our public ignore intellectually productive

Published in *The World Tomorrow*, Vol. 8, p. 202 (1925), under the title, "Have Ideas Prestige Among Us?"

minds in comparison with advertisers and administrators. Thus we not only bestow greater material honors on industrial promoters like Edison and Marconi, but they rather than our Willard Gibbs, Pickerings, or Theobald Smiths are generally regarded as the great scientists. Even a liberal periodical will sometimes express indignation at the fact that scholars put a biologist who has made some technical discovery above J. Arthur Thomson, who has written so many popular books.

But perhaps the best evidence of our low esteem of intellectual work is the attitude toward it of those who are themselves supposed to be scholars, to wit, college and university teachers.

It is not necessary to comment on the responsibility of college teachers for the state of affairs under which students are less genuinely interested in their studies than in extracurricular affairs or in the business of intercollegiate contests euphemistically called sports. Teachers themselves often urge that those who manage a track or football team learn something of greater importance from doing so than from any of their courses; and we may accept this as unfortunately true.

More significant is the way our teachers share without protest the view of the public that to be taken out of teaching and scholarly work and put into the administrative post of dean or president is a promotion. Of course, it is difficult to resist the temptation of increased pay and greater social prestige. But teachers know that administrative work in education, as in transportation, manufacture, or any other important business, is incompatible with a life of creative scholarship.

Our college and university faculties are themselves responsible for the absurd number of petty regulations that involve endless committee meetings to the detriment of the teacher's time and energy. The excuse that these regulations are necessary to compel attendance on the part of the students may be too severe an arraignment of the attractiveness of their own teaching. Teachers themselves are also responsible for multiplying summer schools and other devices which in the end increase the teaching load and reduce the opportunity for productive scholarship. When teachers boast that they are not clock-watch-ers like trade unionists, they forget that increasing the number of teaching hours beyond a certain point can only serve to injure the scholarly quality of their teaching.

Against the foregoing view it has been urged that in a country where there are so many opportunities for practical achievement men of really superior brains are not satisfied to remain mere scholars. It would be vain to deny that this is partly true. We think it natural that literary men like Disraeli or Morley should find a greater sphere for their activity in the field of statesmanship; and the conduct of our great business enterprises offers even greater opportunities for the expression of varied mental gifts than did the old type of statesmanship. As part of his railroad business James J. Hill built up an empire greater than that created by the Caesars. Yet which of us would wish Shakespeare had been a great merchant or Admiral of the Fleet instead of a mere playwright? It is nothing but a stupid and narrow-hearted fallacy to identify brains with material success, as if the brains of Buddha, Socrates, Spinoza, or Newton were not among the highest attainments of humanity.

It would be interesting to discuss the causes of the low esteem in which purely intellectual work is held in America. Here I can only mention the fact that the colonists did not bring with them any vigorous tradition of science and scholarship, and that the conditions of a thinly settled country with an open frontier do not favor the creation of such traditions. The countless denominational differences resulting in prevailingly small and scattered parishes have prevented the growth of any large body of scholarly or liberally learned men among our clergy. As our first genuine university was established only half a century ago, it is no wonder that our lawyers have not as a rule been learned or scientifically trained men but have acquired their practical arts either as apprentices or in trade schools. (The connection between our law schools and our universities was only nominal up to a generation ago.) Nor have we, despite our boasted educational system, as yet developed a large liberally educated public—witness the relatively small number of scholarly books read or published in this country as compared with Germany, England, France, Holland, or the Scandinavian countries. In recent years, to be sure, there has been a marked improvement in this respect. But in the main, serious or "highbrow" books find as little genuine welcome among our college graduates as among our tired businessmen.

A large part of the European public that reads serious books consists of businessmen who generally like to retire at what we regard as an early age. The American businessman, as a rule, dislikes to retire. His education has not taught him how to find real satisfaction outside of his daily routine, and he does not know how to enjoy leisure nobly. Also, where the prestige of money dominates over all, few are willing (even if their wives are) to practice economy in order to make possible an early retirement from business into a quiet, contemplative life. Those who would do so would be regarded as queer.

Only a few enormously wealthy people can spend their leisured old age in using their money on philanthropic ventures. The great mass of our practical men are caught in the vicious cycle of having to make money to keep up their prestige and of being unable to do anything else the more they devote their energies to the making of money.

But possibly the most serious difficulty in the way of building up respect for disinterested intellectual pursuits is to be found in the conditions of democratic education. A system designed to educate everyone cannot pursue high standards. It must emphasize the smatterings of literacy open to all, rather than the severe training that can be pursued only by those mentally gifted. At any rate, our democracy certainly seems to be more disinclined than monarchies or aristocracies to support artistic and intellectual pursuits that do not promise immediate material results.

The prestige of any human occupation is largely a matter of social habit or tradition, and there is nothing that any of us can do at once that will make the community as a whole appreciate the proper worth of disinterested intellectual achievement. All that thoughtful people can do is to exercise the courage of their insight and to insist that, while we may be to the fore in lavish expenditure on educational plants or degree-factories, we are behind in our appreciation and production of the works of the mind that are the crown and essence of liberal civilization.

Thoughtful people should also frown out of good taste the silly notion that pure science exists only for its applications, and the even more silly contrast between scholarship and life— as if rigorous intellectual work were not itself a most intense and thrilling form of human experience. If intellectual workers insist on anything, it should be on the obvious truth that the pursuit of useless science and insight, like the pursuit of useless beauty, and useless happiness, needs no justification. After all, the useful has no intrinsic value and is to be pursued only for the sake of something else which has value in itself. To subordinate everything to the useful is, therefore, to impoverish the heart of life. Possibly, however, no contemporary superstition is so stupid and pernicious as the indiscriminate adoration of the word *life,* used without any definite meaning but effectively hiding the fact that life includes the most loathsome forms of disease and degradation. Sanity and wisdom consist not in the pursuit of life but in the pursuit of the good life, and intellectual pursuits are certainly a major part of the good life.

POSTSCRIPT

THE TWENTY YEARS that have passed since this paper was written have witnessed notable advances, I think, in the intellectual life of this country. The development of graduate schools, centers of adult education, and popular forums, the expansion of governmental and private research agencies, the acknowledgment by courts of the relevance of economic and other social studies in the determination of social issues, and the breaking down of barriers against scholarship in Government posts, are tangible signs of intellectual advance. Even more unmistakable is the retrogression of intellectual standards in most of the other nations of the world during these two decades. If, therefore, this paper implies a disparaging comparison, I hope it will be read not against the somber background of Europe today, but against the brighter horizon of what our own resources, natural and human, might produce and cherish.

33

IN DEFENSE OF THE CONTEMPLATIVE LIFE

LET ME BEGIN by confessing a certain inaptitude in the wording of my theme. The contemplative life needs no defense among those who have had some taste of it here at the university, who have gone out into the world of practical affairs and yet are willing to drop it for a while—to forgo its imperative claims and to return to the university for some brief taste of the studious or contemplative life which the university has to offer.

I am assuming, in other words, that those engaged in the actual business of the world's practical affairs know how unsatisfactory is the life of affairs, of the market place, when our eyes are turned to the grindstone and when we do not have a chance to look up to the sky or see the green fields beyond us. Indeed, at times, men of affairs overestimate the attainment of those who are supposed to be devoted to the contemplative life—in accordance with the old dictum that "the other fellow's lawn looks greener."

It is rather against my colleagues, not necessarily at this university, that I have been preaching the necessity of respect for purely theoretic studies, and in listening to me you are hearing an abstract of what the students of this university have, for good or evil, been subjected to.

To prevent misunderstanding, let me say emphatically that I do not wish in any way to minimize the importance of the

An address given at the University of Chicago.

practical life or attention to those activities which are directed to seeing that the material conditions make life not only possible but tolerable. But I do wish to argue that, because the practical is important and must not be neglected, it does not follow that the theoretical is of no inherent importance, or that it can be justified only to the extent that it ministers to the practical—that pure science, for instance, has no justification as an activity in itself, but has value only to the extent that it finds application in technology and the like. I regard the latter view as intellectually and morally vicious. It is intellectually vicious to assume that, because the heart is important, therefore the brain is not. And it is morally vicious to underestimate the value of pure theory or intellectual vision as an exercise of human intelligence. The latter is one of the most satisfactory exercises of human energy, and to deny its value is to impoverish human life most foolishly.

In European circles the word "Americanism" is used frequently to denote visionless activity, the sort of activity in which a man indulges who raises corn to feed hogs, and feeds hogs in order to raise more corn. Some Europeans find this pure activity without vision embodied in the figure of Mephistopheles, who must be active and activate others without ever seeing the importance of the beatific vision. I do not wish to subscribe to the view that this is a fair picture of America. But to hustle and to be strenuous do seem to be prominent American virtues, and those who pursue intellectual interests for the purpose of ultimate understanding are generally regarded as "highbrows" or "nuts."

This has its roots in the American tradition. The Puritans, with their contempt for worldly enjoyment, for those who danced around the maypole at Merry Mount, set the tone for practical America, in which strenuous physical life for the conquest of a continent left little room for artistic activity or disinterested intellectual curiosity for their own sake. We see it in the disregard which the American people, as a whole, have for the natural beauty of their highways, and other forms of natural beauty which they allow to be disfigured by advertising signs and other hideous contrivances. When some progres-

sive communities have tried to mitigate this evil, our courts—
the natural guardians of conservatism—have frequently interfered. We see it also in the contempt which practical businessmen showed some years ago toward the sentimentalists who
wanted to preserve the scenic beauty of Niagara Falls rather
than to turn it into electric power.

But the glorification of perpetual motion as the blessed life
has become part of a tradition in our literature and philosophy.
There is doubtless a great difference in temper between Longfellow and Theodore Roosevelt, but both believed in what might
be called the philosophy of the busy bee: to improve each
shining moment, to be ever striving upward and onward without ever asking where is upward, and why onward? Ours is
"but to do or die," ours "not to reason why." It is this temper
which makes pragmatism our national philosophy, and the
thinly optimistic faith in the mechanical law of progress the
American Faith.

Against this view, the wisest and best of mankind—those, at
any rate, whom mankind most reveres: the prophets, the great
religious leaders, the artists, the great scientists—are a continuous protest. I shall not invoke the Oriental religions, because I
do not wish to raise the question whether our wisdom is so
much superior. But our own Bible teaches us that men do not
live by bread alone, but need vision. The great religious teachers have taught that the highest happiness consists in the vision
of God rather than in strenuous activity in temporal matters.
In the field of art we have learnt that the vision of beauty is
not merely a luxury, but an attainment of real salvation, for in
it we lose the sense of time and of strife and become identified
with, wrapped up in, the object of our contemplation. The
same is true in the field of pure science. Science progresses not
because of the material rewards that come to those who make
practical inventions. Nor is the scientist activated to make great
theoretic discoveries by the philanthropic desire to help his fellow men. Success comes only to those who have capacity to lose
themselves in the contemplation of the object. It is a great
mistake to suppose that anything but a minor part of mathematics and physics or even biology has found practical applica-

tion. The real driving force in pure science is just natural wonder or curiosity.

We all have it until we are educated out of it, and it provides the supreme joy of the scientist when he solves his problem. It is then that he jumps up and cries, "Eureka, I have it!" This is the key to Aristotle's doctrine of the life of the Gods. The mathematicians are the ambassadors of the Gods.

A false theory as to the history of science has tried to make modern science the child of modern machinery and industry. But the truth is the other way: industry has profited from and has been built upon the work of men like Newton, Laplace, Gauss, Faraday, and Clerk Maxwell, none of whom were interested in any practical application of their theoretic discoveries.

Gladstone asked Faraday what the value of his discoveries was. Faraday answered, "Some day you may tax it." Which is the ultimate *reductio ad absurdum* of the practical theory of utility.

Hegel was busy on *The Phenomenology of the Spirit* when the battle of Jena was being fought. Some people regarded it as absurd, but on reflection, the Battle of Jena is gone and past while Hegel's philosophy is still working—for good or evil.

People argue that Archimedes should have worked for the defense of Syracuse, but Syracuse is gone and Archimedes' work is still influential.

Darwin was taken to task by the London *Times*. "Is this the time to fuss among speculative things when the foundation of our world order is shaken?"

Nobody today is interested in Plato's attitude to Athenian politics, but his philosophy of ideas is still of vital interest.

Practical action must always be a compromise and seldom attains perfection for our hearts' desires. In contemplation we can envisage the absolute best. Such vision is absolutely necessary if our action is to have a direction rather than merely an aimless perpetual motion. But above all, such vision is itself an exercise of the supreme human energy, the energy of a human mind; and, as Sophocles said, wisdom is the major part of happiness.

34

ON TEACHING PHILOSOPHY

THE PROBLEM for discussion at this meeting is not only one of serious importance for the teacher of philosophy but also one that touches more or less directly the problem of the nature of liberal civilization. I am not ready to offer a set of definitive answers to the issues thus raised. Perhaps a few indications of the course of my own limited experience may be suggestive and helpful to others dealing with the problems under discussion.

During the years when I was employed in teaching elementary mathematics, I often asked Professor Woodbridge to lend his influence towards having the American Philosophical Association devote a special meeting to the problems of the teaching of philosophy, its aims and methods; but he always put me off with the remark that the business of philosophy is to philosophize and that the problems of teaching should be left to the pedagogues. Woodbridge called himself a traditionalist, and I attributed his attitude to his unwillingness to change any feature of the traditional program of the American Philosophical Association.

I confess that at first I was inclined to accept his attitude. The word "pedagogue" carried the suggestion of low intellectual virility. With a few notable exceptions that could be counted on one's fingers, I knew of no pedagogues who belonged in the forefront of philosophy. Moreover, I could not share the popular faith in the omnipotence of education. The idea that all

A paper read at a meeting of the New York Philosophy Club, October 1943, as part of a symposium on the teaching of philosophy.

social problems could be solved by education seemed to .me an illusion. Of course, if we knew enough about the solution of all problems we could educate people to solve all the vexed problems of life; but that is to beg the question. It certainly is not true that the spread of schooling will solve all our vexed problems of national and international life. And so I abandoned my efforts to promote discussion by professional philosophers of the aims and methods of teaching their subject.

But I resumed my interest when I began to teach philosophy myself, and asked myself to what purpose I should direct my energies. This led me to reflect on the role of philosophy in a liberal civilization.

Education in the past has always been the possession of the privileged classes, to be used as an ornament and a source of power. Greek education rested for the most part on slave labor, and medieval civilization depended largely on serfdom. The education of the Renaissance was exclusively for the nobility. Even Rousseau could not conceive of education for the multitude. Émile required a private tutor who could devote all of his time to Émile himself. And even modern education could not free itself from the old conception of the substance of education. That is why the substance consisted for the most part of Latin and Greek, with a smattering of Hebrew to continue the theologic tradition. Even American colleges long continued to be ancillary to the theological seminaries. The idea of adapting education to the needs of the great multitude who have to go to work relatively early in life has not yet become an integral part of our national system of education. The struggle to achieve this result is still going on. When at the end of the Mexican War it was proposed to found a free academy in New York, a violent protest was raised by the wealthier classes who objected to the use of public money for that purpose; and the New York *Sun* up to recent days continued to echo the old protests against the institution of the New York City College as a thinly disguised method of robbing the rich to pay for the education of the poor.

When I started to teach philosophy in the City College I found myself devoid of the gift of verbal fluency, and so I naturally resorted to the use of the Socratic method: teaching by means of searching and provoking questions. The head of the Philosophy Department, who was not similarly handicapped —in fact he was exceptionally gifted as a lecturer—at first demurred. "What do you do to make your students into fine fellows?" he asked. To which I replied: "I'm not a fine fellow myself, at least not so much better than my students that I can venture to impose my own standard on them." And this I meant not by way of irony or false modesty but in all sincerity. As a son of immigrant parents I shared with my students their background, their interests, and their limitations. My students were on the whole what may be characterized as emancipated in social matters and politics as well as in religion. They did not share the orthodoxy of their parents. And breaking away from it left them ready and eager to adopt all sorts of substitutes. Though many of their parents were highly learned, as was usual among Russian Jews, my students had gone to American public schools, and the learning of their parents was in the main foreign to them in substance, being permeated so deeply with the Talmudic tradition. City College itself offered a rich variety of courses in languages, literature, and science, and the curriculum allowed few courses in philosophy itself. I therefore saw no adequate opportunity for teaching philosophy along traditional lines, and so I had to give courses in related subjects, hoping to bring philosophic insight to my students through courses on the nature of civilization, the philosophy of law, and the topics covered by Santayana in the last four volumes of his *The Life of Reason*.

Judging by the unprecedented attendance and the eager response I received from my students, I seem to have aroused genuine interest in the problems of philosophy. As a result I developed the conviction that the main purpose of the teaching of philosophy should be to free the minds of students so that they could take a genuine interest in philosophy not only as a matter of opinion but as a liberation from superstitions, new as well as old. By challenging the opinions current among young people at the time—such as the uncritical acceptance of psychoanalysis, economic and other forms of materialist determinism, the complacent cult of progress, and other myths which parade as modern science—I think I succeeded in bringing to some of my students the realization that the problems of philosophy are matters of such vital importance that they have to be faced most seriously in every realm under penalty of otherwise falling into grievous and devastating error.

Subsequently I had the privilege of teaching philosophy in Johns Hopkins, Yale, Chicago, and Harvard, and I was impressed by the prevalence among students of other forms of superstition, such as nationalism and various other varieties of romanticism. As a result of this experience, the conviction grew in me that the main function of teaching philosophy should be the opening of the human mind to new possibilities, rather than the inculcation of any new set of doctrines. To me, this did not mean the old-fashioned liberation of the mind from all traditional beliefs, but rather the supplying of students with new points of view that would genuinely enrich their outlook and thus help them to attain genuine intellectual independence. This in practice amounted to abandoning the traditional attempt to teach philosophy as a self-sufficient body of learning, and instead attempting to teach future scientists, lawyers, economists, and citizens to think philosophically about the problems of science, law, economics, and citizenship.

35

HUXLEY: THE PROPHET OF A GREAT HOPE

M ANY OF US still recall the days when T. H. Huxley appeared a veritable Jack the Giant-Killer of the intellectual and moral world. Ever youthful in ardor, and armed with the shining sword of truth, he fought and killed many ogres who oppressed the children of the light. Pompously fossilized scientists like Owen, sanctimonious statesmen like Gladstone, and Oxford bishops like "Soapy Sam" Wilberforce, as well as the supposedly learned Duke of Argyll—all fell before him.

Was this earlier view unduly worshipful, or is our present age unduly neglectful of that most eminent Victorian? The appearance of these two unusually interesting and substantial books, viewing him in the light of present-day ideas, should help us to answer this question.

Mr. Ayres tackles his job in a singularly forthright manner. His picture is consistently that of the fighter for evolution, and purely personal matters form only the casual framework. Our hero succeeded and was feared because he was right. Those who opposed him were against the truth, and Mr. Ayres wastes no sympathy on them. But posterity has unfortunately accepted Huxley's own overmodest reference to himself as Darwin's bull-dog and has not therefore given him full credit for developing the all-important idea of man's descent from anthropoid stock.

Published in *The New Republic*, Vol. 72, p. 182 (September 8, 1932), as a review of Clarence Ayres, *Huxley*, and Houston Peterson, *Huxley, Prophet of Science*.

It has attributed this idea to Darwin himself, and Huxley has thus fallen into a somewhat secondary place.

Here Mr. Ayres has, it seems to me, put his finger on an important point. Huxley undoubtedly did more than Darwin to establish the facts of man's anatomic and psychologic kinship with the apes, though like Darwin himself he was decidedly weak on the question of the mechanism of the descent. But I think that Mr. Ayres, like most Americans, exaggerates the importance of the whole Darwinian set of ideas for modern thought and civilization.

We in America, and especially those from the University of Chicago, are too close to the evangelical parson's universe to take a cosmopolitan rather than a provincial view of the overthrow of the Mosaic cosmology. As far back as the sixteenth century even a medievalist like Paracelsus could speak of Moses as a teacher of religion only, not of natural science; and no one misunderstood Fontenelle's *mot* that all peoples have mythologies as to the origin of things, but that the Jews, by a special miracle, had only the absolute truth. That Huxley's morphologic studies added considerably to our fund of enlightening and liberating ideas no student of history will deny. But there is no foundation for the claim that our present mechanistic view of human life is due to Huxley. A naturalistic view of man can be traced from the days of Anaximander, Democritus, and Lucretius, to those of Hobbes and the French and German materialists of the eighteenth and nineteenth centuries. Huxley's theory of mental automatism was, in fact, singularly out of vogue in the decade following his death; and the present wave of "behaviorism" is clearly due to the influence of an experimental biology that is more indebted to Europeans like Jacques Loeb and Pavlov than to Darwin and Huxley.

As for the influence of "evolution" on the social sciences, that was already an old story in the days of Hegel and Comte. Historians generally have never been able to take it seriously, and modern students of anthropology like Boas and Lowie are indeed working hard to put away this popular mythology or *a priori* construction of history, to make room for a really scientific study of the facts. Even in biology the term "evolution" is too vague to be a really working scientific concept. Biologists cling to it not only out of verbal piety for the really great services that Darwin and Huxley rendered in their day, but also because, fearing the Fundamentalists and hostile legislation, they do not want to admit to the public how little of the Darwinian set of ideas has remained in contemporary science. Indeed, all but natural selection have gone, and the latter is only a vague term for a number of unknown causes whose effects are partially and only recently confirmed by experimental evidence. In this respect our official leaders of science—men like Osborne, Millikan, and others—are exactly in the position of the original opponents of Huxley, who tried to subordinate truth to public policy. Huxley's effort to introduce fresh air and intellectual cleanliness into the Augean stables of official science has to be undertaken all over again, and will always have to be whenever men of science are more concerned with the effects on the public than with the truth of their science.

As a mere biography, Mr. Peterson's book is richer and more humanistic. If Mr. Ayres is tough-minded, Mr. Peterson is decidedly tender-minded, in regard to Huxley's enemies. The struggle in which Huxley participated is here pictured on a larger canvas and with a wider background—though in this respect better use could have been made of the history of biblical criticism and especially of Bishop Colenso's book on the Pentateuch.

Mr. Peterson has an eye for significant personal detail and we get a more living portrait of Huxley as a man—though, since there is little proof offered for Mr. Peterson's psychoanalytic speculations, a follower of Huxley might well doubt the truth of the portrait. Somewhat in the Stracheyan fashion, subtle doubts are insinuated as to Huxley's absolute rectitude. He protested too much against cant and humbug. He "was a most efficient agent for himself. With all his blunt candor he understood the subtle strategy of reputation. His public appearances were usually well timed. His public retorts had a dramatic fitness."

Now we need not hesitate to admit that in the heat of argument Huxley oversimplified certain issues, and resorted to some arguments that fell short of absolute justice. But was he right on fundamentals? Here Mr. Peterson, like most nonscientifically trained humanists, is decidedly unclear. The subtitle of his book is "Prophet of Science," and the conclusion is that Huxley gained some sort of victory for science. But Mr. Peterson does not himself always believe in science and in its prophet. At times he writes from that dizzy modernistic height where there is no such thing as truth, so that poor Huxley was "psychologically" naïve to believe that it could be found in science. Truth is just a moral prejudice and scientific generalizations are nothing but convenient shorthand of no real validity. Yet Mr. Peterson also criticizes Huxley for that very nominalism or rejection of general ideas in which the latter at times follows Bishop Berkeley. Indeed, we have an appeal here not only to Plato but to Peirce, who blasted the foundations of the anti-realistic attack on, or interpretation of, science. The fact, however, is that neither Huxley nor any other investigator of nature can doubt in the course of his scientific search that there really *are* laws of nature connecting what is sought for with what is already known.

More clear and more orthodox is Mr. Peterson's opposition to Huxley's materialism or "epiphenomenalism." But it rests on a specious argument invented by Spencer and followed by James and others, viz., that since human consciousness is a product of evolution it must have a biologic function or survival value. This argument is either the old theologic assumption that nature operates only according to a providential plan and creates nothing in vain, or else it is a very human conceit that nature operates only like a prudent English businessman who never does anything except for a useful end. But common observation will confirm Huxley's view that nature is a scene of terribly useless prolification which leads to destructive carnage and waste of life, that it produces monstrous growths and functional disharmonies which may last for considerably long periods. Whether, then, human consciousness or intelligence is of biologic advantage or will prevent the extinction of the human species is a question of fact that only the future can answer. It cannot be settled by *a priori* dogmas. Certainly, so long as the stupid or unevolved species continue to multiply as rapidly as they have throughout time, they will thereby show themselves biologically "fit" to survive.

But even if it were true that human consciousness is evolved for a practical purpose, it would still be fallacious to conclude, as Nietzsche, Bergson, and, at times, Mr. Peterson do, that scientific knowledge cannot therefore give us valid truth. Such an inference is the veriest *non sequitur* and clearly self-refuting—since this argument is itself the result of "evolution," and can therefore be only practically useful but not true.

At the heart, however, of Mr. Peterson's opposition to his hero or prophet is the nostalgia for the old faith (shall we not say for the fleshpots of Egypt?) and the persistent idea that "Lilly, Mallock, Balfour and others were correct in predicting that Huxley's views were pointing straight toward moral confusion, if not to chaos." Huxley met this fully in his withering reply to Lilly! As Christian morality came from pagan and Hebrew sources and survived the dropping of the latter, why may it not also survive the disproof of Christian superstitions by modern science? In fact, Mr. Peterson himself does on one occasion agree with Huxley that the problem of morality, of the good life on earth, can be dealt with in terms of human interests and aims, without resort to supernatural interferences. Historically it is rather obvious that recent changes in morals have been so connected with the material conditions of life, with the telephone and the automobile, that it is far-fetched to attribute them to disbelief in the Mosaic cosmology. And who dares to assert that in morality those who hold on to that mythology are always superior to those who have for good reasons rejected it or have even never heard of it? So long as the truth of Huxley's arguments is not even seriously challenged, it must indeed be a poor morality that can be overthrown by them.

There are many admirable people today who suffer from the pathetic fallacy of supposing that their own nostalgia for their old faith and their bewilderment at the newer morality are the peculiar characteristics of their age. In point of fact, this cry over waning faith and growing moral confusion is as old as history; and it is important to realize the absurdity of the claim that it was Huxley who "robbed his generation of its faith and prepared the way for moral chaos." What Huxley really destroyed was a set of rotting conventions that fell to pieces at the first touch of an honest and courageous lance. There were, indeed, few scientists in England who believed in the theory of the special creation of all existing species according to the biblical chronology. But it was considered bad form to disturb the faith of the multitude, just as that Victorian paragon, Mr. Podsnap, would not allow certain topics to be mentioned before "the young person." Huxley had the wit and courage to see that the whole thing could be readily overthrown without serious risk.

It is a curious fact that none of those who attacked Huxley were men of real faith. Mallock, whom Peterson thinks more sagacious than Huxley, was a poor fish, held in contempt by his intelligent contemporaries and none too soon fallen into deserved oblivion. As for Balfour's *Foundations of Belief,* we must look at it in the light of his *Defence of Philosophic Doubt*— that is, as a complacent resolution to doubt all evidence in order to cling to beliefs that have no rational support. If Huxley had not been a dying man in 1895 he would have gone through him as he had through Gladstone and "Soapy Sam." For though Balfour was more urbane and subtle than his predecessors, he had little more than their essential complacency, the Podsnappery which made him argue: Since the Church of England is good enough for us, why is it not good enough for the Welsh?

It is a plain superstition to hold up the morals of Aldous Huxley as a horrible illustration of our loss of faith and morality. The world that Thomas Huxley's grandson paints is far more honest and decent than the early Victorian age depicted in Bulwer Lytton's *Pelham.* What student of history would dare suggest that contemporary sex morals show a decline compared with the brutal and atrociously degrading prostitution which was supported by the British government and defended by Victorian moralists like Lecky as a protection to the "purity" of the home?

Mr. Peterson makes the point that Huxley himself always remained a Victorian in morals and never realized that moral rules could properly change their content with changing conditions of life. This is not only just, but fatally so. Huxley never rose to the ability of questioning the moral assumptions of his age. This shows itself in his essay on "A Liberal Education," in which conventional ideas of property and theft are identified with eternal laws of nature. Logically this led to the view that it was better for Irishmen to starve and let their children starve than to withhold from their English landlords the rent (in the form of grain and food) which the latter's Parliament declared due. Not only on property and labor but on such subjects as birth control there was nothing in Huxley's utterances which we today can regard with any admiration. Perhaps he would not have exerted so much influence on his generation if he had like others dared to be progressive not only in theology but in economics and morals as well. But, to his credit be it said, this was not a conscious consideration with him.

Among Mr. Peterson's psychologic observations I am impressed with the remarks on Huxley's dramatic sense. It seems that Huxley, unlike Darwin, was unhappy when alone, always craved a public, and was at his best when performing before it. And the public before which he moved was ready to discard cosmologic but not economic or moral superstitions. He had an honest if shrewd courage, but not the absorbing penetration which carries one beyond one's generation to martyrdom. Huxley was a great compromiser. He not only shrewdly used biblical terminology but helped those who insisted on the compulsory use of the Bible in the schools. He did not admit that a book that was fallible in its natural science and hygiene might also be fallible in its morals. If today there is an unholy alliance between the official leaders of science and religious modernists to combat all those who demand clear-cut answers to the issues between religion and science, we cannot appeal against it to Huxley. He subscribed to that cheap evasion which asserts that the conflict is only between science and theology—as if any modern religion can or does dispense with a belief in a supernatural, personal God. We can, of course, and we do, stretch the word "religion" to denote any altruistic sentiment, and so we speak of Communism as a religion. But in thus speaking of the avowed enemies of religion as religious, we have stretched the word beyond any useful meaning and have only confused rather than solved the real issues. Huxley, in this respect, suffered from the influence of a Victorian prophet who, if not downright dishonest, was certainly vehemently evasive and confusing in the fundamentals of the Christian religion—I refer to Thomas Carlyle.

The agoraphile inclination which prevented Huxley from brooding over and wrestling with ideas hindered him from penetrating behind the superficial philosophy of Spencer. And he was not sufficiently self-critical to see that despite their many weaknesses T. H. Green and F. H. Bradley were so effectively undermining that philosophy as to leave it no future.

There is a certain justice in the popular judgment which puts Darwin above Huxley. The latter was more of a scientific biologist in the modern sense—i.e., he was more of an experimentalist rather than a mere naturalist as was Darwin. But Darwin, less facile and less brilliant, lived more with his ideas and was less anxious to score a point than to find the truth no matter by whom advanced and no matter how antagonistic to his preconceived ideas. Darwin thus set an example of intellectual honesty which will live long after his particular conclusions are, as they nearly all have been, left behind. As a scientist Huxley will always occupy a very high rank in many fields of biology. But his controversial zeal prevented him from maturing great ideas, principles, or methods as did experimentalists like Faraday or the Abbot Mendel.

Huxley rendered inestimable service to science by his many early technical papers, all showing marvelously acute observations, and by his promotion of the experimental habit of mind in biology. But he will probably be remembered much longer for his services to popular education through his amazingly lucid exposition in such books as his *Physiography* and *The Crayfish*, or in the essay "On a Piece of Chalk." This he achieved, not like Eddington and others through meretricious analogies which produce the illusion of clarity and fool an unmathematical reader into the flattering belief that he understands the quantum theory, but rather by the wise omission of all that can be omitted and by concentration on the essentials of the object before the reader. It was easier for Huxley to do so because he had the realist's faith in the object before him and had no "idealistic" lesson to impose upon it.

To view Huxley as a great liberator in the field of education is perhaps to do most justice to his permanent significance. He was a hero and a prophet of a great hope—the hope that by introducing science into education our human lot would be permanently bettered. Like other hopes of the nineteenth century, such as the one in universal suffrage or in the separation of Church and State, this has met with an outer triumph and inner disappointment. Huxley did not foresee the real obstacles in human nature against the genuine scientific interest. He did not suspect that when the pedagogues and popularizers once got a hold on science they would dilute and cheapen it into a new set of dogmas—something that the erratic Peirce saw very clearly. But if the fate of the human race be to struggle incessantly against obstacles, those who raise and strengthen our hopes will always be nearest our hearts. In this respect Huxley will remain a figure that mankind will not want to forget. He was a valiant fighter and within a narrow field a great strategist in the perpetual struggle for human liberation. He achieved this position not only by his work and through those whom he encouraged, but also by occasional tributes to those who paved the way for him: Descartes, Hume, and Priestley, as well as Darwin. May there always be found equally worthy shoulders to carry on the burden!

IX

RELIGION

36

THE INTELLECTUAL LOVE OF GOD

Introduction

I WISH in this paper to urge the validity of the Spinozistic ideal of the intellectual love of God—the *Amor Dei Intellectualis*—as an ideal which may still serve as a beacon to illumine current tendencies in life and thought.

It would be difficult to mention any contemporary issue in metaphysics or ethical and political philosophy in which Spinoza has not said something that is still laden with pregnant significance. On the questions of humanism or anthropomorphism, naturalism and idealism, on the relation of mind and body, on the method of ethics, on the relation of democracy to government by law, and on the ever-burning question as to the proper scope of governmental activities and the freedom or toleration of political and religious differences, few philosophers contain so much that is still so apt and modern. Spinoza is a central figure in the world's great stream of religious, political, and scientific thought. More than any other philosopher, Spinoza has impressed the imagination of Europe and its literature—witness Lessing, Goethe and Heine, Shelley, Coleridge and Arnold, Taine, Renan, and Leconte de Lisle. Hence the neglect of Spinoza in contemporary Anglo-American philosophic discussion is itself a significant fact for those who wish to judge the intellectual temper of our age, and it is not altogether irrelevant for our present purpose to consider the possible causes of this neglect.

Published in *The Menorah Journal*, Vol. XI, p. 332 (August 1925).

In the first place we have the linguistic difficulty—the fact that since Locke and Kant we have lost the old meaning of terms like subject and object, substance and essence. This offers great difficulty at a time when there is a general disinclination to see how our problems appear when translated into another philosophical dialect. The linguistic difficulty, however, is connected with a real difference of attitude. The struggle between science and theology since Spinoza's day has made it difficult for us to understand his naïve union of radically thoroughgoing naturalism in both ethics and science with the genuine piety toward that which has been held noble and sacred in the spiritual history of man.

Back of this difficulty, which makes naturalism and spiritualism antithetic terms to us, is the development of the modern conquest of nature which makes the modern American and European look exclusively to the control of material objects for the way to happiness, where ancient wisdom sought self-control by spiritual exercise. Metaphysically this shows itself in the tremendous emphasis that modernistic thought places on the category of time. The kernel of my contention in this paper is that if we recognize Spinoza's distinction between time as a category of existence and eternity as a category of essence or meaning, we can reconcile naturalism or, if you please, materialism with the piety which has distinguished genuinely spiritualistic views of life. The doctrine of the intellectual love of God, the central doctrine of Spinoza's philosophy, offers a convenient point of orientation for this contention.

I. The Spinozistic Ideal

If the *Ethics* makes anything clear it is Spinoza's rejection of all anthropomorphic theism. The view that God has any personal traits like will or human intellect, that He can act with a conscious view of promoting what is good for us, is repeatedly and most emphatically rejected. By the term "God," Spinoza obviously denotes what we call today the realm of reality which is the object of all science, the system or necessary concatenation of nature. Matter and meaning (in Spinoza's terms, "extended body" and "idea") are but two aspects of the unimaginable whole called God or Nature. When Spinoza calls the logical aspect or "attribute" of the universe the intellect of God, he expressly warns us that the term "intellect" does not at all mean the same when applied to God as when applied to man. Nor is there any anthropomorphism in the saying that man's intellectual love of God is a part of the love with which God loves Himself. The most consistent atheist—I mean one who denies a personal God, rather than one bent on rejecting any and every use of the word God—can agree with Spinoza that the universe contemplates itself to the extent that it actually contains or involves intellectual contemplation.

All this, however, seems a dreadful play on words to those who complacently assume that the term "God" has not been and cannot be used in any sense other than that of a magnified human person to whom we can pray for recovery of health, or victory in war, and who will be pleased or displeased by the course of our action.

So thoroughly has this language of piety become associated with supernaturalism and prescientific superstitions that there have not been wanting historically unimaginative souls to accuse the fearless Spinoza of having purposely put his atheistic doctrine into pious language in order to ward off personal annoyance. This is pathetically absurd. There can be no doubt that Spinoza was profoundly sincere in rejecting and resenting the charge of atheism, which is associated in his mind with the pursuit of wealth and material goods. Now it would be hard for me to overemphasize the importance of language and the consequent duty of avoiding the confusion which always results from giving new meanings to old words, a confusion which De Morgan has keenly satirized apropos of theologies that convert the stories of the Bible into transcendental psychologies by methods that can make anything mean anything else. But this objection cannot be justly brought against Spinoza, who is the pioneer of our modern historical methods of interpretation. On the contrary, those who object to Spinoza's using "love of God" to denote devotion to philosophic or cosmic truth would cut us off not only from understanding the great neo-Platonic tradition in which Spinoza was nurtured, but from the great human in-sight of teachers since the days of the Buddha and Jesus who have insisted that the kingdom of heaven is within us.

William James, who did inestimable good by insisting on thoroughgoing naturalism in psychology, seems to me to have produced untold harm by the unhistorical assumption that re-ligion must necessarily rest on the belief in the supernatural. To insist that God must necessarily be a person who, if we pray to Him, will help us against our enemies and whom we in turn might help or please by believing in Him, seems to me to rest on an appeal to the unenlightened multitude against the judg-ment of all reflective thought; an appeal as unjustified as the parallel appeal to the multitude in questions of natural science. The unreflective judgment of the multitude is no more decisive on the question of the ultimate values of life than it is decisive in matters such as the motion of the earth around the sun. The unutterable miseries and wretchedness of mankind should em-phatically silence the claim that natural ignorance and unre-flection is the road to blessedness. The God of Spinoza is clearly not the God of Abraham, Isaac, and Jacob, precisely because, on reflection, it is impossible for honest thinkers to believe literally that the infinite ground or rational cause of the universe can sit down to dinner, get angry and punish innocent people, or be guilty of the other absurdities which the consecrated popular conception of God contains. The eternal cannot become iden-tical with the temporal. It is not democracy, but rather the height of sophistication, which can lead a philosopher to appeal here to the judgment of the multitude, very much as the dis-gruntled political aristocrat sometimes appeals to the mob.

On the other hand, those who call themselves naturalists are intensely suspicious of such language as that of Spinoza because of their fear of other-worldliness. But, if other-worldliness means despising the joys which a wise use of nature can afford us, on the ground that mortification of the flesh is in itself preparation for a higher life hereafter, no one has more vigorously opposed such other-worldliness than Spinoza. The popular conception of Spinoza as an ascetic must be corrected by his explicit teaching (*Ethics,* Props. 41-42, 45 note) that mirth is something of which we cannot have too much. The rejection of wealth, sensual pleasures, etc., as absolute ends is always accompanied with the reservation that a wise man will rationally use them as means to happiness.

Those, however, who are exceedingly afraid of other-worldliness frequently use that term in a wide sense to denote any way of life which tends to minimize the importance of immediate gratification of the impulses to which man in natural or artificial society is subject. Other-worldliness, in that sense, is the antithesis of that worldliness which wise men in all generations have called a state of spiritual death. Worldliness is, indeed, the most emphatic denial of the value of philosophy; and no greater blight can fall upon philosophy than to become so preoccupied with human affairs as to become worldly. When naturalism becomes positivistic and loses the speculative or cosmic interests of philosophy, it falls into deadly traditionalism, devoid of all freedom or liberality in ethics. It may sound paradoxical, but in a complex world it seems the sober truth that philosophy can help the man in the market place only by turning its face and fixing its eyes on larger vistas. It may seem cruel to indulge in metaphysical speculations while the great masses are chained to the grindstones; but, as Spinoza has well pointed out, unreasoned pity is a passion of weakness. The physician can help the patient only after hours devoted to impersonal or theoretic issues.

If by materialism we mean to denote the doctrine that every existence is (or refers to) extended body, I do not see how any student of Spinoza can deny that he, like Hobbes, was a materialist. What distinguishes Spinoza from Hobbes and later materialists is his constant distinction between time or duration as a category of existence, and eternity as a category of essence or meaning. This distinction prevents Spinoza from falling into the nominalistic logic which cuts up the universe into a number of hard mutually exclusive terms that have no genuine internal connections, and can therefore be united only by a *deus ex machina*. His insistence that ideas, as logical essences or meanings, are eternal or timeless (that is, not subject to the processes of material change of which time is the measure) enables him to save all the profound human values of neo-Platonism and spiritualism generally.

Modern nominalism arose when physical science was compelled to break violently with the scholastic doctrine of substantial forms. That revolt against scholasticism was humanly necessary and brought much good to mankind. But like other revolts it was also very destructive, and it would have been even more so if mathematics (nourished in the neo-Platonic schools) had not developed the principle of continuity which enables us to see the threads of identity running through the diverse existing things. By taking mathematical method seriously Spinoza was able to maintain—despite some flings at the frailties of scholastic realism—that universals, meanings, or essences (laws, in ultramodern language) unite infinitely different existing terms, but do not form additional particulars, and are not, therefore, subject to the temporal changes of such terms. To see things "under the aspect of eternity"—*sub specie aeternitatis*—is to see their actual meaning. All existing terms are bodies subject to change and therefore located in the time series. But if the whole time order has any meaning at all, the order of meaning includes it and is not exhausted by it.

As subordination of time to eternity (the latter is not to be confused with the everlasting, which endures through all time though in it) distinguishes Spinoza's philosophy from most modernistic thought, some reflections on the modernistic emphasis on time, which we may call temporalism, will not be out of place.

The consciousness of the importance of time separates the modern European from the Oriental as well as from ancient and medieval man. It is intimately related to our modern industrial life. Reflection, however, shows that overemphasis on the importance of time is the root of nearly all the distinctive fallacies of modernism. These can be summed up in the false assumption that the existence of historic antecedents or psychic states does away with the importance of logical reasons. Formally this can be stated more generally by saying that the distinctive error of modern metaphysics is the false elevation of time, which is the necessary condition or aspect of all existent things, into the sufficient condition of all meanings. But it is easy to see that what is an indispensable order for all existing things need not and cannot be exhaustive of all possible orders of meaning.

A bare reference to the typical forms of this fallacy will perhaps make my point clearer. The old fallacy of supposing that you have refuted the truth of anyone's contention by showing that he has an economic motive for saying it has become generalized into a system of politics and historic interpretation. Substitute general psychologic motives for concrete economic ones and you have Freudianism instead of Marxism. Generalize this fallacy still further by saying that the existence of temporally antecedent states contains all the significance and value of anything, and you have historicism, geneticism, or universal evolutionism. All these movements are professed revolts against abstract rationalism. Yet what can be more naïvely and boldly rationalistic than the assumed laws of Marxian social economics or the simplicity with which the different stages of the Marxian dialectic succeed each other; and what could be more crudely rationalistic than the way the subconscious or Freudian unconscious invariably acts like a logical automaton without any emotional disturbances? Popular evolutionism also shows its crude rationalism not only in constructing history into dialectic stages, but also in assuming that all the irrational acts of man are merely survivals from acts that originally served a useful purpose or were thought to do so.

Clear Spinozistic or mathematical rationalism saves us from such vain efforts. The relation of means to end is not at all a characteristic of the order of physical existence. Good and bad are relative to man; and man's power to secure the good depends upon his knowledge. The mathematical form into which Spinoza casts his ethical doctrine is an expression of the faith in universal truth. All forms of professed irrationalism avoid this faith. They passionately embrace some brute particularism, leaving no real ground for rational discussion or toleration or for the ideal of an ever wider integration of our natural interests which is set by the *Amor Dei Intellectualis*.

It is instructive for an understanding of the true character of naturalistic religion to contrast Spinoza's love of God with the Positivist love of humanity. The latter, if humanity denotes the actual human beings we know, involves us, among other difficulties, in the impossible obligation of loving the brute imperfections of our own nature. Now although it is possible to love human beings despite their imperfections (because of the better possibilities which enlightened love can discern), it is not possible to love the unlovable imperfections themselves. Any love that is rationally feasible must involve some norm which will enable us to discriminate that which is admirable from that which is not so; and that is exactly what the *Amor Dei Intellectualis* effects. (The command to love our neighbors needs the love of God as a norm of that which is lovable in them.)

The Spinozistic love of God or nature does not involve a love or acceptance of the world as it is at any particular moment. An intellectual love or understanding of the universe is not possible if our view is limited to a single moment. Such a limitation may help us to form definite images but not adequate ideas, which, Spinoza emphatically insists, must not be viewed as lifeless pictures on a panel (*Ethics* II, 43 note). So far, then, as the love of God involves acquiescence or an acceptance of the universe it is in no way inconsistent with rational effort to improve any particular state or mode of being. Spinoza is as far removed from the violent optimism of Leibniz as he is from the lighthearted pessimism of Schopenhauer. His doctrine is rather the recognition that all rational effort involves an acceptance of the universe; we cannot improve nature except by nature's means. Hence there can be no true happiness or freedom that is not based on a recognition of the causal relation or necessary order which binds together the various parts of nature in time and space.

Though Spinoza's ethical ideal is fundamentally naturalistic —that is, aims at a rational synthesis of natural interests—his insistence that man must visualize his task *sub specie aeternitatis* distinguishes his doctrine from the type of progressivism formulated by the American national poet, Longfellow, in "A Psalm of Life." The latter rejects enjoyment as the end of man and formulates the categorical imperative: So act that each tomorrow finds you one day further than today. This type of popular progressivism rests on the optimistic belief that the cumulative results of personal or communal achievement can endure indefinitely—a belief which appears fantastic in the light of the robust knowledge of the variations of nature. The naïve faith in temporal continuance can only increase the anguish of inevitable disappointment. Of course, a certain amount of progressivism is an indispensable aspect of practical life aiming at commonly attainable external results. In the field of politics, I for one can see no other feasible program. But when progressivism becomes exclusive in its claims, pretending to fill the whole life of man as a religion, it becomes a foolish effort to impoverish life by robbing men of sustaining vision and moral holidays, in the effort to make them satisfied with the petty improvements which are all we can confidently expect from the uncertainties of nature. Here we certainly need Spinoza's reminder: "Human power is extremely limited and is infinitely surpassed by the power of external causes; we have not therefore an absolute power of shaping to our use those things external to us." But we can conquer nature by the act of understanding it.

II. Some Difficulties

I have thus far roughly sketched the concrete Spinozistic ideal without regard to the traditional difficulties which famous expositors have found in the structure of the Spinozistic system. An important group of these difficulties center about the supposed incompatibility between the terms "God," "love," and "intellectual."

Love having been defined as a pleasure or joy, and pleasure as a feeling of transition towards greater perfection, how can it possibly be predicated of God who is all-perfect? We may of course answer this by textual distinctions between the intellectual love of God and the love that is not so qualified. But too sharp an antithesis between the two kinds of love may not help us much to understand Spinoza's doctrine. Let us admit, in the spirit of Spinoza, that any intellectual love which can be actual must have a physical or physiological location in our bodily organism. This physiologic process, so far as it is a transition to greater perfection or a heightening of our vitality, is a bodily process or mode. Like other modes it exists in nature or God—that is, it has its locus in some point of the temporal series. But the essence or meaning of intellectual love of God is the adequate idea or ideal of a complete intuition or insight into the system of nature to which a study of the implication of existing things and especially of our own emotions may lead us. The meaning of this idea is certainly part of the ideal essence or intelligible structure of nature which Spinoza calls God.

But how can love which is an emotion, or passion, be intellectual? Spinoza's explicit declaration that intellectual love is not a passion at all, but an intellectual activity, carries no conviction to the present generation. For since the Romantic movement we no longer look upon passion as literally suffering, but regard it rather as an intense consciousness, expressive of an enhanced vitality. The ideal of passionless reason seems to us, therefore, that of a logical machine without any vital power. To Spinoza, however, "passion" means suffering due to the absence of the light of reason, and the adequate ideas which remove this suffering are not outside of the active conation which is the essence of our being, but are this very conation or will perfected. Here again Spinoza's identification of intellect and will is misunderstood today because we identify the expression of will entirely with external physical motion of practical affairs and exclude thought itself as an expression of human and indeed cosmic energy. This makes us view intellectual insight as a passive state, whereas to Spinoza, as to Aristotle and Dante, it is the most intense activity. The issue here is the same as that concerning the nature of classic art. It is best answered by recognizing that the serenity or absence of distorting passion in classic art is due not to a lack of vitality, but to the literal perfection of it by the mastery of form. If the word "passion" then be used in the modern sense as an intensification of life, intellectual love is the passionate pursuit of truth, which is also the highest expression of the *conatus* to self-preservation.

This will enable us to dispose of those who complacently deny any religious value to the *Amor Dei Intellectualis* on the ground that it is *merely* the scientific interest. This facile and fatal use of the word "merely" was easy in the days when to the transcendental snobbery of theologians scientific knowledge was a relatively unimportant affair. Doubtless, also, so long as the term "scientific" is so often applied to particular investigations which leave the investigator hardly richer in the wisdom of life outside of his narrow specialty, it seems rather violent to identify the scientific and the religious motive. But when we recall that the *Amor Dei Intellectualis* is not knowledge of isolated details, but the union of our mind and nature attained by self-knowledge, we need not hesitate to recognize the profoundly religious value which Spinoza's thought has had for so many.

III. *The Spinozistic Ideal in Contemporary Thinkers*

It may perhaps make my conception of Spinoza's position more clear if I indicate briefly to what extent contemporary thinkers seem to me to embody this *Amor Dei Intellectualis.*

The first name that will readily occur is that of John Dewey. No one today is doing better service in calling attention to the indispensable role of the intellect in making possible a life that can fitly be called human. This is more clear in his recent work, where the emphasis is no longer on the unfortunate term "practical," but on philosophy as vision or illumination of the *significance* of events. In his opposition to authoritarianism, to the romantic return to primitive or natural unreflection and to other forms of anti-intellectualism, he certainly embodies the Spinozistic spirit. Mr. Dewey's divergence from Spinoza results mainly from a too great concentration on the problems of practical education and empirical psychology. Concentration upon practical or social applications have, for instance, led Mr. Dewey to belittle, if not to ignore, the interest in physical or cosmic issues.

For the thorough acceptance of naturalism, both in morals and in science,. perhaps no one today represents Spinoza so closely as does George Santayana. Though Mr. Santayana sweepingly rejects Spinoza's claims at the beginning of *The Life of Reason,* the latter work comes as near being a translation of

Spinoza as is possible for an independent thinker trying to envisage with his own eyes the human scene and its natural background. That the chief human good is not in perpetual physical motion, but in the vision of the essence or significance which illumines the natural scene, is brought out by no one more clearly than by Mr. Santayana. The difference between the latter and Spinoza lies not so much in the emphasis that Spinoza placed on the rigorous or mathematical procedure of science as in the historic circumstances of their respective times. Spinoza wrote at a time when there still flourished the great neo-Platonic tradition which, despite its crust of superstition, had kept alive, while it somewhat cramped, the wisdom of antiquity. Certainly Spinoza's Hebrew teachers, as well as Giordano Bruno, embodied that tradition as a living doctrine. Santayana writes at a time when that tradition, after having nourished the founders of modern science—Copernicus, Kepler, Galileo, and Newton—had run itself into the intellectual underworld, and when the demand all around us is for novelty or originality above all. Santayana, to be sure, has aptly characterized this demand for originality as such as most deadly, and his genius for direct vision into the common life has stood him in good stead. But in a time of general insistence on novelty for its own sake, genius alone is insufficient. One needs also historical study to make the continuity of human life and thought so vivid as to save us from vain efforts. Such study Santayana has not adequately pursued. Hence the results of his thought often appear as illustrations of that which he is most anxious to combat, to wit, impressionism and willfulness.

Mr. Bertrand Russell, in his more strictly philosophical work, has given us a vivid illustration of the Spinozistic belief in the potency of thought and a striking example of what devotion to the truth really means. In this I cannot help thinking his mathematical training has been a great aid. While Mr. Russell's position differs from that of Spinoza in fundamentals, especially in his pluralism, the great difference seems to me rather temperamental. This shows itself in his famous essay, "A Free Man's Worship." Mr. Russell is at one with Spinoza in rejecting the temporalism back of the effort to build up an abiding place for the human spirit in external nature. Nature cares not for our human hopes, and destroys the just and the unjust. Hence there can be no enlightened human happiness without an element of wisely cultivated resignation. But while Spinoza recognizes that human hopes and aspirations are themselves the outcome of nature, and that even in thought we cannot transform nature except by the means with which nature supplies us, Mr. Russell too often allows himself to speak as if nature were an anthropomorphic being, consciously bent on defeating us.

Finally, I must mention one who, perhaps better than any other man, in candor and self-restraint, in depth and profound simplicity, illustrates the Spinozistic *Amor Dei Intellectualis*— F. H. Bradley. Mr. Bradley is at one with Spinoza in the view that insight or intuition into reality is possible only through rigorous intellectual exercise. Mr. Bradley also most thoroughly represents Spinoza in holding that the knowledge of particular things or modes (parceled out among the special sciences) is in itself inadequate for philosophic insight, and needs to be subjected to that persistent inquiry into the nature of the absolute or the whole which we call metaphysics.

By his profound devotion to the pursuit of truth in close reasoning, Mr. Bradley has prepared the way for philosophic modernism, overthrowing the complacency of neo-Hegelians and of the followers of the self-styled critical philosophy. Yet he has not been justly dealt with by this generation. For it is easier to ignore him or revile his doctrine of the absolute than to read him, understand him, and meet him on his own ground. May the recent reprint of his *Logic*, forty years after its first publication, serve to impress contemporary thinkers with the permanent value of his philosophic work.

37

A NOTE ON RABBI JOSHUA
OF NAZARETH

JUDGED by the ordinary rigorous canons of scientific evidence pursued by the scholarly historian, nothing is known with any certainty about the life of Rabbi Joshua of Nazareth, more generally known as Jesus. Very early in the first century A.D. he became identified with the Jewish preternatural view of the Messiah * (as exemplified in the Ethiopian Book of Enoch), and even with the Deity Himself. Stories about his miraculous birth, unknown to Paul, became current even as early as the First Gospel. Even though Paul heard about his crucifixion, Jesus himself appeared to him as the spirit of righteousness and sanctity, seen not in the flesh but heard only in a vision. Thus it has become possible for some scholars to doubt the actual historical existence of Jesus. (See Benjamin Smith's *Der Vor-Kristliche Jesus,* which tries to point out that Jesus was an object of worship before the date commonly ascribed for his birth.) It is indeed remarkable that though Jesus lived in a highly literate age, and was the contemporary of Philo and Josephus as well as of well-known Jewish Rabbis, there are no references to his existence by any historically known contemporaries, notwithstanding the fact that the writers of the gospels wrote as if they were eyewitnesses. Josephus indeed refers to his brother James, but the reference to Jesus himself in Josephus is an obvious and clumsy interpolation. No authentic historical ref-

* The Hebrew word meaning "anointed," translated into Greek as "Christos."

erence to Jesus occurs before the time of Tacitus, who was singularly uninformed about all matters relating to the Jews.

If, instead of demanding rigorous evidence, we satisfy ourselves with human probabilities and take the body of the Gospels or other early Christian writings as a whole, we have a highly plausible account of the main outlines of the life and work of Jesus as the founder of Christianity.

Jesus began his life work as a follower of John the Baptist, who seems to have remained in the orthodox Jewish tradition, preaching repentance and the imminent destruction of the wicked world. Jesus himself believed in the Mosaic law, and according to the Gospels, asserted that not one jot or tittle of it shall pass away; and anyone who preached its abrogation would be least in the Kingdom of Heaven. Even toward the end of his ministry he told his disciples not to go to any of the Gentiles or Samaritans, but "only to the lost sheep of Israel am I sent." But the spirit of his teaching broke through the bonds of Jewish nationalism, and his conception of God as the Father of all mankind laid the basis of a supernational religion, just as Greek philosophy had laid the basis of supernational wisdom in the Socratic idea that wisdom as true knowledge can be taught to everybody, including a slave boy. Indeed, the Hebrew idea of wisdom became identical with the Hellenistic, as exemplified by Philo, who found the Greek garb fitting to the expression of Hebrew ideas. The Stoic philosophers continued to teach that every man is capable of understanding, and the natural law that they preached became identified with the law of God in later Christian writings.

In teaching that every human being is as such a son of God, Jesus freed mankind from ancient fears. According to the Book of Proverbs, the fear of the Lord is the beginning of wisdom. But in viewing God as not only the Creator of Nature and Mankind but also the all-loving Father, Jesus replaced all fear by faith in the love of God for all his creatures.

To be sure, the conception of God as merciful and all-forgiving occurs also in the Old Testament; and the body of the teaching of Jesus, such as the glorification of the humble and the meek, occurs frequently in the Psalms from which Jesus drew his inspiration. But the body of the Old Testament contains so many other things—such as the vengeful conception that God visits the sins of the fathers on their children to the third and fourth generation—that the teaching of Jesus appeared as new and revolutionary. Particularly new was his teaching of the utter unimportance of all material things, compared with purity of heart and the love of God. If anyone takes your coat, give him your cloak also. What has he gained and what have you lost in the Kingdom of Heaven? Indeed, the conception of the Kingdom of Heaven, destroying the importance of all particular material objects, frees us from the petty cares and vexations that absorb life's energies, and thus endows us with freedom to enjoy the universal fruits of the spirit. That, I think, is the most basic and all-liberating of the teachings of Jesus, and indeed the essence of all true religious or spiritual insight.

38

ERASMUS AND LUTHER

ERASMUS is not generally viewed as one of the world's great heroes. In fact, he is often regarded as distinctly unheroic. In the great struggle between the Reformation and the Catholic Church, he refused to take sides and was condemned by both parties as a Laodicean—a trimmer who in the interests of his personal safety evaded the responsibility of joining the one or the other side of a struggle which both sides were inclined to view as identical with that between God and his enemies.

But to rise above the dust cloud of battle and to see things as they are is the primary duty of the scholar, and to that duty Erasmus was faithful in an eminent way. We are apt to admire Luther's directness and absolute firmness which despises all consequences. But it is relatively easy to join the one or the other side and to repeat without qualification the slogans of your party or even to advance the force of your side. It is not so easy to discriminate the elements of truth and falsity in the two sides of a bitter controversy.

Ulrich von Hutten accused Erasmus of cowardice, of being afraid to declare himself or publicly show his colors. It was charged that he who had mercilessly exposed the folly of the established church before scholars had not the courage to join the popular Reform Party that wished to get rid of the evil. Luther, in his usual forthright manner, told Erasmus: "The Lord has not yet endowed you with such constancy, such courage, and such sense as should lead you to fight against this monster boldly, shoulder to shoulder with us." Erasmus, in his answer to Hutten, declared: "In many books, in many letters, in many disputations, I have unfalteringly declared that I refuse to mix myself in the affairs of any party whatsoever. . . . For my part I have said frequently to my friends that, if the Lutherans could feel kindly to me only on condition that I should agree unreservedly with their tenets, let them think what they will, I cannot do so. I love freedom, and I will not and cannot serve any party."

In his letter to Luther, he wrote: "I have worked better on behalf of Evangelical teaching than many who now plume themselves upon the knowledge of the Gospels. I see also that the Reformation has brought into being many corrupt and insurrectionary men. . . . [I] refused to sacrifice the evangel [religious truth] on this altar of human passion."

Erasmus was right in attacking Luther's absolute fatalism— man's utter inability by any work of his own or by any act of contrition to escape punishment for Adam's sin. Luther's position and fanaticism led him to sanction the bloody and cruel suppression of the Peasants' Revolt. "The brute populace must be governed by brute force." "I, Martin Luther, have slain the peasants who died during this rebellion, for I goaded authority to the slaughter. Their blood be on my head."

For Erasmus, Christianity meant peace and humanity. Christ gave his blood that men may love their enemies and avoid conflict. Luther believed in war to the point of extermination.

The war fever cannot be stopped by wise words, such as those of Erasmus, but it can be roused to fury by those, who, like Luther, believe it meritorious to rouse such fury. Erasmus foresaw the torrents of blood that Luther's passion would aid in letting loose. Luther stood for the uncompromising attitude—he was with God. Yet he was not above diplomatic tricks. Assuming that he was quite honest in siding with the princes against the rebellious peasants—he hesitated before his decision—he did try to win over Erasmus after vilifying him. Luther wrote: "If you want to better humanity and reform the Church, you cannot afford to fight shy of a good thumping lie."

There is nothing chivalric about Luther. He liked to trample on his foes. "God is a sturdy fighter"—against whom? Against the Devil. Who is thus as powerful as He?

Erasmus, on the other hand, believed and acted on the motto: "We must not invariably tell the whole truth. Much depends upon how the truth is made known."

Would it not have been better if the reformist ways of Erasmus rather than the revolutionary ways of Luther had prevailed? Catholic France in the eighteenth century was certainly as free as Lutheran Germany, and the whole world might have been spared the Spanish reaction which made the Church in many respects hostile to humanism.

The ideal which Erasmus constantly held before himself was the ideal of peace based on a common culture. The humanistic ideal of breadth of vision and charity of mind has often been regarded as too aristocratic. But the horror of inhumanity is generally felt even though those who express it clearly are few. In the everlasting war against bigotry and fanaticism the hope for a common humanity, which goes back to Greek philosophers and Hebrew prophets, is not to be denied.

Erasmus could not overlook the tortures of the Inquisition, the revolting profligacy of the court of Alexander VI, and the outrageous venality in the sale of indulgences. He recognized the corrupt morals of the Roman clergy and its inability to teach the lessons of spiritual life, but he preferred "things to remain as they are rather than that through my intervention fresh unrest should arise, an unrest which often achieves quite the contrary of that which its moving spirits set out to attain." "I have long since realized how dark and complicated are all human affairs. I know how much easier it is to incite to disorder than to clamp down on such disorder once it is loose."

Fanaticism splits mankind into bitterly opposed fragments. Since it recognizes no other truth or system of ideas than its own, it needs must resort to violence to bring everything under one yoke, and the forcible curtailment of freedom of opinion, every kind of inquisition and censorship, the scaffold and the stake—these evils were brought into the world not by blind violence, but by rigidly stern fanaticism.

Erasmus was a brave fighter in the struggle for a Europe free of national jealousies because it appreciated the debt to the noble sons of each nation. He remains a significant figure in the enduring fight against intolerance and fanaticism and for human consideration and mutual understanding. Such a figure can scarcely appeal to the mob. The mob needs concrete goals and the pungent thrill of hate in order to give vent to its destructive impulses. But passion eventually burns itself out, and in the long run finely pointed words and polished phrases can be more effective than bludgeons. Thus the men of letters did become, in Erasmus, Grotius, and their like, an international power of great historic significance.

Just as Renaissance humanists had sought to purify and restore literature by going back to the classics, so Erasmus sought to purify religion by going back to Scripture (especially the evangels).

People idolized Luther because he fought in a forthright manner for the liberation of mankind against tyranny, ignorance, and corruption. That the Reformation was much needed was admitted by the Church itself in the subsequent Counter-reformation. Even earlier, Dante had put some contemporary popes in Hell; and a later pope, while fully maintaining the holiness of the office, justified him in this.

Luther was put above Erasmus because the multitude could understand him; no sublety was required. Luther represents power, force, intolerance, because he suffered from oppression, and those who suffer from oppression are inclined to use it themselves. Resistance to tyranny, unless modified by intelligence and humane spirit, is thus apt to generate more oppression than it can cure or remove.

Luther was a powerful trumpet who stirred the pulse of mankind. Erasmus was a delicate violin attuned to more subtle harmonies. Who shall say which is the more important in the orchestration of world history?

39

ZIONISM: TRIBALISM OR LIBERALISM?

CONCERNING QUESTIONS of race and religion, even more than those of politics, scientific knowledge is pitifully small and men's convictions are accordingly most intense. But the discussion of Zionism is beset with the additional difficulty that clear and honest thinking is subtly hindered by the fact that really plain speaking is almost unattainable. An exceptionally long history of struggle and suffering has left many sore and sensitive spots in the body of Israel, and the thoughtful non-Jew feels the necessity of excessive caution lest he touch any of these tender spots; while the Jew, no matter how emancipated, cannot completely overcome the effects of a traditional attitude which may put group loyalty above devotion to the simple truth. Self-respecting Jews also cannot help leaning backward in expressions which may risk their being identified with those who for their bellies' sake creep out of the Jewish fold. The discussion of Zionism has thus been largely left to those who are

---

Published in *The New Republic*, Vol. 18, p. 182 (March 8, 1919).

more zealous about the triumph of their righteous cause than scrupulous about the justice of their arguments. In normal times mankind is protected from the clamor of zealous enthusiasts by its profound inertia and by the equally emphatic denials which every zealous group sooner or later provokes; so that those who care for impartial truth can generally wait with some confidence for a favorable time when the still, small voice of reason can make itself heard. But in abnormal days, when small but determinedly loud groups are mistaken for vast multitudes and are causing irreparable harm, one cannot wait for slow time to bring its withering refutations.

At a time when millions of Jews are starving and deprived of all opportunity for resuming human life, one would be uncommonly hard-hearted to say anything against establishing a legally protected home—in Palestine or anywhere else—for homeless Jews. But Zionism is not merely a philanthropic movement to help the homeless. It claims to be a solution of the Jewish problem; and its emphasis on Palestine rests on a nationalist philosophy which is a direct challenge to all those who still believe in liberalism.

Like all practical human movements, Zionism has its roots in a vast variety of complicated human motives, varying from the idealistic and religious to those of frustrated personal and social ambition. It is therefore, like other movements, supported by diverse and often contrary arguments. Some say, Let us go back to Palestine, else Judaism will disappear; while some of the followers of Ahad Ha'am say, Let us go back to Palestine, for there alone can we be agnostic without having to apologize for it to non-Jews. There are those who argue that the Jews are a peculiarly gifted Oriental people, and that only in Palestine can they develop their peculiar gifts; while others passionately deny any such peculiarity, but on the contrary assert that just because the Jews are like other people they should have a land of their own like other people, etc. Back, however, of all conflicting views and arguments and uniting all Zionists by a common antipathy is the opposition to the policy of assimilation which would make the salvation of Jews as well as non-Jews depend on general enlightenment.

The policy of assimilation was clearly expressed by Spinoza, who pointed out that Jews like other groups are held together by the bond of common suffering; and that, as the nations became enlightened and removed their restrictions against the Jews, the latter would adopt the habits of Western civilization and the problem would thus be eliminated. As the removal of the traditional restrictions against the Jews did not begin before the end of the eighteenth century, it was only in the nineteenth century that Jews in large numbers began to adopt the habits of Western civilization and to profess the faith of rational liberalism which has been its intellectual foundation. But, as restrictions against Jews have nowhere been completely removed (witness, for example, the social restriction against Jews among the supposedly enlightened citizens who form our university clubs), it has left the intellectual Jews peculiarly susceptible to the mystic and romantic nationalism which began in Germany as a reaction against the liberalism of the French Revolution, against the old faith in the power of cosmopolitan reason and enlightenment which overthrew medievalism. In a world where most of us frequently suffer the humiliation of being rejected, what can be more natural than that Jews, who undoubtedly suffer more than their share of it, should take comfort in the conviction that their rejection was due not to their personal failing but to the fact of their descent? This constant tendency to emphasize the consciousness of race, tragically intensified by the increased persecutions of recent years, has thus led newly emancipated Jews to adopt the very popular racial philosophy of history, represented on the Teutonic side by Chamberlain's *Foundations of the Nineteenth Century,* or, on the Russian side, by Slavophils like Katkoff. Zionists fundamentally accept the racial ideology of these anti-Semites, but draw different conclusions. Instead of the Teuton, it is the Jew that is the pure or superior race. All sorts of virtues, love of family, idealism, etc., are the characteristic qualities of *its* spirit. Only in Palestine can this spirit find root and only in the Hebrew language its adequate expression.

The scientific adequacy of the ethnologic, historic, and philologic evidence by which all this is supported would be beneath contempt were we not dealing with widespread beliefs of a pathetic intensity and with a cause to which no human heart can deny some sympathy. Nevertheless, these beliefs are radically false and profoundly inimical to liberal or humanistic civilization. History, and Jewish history especially, shows that the claim to purity of race on the part of any civilized people is entirely mythical. It is generally put forth by sacerdotal and other exploiting groups, and when extensively followed leads to narrowness and sometimes to degeneracy. No great civilization was ever achieved except by a mixed people freely borrowing from others in religion, language, laws, and manners. The Jews were such a people when they produced the bulk of biblical literature, and they certainly increased their contribution to civilization when they left Palestine and mixed with other peoples, as the names of Philo, Spinoza, Heine, Karl Marx, Dr. Ehrlich, Antikolski, Bergson, and Flexner will readily indicate. Have the French been hindered in their civilization because they gave up their native Gallic for the language of their Roman conquerors? Only a Germanic pedant like Gierke would advise a modern European people to give up being ruled by Roman law because it was imposed from without and did not grow out of the national spirit.

Though most of the leaders of Zionism in America are sincerely and profoundly convinced of the compatibility of Zionism and Americanism, they are none the less profoundly mistaken. Nationalistic Zionism demands not complete individual liberty for the Jew, but group autonomy. What this may mean in practice can be gathered from a general tendency to deny to anyone born a Jew the right to follow his conscience and to abandon the Jewish religion. Indeed, how could a Jewish Palestine allow complete religious freedom, freedom of intermarriage, and free non-Jewish immigration, without soon losing its very reason for existence? A national Jewish Palestine must necessarily mean a state founded on a peculiar race, a tribal religion, and a mystic belief in a peculiar soil, whereas liberal America has traditionally stood for separation of Church and State, the free mixing of races, and the fact that men can change their habitation and language and still advance the process of civilization. The supposition that the Jews in Palestine will be more fortunately situated to make contribution to civilization than the Jews of America is contrary to all human experience. There is not a single opportunity offered by Palestine that is not open, to a larger extent, here. Even the Jewish University of Jerusalem will not offer a single course that a student could not just as well, or better, pursue in one of our American universities. The fact, however, is that the American ideal of freedom is just what the Zionists most fear. At bottom they have no confidence that with complete toleration and full freedom Judaism can hold its own in the open field.

Zionists always speak of themselves as idealists and regard the great majority of Jews who refuse to be moved by their appeal as materialists. The word "idealism" covers a multitude of sins, and one of these is a disinclination to look actual difficult problems in the face and a tendency to take refuge, instead, in arbitrary dreams. (Incidentally, the idealistic Zionists are quite willing to ignore the rights of the vast majority of the non-Jewish population of Palestine, almost like the Teutonic idealists with their superior Kultur. An ominous sign of this is the intense opposition to Dr. Magnes's effort to arrive at a peaceful understanding with the Arabs [Brith Shalom].) The actual Jewish problem in all countries is a problem of adjustment, how the members of a certain historic group may learn to live in peace and mutually profitable intercourse with their fellow countrymen. As the number of Jews that can in any year be settled in Palestine is much less than the annual natural increase of the Jewish population in such countries as the United States or Russia, it follows that the Jewish problem is one that must be settled in each country separately. How will the establishment of a small, politically autonomous Jewish community in Palestine help the much greater body of Jews in the world at large to play their part worthily in the civilization in which they find themselves? The supposition that the Jews of Palestine will necessarily be on a higher spiritual plane and serve as an inspiration to Jews throughout the Diaspora is like the argument that an independent Liberia will elevate the position of

Negroes elsewhere. Indeed, there are few arguments for Palestine that do not find their parallel on behalf of Liberia.

One of the great leaders of American Zionism, a man whom I highly revere, said: "The policy of enlightenment has failed. Enlightened countries like France, Germany, and England have not solved the Jewish problem. We must try to solve it ourselves in Palestine." This seems to me an easy but profound error. Enlightenment is not something that any country has as yet perfectly achieved, but it is true that to the extent that the nations have become enlightened the condition of the Jews has become ameliorated. Enlightenment is a painfully slow process, as painful as the winning of our daily bread from the soil; hence our frail humanity is always ready to listen to some romantic get-rich-quick scheme to attain a heaven-on-earth where all of us can live happily forever afterwards. A favorite device of this kind is the attempt to revive a supposed glorious past. But, even if the history of Palestine were glorious—which the reader of the Book of Kings or Josephus can see was hardly the case—the glory of Palestine is as nothing to the possible glory of America. If history has any lesson at all, it is that never have men accomplished anything great by trying to revive a dead past. Great things are accomplished not by imitation of the past, but by resolutely facing the actual definite problems before us; and to those who face the problems of the harmonious adjustment of the Jew to American life Zionism is an evasion, not an answer.

Yet life has its peculiar ironies, and it would be an unusually ill wind that blew no good. Despite its emphasis on tribal loyalty, Zionism has clarified the problem of the Jew by giving it a more just setting. The older ideal of assimilation had degenerated into an ideal of blind aping of Gentile ways. Yet, obviously, Jews could not make any significant contribution to American civilization by mere imitation or acceptance. Zionism has rendered the supreme service of increasing men's self-respect, and has helped men to realize that they must be ready to give of their own past experience as well as to accept. For this, the American ideal of civil and political liberty still provides a fair field.

331

Liberalism is the traditional American policy, our heritage from the eighteenth-century philosophy which expressed itself in two revolutions. But precisely because it is a tradition it is apt to fall into desuetude and to receive an empty lip-worship. The stress of recent events calls out loudly the need for a refreshing faith in individual freedom and enlightenment. The ideal of liberal enlightenment is a difficult one. Progress toward it is painful and by no means certain. With the fall of the Roman Empire civilization received a terrible setback, and it is by no means impossible that as a result of this war and the intensification of the small-nationality idea Europe and a great deal of the rest of the world will be Balkanized—that is, organized on a tribal basis, as it was in the Dark Ages. But, whether tribalism triumphs or not, it is none the less evil, and thinking men should reject it as such.

POSTSCRIPT

IN REPUBLISHING a piece written twenty-six years ago on a problem that has been buffeted by many storms in our generation, I feel that I should disavow some views that have been falsely associated, in the public mind, with opposition to Zionism. In the first place, it should be made clear that one need not be a Zionist to protest against British laws and regulations which, in defiance of international compacts, deny to would-be immigrants the right to enter Palestine merely because they are Jews. Laws that discriminate against any creed are abhorrent to the conscience of liberal humanity, whether they are the Nuremberg laws of Hitler, the British laws limiting Jewish immigration and land purchase in Palestine, or the United States immigration laws which make ancestry the test of admissibility to our shores and discriminate against those immigrant groups which have come to our land since 1890. When the United States in the 1920s abandoned its traditional policy of allowing free entry to the oppressed and downtrodden of the Old World, and adopted instead the policy of limiting immigration on the basis of so-called national origins, it abandoned the liberal faith for a form of ancestor-worship based on demonstrably false racial theories. In taking this step, we not only curtailed the rapid expansion of our population and industry, which had been the basis of our national prosperity, but gave world currency and prestige to racist legislation in fields of immigration and in other fields as well. It is a small step from excluding Jews or East Europeans from a country to excluding them from a profession or trade. Tribalism is a creed that leads to grief and massacre, whether it bears the label of Zionism, Aryanism, Anglo-Saxon America, or Pan-Islam.

In the second place, it should be noted that just as crimes may be committed in the name of liberty, so good deeds may be done under the banners of a false creed. The admiration of the civilized world is due to the achievements of the Jewish settlements in Palestine over the past quarter of a century, and to the courage, wisdom, and faith in life's better possibilities that have made these achievements possible. Impartial technical observers like Lowdermilk (*Land of Promise*) have hailed the demonstration made in Palestine of the great possibilities of scientifically and humanely conducted agriculture, free from the illiberal tax policies that, through centuries of Turkish rule, hindered the conservation of the soil and the development of human enterprise. These achievements, however, did not presuppose the establishment of a Jewish state, and I trust that they may be advanced and extended in years to come within the framework of a nonsectarian state that allows equal rights to all—Jews, Christians, Mohammedans, and atheists alike.

40

BASEBALL AS A NATIONAL RELIGION

I N THE WORLD'S HISTORY baseball is a new game: hence new to song and story and uncelebrated in the fine arts of painting, sculpture, and music. Now, as Ruskin has pointed out, people generally do not see beauty or majesty except when it has been first revealed to them in pictures or other works of art. This is peculiarly true of the people who call themselves educated. No one who prides himself on being familiar with Greek and Roman architecture and the classic masters of painting would for a moment admit that there could be any beauty in a modern skyscraper. Yet when two thousand years hence some Antarctic scholar comes to describe our civilization, he will mention as our distinctive contribution to art our beautiful office buildings, and perhaps offer in support of his thesis colored plates of some of the ruins of those temples of commerce. And when he comes to speak of America's contribution to religion, will he not mention baseball? Do not be shocked, gentle or learned reader! I know full well that baseball is a boy's game, and a professional sport, and that a properly cultured, serious person always feels like apologizing for attending a baseball game instead of a Strauss concert or a lecture on the customs of the Fiji Islanders. But I still maintain that, by all the canons of our modern books on comparative religion, baseball is a religion, and the only one that is not sectarian but national.

The essence of religious experience, so we are told, is the

Published in *The Dial*, Vol. 67, p. 57 (July 26, 1919).

"redemption from the limitations of our petty individual lives and the mystic unity with a larger life of which we are a part." And is not this precisely what the baseball devotee or fanatic, if you please, experiences when he watches the team representing his city battling with another? Is there any other experience in modern life in which multitudes of men so completely and intensely lose their individual selves in the larger life which they call their city? Careful students of Greek civilization do not hesitate to speak of the religious value of the Greek drama. When the auditor identifies himself with the action on the stage —Aristotle tells us—his feelings of fear and pity undergo a kind of purification (catharsis). But in baseball the identification has even more of the religious quality, since we are absorbed not only in the action of the visible actors but more deeply in the fate of the mystic unities which we call the contending cities. To be sure, there may be people who go to a baseball game to see some particular star, just as there are people who go to church to hear a particular minister preach; but these are phenomena in the circumference of the religious life. There are also blasé persons who do not care who wins so long as they can see what they call a good game—just as there are people who go to mass because they admire the vestments or intoning of the priest—but this only illustrates the pathology of the religious life. The truly religious devotee has his soul directed to the final outcome; and every one of the extraordinarily rich multiplicity of movements of the baseball game acquires its significance because of its bearing on that outcome. Instead of purifying only fear and pity, baseball exercises and purifies all of our emotions, cultivating hope and courage when we are behind, resignation when we are beaten, fairness for the other team when we are ahead, charity for the umpire, and above all the zest for combat and conquest.

When my revered friend and teacher William James wrote an essay on "A Moral Equivalent for War," I suggested to him that baseball already embodied all the moral value of war, so far as war had any moral value. He listened sympathetically and was amused, but he did not take me seriously enough. All great men have their limitations, and William James's were due to the fact that he lived in Cambridge, a city which, in spite of the fact that it has a population of 100,000 souls (including the professors), is not represented in any baseball league that can be detected without a microscope.

Imagine what will happen to the martial spirit in Germany if baseball is introduced there—if any Social Democrat can ask any Herr von Somebody, "What's the score?" Suppose that in an exciting ninth-inning rally, when the home team ties the score, Captain Schmidt punches Captain Miller or breaks his helmet. Will the latter challenge him to a duel? He will not. Rather will he hug him frenziedly or pummel him joyfully at the next moment when the winning run comes across the home plate. And after the game, what need of further strife? When Jones of Philadelphia meets Brown of New York there may be a slight touch of condescension on one side, or a hidden strain of envy on the other side, but they take each other's arm in fraternal fashion, for they have settled their differences in an open, regulated combat on a fair field. And if one of us has some sore regrets over an unfortunate error which lost the game, there is always the consolation that we have had our inning, and though we have lost there is another game or season coming. And what more can a reasonable man expect in this imperfect world than an open chance to do his best in a free and fair fight?

Every religion has its martyrs; and the greatest of all martyrdoms is to make oneself ridiculous and to be laughed at by the heathen. But whatever the danger, I am ready to urge the claims of international baseball as capable of arousing far more national religious fervor than the more monotonous game of armaments and war. Those who fear "the deadly monotony of a universal reign of peace" can convince themselves of the thrilling and exciting character of baseball by watching the behavior of crowds not only at the games but also at the baseball score-boards miles away. National rivalries and aspirations could find their intensest expression in a close international pennant race, and yet such rivalry would not be incompatible with the establishment of the true Church Universal in which all men would feel their brotherhood in the Infinite Game.

41

THE DARK SIDE OF RELIGION

THE *advocatus diaboli*, as you know, is not a lawyer employed by the Prince of Darkness. He is a faithful member of the Church whose duty it is, when it is proposed to canonize a saint, to search out all the opposing considerations and to state them as cogently as possible. This wise institution compels the advocates of canonization to exert themselves to develop arguments vigorous enough to overcome all objections. In this symposium on religion, I am asked to serve as *advocatus diaboli:* to state the Dark Side so that those who follow may have definite positions to attack and may thus more fully develop the strength of their case.

While there have not been wanting atheists and other freethinkers who have attacked religion root and branch, these assailants have often shared the indiscriminate or fanatical intensity which has characterized so many upholders of religion. It has therefore been possible to pass over the argument of men like Voltaire, Bradlaugh, or Ingersoll, as inaccurate, superficial, and too one-sided. The truth, however, is that religion is something about which men generally are passionate; and it is as difficult to be patient with those who paint its defects as it is to listen attentively to those who point out our most intimate failings or the shortcoming of those we love most dearly, of our family or of our country. Indeed, to most people religion is just a matter of loyalty to the accepted ways hallowed by our

The substance of this essay appeared as a contribution to the symposium volume, *Religion Today, a Challenging Enigma,* edited by Arthur L. Swift, Jr. (1933).

ancestors; and to discuss it at all critically is just bad taste, very much as if a funeral orator were to treat us to a psychoanalysis of our lamented friend.

A curious illustration of the confusion resulting from the absence of a critical discriminating attitude in the discussion of religion is the fact that the heterodox opponent of the established religion has often much more real faith than most of its followers. Thus Theodore Roosevelt was probably representative of Christian America when he referred to Tom Paine as "a filthy little atheist." Yet a comparison of their respective writings can leave little doubt that Paine had far more faith than his contemner in a personal God, in the immortality of the soul, and in moral compensation hereafter. But Theodore Roosevelt never said a word against established religion or the church and so remained respectable—though his conception of religion as identical with such good works as the taking of Panama and the building of the Canal [1] literally ignores the whole spiritual essence of the historic Christianity which our churches profess. The common identification of religion with the unquestioning acceptance of traditional conventions or good manners is shown in the popular distrust of anyone who thinks about religion seriously enough to change his religious affiliations or to depart from the religion of his fathers. Even lower in general esteem are those who think out a religion for themselves. Thus the Russians say: "The Tatars received their religion [Mohammedanism] from God like the color of their skins; but the Molokans are Russians who have invented their faith." [2]

The general disinclination to conscientious or scrupulously logical examination of religious beliefs is shown by the way even educated people judge religious doctrine by their labels rather than by their content. Thus we talk about Spinoza as a God-intoxicated man because he used the *word* "God" and the language of traditional piety. But those who repeat his opposition to that anthropomorphic theism which is the essence of all popular religion, and who do not write nature with a capital N,

[1] See his Noble Lectures at Harvard.
[2] D. M. Wallace, *Russia*, Chapter X.

are just atheists. Indeed a writer who has made a considerable impression on our contemporary public by his books on religion identifies the latter with a belief in *Something*. What should we have thought of his doctrine if we merely heard it, or if we had only one case of type?

One of the effective ways of avoiding any real discussion of religion or discriminating its darker from its brighter side is to define or identify it as "our highest aspiration." This is very much like defining a spouse as the essence of perfection or our country as the home of the brave and the free. Some particular religion, like some particular wife or country, may perhaps deserve the praise. But we must first be able to identify our object before we can tell whether the praise is entirely deserved. To define religion as our highest aspiration, and then to speak of Christianity, Islam, or Judaism as a religion, is obviously to beg the whole question by a verbal trick of definition.

In the interests of intellectual honesty we must also reject the identification of religion with the mere sentiment of benevolence or with altruistic conduct.

This is the favorite vice of our modernists and of scientific leaders like Millikan who try to harmonize religion with science in general (not with their own special field). We may dismiss these harmonizers as plainly ignorant of the history of religion. For to identify all religion with vague altruism [3] rules out not only all the historic tribal and national religions, Hinduism, and most of the Old Testament, but also Christianity of the Orthodox, Catholic, and Fundamentalist-Protestant type. All post-Hellenic cults have insisted on sacraments like baptism and on the acceptance of dogmas about the Trinity, the Incarnation, the Fall of Man, the Atonement, eternal Hell, etc. Worse than that! This "liberal" or nondogmatic view is logically bound to apply the term "religious" to philanthropic atheists and Communists who, in the interests of humanity and to stop the exploitation of the masses by the clergy, are the avowed enemies of all religion. And indeed there are many who do speak of Communism as a religion. But this surely is to cause

[3] See Coulter, J. M. and M. C., *Where Evolution and Religion Meet.*

hopeless confusion. There is no real liberalism in ignoring the historical meaning of words; and no one who knows anything of the historical and general use of the word "religion" can well use it to include atheists like Shelley or Lenin and exclude men like Torquemada, Calvin, and Jonathan Edwards. Such "liberalism" does not really strengthen the case for religion. Consider the vast varieties of religions ancient and modern. Are they all expressions of our highest aspirations? Is each one an effort at universal benevolence? If so, why do they differ? And since they do differ, and each regards the others as inferior, can they all be true? Nor is the case improved if we say that each religious group seeks what is highest or noblest, for there can be no question that error, ignorance, stupidity, and fanatical prejudice enter into what men think.

Instead, then, of darkening counsel by beginning with arbitrary and confusing definitions of religion, let us recognize that the term "religion" is generally used and understood to apply to Christianity, Judaism, Islam, Hinduism, etc., and that these represent certain forms of organized life in which beliefs about God and a supernatural realm enter more or less articulately. Religion is first of all something that makes people do something when children are born, when they become mature, when they marry, and when they die. It makes people go to church, sacrifice, fast, feast, or pray. A religion that does not get so organized or embodied in life is a mere ghost, the creature of a cultivated imagination. Generally speaking, people get these habits by social heredity, according to the community in which they are born. The beliefs thus involved are more or less tacitly assumed. But such tacit beliefs do become at times explicit, and when this happens men cling to the verbal formula with the most amazing intensity and tenacity. Men are willing to burn others and to be burned themselves on the question whether they should cross themselves with one finger or two, or whether God is one person of various aspects or natures, or three persons of one substance.

Now if we thus view religion as an historic phenomenon in human life, we are prepared to believe—from what we know of human nature and history—that religion like all other social institutions has its darker as well as its brighter side.

1. Religion Strengthens Superstition and Hinders Science or the Spirit of Truth-Seeking

Since the days of the Greek philosopher Xenophanes, theistic religion has been accused of foolish anthropomorphism. And since Epicurus and Lucretius it has been identified by many thinkers with superstition. Eighteenth- and nineteenth-century writers like Voltaire, Gibbon, and Condorcet, Lecky, Draper, and A. D. White have so traced the history of the conflict between scientific enlightenment and religious obscurantism as to make this point a commonplace. But the attempt has been made to make it appear that this conflict is not between religion and science, but between the latter and theology. This seems to me a cheap and worthless evasion. In the first place, none of the religions that are in the field today ever have dispensed or can dispense with all theology. What would be left today of Christianity, Judaism, or Islam without a belief in a personal God to whom we can pray? In the second place, we do not understand the roots of religion if we do not see that the historic opposition to science has not been a vagary of wicked theologians but has risen out of the very spirit which has animated most, if not all, of the religions which have appeared in history. We must start with the fact that with rare exceptions men cling to the religion in which they are born and to which they have been habituated from childhood. We inherit our traditional ritual with its implicit faith and emotional content almost with our mother's milk; and we naturally cling to it as passionately as we do to all things which have thus become part of our being, our family, our country, or our language. When religious opinion becomes formulated, it naturally expresses itself in absolute claims. Doubts are the fruit of reflection. To one brought up in a Mohammedan village, it would sound blasphemous to say that there probably is a God, Allah, and that he is probably more benevolent than malevolent; and that Mohammed has a fairly good claim to be the most reliable of prophets. Similar considerations hold in the case of every other simple religious person. But science regards all established truths (other than the logical methods of proof and verification) as subject to possible doubt and correction. Consider the attitude of a simple man or woman to anyone who offers to prove that we come from an inferior stock, or that our country is inferior in merit to its traditionai rivals. Who can doubt that the first and most patent reaction will be resentment rather than intellectual curiosity? And the same is bound to be our attitude as regards religion, so long as the latter integrates in simple piety all traditional and habitual loyalties to the sources of our being. Thus arises the fierce intolerance of religion as contrasted with the cultivated open-mindedness of science. To religion, agreement is a practical and emotional necessity, and doubt is a challenge and an offense. We cannot tolerate those who wish to interfere or break up the hallowed customs of our group. Science, on the other hand, is a game in which opposing claims only add zest and opportunity. If the foundations of Euclidean geometry or Newtonian physics are suddenly questioned, some individual scientists may show their human limitations; but science as a whole has its field widened thereby, great enthusiasm is created for new investigations, and the innovators are objects of grateful general homage. Science does not need, therefore, to organize crusades to kill off heretics or unbelievers. Science, like art, enjoys its own activity and this enjoyment is not interfered with by anyone who obstinately refuses to join the game or scoffs at what the scientist has proved. The scientific banquet is not spoiled by our neighbors' refusing to enjoy it.

Thus it comes to pass that religion passionately clings to traditional beliefs which science may overthrow to satisfy its insatiable curiosity and its desire for logical consistency. The conflict between religion and science is thus a conflict between (on the one hand) loyalty to the old and (on the other) morally neutral curiosity about everything.

Let us glance at some actual forms of superstition that have been strengthened by religion.

(*1*) *Demoniac Possession.* Whatever be our theories as to the origin of religion, there can be no doubt about the antiquity and persistence of the belief in disembodied spirits, benevolent and malevolent; and all existing religions involve the belief in such supernatural beings, called gods, ghosts, spirits of ancestors, demons, angels, etc. Organized religion is largely based on and develops credulity in this domain. It insists on certain approved ways of conciliating these spirits or obtaining their favor by some ritual of sacrifices, prayer, incantations, the wearing of amulets, or the like. Priests are experts in these rituals, and their influence is certainly not to destroy the belief on which their occupation rests. Consider, for instance, the oracle at Delphi, based on the belief that the raving priestess was possessed by the God Apollo who spoke through her. Religious people like Plato or the Platonic Socrates believed this and held the oracle in great awe. Yet even contemporaries realized that the managing priests were manipulating the final answer under the guise of interpreting the raving utterances of the priestess. The sober Thucydides went out of his way to remark on the only occasion on which the oracle guessed right. Similar observations may be made about the raving prophets mentioned in the Book of Samuel. We find their analogue today in the dancing dervishes of Islam.

One form of this superstition of demoniac possession plays a prominent role in the New Testament. The power of Jesus and his disciples to cast out devils was obviously regarded by the writers of the Gospels as a chief pillar of the Christian claim. The New Testament, to be sure, did not originate this ancient theory of the nature of certain mental aberrations; but its authority has certainly hindered the effort to dispel this superstitious view of the cause of insanity and hysteria—a view that resulted in a most horrible treatment of the sick.

(2) *Witchcraft.* The fear of witchcraft is a natural outcome of the belief in spirits and in the possibility of controlling or using them. If religion did not originate this superstition, it certainly did a good deal to strengthen it. Indeed, Protestant as well as Catholic Christianity at one time bitterly persecuted those who did not believe in the efficacy of witchcraft. For the writers of the Bible certainly believed that witches could recall even the

prophets from the dead; and the Mosaic law specifically commanded that witches should be put to death.[4]

The effects of this Biblical command were quite horrible. Not only were thousands burned within a short time at Trèves, but the torture of those suspected (in order to make them confess) was perhaps even more frightful. The victims of mere suspicion had their bones broken, were deprived of all water, and suffered unmentionable cruelties. Perhaps even worse was the resulting general insecurity and the terrible feeling of fear and of distrust. Yet so clear was the Biblical injunction that enlightened men like More, Casaubon, and Cudworth denounced those who disbelieved in witchcraft. For to give up the belief in witchcraft is to give up the infallibility of the Bible.

(3) *Magic.* Closely related to witchcraft is magic.

Recent writers like Frazer are inclined to draw a sharp distinction between magic and religion. But though the Church hindered the progress of physics, chemistry, and medicine by persecuting magicians,[5] the belief that the course of nature could be changed by invoking supernatural agencies or spirits is common to both religion and magic. The magician cures you by an incantation, pronouncing a strange formula; the priest or rabbi does it by a blessing; the saint does it posthumously to anyone who touches his relics. The magician brings rain by rubbing a stick, the priest by a prayer. If a formula or ritual invokes the accepted god and is performed by the authorized person, it is religion. If the god, the act, or the agent is not an authorized one, the first is referred to as a devil, the second as a sacrilege, and the third as a magician. The Church itself regarded the pagan deities as demons. Both religion and magic generally involve the influence of the supernatural—though the magicians more frequently studied the physical or medicinal properties of the substances they used. The fetish-worshiper attaches magical potency to stones, but so does the Bible. Touching the Ark, even with the most worshipful intention, brings death.[6] Christianity frowns on idol-worshiping but it still at-

4 Exodus 22:18; Leviticus 20:27.
5 It burned Peter of Abano even after his death.
6 II Samuel 6:6-7.

taches supernatural power to certain objects like the cross, relics of saints, etc. Holy water wards off devils. Miracles are a part of Christian faith and are offered as evidence of its truth. But the evidence in favor of the Virgin Birth, of the stopping of the sun and the moon at Ajalon, or of the Resurrection, etc., cannot support its own weight. A small part of mankind finds it adequate, and this only because of the fear of being damned or anathematized for unbelief. It is inconceivable that an impartial court would convict anybody on such evidence. In fact, no event would be considered miraculous if the evidence in its favor were as cogent as that which makes us believe wonderful but natural occurrences.

Another religious belief that the progress of science has shown to be superstition—i.e., to have no basis in rational evidence—is that the rainbow, comets, and other meteorological phenomena are not natural events but special portents to warn mankind against sin.[7]

(4) *Opposition to Science.* It is not necessary for me to recount the fight of Christianity against the Copernican astronomy, against modern geology or biology, or against the scientific treatment of Biblical history. They have become commonplace, and I may merely refer to the works of Lecky, Draper, A. D. White, and Benn. The point to be noted is that the old adherents of religion did not want to know the truth, and that their religion did not encourage them to think it worth while to seek any truth other than their accepted particular faith. Religious truth is absolute and its possession makes everything else unimportant. Hence religion never preaches the duty of critical thought, of searching or investigating supposed facts.

From this point of view it is interesting to read the testimony of Bishop Colenso as to what led him to write his book on the Pentateuch. When he tried to teach Biblical history to the South African natives, he was amazed at the obvious contradictions which these simple savages discovered in the various accounts of the patriarchs. Yet millions of astute and learned Christians had not noticed these discrepancies.

[7] Genesis 9:13; Joel 2:30, 31.

Consider, for instance, the Biblical statement that the hare chews the cud. This can easily be tested. Does your orthodox Christian do that? This disinclination to question things also appears, of course, elsewhere; but nowhere so emphatically and persistently as in the field of religion. Believe in the Koran or be damned forever!

Not only does religion fail to regard critical intelligence and the search for natural truth as a virtue, but the ideal which it holds up frequently makes light of truth itself. Even when God lays down a moral law, He is Himself above the moral law. He sends a lying spirit to Ahab, and his Church for a long time did not think a promise to heretics binding. In the fourth century organized Christianity adopted the view that deceit and lying were virtues if in the interests of the Church (*cf.* Mosheim). The duty of truthfulness is much more exemplified in science than in religion.

In this respect "liberal" modernism seems intellectually much more corrupting than orthodox Fundamentalism. Confronted by natural absurdities—such as the sun and the moon stopping in their course, or the hare chewing the cud—the Fundamentalist can still say: "I believe in the word of the Spirit more than in the evidence offered by the eyes of my corruptible flesh." This recognizes a clear conflict; and the intellectual hara-kiri of the Fundamentalist is a desperate venture that can appeal only to those whose faith is already beyond human reason or evidence. But the modernist who gives up the infallibility of the Bible in matters of physics, and tries to keep it in matters of faith and morals, has to resort to intellectually more corrupting procedure. By "liberal" and unhistorical interpretations he tries—contrary to the maxim of Jesus—to pour new wine into old bottles and then pretend that the result *is* the ancient wine of moral wisdom.

In any case, religion makes us cling to certain beliefs, and often corrupts our sense of logical evidence by making us afraid to regard arguments in favor of religion as inconclusive or to view arguments against it as at all probative. The will to believe even contrary to demonstrative evidence, *credo quia absurdum,* is often lauded as a religious virtue.

It has often been claimed that the superstitions of religion are merely the current superstitions of the people who at the time profess that religion. If this were true, it would only prove that religion is powerless to stop superstition—that it is intellectually parasitic and not creative. But the intimate connection between religion and supernaturalism, and the passionate attachment to the old ways which every religion intensifies, cannot but strengthen superstition and hinder the progress of science towards the attainment of new truth as to human affairs. And this is altogether independent of the personal profit in power, prestige, or even revenue which leads many in and outside of the churches to exploit the credulity of the multitude.

2. *Religion as an Anti-moral Force*

It is often claimed that religion is the protector of morals and that the breakdown of the former inevitably leads to a breakdown of the latter. While there may be some correlation or coincidence between periods of moral change and periods of religious change, there is no evidence at all for the assumption that the abandonment of any established religion leads to an enduring decline in morality. These is more evidence to the contrary. Those who break away from religion are often among the most high-minded members of the community. The chaplains of our prisons do not complain of the prevalence of atheism or lack of religious affiliation among the criminals to whom they minister, while there certainly has been uncontested complaint that religious leaders, high priests, popes, and cardinals have led rapacious and most licentious lives. As faithful a son of the church as Dante puts popes in Hell, and it was in an age of general religious faith that Boccaccio put into the mouth of a Jew the *mot* that the Church of Rome must be of divine origin or it could not stand despite such government. But this is an ungracious task from which we may well turn.

Let us look at the matter more philosophically. What do we mean by morality? Generally we mean those rules of conduct that appeal to people as generally conducive to a decent human life. It follows therefore that, as the conditions of human life change, the content of wise moral rules must change accordingly. Religion, being passionate and absolute in its claim, formulates moral rules as inflexible taboos. It thus prevents needed change and causes tension and violent reaction. But science, studying the principles involved, can distinguish the permanent elements of human organization and safeguard them amidst necessary adjustments to new situations. It is secular social science and philosophy rather than religion that have the wisdom to see the necessity of conserving human values in the very process of facilitating desirable changes.

The absolute character of religious morality has made it emphasize the sanctions of fear—the terrifying consequences of disobedience. I do not wish to ignore the fact that the greatest religious teachers have laid more stress on the love of the good for its own sake. But in the latter respect they have not been different from such great philosophers as Democritus, Aristotle, or Spinoza, who regarded morality as its own reward, like the proper playing of a musical instrument. But the great body of established religions have emphasized extraneous punishment. In the religion of the Old Testament, as in that of almost all Oriental and classic Greek and Roman religions, the punishment meted out to the individual or people is entirely temporal, and the rewards of virtue are in the form of material prosperity. When people realize that this is not true, that the wicked do prosper and that, contrary to the pious Psalmist, not only the righteous but their children are often in want of bread, they either put the whole thing in the realm of theological mystery (as in the Book of Job) or else resort to the pious fiction that the bad man is troubled by his conscience. But the latter is obviously not true. Only those who are trained by religion to cultivate their conscience are troubled that way. The bad man gloats over his evil if he succeeds, and is sorry only if he fails. For this reason, Judaism, Christianity, and Islam have developed and stressed the doctrine of Hell, of eternal and most terrifying punishment. But it is doubtful whether the deterrent value of all these terrors is really large. Living in the presence of a constant terror does not eliminate carelessness. At best, fear secures only conformity. The development of enlightened inclination or disposition depends on educational wisdom and science. Some religions have talked much about love. But the predominant emphasis on the motive of fear for the enforcement of absolute commands has made religious morality develop the intensest cruelty that the human heart has known.

Religion has made a virtue of cruelty. Bloody sacrifices of human beings to appease the gods fill the pages of history. In ancient Mexico we have the wholesale sacrifice of prisoners of war as a form of the national cultus. In the ancient East we have the sacrifice of children to Moloch. Even the Greeks were not entirely free from this religious custom, as the story of the sacrifice of Iphigenia by her father testifies. Let us note that while the Old Testament prohibits the ancient Oriental sacrifice of the first-born, it does not deny its efficacy in the case of the King of Moab (II Kings 3:2) nor is there any revulsion at the readiness with which Abraham was willing to sacrifice his son Isaac. In India it was the religious duty of the widow to be burned on the funeral pyre of her late husband. And while Christianity formally condemned human sacrifice, it revived it in fact under the guise of burning heretics. I pass over the many thousands burned by order of the Inquisition, and the record of the hundreds of people burned by rulers like Queen Mary for not believing in the Pope or in transubstantiation. The Protestant Calvin burned the scholarly Servetus for holding that Jesus was "the son of the eternal God" rather than "the eternal son of God." And in our own Colonial America, heresy was a capital offense.[8]

Cruelty is a much more integral part of religion than most people nowadays realize. The Mosaic law commands the Israelites, whenever attacking a city, to kill all the males, and all females who have known men. The religious force of this is shown when Saul is cursed and his whole dynasty is destroyed for leaving one prisoner, King Agag, alive. Consider that tender psalm, "By the rivers of Babylon." After voicing the pathetic cry "How can we sing the songs of Jehovah in a foreign land?" it goes on to curse Edom, and ends "Happy shall he be, that

[8] This, of course, is based on the Bible: Deuteronomy 17:2-5 and 18:20.

349

taketh and dasheth thy little ones against the rock." Has there been any religious movement to expurgate this from the religious service of Jews and Christians? Something of the spirit of this intense hatred for the enemies of God (i.e., those not of our own religion) has invented and developed the terrors of Hell, and condemned almost all of mankind to suffer them eternally—all, that is, except a few members of our own particular religion. Worst of all, it has regarded these torments as adding to the beatitude of its saints.[9] The doctrine of a loving and all-merciful God professed by Christianity or Islam has not prevented either one from preaching and practicing the duty to hate and persecute those who do not believe. Nay, it has not prevented fierce wars between diverse sects of these religions, such as the wars between Shiites, Sunnites, and Wahabites, between Greek Orthodox, Roman Catholics, and Protestants.

The fierce spirit of war and hatred is not of course entirely due to religion. But religion *has* made a *duty* of hatred. It preached crusades against Mohammedans and forgave atrocious sins to encourage indiscriminate slaughter of Greek Orthodox as well as of Mohammedan populations. It also preached crusades against Albigenses, Waldenses, and Hussite Bohemians. And what is more heartrending than the bloody wars between the two branches of the Hussites over the question of the communion in two kinds? This war desolated and ruined Bohemia.

The Inquisition is fortunately now a matter of the past. Let us not forget, however, that the Church has not abandoned its right and duty to exterminate heretics; and it will doubtless perform its duty when conditions permit it. Spanish and Portuguese saints have expressed deep religious ardor in burning heretics.[10] Ingenuity in inventing means of torture was the outcome of religious zeal on the part of the pious clergy who belonged to the Office of the Holy Inquisition.

The essential cruelty of religious morality shows itself in the peculiar fervor with which Protestant Puritans hate to see any-

[9] Tertullian, Saint Augustine, and Saint Thomas are among those who have so expressed themselves. See *Summa Theologica Suppl.*, Qu. 94, Art. I.
[10] In our time Unamuno, while not orthodox, defended the Inquisition because he would not accept the secular rationalism which abolished it.

one enjoy himself on Sunday. Our "Blue Sunday" legislation is directed against the most innocent kinds of enjoyment—against open-air games like baseball, concerts, or theatrical plays. And while there may be some serious social considerations in favor of liquor prohibition, there is little doubt that an element of sadism, a hatred of seeing others enjoying beer or wine, is one of the motives which actuate religious fanatics. For that is in the great historic tradition of the Protestant Church.

Cruel persecution and intolerance are not accidents, but grow out of the very essence of religion, namely, its absolute claims. So long as each religion claims to have absolute, supernaturally revealed truth, all other religions are sinful errors. Despite the fact that some religions speak eloquently of universal brotherhood, they have always in fact divided mankind into sects, while science has united them into one community, which desires to profit by enlightenment. Even when a religion like Christianity or Islam sweeps over diverse peoples and temporarily unites them into one, its passionate nature inevitably leads to the development of sects and heresies. There is no drearier chapter in the history of human misery than the unusually bloody internecine religious or sectarian wars which have drenched in blood so much of Europe, Northern Africa, and Western Asia.

Even in our own day, a common religion of Christian love does not prevent war between Christian nations. Rather do the churches encourage the warlike spirit and pray for victory. If the conflict among the various creeds of Christianity in our own country is not so bloody, it is not because the spirit of intolerance has disappeared. The Ku Klux Klan and the incidents of our presidential campaign in 1928 are sufficient indications to the contrary. The disappearance of religious persecution is rather due to the fact that those who would persecute do not any longer have adequate power. It is the growth of science, making possible free intercourse among different peoples which has led to that liberation which abolished the Inquisition and has made it possible for free thinkers to express their views without losing their civic and political rights.

The complacent assumption which identifies religion with higher morality ignores the historic fact that there is not a single loathsome human practice that has not at some time or other been regarded as a religious duty. I have already mentioned the breaking of promises to heretics. But assassination and thuggery (as the words themselves indicate), sacred prostitution (in Babylonia and India), diverse forms of self-torture, and the verminous uncleanliness of saints like Thomas à Becket, have all been part of religion. The religious conception of morality has been a legalistic one. Moral rules are the commands of the gods. But the latter are sovereigns and not themselves subject to the rules which they lay down for others according to their own sweet wills.

In all religions, the gods have been viewed as subject to flattery. They can be persuaded to change their minds by sacrifices and prayers. A god who responds to the prayers of the vast majority of people cannot be on a much higher moral plane than those who address him. And what would become of religion, to the majority, if prayers and sacrifices were cut out?

It is doubtless true that some of the noblest moral maxims have been expressed by religious teachers—the Buddha, the Hebrew prophets, Jesus, and Mohammed. But in organized religion, these maxims have played but an ornamental part. How much of the profound disillusion and cultivated resignation of Prince Gautama is to be found in the daily practice of the Bhikhus or beggar monks, or the common ritual of prayer-wheels and talismanic statuettes of the Buddha? This, however, is too long a theme. It would require an examination of the actual practices of the various religions which would exhaust many hours.

Let me, however, consider one point. It is often alleged that the later Hebrew prophets beginning with Amos were the first to introduce a strictly moral conception of God. "An honest God's the noblest work of man." Now it is true that men like Amos, Isaiah, and Micah did among other themes preach social righteousness, feeding the widow and orphan, rather than the national cultus of Sabbaths, holy days, and sacrifices. But will anyone dare to assert that the feeding of widows and orphans, and similar deeds of mercy, constitute the distinguishing essence of the Jewish religion? Surely others before and after the prophets believed and practiced such admirable commandments. Some of the philosophers even ventured to discuss and generalize them so that we might have some clew as to when a given act *is* just and merciful, and when it is not. Yet if a Greek or a Persian should "do justice, love mercy, and walk humbly with God" (the last defined, let us say, in Aristotelian or Spinozistic terms), would he be regarded as a Jew in religion? Surely not so much as one who should be rather negligent in regard to justice and mercy, but should practice circumcision and observe the dietary laws, the laws of the Sabbath and of the Day of Atonement, etc. So also a Persian who in fact believed in the ethical commands of Jesus would not be considered a Christian in religion if he had not been baptized into any church, and did not subscribe to the doctrine of the Trinity or the Virgin Birth. Admirable moral practices on the part of a Hindu or an Inca would not make either of them a Christian. One's religion is judged by the organized group or church of which he is a member. My revered teacher Josiah Royce has justly identified religion, and especially Christianity, with communal life.

In the struggle for social justice, what has been the actual influence of religion? Here the grandiose claims of religious apologists are sadly belied by historic facts. The frequent claim that Christianity abolished slavery has nothing but pious wishes to support it. Indeed, in our own country, the clergy of the South was vigorously eloquent in defense of slavery as a divine institution. Nor was it the Church that was responsible for the initiation of the factory legislation that mitigated the atrocious exploitation of human beings in mines and mills. It was not the Church that initiated the movement to organize workmen for mutual support and defense, or that originated the effort to abolish factual slavery when men were paid in orders on company stores—a practice that has prevailed in some of our own states. The Church has generally been on the side of the powerful classes who have supported it—royalists in France, landowners in England, the *cientifico* or exploiting class in Mexico, etc. Here and there some religious leader or group has shown sympathy with the oppressed; but the Church as a whole has property interests which affiliate it with those in power.

3. Religion and the Emotional Life

Kant has regarded religion as concerned with the great question of *What We Can* (ultimately) *Hope For*. In so far as hopes are resolutions, they are irrefutable by logical arguments. For arguments can only appeal to accepted premises. But hopes may be illusory or ill-founded—they may even attach to what is demonstrably impossible. Such, in the light of modern science, is the hope of the actual resurrection of the body. But what is more important is that many of the hopes that religion has held out to men—e.g., the Mohammedan heaven—are now seen as thoroughly unworthy and even sordid.

Does religion enrich the emotional life? It is customary to speak of religion as if it were always a consolation to the bereaved and a hope in times of trial and distress. Doubtless it often is so. Let us not forget, however, the great fact that religion is based on fear and promotes it. The fear of the Lord is the beginning of religious wisdom, and, while the Lord is sometimes merciful, he is also a God of Vengeance, visiting the sins of the fathers upon the children to the third and fourth generations. The fires of Hell or other forms of divine punishment are a source of real fear whenever and wherever religion has a powerful grip on people generally. Indeed, when the belief in the Devil or evil gods tends to wane, the belief in a personal god tends to evaporate.

The gods are jealous of human happiness. Schiller has portrayed this in *The Ring of Polycrates,* following the good authority of Herodotus and others. When Jehovah is angry at David, he sends a plague killing seventy thousand innocent Israelites. Indeed, throughout the books of Judges, Samuel, and Kings, we have numerous instances of Jehovah's action being above the moral law. In the Book of Job the question is put directly: "Who is man that he dare pass judgment on God's ways?" God's ways are beyond us and nothing is secure for us.

It is the keen dread of the gods and their wanton interference in human affairs that has made men like Lucretius hail the

Epicurean philosophy with joy as a great emancipation from continual fear.

Many of the supposedly spiritual comforts of religion are meretricious. The great elation which people experience when they "get religion" is often a morally disintegrating force, as all forms of irrational or uncontrolled excitement are likely to be. We can see this effect in the religious orgies of Semitic times, euphemistically referred to as "rejoicing before the Lord." And we have ample records in America of the breakdown of morale as a result of the hysteria engendered by ignorant revivalist preachers, leading at times to sexual frenzies. Nor is this a new note in religion. Among the Mohammedans, where the sex element is rigorously removed from religious ritual, frenzies take the form of dervish dancing, which results in complete loss of self-control. Such organized hysteria is to be found in all religions.

No one can read religious literature without being struck by the abject terror that the notion of sin has aroused in human consciousness. Religious sin is not something that mortal man can avoid. It is a terrible poison which infects the air we breathe and every fiber of our flesh and blood. For our very existence in the flesh is sinful. How can we avoid this body of death and corruption? This is the terrible cry which rings through the ages in the penitential prayers of the Assyro-Babylonians, Buddhists, Hebrews, medieval monks, and Calvinistic preachers.

> Quid sum miser tunc dicturus,
> Quem patronum rogaturus,
> Cum vix iustus sit securus?

Religion has encouraged men to dwell on the torments of Hell and to inflict on themselves diverse spiritual agonies (see *The Spiritual Exercises* of Saint Ignatius Loyola).

Religion breeds terrors of all sorts. Who, for instance, would worry about the appearance of Halley's Comet if pious readers of the Bible did not conclude that this was a warning from heaven and a portent of evil to come? Yet Europe suffered the most agonizing terror, the veriest paroxysm of fear, because of it. This fear strengthened ecclesiastical tyranny and hatred against

355

unbelievers when the pope himself exorcised that distressing sign in the sky.

Consider the terrors which the religious belief in demons and their control of earthly affairs has aroused in the daily lives of simple-minded men and women. We think it cruel to frighten children by threats of the "bogey man"; yet religion has systematically frightened most of mankind through the doctrine of demons, who have the power to make us sin when we do not know it and to torture us at their evil pleasure. What greater terror can there be than the fear of having witchcraft or even a powerful prayer or curse directed against you by some unsuspected enemy? Perhaps the fear of not believing in miracles which seem to us impossible and thus being guilty of mortal heresy is not now widespread. But it is of the essence of religious thought even today that, unless you can get yourself to believe certain inherently improbable propositions, you must abandon all hope. And how can anyone be free from all doubts when opposed views are actively expressed by some of our most respected fellow men?

Consider also the tragedy of enforcing monastic celibacy on young people because their parents promised them to the Church. Or consider, on the other hand, the opposite harms to family life resulting from the Church's opposition to birth control, no matter how rationally indicated by hygiene and common decency. Whatever motivates the Church's opposition, the source of its strength on this point is the old religious taboo against touching the gates of life and death, a taboo which science daily disregards. This taboo shows itself in the prohibition of any form of euthanasia or suicide, no matter how hideous or tortured life becomes. Even supposedly liberal clergymen are ready with unfeeling arrogance to brand as a coward anyone unfortunate enough to find life unbearable. But despite the depth of this religious fear of touching the gates of life and death, we do not or cannot carry it out consistently. We do control the birth rate and the death rate of any community by economic sanitary and political measures. By excluding the Chinese from our own country and confining them to their inadequate lands we force many of them into starvation. The

Church does not condemn this way of controlling the birth or death rate. It does not even condemn the wholesale death-dealing and birth-prevention of war.

While religion has encouraged certain feasts and holidays, it has not been the active friend of that more steady enjoyment of life which comes from developing the industrial and the fine arts. The Old Testament and the Koran, with their prohibition against graven images, have repressed sculpture and representative painting; and the record of the Christian Church for the two thousand years of its existence hardly supports the contention that it has been the mother and patroness of the fine arts. The monasteries, to be sure, developed the art of illuminating manuscripts, and many magnificent structures were erected by bishops and popes like Leo X, who in their personal lives openly flouted the Christian religion. But when did religion or church do anything to nurse the arts and bring them into the homes of the great mass of people? Censorship rather than active encouragement has been the Church's attitude.

In regard to the terrors as well as the superstitions and immoralities of religion, it will not do to urge that they are due only to the imperfections of the men who professed the various religions. If religion cannot restrain evil, it cannot claim effective power for good. In fact, however, the evidence indicates that religion has been effective for evil. It might be urged that certain terrors have likewise been aroused by popular science— e.g., the needless terrors of germs, the absurd and devastating popular theories of diet, etc. But the latter are readily corrigible. Indeed it is the essence of science to correct the errors which it may originate. Religion cannot so readily confess error, and the terrors with which it surrounds the notion of sin are felt with a fatality and an intensity from which science and art are free.

I have spoken of the dark side of religion and have thus implied that there is another side. But if this implication puts me out of the class of those who are unqualified opponents of all that has been called religion, I do not wish to suggest that I am merely an advocate, or that I have any doubts as to the justice of the arguments that I have advanced. Doubtless some of my arguments may turn out to be erroneous, but at present

I hold them all in good faith. I believe that this dark side of religion is a reality, and it is my duty on this occasion to let those who follow me do justice to the other side. But if what I have said has any merit, those who wish to state the bright side of religion must take account of and not ignore the realities which I have tried to indicate. This means that the defense of religion must be stated in a spirit of sober regard for truth, and not as a more or less complacent apology for beliefs which we are determined not to abandon. Anyone can, by assuming his faith to be the truth, argue from it more or less plausibly and entirely to his own satisfaction. But that is seldom illuminating or strengthening. The real case for religion must show compelling reasons why, despite the truths that I have sought to display, men who do not believe in religion should change their views. If this be so, we must reject such apologies for religion as Balfour's *Foundations of Belief*. One who accepts the Anglican Church may regard such a book as a sufficient defense. But in all essentials it is a subtle and urbane, but none the less complacent, begging of all the serious questions in the case. For similar reasons also I think we must reject the apology for religion advanced by my revered and beloved teacher William James.

Let us take up his famous essay on "The Will To Believe." Consider in the first place his argument that science (which is organized reason) is inapplicable in the realm of religion, because to compare values or worths "we must consult not science but what Pascal calls our heart" (p. 22). But if it were true that science and reason have no force in matters of religion, why argue at all? Why all these elaborate reasons in defense of religion? Is it not because the arguments of men like Voltaire and Huxley did have influence that men like De Maistre and James tried to answer them? Who, the latter ask, ever heard of anyone's changing his religion because of an argument? It is not necessary for me to give a list of instances from my own knowledge. Let us admit that few men confess themselves defeated or change their views in the course of any one argument. Does this prove that arguments have no effect? Do not men frequently use against others the very arguments which at first they professed to find unconvincing? The fact is that men do argue about religion, and it is fatuous for those who argue on one side to try also to discredit *all* rational arguments. It seems more like childish weakness to kick against a game or its rules when you are losing in it. And it is to the great credit of the Catholic Church that it has categorically condemned fideism or the effort to eliminate reason from religion. Skepticism against reason is not a real or enduring protection to religion. Its poison, like that of the Nessus shirt, finally destroys the faith that puts it on. Genuine faith in the truth is confident that it can prove itself to universal reason.

Let us look at the matter a little closer.

James argues that questions of belief are decided by our will. Now it is true that one can say: "I do not wish to argue. I want to continue in the belief that I have." But is not the one who says this already conscious of a certain weakness in his faith which might well be the beginning of its disintegration? The man who has a robust faith in his friend does not say, "I want to believe that he is honest," but "I know that he is honest, and any doubt about it is demonstrably false or unreasonable." To be willing to put your case and its evidence before the court of reason is to show real confidence in it.

But James argues that certain things are beloved not on the basis of rational or scientific weighing of evidence, but on the compulsion of our passional nature. This is true. But reflection may ease the passional compulsion. And why not encourage such reflection?

The history of the last few generations has shown that many have lost their faith in Christianity because of reflection induced by Darwinism. Reflection on the inconsistencies of the Mosaic chronology and cosmology has shown that these do not differ from other mythologies; and this has destroyed the belief of many in the plenary inspiration of the Bible. It is therefore always possible to ask: Shall I believe a given religious proposition as the absolute truth, or shall I suspend final decision until I have further evidence? I must go to church or stay out. But I may do the latter at least without hiding from myself the inadequacy of my knowledge or of the evidence. In politics I vote for X or Y without necessarily getting myself into the belief that my act is anything more than a choice of probabilities. I say: Better vote for X than for Y; although if I knew more (for which there is no time) I might vote the other way. In science I choose on the basis of all the available evidence but expressly reserve the possibility that future evidence may make me change my view. It is difficult to make such reservations within any religious system. But it is possible to remain permanently skeptical or agnostic with regard to religion itself and its absolute claims.

The momentous character of the choice in regard to religion may be dissolved by reflection which develops detachment or what James calls lightheartedness. What is the difference between believing in one religion or in another or in none? A realization of the endless variety of religious creeds, of the great diversity of beliefs that different people hold to be essential to our salvation, readily liberates us from the compulsion to believe in every Mullah that comes along or else fear eternal damnation. James draws a sharp distinction between a living and a nonliving issue. To him, I suppose, the question of whether to accept Judaism, Islam, or Buddhism was not a living one. But the question whether to investigate so-called psychical phenomena as proofs of immortality was a living one. But surely reflection may change the situation, and a student of religion may come to feel that James's choice was arbitrary and untenable.

The intensification of the feeling that religious issues are important comes about through the assumption that my eternal salvation depends upon my present choice, or—at most—on what I do during the few moments of my earthly career. There is remarkably little evidence for this assumption. If our life is eternal, we may have had more chances before and we may have more later. Why assume that the whole of an endless life is determined by an infinitesimal part of it? From this point of view, men like Jonathan Edwards, to whom eternal Hell is always present and who makes an intense religious issue out of every bite of food, appears to be just unbalanced, and in need of more play in the sunshine and fresh air and perhaps a little more sleep. I mention Jonathan Edwards because his life and teachings enable us to turn the tables on religion by what James regards as the great pragmatic argument in its favor. Accept it, James says, and you will be better off at once (pp. 25, 26). As most religions condemn forever those who do not follow them, it is as risky to accept any one as none at all. And it is possible to take the view that they are all a little bit ungracious, too intense, and too sure of what in our uncertain life cannot be proved. Let us better leave them all alone and console ourselves with the hypothesis—a not altogether impossible one—that the starry universe and whatever gods there be do not worry about us at all, and will not resent our enjoying whatever humane and enlightened comfort and whatever vision of truth and beauty our world offers us. Let us cultivate our little garden. The pretended certainties of religion do not really offer much more. This is of course not a refutation of religion, or of the necessity which reflective minds find to grapple with it. But it indicates that there may be more wisdom and courage as well as more faith in honest doubt than in most of the creeds.

X

PHILOSOPHIC CURRENTS

42

VISION AND TECHNIQUE IN
PHILOSOPHY

IT IS not without awe that one brought up in Oriental regard
for his masters can venture to address you from a post formerly occupied by his revered teachers, Royce, James, Woodbridge, Sheldon and Adler. What melody can my frail harp
bring forth that is comparable to their rich music? But the kind
suffrage which has elevated me to this position imposes its ob-
ligations. I must speak to you of Divine Philosophy, as she appears to my own poor eyes, even when what I see differs from
what is revealed to those that I revere most highly. And this
has dictated my theme. The subject of vision and technique
not only touches all our common philosophic interests and
brings them into relation with the general intellectual temper
and issues of our age, but also enables me to use my brief moment of authority to sound a warning against what seems to me
an insidious danger to philosophy, a danger which neo-Roman-
ticism and the genius of William James have served to
strengthen. I mean the sharp contrast between vision and technique to the disparagement of the latter. Let me begin with the
last point.

Years ago, when, with boyish ardor for economic science and
zeal for social reform, I first approached the temple of philosophy, its official servitors and priests seemed to me too preoc-

The presidential address to the Eastern division of the American Philosophical Association at New York, December 30, 1929, published in *The
Philosophical Review*, Vol. 39, p. 127 (March 1930).

cupied with ritual or technique and too little with the problem of feeding the multitude at the gate with genuinely sustaining intellectual food. It was therefore with much sympathy that I first heard William James declare that the essence of philosophy is vision, and not technique; that where there is no vision the people perish.

Pride in merely technical competence has always been deadly to further intellectual achievement. A good deal of the unsubstantiality of later Scholasticism was certainly due to the fact that, after it had elaborated a subtle and most useful set of technical distinctions, men felt themselves to be learned by the mere acquisition of this apparatus, by the mere ability to speak in a learned language. The change from Latin to the vernacular revealed this emptiness and forced greater attention to substantial content. But since then new technical vocabularies have been developed in philosophy as in the related fields of popular psychology and sociology, so that exercises in these terminologies often hide the paucity of genuine insight. Let us then not forget, amidst our professional preoccupations, that philosophy is literally and truly a form of love, the love of a certain elevated universal or cosmic knowledge anciently called wisdom. Unless we love this knowledge for its own sake and regard all technique as instrumental for the attainment of the vision of supreme truth, we surely bear the name of philosophers in vain. Unless our toil is above all for the delight which the mere vision of philosophy as the supreme mistress of our mind and devotion brings, we may be paid servants in her household but never her true lovers. Yet the true or devoted lover must also serve, as the institution of chivalry well recognized. To insist on vision without technique has actually and historically proved a perilous half-truth. It needs to be accompanied with the observation that without laborious and thoroughgoing technique neither art nor science nor philosophy can prosper or live worthily. Titanic genius such as William James's may seem to create its own method or technique. But those of us to whom philosophy is not a matter of blind faith in the vision of others, and who cannot assume the perilous responsibility or irresponsibility of the genius or prophet, must view the work of the philosopher, like that of the scientist, as part of humanity's organized search for universally ascertainable truth, a truth that can withstand partisan contention and critical doubt. Whether we view it realistically, idealistically, or pragmatically, truth is more than a private, arbitrary opinion or impression. Not only must the truth of a proposition be tested by its consequences, but its very meaning, if it is universal, is constituted by its implications or logical consequences. Thus the meaning of any of Euclid's axioms, of Newton's laws of motion, or of the rule of respect for personality or property, is constituted by the system of propositions that can be deduced therefrom. The philosophy therefore which seeks to attain truth requires continuous and organized means of penetrating into the hitherto unknown, and definite ways of so consolidating our findings that others engaged in the same task may build upon them. Otherwise each individual begins anew without any hope of aid for himself or prospect of helping others. The orator may impose his vision upon us through his eloquence, the vision of the poet may charm us by the beauty of his magic lines, and the vision of the prophet may stir us to our depths by the awful conviction that "thus saith the Lord." But the vision of the philosopher, like that of the theoretic physicist or biologist, finds its justification in the light it brings to diverse searchers for ascertainable and verifiable truth. Unless, therefore, our philosophic vision receives technical development and is verified in many fields, it may rightly be condemned as unsubstantial and visionary.

Now I am far from denying all value to the vision that runs ahead of verifiable fact. How shall we ever develop and verify hypotheses unless we first entertain them in their unorganized and unverified form? Humanity's safety and natural growth depend upon the adventurous or pioneer mind that can penetrate the dark jungle that surrounds the little clearing that knowledge has conquered in the domain of infinite ignorance. But the pioneers who lose contact with their fellowmen and with the familiar signposts all too often get lost, and those who return are frequently bewildered so that they are not always safe guides to the green fields that they imagine they have discovered. Humanity therefore does well to be critical in following its visionaries. We must examine the ground of proposed new paths care-fully and cautiously. The cosmic vision of romantic philosophers like Schelling must submit to the painfully laborious methods of rigorous mathematical demonstration, experimental methods of counting, measuring, weighing, and the like.

At no time has the need for correcting the aberrations of romantic philosophy been more urgent than today.

We are living in an age which, though aware that it is based on the achievements of technical science, still harbors a strong aversion for laborious technique and a strong predilection for seemingly easy romantic ways of getting rich quick in the arts and in wisdom as well as in purely financial matters. In paint-ing, music, and literature the thorough mastery of one's art is nowadays often reviled as academicism, and in popular science the public demand is certainly for romantic results cut off from the evidence or the technical methods without which they are meaningless. Whether it is because of the impatience of King Demos and the cowardice of his courtiers, who dare not tell him that there is no royal road to knowledge except the steep climb up the Hill of Vision, or whether it is that the rapid staccato rhythm of our mechanical age breaks up our time and makes long-sustained efforts in intellectual work almost impossible, the fact is that there is a noticeable waning of faith in and re-spect for technical competence in philosophy. We need, there-fore, to be reminded that not only the greatest philosophers, Plato, Aristotle, Saint Thomas, Leibniz, Kant, and Hegel, but the men of highest genius in all the arts, Dante, Leonardo da Vinci, Newton, Napoleon, and Beethoven, devoted very pains-taking study to the technique of their respective work. (Even that romantic egotist, Richard Wagner, attests this.) As the technique of painting not only helps the painter to express more adequately what he sees, but also helps him to see more accurately, as without its technical methods the vision of science would be indistinguishable from mythology, so, apart from rigorous technical development, philosophic vision is thin and devoid of substance—either irresponsibly capricious or else a dark night in which all cows are black.

In the bald form in which I have put them, the foregoing remarks doubtless sound trite and commonplace. But philosophy need not fear ancient truth more than novel error. Indeed, the craving for novelty is indicative of low intellectual vitality. Eternal truths bear eternal repetition. And to me, I confess, these rudimentary truths seem peculiarly timely.

When the public at large is urging us, on the authority of our leading representative, Professor Dewey, to abandon the technical problems which occupy philosophers and to go back to the problems of men, it is surely opportune to insist in all seriousness that we shall never help humanity very much by neglecting our own special task, the only task for which we are as philosophers properly trained. It is true, of course, that in science as in the arts technical problems tend to become too complicated, and it is often advisable to retrace our steps and to find a new path through our tangled difficulties. But the value of a new approach is to be tested by whether it enables us to see the old problems in a new light. He who is constantly making new starts never gets anywhere. It is well at times to return to naive experience to make sure that we have not overlooked some important fact. But the myth of Antaeus doubling his strength by contact with the earth does not mean that all progress is a return to the mud whence we have sprung and in which we are still all too deeply sunk. The past has its ineradicable marks in us, and it is vain to try to regain our youth completely by throwing away the experience of the years in favor of some romantic elixir which so often turns out to be a very ancient intoxicant. William James has almost persuaded our present generation that progress in philosophy depends on the easy device of avoiding Kant rather than on the difficult job of going through him. But this advice, flattering to our vanity if not to our indolence, has not brought any noticeable gains to philosophy. Confused as Kant was in some of his pedantically technical preoccupations, we can still gain strength by putting our minds on his problems and thinking his thoughts, even if in the end we may reject his assumptions and conclusions. The more difficult path is the more profitable one.

Vision and Technique in the History of Philosophy

There can be no doubt that the history of philosophy is properly a branch of history, subject to the same tests of scholarship. This means that not only must all references to the views of Aristotle, the Scholastics, Kant, or Hegel, rest on some actual text—something which seems to be going out of fashion today—but our knowledge of the text must be so adequate as to enable us to decide whether certain quotations are or are not truly representative. If anyone refers to Democritus as a merely speculative philosopher, to Galileo as a mere experimentalist, or to Hegel as a psychologic or subjective idealist, we can say that he has not conformed to the requirements of technical history.

Unless we go back to the actual writings of individual philosophers and apprehend them by the principles of interpretation followed in all critical history, we shall continue traditional myths that grow more and more conventional with repetition.

But the philosopher's interest in the history of his subject is *more* than historical. The history of philosophy is for us more than philology or the archeology of ideas. The lives and opinions of philosophers, whether told in the ancient or the modern style, are not a history of philosophy. We want to know the truth of these opinions or ideas. This is indispensable because it is logically involved in the question which of those who have emitted opinions have been real philosophers; and this means that the history of philosophy must involve philosophic vision and technique over and above that which may satisfy the historian of civilization.

This conception makes of the history of philosophy a laboratory of intellectual experiments, where we may learn from past thinkers by observing the results of their experiments.

Though the word "social" is heard all too often in the din of current discussion, few of our pragmatic friends seem to care for this form of intellectual co-operation with those who preceded us in the search for truth. Truth is, in fact, not a highly regarded idea today. It is easier to invent social explanations of what caused the ancient philosophers to hold their opinions, than to determine whether these opinions were true. Professor Dewey's paper at the last congress of philosophy, with its contention that truth is inapplicable to the cultural meaning of philosophy, may be taken as the authoritative expression of this tendency.

But truth cannot be so readily disposed of. For the question whether certain views of Plato, Kant, or Hegel were or were not dictated by certain political situations in Athens or Germany is itself to be answered either truly or falsely.

We smile complacently nowadays at men like Descartes and Spinoza who conceived of philosophy as a search for clear and adequate ideas and thought that they themselves had arrived at truth. I wish to suggest in all seriousness that their claims are better founded than many of the current explanations of the social or political origins of the cosmic views of diverse philosophers. It seems remarkably naïve to assume that all philosophers have been predominantly preoccupied with the social and political condition of their time, rather than with the more permanent conditions of human life and cosmic existence.

Philosophers have generally been men of a speculative turn of mind, and therefore indifferent to many things that absorb the attention of the multitude in their time. And it is for that very reason that they interest us today. Plato speaks to us not because he was interested in the affairs of Athens, but because he was more than an Athenian. His criticism of the Greek democratic method of electing officers by lot was based on little insight into its actual role. But when he speaks on the doctrine of ideas he touches on something which has been a beacon-light to human thought throughout the ages. Aristotle, the most influential of philosophers, seems never to have been concerned about the conquest of the world by his pupil Alexander.

We may, with Professor Dewey, see in Kant's moral theory a reflection of the Prussian regime of the Great Frederick. But may not the influence of the Stoic classics, and Kant's preoccupation with the laws of mathematical physics, afford a more apt explanation? We know that Kant's catholic and many-mansioned mind was not much solicited by contemporary political affairs. The invasion and occupation of his native city by the Russians does not seem to have affected him in any way. He applied to the Russian Empress for promotion in the same way and with the same negative results as he had to the Prussian authorities. Nor is there anything distinctive of his philosophy in his mild and qualified sympathy with the French Revolution or in the restraint which the Prussian Government put for a time on his freedom of publication.

It is true that Hegel late in life gave the Prussian state a high place in his philosophy. But Hegel's formative influences were theology and the classics. The national struggle against Napoleon did not interest him. He put the finishing touches to his unearthly *Phänomenologie* as the Battle of Jena was about to be fought almost at his door. His glorification of the State is probably due more to his study of Aristotle than to any political event of his day. If his dialectic evolutionism dominated the thought of both revolutionists and conservatives of the nineteenth century (and still dominates us), it is because of its intellectual appeal, or, if you will, because it offered a convenient technical terminology.

I do not wish to deny that a knowledge of the history of civilization, like any other knowledge, widens our vision of philosophic truth. But cultural explanations of how certain opinions arose are themselves highly speculative, seldom based on adequate evidence, and cannot in any case enable us to dispense with the often simpler philosophic issue as to the truth of the opinions studied. The technique of the history of civilization cannot replace the technique of philosophy itself. Pericles, Alcibiades, and Demosthenes had definite views which reflected the conditions of their time and influenced the views and conduct of their fellow men. But they do not belong to the history of philosophy as do such men as Parmenides, whose monistic views might have been enunciated ages before or ages after. The life and geographic environment of Thales are really irrelevant to the truth of the mathematical propositions and proofs which he discovered. The same is true of Democritus' theory of atoms, Spinoza's theory of substance, Berkeley's nominalism, or Kant's deduction of the categories. Yet philosophically these issues are of the highest importance.

Those who, in the history of philosophy, would subordinate logic and metaphysics to the study of political and other social conditions generally profess an extremely empiricist philosophy, as do most followers of historicism, geneticism, and evolutionism. But a careful examination of the implications of their position shows them to be logically, if not historically, descended from the panlogistic Hegel, according to whom the philosophy and general culture of any age are but an incarnation or emanation of the absolute, developing according to a necessary logic. It is a philosophy which will not recognize that the actual world contains many things which are irrelevant to each other. Those who profess it have been driven to this position by the fact that actual history is too fragmentary to give us the complete rounded story that popular taste requires. Hence those who begin with professed anti-intellectualism naturally fall into the most extreme and abandoned form of cryptorationalism. A more realistic approach to the problem, however, shows that the most significant factor in determining the path of philosophizing is the fund of available analogies that prove fruitful to diverse minds. Those analogies which by persistent thought become fruitful hypotheses are suggested to philosophers by their own reflection or by the reflections of other intellectual workers. Thus contemporary philosophies find their starting-points in certain ideas of physics, like that of law or causation, or in biologic ideas, like evolution, natural selection, and the like. And this seems always to have gone on. Plato's, Descartes', and Spinoza's views were largely suggested by mathematical studies; and Leibniz's by these and also by his juristic studies. Aristotle's logic seems to have been largely molded by his interest in classificatory zoology. Kant's theoretic philosophy was largely molded by the form of Newton's *Principia*. This means that the history of philosophy should be studied in close connection with that part of the history of civilization which is most relevant to it, namely, the history of science. Philosophy and science not only were originally indistinguishable parts of the same body of learning, but still have in common a devotion to truth and to critical methods of testing the latter by rational evidence. The divorce between the history of philosophy and the history of general science has been most unfortunate for both. The traditional form of the history of philosophy was fixed by Cicero, Diogenes Laertes, and Saint Augustine, until the older Aristotelian view of the history of philosophy, as a gradual evolution of the full truth, was revived and transformed according to an absolute logic by Hegel. Meanwhile our histories of science have been dominated by the superficial philosophy of Voltaire, that the world lived in utter darkness about science until the advent of the prophet Bacon. It is only recently that, thanks to such labors as those of Duhem, we are recovering a saner view of the continuity of the history of science, and are realizing the baselessness of the empiricistic ideology—or rather demonology—according to which theology and speculative philosophy are the two devils that have hindered the growth of science throughout the ages.

In this connection I should like to note the shameful neglect of the study of the interrelation of the history of philosophy and the history of medicine. For ages after Empedocles, Democritus, Hippocrates, and Galen, the physicians were the official custodians of physical philosophy. It is only recently that the terms physicist and physician have become distinct. It is well to remember that the University of Padua, with which are connected the greatest names among the founders of modern science (Copernicus, Vesalius, Galileo, Harvey, and Gilbert), was the university of the Averroist tradition in medicine and philosophy. The logical writings of Zabarella, the colleague of Galileo, show how unjustly the Averroists have been judged. Schelling's romantic philosophy of nature was influenced by the medical system of Dr. John Brown. These ideas of irritability and excitability, of stimulus and response, have molded our modern conception of psychology. The influence of medicine on psychology has continued from the days of Lotze to those of Freud.

I must also in passing call attention to the fact that the romantic philosophy of nature rendered most important services to the growth of natural science, as Oersted's discovery of electromagnetism, von Baer's work in embryology, and Johannes Müller's work on the physiology of the sense-organs amply testify.

374

Due regard for the intimate connection between vision and technique in the history of philosophy will also aid us in disposing of the Philistine assumption that philosophy should deal with the present and let the dead past alone. Both history and philosophy show the impossibility of an absolute separation of the present from the past; and that the more intelligent our apprehension of the present, the more it involves the past. Conversely, a philosophic analysis of the technique of historical method shows that a knowledge of the past is impossible to those who do not understand the present. The whole of history is a logical inference from facts which exist in the present, but are interpreted as remains of the past. Our knowledge of the past is thus a necessary extension of our knowledge of the present.

Vision and Technique in Logic and Metaphysics

Logic and metaphysics form the nucleus of philosophy, and the relation between them is perhaps the best illustration of the relation between technique and vision.

The panlogist identification of logic with metaphysics, of rationality with existence, has always brought forth opposition. This opposition often maintains that logic is a merely technical device either for the manipulation of words, or else for the attainment of mere consistency of thought. In neither case, it is claimed, does it give us truth or deal with reality which is more than words or thought.

It is a characteristic irony of fate that those who object to logic as dealing with mere words make an idol of the word "reality," and generally use it with a sort of emotional afflatus that carries no definite meaning, just as our less sophisticated brethren and sisters use the word "grand." Obviously, however, if the word "reality" is a symbol pointing to something beyond it, so may other words be; and a manipulation of symbols may give us truth to the extent that there is some correspondence between these symbols and the realities to which they point. It would be well if American philosophy could devote more attention to philosophical grammar. For a logical analysis of the categories of language, of the nature and function of communication, can carry us into the heart of metaphysics.

Who can doubt that language is an aid to thought? Do not children learn to think after they have learned to speak? Do not our thoughts grow as we learn to express them? Intelligent discourse can no more be completely divorced from thought and the things thought about than it can be from the action of the organism of which it is the expression.

But language, if it is understood, also involves those to whom it is addressed; and this means a world of thoughts and objects common to the speaker and hearer. Symbols then connect the world of thought with the world of things, and a logic of symbols cannot be removed from the substance of philosophy. It is one of the many profound contributions of Charles S. Peirce to philosophy to have put symbols beside thoughts and things as a fundamental category.

It is, therefore, extremely unfortunate for philosophy that in no field is the divorce between vision and technique as marked as in that field of exact logic in which the use of special symbols is such a great aid. There is an undisguised feeling of superiority with which most philosophers turn away from any exposition that involves quasi-mathematical symbols. They say they are interested in reality, not in artificial language. Yet there can be no doubt that without appropriate symbols many branches of mathematics and physics would not have been developed—for example, Maxwell's electromagnetic theory. If the equations of electromagnetism were written in ordinary non-technical words, they would sound so complicated and would occupy so much space that we could not grasp them as totalities or see the necessary distinctions. Without the proper nets we cannot catch schools of fish, and without proper lenses we cannot see the phases of the planet Venus or the structure of protoplasm. The use of proper symbols has enabled us to come closer to an adequate representation of the actual course of mathematical demonstration, and in this way it has not only facilitated certain mathematical inquiries but enabled us to give a coherent account of the nature of infinity and continuity, so that these ideas are no longer recurrent occasions for gaping awe or intellectual violence.

Symbolic logic helps us to make our assumptions explicit, and our deductions rigorously concatenated. This clarifies the structure of our system, and enables us to see more exactly what it is that we are asserting or believing, and what evidence we have for it.

All this, however, does not deny that symbolic logic is apt to become sterile if it isolates itself completely from the content of philosophy. The very elegance of symbolic expressions, and, at times, a justifiable repugnance to the looseness of ordinary philosophic discourse, prevents us from advancing the subject so as to bring it nearer to the more concrete problems of reason in the sciences. Thus symbolic logic defines a proposition as that which is true or false; but it does not go on to work out any criterion as to what assertions have that property. It is obviously not true that every sentence that has the form of a proposition—e.g., "Jones is wise"—is true or false. The latter is in fact an incomplete statement; so that when one is asked whether it is true or false, the answer might well be: "That depends." That is to say, further qualifications may be necessary to make an assertion true or false.

Let us now consider the second objection, that logic is a mere technical device for securing consistency, and that this is not the same as truth.

This view gains force through the abuse of the word "mere"— the most dangerous word in our language because it is the only one that has a superlative but no comparative. Logic *is* an organon for attaining consistency, but this does not mean that truth and consistency though distinguishable are mutually exclusive. What would truth be or mean if it did not involve consistency? Unconscionable mischief has resulted from the unfortunate controversy between those who believe in the coherence-theory and those who believe in the correspondence-theory of truth. A regard for the actual technique of science shows that both are involved in the attainment of truth about nature. The removal of inconsistencies in our theory or account of any field is a necessary step in, and stimulus to, scientific progress. But there must also be experiential correspondence or identity of logical structure between the elements of our theory and the experimental results to which they point.

This means that mere logical consistency is not sufficient to guarantee existential truth about nature. But this itself is a most illuminating proposition. For it sums up the lesson that belated rationalists have refused to learn from the discovery of the possibility of non-Euclidean geometry, of divers types of algebra other than the traditional one, and of non-Newtonian mechanics. Logical or mathematical proof can never get rid of unproved assumptions, and the truth of these assumptions is not guaranteed by logic—except in the case of propositions whose denial involves self-contradiction, such as: "There are assertions, propositions, things talked about, etc." In every scientific system there are propositions that are presupposed and cannot therefore be refuted within that system, and it seems that all possible logical or systematic truth involves some presupposition of this kind, which we may thus call absolute, *a priori*, or invariant. But, leaving those out of account for the present, we may admit that logical proof of consistency does not prove our results any truer than our unproved assumptions. But while logic cannot then in general prove the truth of our assumptions, it does develop their fuller meaning; and we cannot establish the truth of the meaningless. Thus while modern mathematical or exact logic, as a technique for attaining consistency, has through such a discovery as that of non-Euclidean geometry clipped the wings of the old arrogant rationalism, it has also shown the futility of myopic empiricism and the view that the propositions of pure mathematics are inductions. You cannot by the observation of a few cases prove a rule, unless you have already assumed that these cases are instances of the rule. Psychologically, of course, the consciousness of the universal rule may follow the consciousness of the particulars which assume it. But the psychologic order in which we learn propositions is not the same as the order of logical dependence of the propositions learned, just as the order in which we learn of certain historical events may be different from the order in which they occurred.

Reasoning as a psychologic or temporal event in an individual biography is seldom either deductive or inductive. We seldom start with the right premises to go on in a definite order to the proper conclusion. Often we start with some vague idea of the solution or logical conclusion at which we wish to arrive, and seek for premises to support it. More often still we start somewhere in the middle and fumble backwards and forwards to discover presuppositions and implications. As we do not know our way in the unknown, we seldom reason in straight lines. Our time is for the most part spent in hesitation, false starts, and painful retracing of our steps. It takes time before the proper logical order of axioms and theorems can be discovered in a mathematical system like mechanics. Indeed, it took many centuries before the proper axioms for Euclid's geometry were formulated. The logical order thus discovered is an order of our subject-matter.

If logical order is thus a characteristic of the world studied, logic is a part of metaphysics, and its technique opens our vision in the field of abstract possibility. Natural science, of course, is never satisfied with mere possibility, but seeks those possibilities that can be embodied in verifiable experiments. But natural science can proceed only on the basis of some theory, and this means that mathematics or logic is applied to nature. If proof is applicable in natural science, it is because there are relations of identity which remain invariant throughout natural changes. The rules of logic and mathematics are rules of transformation in a universe where repetition of some sort is possible and where change is thus always relative to something constant.

The metaphysics or world-view involved in logical procedure, especially as applied in the exact sciences, is a vast and promising field of study. It offers a much needed alternative to recent romantic philosophies, like those of James, Bergson, and Croce, which indeed have stirred genuine enthusiasm by trying to be constructive, but have been too impatient or capricious to pay close attention to logical and scientific technique. In vain does this impatience try to justify itself by the view that rational science is a mere practical device devoid of genuine theoretic or philosophic insight. Metaphysical or philosophical

379

vision must doubtless extend beyond rigidly demonstrative science. But serious philosophy must be something more than a poetic image or prophecy. The views of poets and prophets have in fact often proved narrowly one-sided, conflicting, incoherent, and illusory. To introduce order and consistency into our vision, to remove pleasant but illusory plausibilities, to contrast various views with their possible alternatives, and to judge critically all pretended proofs in the light of the rigorous rules of scientific evidence, is the indispensable task of any serious philosophy that can pretend to hold a consistent doctrine. The seed which ripens into vision may be a gift of the gods, but the labor of cultivating it so that it may bear nourishing fruit is the indispensable task of arduous scientific technique. Scientific method, rather than any body of scientific results, lies before us today as the safest road to truth. While results are constantly being corrected, this takes place only in the light of logical rules of evidence. Hence any philosophy that ignores or attempts to belittle this method or technique for attaining truth lives in a fool's paradise, which is proverbially of short duration.

Yet it is not altogether unjustly that *Logicismus,* formalism, and logomachy are terms of reproach in philosophy. Metaphysics is more than logic, even as existence is more than empty form or bare possibility. As an attempted view of the world in which we live, metaphysics cannot well ignore the facts which form the content of the natural sciences. It must deal, as in its vigorous days it always has dealt, with the questions of natural existence, of time and space, of law and cause, of matter and life, of mind and body, of the origin and course of our actual physical world, and of the ultimate fate of life in it. How could philosophy pretend to have anything to say on truth and reality if it ignored these issues?

As the philosopher, however, is not generally trained in all the special sciences, how shall he escape the humiliating ridicule which fate always has in store for those who venture beyond what they know? Can we uncritically rely on authority for the so-called results of science? That would indeed be abandoning philosophy's birthright. For since metaphysical assumptions of some sort are inevitably made by everybody, and since these assumptions are not the sounder when they are not critically examined, it follows that if we passively accept the latest (and perhaps unripe) physical theories, we shall swallow a lot of bad and even obsolete metaphysics. The history of materialism, of phenomenalism, of the various evolutionary theories from Spencer to Bergson, and the popular-scientific writings of physicists turned into metaphysicians such as Professor Eddington—despite the admirable character of the latter's strictly mathematical work—amply illustrate this danger.

A sane and decent regard for our own work demands, therefore, that we be not seduced to abandon it for what may seem the greener fields of our neighbors.

We shall distinguish our work from that of others all the better if we recognize that our fields are bound to overlap in some respects. The physicist like other human beings may be interested in world-views or cosmic pictures; but this is subsidiary to his search for definite hypotheses or laws from which consequences can be deduced that will agree or disagree with experimental results. Thus Newton, like Kepler and even Galileo, was greatly interested in neo-Platonic metaphysics, and copied out many pages of Boehme. But since he was a physicist, every idea had to lead to mathematical computation and experimental verification. Metaphysics, however, is not interested in the discovery or formulation of specific laws of nature or the prediction of specific facts. It is primarily concerned with what Plato and Kant called ideas—i.e., with formulations of those ultimate totalities (or absolutes, if you please) which a changing world can show.

I do not mean to rule out from philosophy those who like myself see insuperable difficulties in any idea of an actual total universe. The world of existence is unfinished in time, and our subjective notions of it must always be fragmentary and inadequate. Despite all of our efforts the diversities of existence are always greater than we can reduce to substantial unity, so that the formal unity of our world is only that of an incompletely reduced plurality. But the idea of an absolute or ultimate totality of existence is necessarily involved, as a limiting concept, in all judgments that anything is incomplete, relative, or conditioned. We must have an ideal of absolute straightness to judge any particular line as a departure from it. If we discriminate between the formally and the materially absolute totality, we need not hesitate to claim absolute knowledge of the former. Indeed, those who assert the impossibility of absolute knowledge must claim their assertion to be true in that very sense. And any rational inquiry into the limits of the knowable is possible only on the basis of certain metaphysical assumptions, such as that there are substantial minds that can introspect their content, that have certain relations to the external world, etc. The recognition therefore of the fragmentary character of our experience and of our factual knowledge does not remove but rather necessitates the metaphysical idea or ideal of a system or world of time and space to which all of our actual experience and knowledge more or less approximates. To seek the ultimate presuppositions and implications is as necessary for metaphysics as is the effort at finality of expression in art, or perfect demonstrability in exact science.

This distinction between the formal and the material, between what Kant called the regulative and the constitutive use of the ideas of reason, is obvious and rudimentary. I venture to put it before you because I believe it helps to put the proper emphasis on the distinctive traits of metaphysical vision and technique. The two poles of metaphysics are (a) the nature of the elements which enter into anything at all, and (b) the nature of the totality of everything. The former gives rise to the problems of ontology, the distinctions between actual and possible existence, unity, totality and plurality, appearance, essence and reality, universality and individuality, etc. The second or cosmologic pole leads to the problems of time and space, the nature of causal laws, life and mind, and to the question whether there is anything beyond merely natural existence. In neither set of problems can we ignore factual content. We need the results of actual experience to support or limit our free speculation. Yet empirical facts or laws can never be conclusively adequate for metaphysics. We need dialectic method. We must cultivate not only the power of pursuing the logical presuppositions and consequences of our assumptions but also the strength to hunt out logical difficulties, antinomies, or paradoxes in our own views. This is our guard against easy but one-sided conceptual impressionism. It compels us to seek greater comprehensiveness and thoroughness.

This essential trait of metaphysical technique shows itself in the attitude, already developed by Aristotle, of taking account of our predecessors and discriminating between the true and the false in their diverse views. It shows itself also in his exhaustive surveys of different possible views that are opposed to each other and thus generate *aporiae* or difficulties. The method of seeking truth by finding the discrimination that will harmonize apparently conflicting views is the essence of the scholastic method of Saint Thomas and of practical good sense. Modern philosophy since Kant has renewed the still older method of Zeno and Plato, of seeking necessary antinomies or contradictions within our views and thus showing their limitations. This has manifested itself in such diverse fields as the paradoxes of the *Mengenlehre,* which have led to Russell's and Whitehead's theory of types, and to Hegel's logic in which contradiction is essential to the meaning and fruitful application of the concepts of the understanding. While the romantic abuse of the distinction between reason and understanding has discredited this view, there is a growing appreciation of the necessary polarity of ideas, that fruitful thought must use opposite categories in every situation to get adequate insight.

Let me illustrate the distinctive traits of metaphysics by three examples.

(1) In physics the idea of causality is only a postulate that there are causal connections in nature to be discovered. It is a one-sided metaphysical dogma to generalize this into the proposition that the world is a machine in which there is no room for chance or contingency. A more adequate dialectical development of the implications of a world in which the principle of causality prevails shows that contingency of facts and of the laws themselves cannot be eliminated.

(2) The primary task of the biologist is to investigate the phenomena of life and to explain them according to general principles. If he goes on to speculate, as he well may, as to

whether life is essential to all existence, or whether the world as a whole can be said to be alive, he clearly enters the realm of metaphysics. If, like Bergson, he tries to explain some specific biologic phenomenon not by specific biologic conditions but by invoking a theory of the nature of life as a whole, we can certainly say that he is confusing metaphysics and natural science to the detriment of both. Similar remarks may be made with regard to the use of the supposed law of evolution by Spencer and others.

(3) The problem of the nature and existence of deity, involving as it does the question whether the world is indifferent or responsive to man's inner striving, is central to any serious attempt at a world-view. Any atheistic or agnostic naturalism that pretends to be more than an arbitrary opinion must face this problem and give adequate consideration to all the issues involved. Yet the neglect of vigorous and appropriate intellectual technique, as well as the difficulty of making disinterested love of truth prevail over intense sectarian loyalties, has brought it about that the results of philosophic discussion on this highest of all themes are now seldom of more than trivial importance. We befuddle the issues with essentially vague and question-begging terms like "religious experience," very much as the old Scottish theological realists elevated questionable dogma into a fundamental intuition of the human mind. Nor can we cover the abject poverty of our results by the venerable use of capital letters, so that a belief in Something is deemed sufficient for a book on the philosophy of religious experience.

Assuredly the philosophy of religion must not ignore the light which recent psychologists and anthropologists, like the older historians, have thrown on the phenomena of religious conduct—though we may wish that some of them, notably J. G. Frazer, had a little more sense of what constitutes evidence for an alleged fact. It is also desirable that the claim of religion to moral value be viewed more critically in the light of the long catalogue of moral evils due to established religion. But in the end a philosophy of religion must involve metaphysics, a theory of mind, the physical world, and the relation between them.

Technically the problem of rational theism is that of combining the notion of personality, borrowed from human analogies, with such unlimited concepts as omniscience, omnipotence, and omnibenevolence. The question whether these concepts are compatible, and in what sense, if any, existence can properly be applied to their combination, is admittedly one which has strained human reason without producing results commanding universal assent. Nevertheless the effort has not been without great service to philosophy. The ideal of a transcendent and holy being serves to limit our intellectual and moral pride. Whether the gods do or do not exist, we certainly lack their power and moral perfection. It is one of the profoundest lessons which the discipline of the great organized religions has brought to the faithful; and even to a purely intellectual view of the world no lesson can be more important.

Vision and Technique in Ethics

Twenty-one years ago, when I read my first paper before this Association, my official critic remarked on the scarcity of ethical topics on our programs. Since then the war, the rapid expansion of what is called social science in our universities, and the powerful influence of Professor Dewey, in whose philosophy the cosmic and the existential are completely subordinated to the human and the moral, have all led to greater emphasis on philosophy as a *Lebensanschauung* instead of a *Weltanschauung*. As I survey our work in this field I am tempted to say that while in the field of logic and metaphysics we are inclined to underestimate the value of sound technique, we are, in the field of ethics, disposed to minimize the importance of free or liberal vision. (Though of course genuine philosophic vision involves its own logical technique.) For moral issues move in an atmosphere that is more highly charged with emotion, and it is more difficult to maintain the detachment which distinguishes philosophic vision from partisan contention. While on the problems of logic and metaphysics the community leaves us free to arrive at any conclusion, this is not equally true of such problems as socialism, birth-control, patriotism, and the like. It is not only difficult to resist the judgment of the public about us as embodied in our daily speech, it is even more difficult to resist the temptation to announce our conclusion before we have had time to consider the complicated evidence for it. Most insidious of all is the danger of subordinating free philo- sophic inquiry to what we regard as the good of mankind. In- deed, distrust of the pursuit of knowledge for its own sake is a part of the moralist tradition from the days of Seneca and Thomas à Kempis to the group of philosophers that I shall for the sake of identification rather than description refer to as the Chicago School. Philosophy according to this view must be dominated by a sense of its social responsibility. Even the physi- cist and the biologist may pursue their work only if they emerge from their laboratories with some results that bear on human destiny. Philosophic ethics then, according to this view, must endeavor to help us to solve the problems that distress man- kind, how to obtain better political representation, better ad- ministration of justice, better milk for babies, and the like.

In a world where narrow selfishness and lack of active good- will are all too frequent, regard for the common good is a bright jewel against a dark background. Moreover, not only is such active good-will admirable in itself, giving a touch of warmth to an otherwise cold world in which the winds of circumstances too often chill our hearts, but we may go further and say that compassion for human suffering is closely allied with spiritual insight. This seems to be the case with the great religious lead- ers, whose insights into the human heart and into the ways of overcoming the miseries that arise from it form the enduring basis of their influence. And here also technique may help vision. Our views as to the nature of knowledge may receive a more definite and richer meaning when applied to the technical problem of education, and theories of social interests or causa- tion may be illumined when applied to the problems of the legal order.

Yet when all this is said, we must admit with the serene Spinoza that passionate pity is a human weakness. The benevo- lent desire to play the part of God or Providence to other mortals is a fruitful source of illusion.

It is well not to lose all sympathy with our fellow men. But it is not well so to identify ourselves with them that we become infected with their passionate confusions and compulsions. He who wishes to preach to those in the market place must see more than the market place. He must go up alone to the mountain to pray, not only to recreate his spirit and learn to articulate his insight, but also to set an example of the wisdom of learning to live alone with one's ideal. Without such ability, society is contemptibly cheap, constituted by a lot of empty ciphers.

The benevolent philosopher is all too apt to be dominated by some narrow or partisan view as to what is good for all men. Too often are those who embark on the sea of moral discovery determined not to go too far from the port whence they start, so that they return only as apologists for what happens to be the established order. And those who call themselves radicals or revolutionists are also dominated by certain catchwords and by a childish eagerness for fashionable novelty, reflected in such words as *advanced, emancipated, forward-looking,* and the like, so that they are prevented from giving their visionary proposals the critical examination which the detached scientist or philosopher gives to a new theory of the atom.

Reflection on human good is not worthy to be called philosophy unless it is scientifically neutral about the various ethical or moral issues—i.e., unless it regards its own thoroughly logical procedure as more important than any of the results of such critical study. Unless we are willing to examine minutely and critically all the logically possible alternatives to the various accepted moral judgments with the same detachment with which the mathematician studies non-Euclidean geometries, the physicist non-Newtonian mechanics, or the biologist new theories of pathology, we are advocates, not genuine philosophers.

Intelligence, we are told, must not become an otiose observer divorced from human problems, and only by its devoted use can the latter be solved. But real intelligence must recognize its own limitations. The philosopher who wants to be a physician to the ills of the body politic should first study most carefully what is within his competence and what is beyond it. Above all he must critically examine and disinfect his instruments, lest he infect others with his own passionate errors. Nothing is so ill-fitting to the philosopher as intellectual arrogance. Intellectual decency should compel us to recognize that our philosophic studies or reflections do not enable us to take the place of the statesman, the administrator, the social worker, or the others who are more conversant with the facts and agonies of social life. But above all it is incumbent on the philosopher to look fearlessly at the inevitable shadows of human existence, the incurable ills such as death, destruction through cosmic forces beyond us, and, above all, the ignorance which despite all possible growth of knowledge will always be characteristic of finite beings.

Nor need this courageous looking into the darkness depress us. On the contrary, it can give us one of the greatest of all goods, peace through understanding. If philosophy cannot help men in the market place to attain the various ends which they so restlessly pursue, it can give them something which may at times be of greater moment. It can teach them to lift their eyes to the heaven above the human scene and in its beauty free themselves from the compulsion of their vain and petty desires.

Too much absorption with human problems is intellectually narrowing and destructive of a certain natural sweetness of life. We need to be liberated from the insatiate preoccupation with improving every shining moment. It is a great help in this direction to see that our present life is but an episode in the history of mankind, and the latter but an insignificant incident in cosmic history. Such wider vision not only diminishes the exaggerated importance which we attach to most of our practical concerns, but is, as an exercise of supreme intellectual energy, a good in itself if anything is good. Human life would be only impoverished if this intrinsic good were minimized. Wisdom is a major part of happiness, as Sophocles said long ago. This brings us to our last point.

The Philosophy of History

In the form of a theodicy or divine plan of human existence the philosophy of history is very ancient; and as a general background for the understanding of the present human scene and its prospects, it is indeed indispensable. Why is it then the most undeveloped branch of philosophy? The answer is that the vision of the old theodicies, the way they conceived the divine plan, was narrow and provincial, so that wider and deeper knowledge of human history has made them obsolete; and those who have rejected all theodicy have not worked out any satisfactory technique for dealing with the fundamental conceptions or ideas of human history. The various so-called scientific theories of history, the geographic, the biologic, the economic, and the like, have all brought some gifts to the understanding for which we may be grateful. But they have all run afoul of the great truth that the facts of history as dated are each unique and unrepeatable, and that the scientific determinism of abstract laws can never exhaust the concrete fullness of the individual thing or event. To try to deduce all history from the laws of climate, Mendelian heredity, or the economic law of supply and demand is an expression of the monistic mania that obviously involves an insensibility to the rich diversity of human life. Nor do we get much aid from the evolutionary philosophy, according to which all peoples must pass through certain stages in their social institutions. If the western slopes of the Andes provide no cattle, the poor Peruvians cannot pass through the pastoral stage despite all the laws of evolution.

Impressed by this difficulty Windelband, Rickert, Münsterberg, and the followers of Dilthey have abandoned all attempt to explain human history in terms of laws, an attempt which they regard as appropriate only to physical science. Historical and cultural events are to be appreciated in terms of a philosophy of value. But if a philosophy of value contains significant propositions or categories, they are applicable to classes of events; and we thus have the metaphysical problem of the relation of the universal to the particular over again. We cannot describe any individual event such as the death of Socrates, the fall of the Roman Empire, the Industrial Revolution, the Dreyfus case, or the World War, except in universal repeatable traits. And our appreciation or evaluation of an historical event must relate to some definite phase of it.

The dilemma between law and individuality is solved practically by critical historians like Maitland, who succeed in giving us concrete vivid pictures based on the painstaking weighing of evidence that is characteristic of science and, of course, involves the assumption of general laws. We must recognize not only that historical causation involves social-psychologic as well as physical factors, but that cultural events have a cumulative character which makes us refer to them often as our social heritage. Careful reflection, at any rate, will show no inconsistency but rather mutual implication between true scientific determinism and the notion of unrealized possibilities in history. If there are causes or conditions *sine qua non,* then it is surely significant to maintain that if certain factors had been absent the actual results of history would have been different. Had Alexander the Great been drowned when crossing the Granicus, his generals, as was later shown, could not have carried on his work. Had the Hasmonean revolt against Syria been suppressed, Judaism might not have survived, and Christianity might have remained unborn. Historians do not like to indulge in such reflections as to what might have been. But to assert the significance of any given event involves the judgment that it is a condition *sine qua non* for what followed, and this means that if it had not taken place subsequent history would have been different.

The logical and metaphysical elaboration of historical possibility, and the evidence for what might have been, restore our sense of the living drama of history, the pathos of its tragic defeats as well as the glory of its triumphs.

The vision of history which sees in it lost opportunities or the frustration of finer possibilities makes it more fit for a free and humane ethics than the evolutionary-progressive view according to which every event makes a step upward and onward for the better. The latter logically leads to an indiscriminate worship of brute power when the latter happens to triumph. Only a vision of history in which the finer possibilities of the past are visible to us can support a liberal ethics.

The ancients put the golden age in the past, and the moderns are inclined to put it in the future. Wise men like Thomas More have placed it nowhere—Utopia. The writing of Utopias is an exercise of visionaries, but a wholesome corrective to those who slavishly worship the brute actual. The writing of *Ouchronias,* of that which never happened but might have happened, such as Renouvier attempted, would similarly liberalize our view of human history, and give the actual greater significance. Recent philosophy has developed a most unfortunate fear of other-worldliness. It is the function of art as the vision of beauty, and of religion as the vision of sublimity, to lift us above the dead actualities to the realization of higher or wider possibilities. Theoretic science and philosophy fulfill the same function, but must take care to do so by rigorous logical technique that shows the actual included in the possible, and the possible as a logical extension of the actual. Logic as the exploration of the field of possibility is thus the life-blood of philosophy, and also that which keeps it from disintegrating into arbitrary opinions.

Philosophical vision or contemplation is a most vital and strenuous intellectual activity, if carried on under the exacting rules of logical technique. It is worthy of our utmost devotion.

43

THE FOUNDER OF PRAGMATISM

LESS THAN THIRTY YEARS AGO William James and Josiah Royce, anxious that their students should have the opportunity of hearing Charles S. Peirce, their master in philosophy, sought to arrange such a meeting. President Eliot, widely known as a courageous champion of academic as well as of other kinds of

Published in *The Nation,* Vol. 135, p. 368 (Oct. 19, 1932), as a review of the first two volumes of the *Collected Papers of Charles S. Peirce,* edited by Charles Hartshorne and Paul Weiss.

freedom, refused to allow Peirce to enter any room of Harvard University, and James and Royce had to hire a private hall. Now Harvard University is, at considerable expense, publishing Peirce's *Collected Papers* in ten magnificent volumes. This contrast between the scorn for the living and the glorification of the dead is not only dramatic but significant.

Those who see history in terms of sex morality, or of some other variant of the motto "Cherchez la femme," may well say that Peirce was excluded because the incidents of his divorce shocked the Mrs. Grundys of his day; and that since then public opinion has changed in this respect. Those who follow the economic interpretation of history may insist that since 1903 American university teachers have become better organized, more conscious of their professional claims, and therefore firmer in their academic demands. In any case we can look upon this splendid edition of Peirce's works as a symbol of the truth that academic America can, like Rome, erect monuments to, and sanctify, those that it has burned—except that New England does not wait centuries thus to atone for its past errors.

There can be no doubt that Peirce's intellectual gifts were to an irreparable extent spurned by the prevailing hostility of his generation. He was endowed with a mind that was extraordinarily subtle, free, and fertile in general ideas, and his training gave him a knowledge of the whole field of science that was unmatched among philosophers in its extent and depth. The son of one of America's greatest mathematicians, and brought up as it were in a laboratory, Charles Peirce himself made noteworthy contributions in diverse fields of science, in logic and mathematics, in photometric astronomy, in geodesy and gravitation, and in experimental psychology as well as philology. Here, indeed, was the ideal teacher for any young, active mind that was ready to receive ideas and to devote life's best energies to developing the wealth of their implications.

But, alas! The very untrammeled nature of Peirce's mind, which made him so valuable in the field of thought, made him intolerable to officials whose demands for practical team work could not brook his essential capriciousness and outright waywardness. For only a few years, at Johns Hopkins, was an academic career opened to him. And there he showed not only an unparalleled power to fructify active minds—Professor Jastrow and the late Mrs. Ladd Franklin have given ample proof of this —but his own thought was clarified by the impulse to coherent intelligibility which good teaching stimulates. Deprived of this needed opportunity and stimulus, he became more and more self-involved, fragmentary, and almost willfully obscure. In his later years he lived entirely as a recluse, shut up in his garret with his rope ladder pulled up after him. His work thus suffered from the absence of intellectual intercourse between him and those who, like Peano, Frege, and Russell, were working in the same field. He thus lost the impulse to check his own fanciful opinions (as, for instance, his spiritual interpretation of ladies' perfumes) and became crabbedly and captiously opinionated about things beyond his knowledge, as in his references to the higher criticism of the Bible and to Claude Bernard. He thus sometimes failed to complete his knowledge on essentials, for example, in regard to Leibniz, who blazed many of the trails along which Peirce and other modern logicians have been proceeding.

It is necessary to keep the foregoing in mind to judge properly the volumes before us. Of the first volume only a negligible fraction was ever prepared for publication by Peirce himself. Following a somewhat questionable policy, the editors have relegated to later volumes Peirce's finished or published papers, which give a more concrete picture of his general philosophy. But even the whole of what Peirce has left us consists only of fragments of a great system along logical lines on which he was working, not continuously, but by fits and starts from diverse angles. Even if he had lived to finish it, it would have been caviar to the general. For he was essentially a pioneer who lived with new and strange ideas; and he wrote for those willing to think for themselves and find out the truth, not for those who wish philosophy ladled out to them. "There are philosophic soup-shops at every corner, thank God!"

Despite, however, the unfinished character of Peirce's philosophy, his many variations and even contradictions, one great principle remained his polestar—and that was the reality of general ideas or universals. In this he was opposed to the general nominalistic tendency of all modern philosophy to believe that only particular things in time and space are real. Repelled by the abuses of later scholastic realism, and on the other hand by the suicidal character of the idea that all general terms are mere sounds or marks devoid of any objective meaning, modern philosophy has for the most part adopted a disguised form of nominalism that is called conceptualism; that is, it has given universals a dubious existence by placing them "in the mind only." But abstract predicates, relations, and laws are asserted not only of the mind but of objects in the natural or physical world. We say *things* remain identical, are equal in length, or change according to the law of multiple proportion. It is therefore irrelevant to the truth or falsity of such objective statements to drag in ideas which exist only in individual minds to which the objective world is "external." If the chemical law of multiple proportion is true, it was true before any human beings came on the scene. Moreover, if there is one thing that Bishop Berkeley *did* prove, it was that the difficulty concerning universals is in no way removed by placing them in the mind. The basic opposition to the conception of universals as real parts or phases of nature comes from the inveterate "practical" or materialistic prejudice in favor of the tangible objects of our sense perception, so that we tend to think of abstract "humanity" or "triangularity" as if it were an additional man or triangle. It is this latter view that is readily refuted by asking: Where is this general man or general triangle that is not anything or anywhere in particular? But the question *where* literally applies only to concrete objects in space. True universals or laws of nature are not additional objects, but the conditions of objects' being what they are. Thought, to be sure, is required to apprehend the universal relations which constitute the meaning of things. But our individual thinking only brings before us, and does not create or determine, the character of the objects thought about. The truths of mathematics and logic, Peirce insists, have to be discovered, and are no more subject to our fiat than are the truths of astronomy. A false inference remains false even if we cannot resist the tendency that makes us wrong.

Peirce's realism has important consequences. Theoretically it leads to the study of the character of objects apart from the psychologic processes that may go on in the individuals who think about these objects. Peirce thus anticipates the science of phenomenology by which Meinong, Husserl, and their disciples have revolutionized German thought in the last two decades. It will, I think, be found that Peirce has more substance and less pedantic machinery than the German movement. Realism also leads Peirce to make significant contributions to the important but neglected problem concerning the nature of significant signs, the basis of any adequate philosophy of language that can be an aid to logic and to social science.

The practical consequence of Peirce's realism is his sharp distinction between what is useful and what is true. The founder of pragmatism insisted that theoretic science can aim only at knowing the truth, and consideration of utility is foreign to it. Anyone who subordinates the pursuit of truth to any other end, even if it be the welfare of others, ceases to be a scientist to that extent—even if it be claimed that he becomes something better. If the physiologist or pathologist, when cutting up an animal, thinks of how many human lives may be thereby prolonged (into happiness or misery), he will be devoting so much less needed attention to the problem before him. The solution of these problems of science depends primarily on critical care and not on philanthropic motives. As a logician Peirce is rightly jealous of the integrity of scientific procedure. He is impressed, as all honest men should be, by the extent to which practical interests corrupt our reasoning power and make us ignore logical consequences in favor of desired conclusions that are in no way justified by their premises. The backward state of philosophy is due to the fact that its devotees "have not been animated by the true scientific Eros," but have been "inflamed with a desire to amend the lives of themselves and others." "Exaggerated regard for morality is unfavorable for scientific progress." For morality, "the folklore of right conduct," is essentially conservative and thus hostile to free inquiry. Morality is necessary for the good life but is not the whole of it.

Excessive preoccupation with what are regarded as matters

of vital importance is the essence of illiberality and leads, according to Peirce, to the American worship of business, which kills disinterested science and makes for barbarism. Peirce's pragmatism asserts that the meaning of an idea is to be found by considering all the *possible* practical consequences that would follow from believing the proposition that embodies it. But the deduction of practical or other consequences is a matter of science. Peirce did not—certainly not in his later years—believe that action was the ultimate end of man. He regarded that view with abhorrence. Science is degraded if turned to potboiling, "whether the pot to be boiled is today's or the hereafter's." Absorption in science has a much higher value. The pursuit of truth like that of beauty gives us the divine spark of blessedness.

Another fundamental idea which distinguished Peirce and set his generation against him was the idea of real chance or radical indeterminism. This is an idea which is rapidly coming into vogue today through the statistical view of nature; but it needs more critical attention than it has as yet received. For the fact that phenomena do not precisely satisfy any known laws does not prove that their course cannot be formulated in more complicated laws. But this is a topic which is only faintly indicated in the two volumes before us. Peirce gave it more thorough attention in some published papers which I have reprinted in the second part of "Chance, Love and Logic," and which will, no doubt, be included in the fifth and sixth volumes of the present edition.

What has Peirce to offer to our present generation? Any attempt at a definitive answer now would be premature. We can only say that men like James and Royce have been nourished by fragments of his philosophy, and that our present generation has caught up with him and is in a better position profitably to develop more of his fruitful ideas. Certainly in the field of exact science, in logic and mathematics, those who, like Russell, have worked along his lines have molded our most advanced thinking.

There is, however, one general observation which the history of philosophy justifies us in making with considerable confidence. Anglo-American philosophy since Locke has, on the whole, been unduly centered about man's psychologic nature and moral duties. Such concentration on human affairs has always made philosophy narrow and illiberal—witness the Roman and later Greek periods. For it impoverishes philosophy to minimize those cosmic interests which have always constituted its life-blood. And our view of the human scene becomes narrow, unillumined, and passionate if we do not rise above its immediate urgency and see it in its cosmic roots and backgrounds. Plato is reputed to have written over the door of his academy: Let none ignorant of geometry enter here; and, later, Spinoza showed the high serenity which comes from bringing to the discussion of human passions the spirit in which the mathematician discusses lines and circles. Recent revolutionary developments in mathematics and physics have stimulated men's imaginations to a remarkable extent, and have invited philosophy to re-enter its neglected domain. To aid in this, no philosopher offers more direct help than does Charles S. Peirce. Though he has been dead for many years, he was in live contact with the forces which have molded modern mathematics and physics; and perhaps the very fact that his ideas are not completely articulated may make them all the more serviceable in the necessary task of reorganizing our general views of the cosmos so as to make them more in harmony with recent experimental discoveries. "Blessed are we if the immolation of our being can weld together the smallest part of the great cosmos of ideas."

It would be unfair to write anything at all about this edition of Peirce's papers without expressing admiration for the work of the editors. Only one who saw the manuscripts in their original chaos can fully appreciate the imaginative labor involved. Doubtless there will be differences of opinion on questions of arrangement, and especially about breaking up the "Grand Logic" which Peirce himself prepared for publication. But no one can fail to be grateful for the thorough and patient intelligence which has made Peirce's work so available.

44

AN ADVENTUROUS PHILOSOPHER

IN THE PRESENT VOLUME Professor Whitehead has given us not only a restatement of his metaphysics (in Book II) but also an application of the latter to the interpretation of history and to the idea of civilization as the embodiment of Truth, Beauty, Adventure, Art, and Peace.

Although Professor Whitehead has come to philosophy after a distinguished career as a mathematical logician, his later writings are motivated more by the interests of a cultivated man and a liberal Christian than by those of a scientist. This volume consequently exhibits greater regard for substance than for form or method. At a time when technical philosophy seems barrenly timid, even at times denying the very possibility of metaphysics, it is refreshing to find one philosopher intellectually daring and adventuresome, showing a benign disregard for the difficulties and pitfalls which have defeated previous heroic efforts. This comes out most clearly in the author's treatment of history.

The effort to grasp the essence of nature and of human history by speculative methods came to grief in the first part of the nineteenth century. And when it was thus suffering from general discredit, philosophy turned to formal epistemology. Undaunted by all this, Professor Whitehead sees that no metaphysics can be complete without a philosophy of history—that

The substance of this paper was published in *The Yale Review,* Vol. 13, p. 173 (Autumn, 1933), as a review of Alfred North Whitehead, *Adventures of Ideas.*

is, without applying ideas to the interpretation of the temporal process of human civilization. Although not avowedly Hegelian, Professor Whitehead's vision is largely the vision of Hegel, modified by the Victorian version of idealistic liberal Christianity made a little more pungent by dashes of Bergson's romantic intuitionism. Without using Hegel's terminology or dialectic method, Whitehead accepts Hegel's view of history as essentially a development of ideas, more especially of progress in freedom. In addition, he also shares the latter's low opinion of abstractions and of purely empirical or unspeculative science.

Whitehead's insistence on the effectiveness of ideas, not only in transforming society but also in conserving our human gains, does not prevent him from recognizing the primacy of the organic and emotional life of which mentality is an outgrowth. He rightly emphasizes the importance of custom and routine and admits that in the end nothing is effective except "massively co-ordinated inheritance." In specific situations he recognizes the controlling influence of geographical and economic factors, such as trade routes, the opening of new continents, and so on. But as a philosopher he is naturally and emphatically interested in the Platonic and Christian idea of the soul, which he thinks is the key to the progress from slavery to freedom and from force to persuasion that has characterized West European history for the last two millennia.

There are certain obvious objections to this thesis, which a more systematic treatment would have tried to meet.

Is the progress from slavery to freedom a historical fact? Our genial author speaks of factory conditions in nineteenth-century England as a form of slavery. Even if we take slavery in the conventional legal sense, the question may well be raised whether there were not proportionately more slaves in the Southern States of this country in the middle of the nineteenth century than in Periclean Athens. In any case, one may well deny that the abolition of slavery can properly be attributed to the Platonic and Christian traditions. The chief disciple of the former explicitly justified slavery, and the greatest of the Apostles preached that servants should obey their masters. The Christian fathers and the great teachers like Saint Thomas did not protest against slavery. For a long time Christianity refused to admit the children of serfs to the priesthood. In fact, the practical enslavement of free land-owners into serfs in Russia and in the rest of Europe came after the introduction of Christianity, and in our Southern States the Methodist Church and other Christian denominations defended slavery as a divine institution until 1865.

Professor Whitehead, in another passage, attributes the liberation of slaves to the Enlightenment of which Voltaire and Rousseau were chief exponents. This does not seem to have been the case in America and the French colonies. These liberal ideas were championed in America in the writings of Jefferson but were refuted, practically, by the invention of the cotton gin. Nor is the statement that "it was democracy that freed the slaves" true either of the United States or of Russia. It was rather the uneconomic character of slavery under modern technological conditions that led to its abolition.

It would be pleasant to believe that we rely today more on persuasion than on force. But is there sufficient evidence to prove that this is so? Possibly we differ from the ancients in the fact that in our modern complex society the exertion of force is much more indirect. But ultimately economic and political force cannot exist without physical force. The present wave of dictatorships in Europe only emphasizes in a brutal way the force with which no government can completely dispense.

There seems no evidence to support Professor Whitehead's contention that Eastern civilization declined through "the stoppage of the growth of persuasive intercourse." In general, it seems rather strange to deduce the specific traits of Western civilization from the Platonic and Christian view of the soul, when the latter is essentially Oriental—that is, Egyptian, Persian, and Semitic.

Professor Whitehead speaks of the sense of unity promoted by Christian ethics. Not only does this unity seem noticeably absent in the world today, but one finds little trace of it in the entire history of the last eighteen centuries. Division among Christians was a notable cause of the triumph of Arabs and Turks in Eastern Europe, Asia, Africa, and Spain. Can we say that there was less sense of human unity before the triumph of the Christian Church in the fourth century A.D.?

The strain of anti-intellectualism running through this book comes to the fore in the statements that "History, devoid of aesthetic prejudice, is a figment of the imagination," and "Mere knowledge is a high abstraction which we should dismiss from our minds." May not the ideal of unprejudiced knowledge be like the idea of perfection which Professor Whitehead so eloquently preaches and which no one supposes to be completely attainable by man on earth? Men have certainly made as much progress in scientific knowledge as in any other virtues.

On the whole, Professor Whitehead seems to me not only to underestimate the importance of science, or accurately tested knowledge, as an influence in the transformation of human life, but also to be most unfortunate in pressing the charge of dogmatism or Alexandrianism against the positive sciences. Individual scientists, of course, may be as dogmatic as individual theologians or metaphysicians. But surely modern physics and biology, with their constant readiness to overthrow old theories and to entertain new hypotheses, can hardly with fairness be called dogmatic or Alexandrian.

In considering the charge that the metaphysical basis of science is inadequate, it is well to remember Professor Whitehead's own admission that "metaphysical knowledge is slight, superficial, and incomplete." As human beings it is surely not wise for us to blind ourselves to the various values of life outside the scope of the exact sciences, but it would be a calamity if these sciences deserted the ideal of accurate and verifiable systematic knowledge for its own sake.

Not being a trained historian, Professor Whitehead naturally commits himself to a number of propositions which careful study will not warrant. It would be an ungracious task to catalogue them, but a few must be mentioned, not only because they are common, but because Professor Whitehead and others build a good deal on those uncertain foundations.

There is no adequate ground for supposing that the Hebrew prophets were interested in speculative ideas or that organized Christianity began among the Galilean peasantry. Although the most influential of Christ's disciples were Galileans, there is no record of any church in Galilee during the first century. One might also question whether the influence of Saint Augustine did in fact prevent Western Europe of the eighth and ninth centuries from being as superstitious as Christian Abyssinia.

Statements about the population of Europe during the Middle Ages are necessarily hazardous, and I do not see how Professor Whitehead can justify his statement (directed against Malthus) that from the age of Charlemagne to the present day there has been a persistent increase in population accompanied by an equally persistent rise in the standard of living. For the seven centuries up to 1492, according to the best evidence, the population of Europe increased only slightly and sporadically, as the food supply increased—a fact which certainly does not refute Malthus.

The statement that Eastern civilization collapsed under the impacts of Tatars and Turks may also be questioned. Persian literature flourished after the Mongol invasion, and the Turks' conquests in Asia Minor and Eastern Europe brought a general prosperity greater than that under the government of Greek princes.

Even more than in his other writings Professor Whitehead here shows that the philosopher absorbed in ideas can have shrewd insights. Businessmen, he says, can anticipate special but not general demands. Lawyers might well learn from him that contract and custom are interdependent and that today "private property is mainly a fiction." Political scientists will do well to remember that the concept of the original contract helped "to dismiss the Stuarts into romance," to found the American republic, and to bring about the American Revolution, though it overestimated the political importance which reason, or rational consideration, at any time actually exerts. Those genuinely interested in social improvement should profit by the reminder that the spirit of adventure is not stimulated but weakened by poverty. Useful, too, is the observation that what is important in politics is not only who governs but whom the government tries to satisfy, and that the class of the latter is relatively restricted if the majority is quiescent. The importance and dangers of the professional spirit are also the objects of comments that are both acute and sound. An instance of brilliant reconstruction of history is seen in what Professor Whitehead says about the rise of agriculture as a form of human prevision. The actual history was probably more gradual, accidental, and prosaic; but what Professor Whitehead says stimulates the imagination.

45

THE NEW PHILOSOPHER'S STONE

Mr. RUSSELL'S VISIT to this country in 1914 did not attract as much attention from the general educated public as did the previous visits of Bergson or Eucken. Yet there can be no questioning the fact that American philosophy is far more indebted to Russell than to either of the more widely known men. Not only have our young neo-realists been dependent upon him for inspiration and substantial arguments, but the center of interests and the prevailing standards of philosophic workmanship have been largely influenced by his work. Certainly no one acquainted with recent philosophic literature will disagree with the judgment of such independent thinkers as Professors Dewey, Adler, Woodbridge, Thorndike, and Bush, who recommended that the Butler medal be conferred upon him "for the most important contribution to philosophy in the last five years." But though Mr. Russell writes with unusual clarity and with a nobility of style that is remarkable, he is not likely

Published in *The New Republic*, Vol. 3, p. 338 (July 31, 1915), as a review of Bertrand Russell, *Our Knowledge of the External World as a Field for Scientific Method in Philosophy*.

ever to become popular. He brings no kindly message to the common man. Most people who ask advice really crave confirmation, and certainly the great majority come to philosophy not to learn new truths, but to find support for such cherished beliefs as those in immortality, progress, and the like. Mr. Russell, however, does not conceive it to be the duty of philosophy to serve merely as an aid to bolster up theologic or other comforting certainties. Scientific philosophy must devote itself entirely to the attainment of demonstrable or verifiable truth. This may sound like a thin platitude. Of course philosophy must seek the truth. Who doubts it? In point of fact, however, the love of truth for its own sake *is* very rare, and perhaps becoming rarer in this hasty utilitarian age. Even if we disregard the unripe and seedless wisdom of those who deny the very existence of truth or the possibility of our being interested in any truth that is not of some practical use, it is certainly a fact that the prevailing tendency today subordinates pure science to its practical application, and philosophic truth to social or spiritual edification. Hence it will come as a shock to many readers to find that Mr. Russell claims for philosophy the right of ethical neutrality. The philosopher ought no more to be called on to justify the ethical or social importance of his propositions than the mathematician or physicist should be called on to justify the ethical importance of equations or atoms. Indeed, astronomy became a true science only when it lost its main human interest by giving up its astrologic pretension to foretell the outcome of human ventures, and restricted itself to such apparently unimportant and neutral facts as that the paths of the planets could be expressed in mathematical relations.

The importance of thus taking the scientific motive seriously is seen in Mr. Russell's attitude to the dominant types of philosophy of today, the classical and the evolutionary. The classical tradition, according to Mr. Russell, has its roots in the Greek unquestioning confidence in the power of deductive reason—due to the triumphs of geometry—and the medieval assumption that the world is an essentially tidy affair. Mr. Russell recognizes the great value of the classical systems of philosophy as aids to the imagination. As claimants of truth they not only

contradict each other but make glib generalizations with regard
to the totality of things that certainly go beyond our limited
stock of verifiable knowledge. At any rate most of these generalizations are as to matters of fact which are or ought to be the
objects of special sciences. The peculiar problems of philosophy
relate to certain more general and abstract issues for which
logic is the organon. (The logic of Mr. Russell is not only
analytic but also synthetic, liberating the imagination as to
what the world *may be,* though refusing "to legislate as to what
the world is"—p. 8.)

The word "evolution" has acquired such a potency that the
mere fact that certain philosophies like those of Spencer or
Bergson use it causes them to be regarded as scientific. But as
a few drops of holy water cannot transform a sinner into a saint,
so a few empirical generalizations and technical terms cannot
transform mythologic pictures of the universe into genuine
science. The scientific spirit, like the spirit of sanctity, can be
acquired only by the arduous methodical discipline. It requires
a chaste self-control in the presence of tempting hypotheses and
alluring generalizations that would ensnare the scientific Ulysses
into a voluptuous rest. Is this true of the evolutionist philosophies, with their easy, sweeping generalizations about the
totality of things based on a few inaccurately reported facts?
If we look closely we can see beneath the scientific cosmetics
the old shrew Theology. Instead of the old Providence, we have
the struggle for existence, the social organism or the *élan vital;*
instead of the far-off divine event we have the goal of progress;
instead of the triumph of the will of God we have the survival
of the fittest, etc.—but the substance is the same: an elaborate
system of apologetics for the powers that be.

Scientific method in philosophy, according to Russell, is not
some esoteric procedure but simply a method of ordinary knowledge rendered as critically careful as possible. We start with
common knowledge, "vague, complex and inexact as it always
is," yet in some sense true; and we advance by analyzing our
question, finding its precise meaning, what kind of answer it
calls for, and trying to construct the required solution from the
available or possible material. Hence readers who take up this

volume expecting to find new, secret, or mystic knowledge with regard to the external world will be disappointed. But the patient reader will be amply rewarded by learning that such concepts as continuity, infinity, and causality need no longer serve as objects of gaping awe or intellectual violence. By the aid of modern mathematics philosophy has solved the infinite as definitely as the general quadratic equation has been solved.

As an ardent worshiper of Mr. Russell's *Principles of Mathematics,* I confess that my faith is sorely tried by those parts of the book which deal with the relation of sense to physics. There seems to me here too much concession to the Kantian psychology, whereas the intellectual or Platonic realism which Mr. Russell rediscovered for the modern world renders the whole epistemologic problem unnecessary. Mr. Russell, however, does not claim finality for his results (except in the arguments concerning continuity and infinity). The method alone is offered as a permanent contribution. Like other scientific contributions, it is in the nature of the case not something brand new but a carrying to a higher point of that which others have done. Thus Mr. Russell's method contains elements of the Platonic dialectic, the Aristotelian method of definition, and the method of presupposition which Kant calls transcendental. The method has been in great part embodied by Mach and Poincaré, and by Mr. Russell's collaborator, Mr. Whitehead, in a wonderful memoir on "The Concepts of the Material Universe." The latter, however, being written in the terse and elegant language of Peanese symbolism, has remained·an inaudible music. Even the mathematical physicists who have most to learn from it have allowed it to remain buried in the Transactions of the Royal Society.

By insisting on the scientific spirit in philosophy Mr. Russell, of course, abandons the problems that have a wider human appeal. The need for some imaginative picture of the universe, some plan or scheme of things entire, seems too fundamental a human need to be ruled out of court. And if scientific knowledge is not adequate, why not rely on faith, intuition, etc.? Here, however, Mr. Russell is at his best. Without pretending to be able to deny that by intuition or mystic experience we may guess or in some way attain insight, he points out that so long as such insight is untested and unsupported it carries no guarantee of its truth. It is most important, however, that we keep the currents of our intellectual life clean and undefiled. Impatience with the painfully slow progress of science, and a too eager desire for immediate visible results, makes philosophy an easy prey to get-rich-quick schemes and other romantic ways of avoiding the laborious and monstrous routine that scientific work involves. But the hunters after the philosopher's stone, after magical formulae to solve the riddles of the universe so that we shall live happy forever afterwards, like the circle-squarers and the purveyors of physical and social panaceas, exhaust themselves in vain. We cannot all win the first prize. It is better, then, to make the great renunciation: that omnipotence and omniscience is not ours. If such renunciation does not seem heroic it at least saves us from being ridiculous.

Mr. Russell's emphasis on the narrower and soluble problems of philosophy does not, of course, mean an insensibility to the more poignant problems of human existence. On the contrary, few men seem to me to have so justly dealt with the problem of conscious personal existence from the modern standpoint. But precisely because of Mr. Russell's belief in the transcendent importance of intellectual honesty, he is so clear-headed in rejecting the petty ointments by which quacks pretend to cure the mortal ills of finitude.

46

PHILOSOPHY IN THE MODERN
CURRICULUM

WHEN THE OPENING of one of our largest western universities was planned in the early nineties, the president decided to dispense with any department of philosophy. Logic was to be taught by the department of mathematics, psychology by the department of physiology, esthetics by the department of art, ethics in part by the department of economics and in part by the divinity school (courses in sociology and philanthropy were not then generally given). The divinity school could also teach metaphysics; and the history of philosophy was to be better taught, as a part of the history of civilization, by the department of history. For a university president not especially trained in philosophy, this suggestion showed rare insight into the modern status of philosophical studies. In a thoroughly departmentalized university, there is really no room for philosophy, any more than there is room for information in general in an alphabetic encyclopedia. Yet our university president's brilliant and economical schemes failed, and he finally found himself compelled to call in a famous eastern philosopher to help him build up what is now a regular and flourishing department of philosophy. Without pressing any inquiry into the exact circumstances of the case, this incident suggests significant reflections.

Philosophy, as is well known, began among the ancient Greeks as the sum of all theoretic knowledge, i.e., as the totality of

Published in *City College Quarterly*, Vol. 17, No. 3, p. 4 (October 1921).

knowledge which satisfies man's wonder or rational curiosity about the world in which he lives. But the progress of science soon demonstrated that such a synthesis of all available knowledge was beyond the limits of any one individual. Very early in the history of philosophy mathematics broke away and set up as an independent field of inquiry. Aristotle, like many of his successors, was a poor mathematician, while Euclid, Archimedes, and Diophantus found plenty of room for the exercise of their genius in purely mathematical inquiries. In some British publications, and in the register of our own college, physics is still referred to as "natural philosophy," and in that most conservative institution, the U. S. Academy at West Point, it is referred to more simply as "philosophy." But the separation really came about in the middle of the seventeenth century, when physics began to use a technical mathematical language, to the great discomfiture of the older philosophers, best represented by Hobbes. The undoubtedly powerful and wonderfully keen mind of the latter could not prevail against the accurate experiments and rigorous mathematical reasoning of men like Boyle and Wallis. Philosophers thereafter avoided these difficult realms and restricted themselves more and more to mental and moral subjects. But the great success of mathematics and physics as independent sciences has led mental philosophy to transform itself into empirical psychology closely modeled on the experimental methods of physics. So, likewise, has the subject matter of moral philosophy been recently parceled out among the modern social sciences of economics, jurisprudence, politics, etc. Students of the physical sciences sometimes laugh at the term "social science," and there can be no doubt that the latter lacks the rigorous knowledge that will enable us to predict the course of phenomena with the accuracy that we can attain in physical matters. Yet, despite the fact that the social sciences are apt to attract minds whose primary interests are philanthropic or practical rather than scientific, their imitation of physics makes them aim at an accuracy and regard for fact rather above the traditional methods of philosophy. One who takes the whole universe as his province cannot be so attentive to individual historic facts—there are too many of them—and he is less likely to resist the strong temptation of broad and sweeping generalizations. It is certainly easier to suspend judgment and wait for fuller returns in a science that is constantly gathering new facts than in a philosophic enterprise that must necessarily either float above the level of facts or else attempt to generalize as to the nature of the whole on the basis of slight familiarity with some special part.

Some have tried to meet the situation by saying that the philosopher need not bother with the details that take up so much of the attention of the specialist. It is sufficient for the philosopher to know the general principles and methods of the various sciences. But modern study has shown the vanity of the pretended knowledge of principles and methods that is not based on intimate knowledge of actual facts and problems. Without the latter, discussion of principles is apt to be just verbal play. Genuine discovery of principles and their meaning is more readily made by those seriously concerned in the analysis of the facts that experience presents. In recent times, the most substantial contributions in the field of general ideas have been made by those who began their studies in some special science. It would certainly be difficult to mention any modern professional philosopher whose contribution in the field of general ideas has been as original and fruitful as those of the philologist Nietzsche, the biologists Darwin and Driesch, the mathematicians Cantor, Frege, and Russell, or the physicists Mach, Poincaré, and Einstein.

This, in brief, is the case against the traditional conception of philosophy as a separate and somewhat superior study. The defenders of the latter may pick flaws in these arguments, but the main trend of evolution is certainly against them. The growth of science and specialization puts the mastery of the essentials of all the sciences as much beyond our reach as is the mastery of the total universe which these sciences study. Those modern philosophers who, like Hegel, Comte, and Spencer, have attempted such complete syntheses have clearly failed in this respect.

There is, however, an argument for the traditional conception of philosophy as a separate discipline, which frankly accepts the above arguments but regards them as inconclusive. It maintains that just because the modern college or university offers the student so many diverse departments of knowledge, it ought also to offer him one department where the effort will be made not indeed to add to the diverse masses of knowledge, but rather to help him to co-ordinate and digest what he has already acquired, as well as to give him some idea of its limitations and a sense of horizons beyond his reach. Without philosophic breadth of view, specialization defeats itself, losing sight of the woods for the trees, or developing a world where everyone is a specialist and no one can understand his neighbor. Granted that a perfect synthesis of all the sciences is beyond the power of any individual, yet the ideal of it is indispensable for everyone who wants to live a rational life. As rational beings we must all form some provisional plan or picture of the world in which we live and of the goal of our human efforts, and this is precisely where philosophy alone can be of direct help. As we cannot stop the enterprise of life until we get absolutely perfect knowledge, we must learn to make the best use of what we have. Surely human wisdom demands that we learn to live, not alone in the light of the perfect, but also in the light of the best attainable. As a result of their social inheritance, of being brought up in a community where certain ideas and attitudes are dominant, most people develop a more or less coherent system of beliefs, which may be called a philosophy of life and which is certainly none the better for being uncritically accepted and remaining generally unconscious or unavowed. The study of philosophy can thus certainly help to make us conscious of the precise meaning of our actual fundamental assumptions and of the responsibilities which they involve.

This argument involves a psychologically true, but logically dangerous, admission, viz., that the actual synthesis of philosophy is not carried on rigidly according to the rigorous canons of science, but is actuated rather by the myth-making faculty and the need to dramatize our picture of the world. There can be no doubt that the great philosophic systems continue to live, not through their forbidding terminology or argumentation, but rather by their appeal to the imagination which they quicken to insight. Nevertheless, to abandon altogether the ideal of a completely scientific synthesis because it is unattainable would be destructive of all that is most valuable and distinctive about philosophy. How does philosophy as the love of wisdom differ from philodoxia or the love of opinion, if not by its unswerving determination to seek the truth by rigorously logical evidence? Who will claim that there is any pressing need for multiplying the number of opinions loose in our modern world or for intensifying the blind devotion with which so many of them are held? What we need is rather the keenest questioning of our first principles, to examine most patiently the evidence for them, and to learn to estimate the precise degree of probability that is rightly due to our cherished conclusions. We all start with the ideas which are the mode in our time, place, group, and station. These ideas become fixed in most of us by repetition and imitation. We become intellectual free men, free from the dead hand of the past and the blind acceptance of the accidental, only through philosophy as the rigorous effort to come to grips with fundamentals and to evaluate their true claims. This can be done only by the most exacting scientific logic, which can never remain satisfied with fragmentary or partial arguments. In our practical activities, we may always have to compromise and choose the best available rather than unattainable perfection. But it is fatal to do so in the inner life of religion, philosophy, or the appreciation of fine art. For to give up our loyalty to the ideal and worship something that is bad, merely because it is attainable, is nothing short of treason to the integrity of our inner life. Even in practical life, the spirit of compromise has its limitations. We may have to vote for the lesser of two evils, but there is surely no gain in failing to see the situation as it is, in fooling ourselves into the belief that the man or measure that does get our vote is the actual embodiment of the ideal. The blighting idolatry of the "practical" may make us wise as to means, but it blinds us as to our ends.

The conception of philosophy which emerges from this discussion is that of a method of integrating our knowledge rather than an addition to its sum. It is humanistic in its sympathies, but must be based on rigorous logic and scientific knowledge. The recognition of the fragmentary character of our knowledge only means that we must learn the scientific virtue of suspending judgment, to live intellectually in the open air, or, if you prefer to call it so, in the desert of doubt. Formerly men looked to philosophy for magical panaceas and elixirs of eternal life. Today we can expect of philosophy only that it should be an antiseptic, disinfecting our minds and our intellectual tools. Philosophy must give up the effort to solve the riddles which baffle the statesman, the economist, and the jurist. The philosopher has indeed had little success in that regard since the cities of southern Italy revolted violently against being ruled by Pythagorean sages. But philosophy has rendered and still renders the greatest service to all men, whatever their specialty, by maintaining the supreme and even unattainable ideals by which our limited achievements should be measured.

Even from a rigidly practical point of view, philosophy does not lose in human worth by thus emphasizing intellectual processes rather than results, for the way in which we believe is actually as important as what we believe. He whom I regard as one of the wisest of men has remarked that "to have doubted one's own first principles is the mark of a civilized man." This does not involve any weakening of the ardor with which we must fight for what we necessarily regard as the true principles. But the experience of such doubt makes us realize that this world has more than one center or point of view and that our opponents must, from their point of view, fight against us. This is the basis, not only of knightly chivalry, but of that virtue which is fundamental to Western or Hellenic civilization—liberal tolerance, or courtesy. It was the Greek, and especially the philosopher Socrates, who taught the world true courtesy, which must be distinguished both from the servility due to absence of vitality and from the insolence due to an untamed vitality. Oriental literature, though full of profound wisdom, is based on a slavish acceptance by the pupil of the authority of the master. Modern polemic literature amply illustrates the weaknesses of intellectual insolence. In the philosophic tradition, which begins with Socrates and finds its expression in the dialogues of Plato, we have the classic expressions of the well-bred courtesy of free men; and I think that in times of bitter strife between classes and nations men will do well to study these philosophic classics.

XI

SCIENCE AND MYTHOLOGY

47

A CLASSIC THAT SURVIVES

THE OTHER DAY our cousin Sam rushed into my room flourishing a handsome volume containing an English translation of Galileo's *Dialogues Concerning Two New Sciences,* and with his usual brusqueness began: "Now look here, answer me outright, is this an accurate translation or not?"

"Well," I said, "I never set up as a great Italian scholar, but so far as I can tell it is substantially accurate. Why are you so excited about it?"

"Because," he answered, "you have for years been bullying me about Galileo and about his *Dialogues* being one of the greatest works of the human mind, and now that I have the book in English I don't want you to wriggle out by throwing the blame on the translators."

"Go ahead and relieve your mind," I said. "Never mind the translators. Have you read the book through?"

"No—but enough of it to indict you for inducing me under false pretenses to part with my hard-earned money and waste my time in addition. Look here! This book pretends to be a series of dialogues, but the speakers are mere puppets. There is as much dramatic interest in it as in a catechism on Euclid."

"Not quite," I said; "but for the peace of the family I grant it."

"Well, then, as to the substance? Does it contain anything

Published in *The New Republic,* Vol. 11, p. 85 (May 19, 1917), as a review of a translation by Henry Crew and Alfonso De Salvio, of Galileo's *Dialogues Concerning Two New Sciences.*

more than a prolix account of what one can more easily find in any high-school book on mechanics?"

"I might take you up," I rejoined, "and point to a number of things—for example, to the solution of the problem of the infinite, a problem that had stumped the mind of man for ages. But that is, after all, a secondary matter. The important thing is that in this book Galileo for the first time laid down the plan and foundation of the science of mechanics and the true method of modern physical science. Your high-school textbook on physics must have dulled and flattened your conception of what a marvelous creation of the human mind physical science is. But because a photograph of Matterhorn, of Niagara, or of the starry sky is not a great work of art, don't jump to the conclusion that there is no grandeur or sublimity in the object represented."

"What you say may be true," Sam retorted, "but I don't see any sublimity in this book. The fellow who invented rolling friction or the art of drawing fire from flint may have been a wonderful genius and a great benefactor of the human race. But I can't see any sublimity in the wheel of a wagon or in the old pieces of flint that they keep in the museum."

"The seeing of the sublime," I tried to explain, "does not depend on the object only. You must also be in the proper position and readiness. Your heart as well as your ear must be attuned to catch the Music of the Spheres. I can only suggest to you to reflect how for ages men were ruled intellectually as well as physically by authority. Like sheep, men followed those who happened to be before them. Even the god-defying Promethean Titans rushed about and lost themselves in vain because they could not find any sure path through the labyrinth of nature's perpetual changes. The Greeks helped to lift man to equality with the gods by discovering geometry, the first body of absolutely certain knowledge capable of infinite development; but almost two thousand years passed before Galileo discovered that nature may be so manipulated that mathematical laws may be applied to it. Thereby he not only increased our power over nature but gave us the gift of vision into the illimitable past and future, far beyond the brief space which marks the petty life of men."

"The trouble with you bookish chaps," Sam exclaimed impatiently, "is that you lack practical sense. What if Galileo *did* overthrow Scholasticism and establish the method of modern science? That happened and was finished three hundred years ago. Why keep on reading and wondering about it forever? Why not wake up to some of the important things going on in the world right now? Are there not new things being produced today, and isn't it likely that some of them are more wonderful —and more important to us—than this work of your wonderful Italian?"

"Most likely," I replied. "But you are mistaken, dear Sam, in thinking that Scholasticism is dead, that Galileo's work is finished. Read the decisions of our highest courts and note how they dispose of the most urgent practical questions of the day by the regular Scholastic method of formal definitions and reliance on the authority of men long dead who could not possibly have known about railroads or modern labor conditions. Note how often the daily papers dispose of questions by invoking the authority of men who could not possibly—"

But by this time Sam's patience was exhausted and with an "Oh, you're hopeless!" he deserted me, leaving me to reflect how futile and childish Galileo's concern with the laws of falling bodies must have appeared to the serious and devout persons of his day, who, like the pragmatists of today, were deeply concerned that philosophy should show immediate practical results.

48

MYTHICAL SCIENCE

THERE IS A TRADITION—which, not having seen in print, I may designate as folk-lore—that at Oxford, Sir James G. Frazer is recognized as the only Cambridge man who can write well. Without wishing to subscribe to any invidious distinction against Bertrand Russell and others, I may, at the outset, testify to the magical quality of Frazer's way of writing. Only some sort of magic can compel one to read through a three-volume book of over sixteen hundred pages from beginning to end, and this too, despite a most thoroughgoing dissent from the fundamental ideas and methods at the basis of all of Frazer's anthropologic work.

Following the procedure of his *The Golden Bough,* a number of passages in the Old Testament are used as pegs on which to hang vast collections of myths, magic rituals, and popular beliefs of "primitive" people, collected from all possible and many impossible sources. Frazer is a born story-teller, and the collocation of biblical themes with primitive superstitions—all done with rather naïve humor—produces most charming results. The treatment of the stories about the patriarchs as if they were actual history produces rather broadly humorous results—e.g., when Jacob is spoken of as squeezing Laban dry as a lemon, and the latter as being as inferior in the gift of gab as in the finer reaches of cunning.

Without meaning to be in the least irreverent, he is certainly

The substance of this paper appeared in *The New Republic,* Vol. 28, p. 51 (1921), as a review of J. G. Frazer, *Studies in Comparative Religion.*

piquantly human in his description of the irascible but kind-
hearted deity who indulges in copious curses to ease his feelings
(when Adam and Eve disobey him) and who waives scruples
over the sin of David's census on the receipt of half a shekel per
human head. The value of a free, even if somewhat uncontrolled, imagination shows itself in the suggestion of how the
story of Samson and Delilah must have been told by the Philis-
tines whom that lady freed from the burly freebooter. But perhaps the best illustration of an imaginative liberation from
traditional ideology is shown when Frazer views the Deutero-
nomic reform and the destruction of the local "high places" as
similar to the destruction of local or village churches to compel
people to go to town. But though a pupil of Robertson Smith
and able to quote many books on the higher criticism, Frazer
is entirely devoid of a critical historical sense. There is no sharp
difference in his mind between actual fact and the content of
popular myths about legendary figures like Moses. Hence, despite the almost unrivaled industry that these three volumes
show, there is rather little light thrown on the Old Testament
or on the life of the people who produced it. Zeal in the collection of facts cannot compensate for the absence of the critical
spirit which is the essence of scientific procedure.

It may seem ungracious, especially after one has derived much
innocent pleasure from the book, to quarrel with the author
on the score of scientific method. Indeed, in the preface, Frazer
explicitly renounces any claim for his general views except as
tentative or provisional hypotheses, pigeonholes in which the
multitude of facts can be temporarily arranged. But despite this
genial prefatory profession of scientific modesty, Frazer cannot
be absolved from the gross intellectual confusion at the basis
of his unhistoric and undiscriminating use of the comparative
method and of the method of interpreting everything as a "survival." The fact that these methods are now almost universally
accepted in our popular social science, and are supported by
the supposed scientific character of the doctrine of social evolution, only serves to make the charm and the imposing bulk of
Frazer's book all the more dangerous.

Despite the fact that degeneration is as much a biologic and historic fact as progress, the belief in the universality of the latter is so fashionable that few dare to doubt the pleasant dogma that there are certain necessary stages through which all people must pass, and that the savage or lower races of today represent the stages through which all civilized or higher peoples must at one time have passed. This belief, like the older popular account of the social contract, has the advantage of enabling us to write history *a priori*. We need not trouble to find the actual facts of the past when our formula can tell us what they must have been. The method of explaining every puzzling social fact as a survival is thus an ingenious device for capitalizing our boundless ignorance of the past and making it an unlimited reservoir of easy explanations.

Those who push this method in the social sciences think themselves scientific because they imagine they are following a method that has triumphed in biology. But apart from the criticism which vague and speculative ideas like evolution have received from modern experimental biologists like Jacques Loeb, there are important differences to be noted. Unlike the social evolutionists, biologists take great pains to make sure of their facts before explaining them. The works of the social evolutionists from Spencer to Frazer are indeed monuments of credulity. Printed reports by globe-trotters, missionaries, trained or untrained observers, are all taken at a hundred percent of their face value. These writers have no use for the undemocratic question as to the competence of the observer or reporter. Some years ago when it was fashionable to write up the East Side of New York, literary gentlemen used to visit our cafés, where we generously fed them the kind of stories they wanted to hear. In this respect we were not unlike the savages who also like to please the traveler looking for striking details and local color. But the resulting books, though pleasant to read, are surely not competent to support scientific generalization. Social facts are more complicated than biologic ones, and their careful observation for scientific purposes demands an even more cautious and elaborate technique. When Frazer, like Spencer and others, generalizes on the basis of myths and practices drawn from different peoples, without knowing the actual history or descent of these myths, his procedure is more absurd than that of a biologist who would generalize from the conduct of animals belonging to different phyla—e.g., the flying of bats, birds, and bees. Comparisons are not significant unless we are comparing facts of the same order; an outer likeness of legends is no guarantee of similar origin.

Frazer is on seemingly firmer ground when he deals not with legends but with laws or practices. Magical ideas as to the harm that might happen to an animal if its milk (or some part of its body) is heated do seem to explain in part the curious importance attached to one of the original Ten Commandments, viz., not to seethe a kid in the milk of its mother. But the subsequent development of this rule and its elaboration by the Talmudists into the dietary code and kitchen ritual which governs the orthodox Hebrews to this day completely escapes Frazer. For here we are on historic ground and the actual development of this ancient taboo illustrates the inadequacy of the method of "survival." Indeed, no institution is really explained by the mere fact that it is a survival. There is always something in the present which makes some old practices continue while others disappear. What determines the difference is a question of historical fact, and not of *a priori* assumption.

It is curious that Frazer like other amateur psychologists dealing with the oddities of human conduct should fall into the naïve rationalism of the assumption that all the queer things we do, we do because they were formerly deemed useful. This really amounts to the assumption that man is originally a rational or economic creature. But the facts of history clearly indicate that as far back as we can go we always find man just as full of irrational and inexplicable quips as are the most civilized races today. Rationality or economic action comes, when it comes at all, not at the beginning of human history but as the end of a process of eliminating primordially wasteful and meaningless motions. The lapse into the naïve rationalism of our popular theories of magic is all the more curious in Frazer because his teacher Robertson Smith long ago pointed out the priority of ritual or conduct over myth and belief. The aversion for boiled milk may be older than certain beliefs in magic; and belief in magic may have as little to do with the Bantu's aversion for the use of water as is the case with many children and vagrant adults in our own midst. So also the wearing of bells by the priest, to which Frazer devotes so much alluring erudition, may be much earlier than the belief that he would die if he did not. Must we suppose that every farmer puts a bell on his cow in order to frighten off evil spirits? I once heard two very learned modern scholars explain the stamping and shuffling of feet at unpopular lectures as a survival of sympathetic magic. But a little reflection might have recalled to their attention that at German university lectures the stamping of feet is a sign of approval.

Besides displaying on a large scale the frailties of our popular evolutionary social science, Frazer's book illustrates the oft-overlooked difference between imagination and insight. Frazer's type of imagination is the one that he himself glorifies as poetic fancy "without which no one can enter the heart of the people." "A frigid rationalist will knock in vain at the magic rose-wreathed portals of fairy-land." But the simple fact is that the scientific understanding of the nature of fairy-tales actually comes not from the poetic fancy of credulous children but from rationally trained minds, and that here we have the cause of the barrenness of Frazer's work. This conclusion imposes itself all the more when we compare Frazer with men like Maitland or Robertson Smith who use their imagination on the fragmentary material of history to open up for us new vistas on the life of the past. The latter are able to reconstruct the life of the past in its concrete fullness, only because their realistic imagination is supported by the critical sifting and checking up of evidence. It is only the abstract or lazy imagination that is repelled by the laborious methods of science. The imagination which is creative of insight finds in these methods indispensable nourishment and sorely needed support against irresponsible vagaries.

49

DOGMATISM IN THE NAME
OF SCIENCE

PROFESSOR CURTIS'S BOOK unintentionally indicates why scientists do not, as a rule, go in for writing on the larger bearings of science for human life. The developed sciences are precisely those that, like physics, chemistry, and biology, deal with the simpler aspects of the world; and as it requires the major part of a man's intellectual energy to master his own special field, the cautious scientist realizes that he cannot give to the larger and more complicated problems of human life as a whole the same thorough and conscientious work which he devotes to the relatively simpler technical problems that are his specialty. Under the circumstances, two types venture to deal with science as a whole. On the one hand there are a few philosophers like Santayana who are profoundly conscious of the limitations of their knowledge, but realize that life is an adventure with uncertainties which cannot be halted until certain scientific knowledge is available. On the other hand there are a larger number who, though they may exercise scientific caution in their own field, have no hesitation in swallowing quite uncritically that which they gather at second hand to be the teaching of science as a whole. It is one of the ironies of fate that men are never so certain about the things which they have investigated for themselves as about the things which they have accepted on the authority of others. In the process of retailing

Published in *The New Republic*, Vol. 32, p. 255 (November 1, 1922), as a review of W. G. Curtis, *Science and Human Affairs*.

the investigations of others all the qualifications and doubts that distinguish critical science from hearsay knowledge tend to drop out.

Of the three parts of Professor Curtis's book the middle one is the only one that falls within the author's special competence, viz., zoology. Here we have a fairly clear statement of some of the principal problems of modern biology—perhaps most satisfactory on the problem of heredity. But the reader will be quite misled if he takes the author's word for it that universal evolution is an undisputed fact. It certainly is not a fact of direct observation but rather a highly speculative theory. Moreover, apart from the rejection of the Biblical myths as a pretended scientific cosmology, "evolution" is too vague and meaningless a term to be of any use in scientific experimental biology. Leading experimenters like Jacques Loeb have not hesitated to say so, but the great majority are afraid to say this for fear of lending support to fanatical ignoramuses like Bryan, McCann, and Company. But this is a great mistake. Science has much less to fear from external dangers like hostile legislation than from the internal danger of abating the enunciation of truth by considerations of public policy or expediency. It is precisely because Darwin ignored questions of expediency and stated his case with transparent honesty, indicating fully the available evidence against as well as that in favor of his thesis, that he was able to impress the public as well as advance biologic science.

In the other two parts of the book, devoted respectively to the history and to the present significance of science, the author's complacent dogmatism is not mitigated by first-hand knowledge. One who compiles any history on the basis of secondary sources will, of course, fall into errors from which reference to primary sources might have saved him. What is worse, however, is that he will accept and retail as fact that which is but questionable interpretation. Thus Professor Curtis, following his guides, Draper and A. D. White, most complacently repeats the assertion that the principle of authority, and especially theology and Scholasticism, have been the great hindrances to scientific development. Now there can be no doubt that many theologians have been hostile to science; and no enlightened person can withhold from Draper, White, and the other continuators of the Voltairean tradition the high praise due to those who have delivered telling blows in the interests of toleration and freedom of thought—great goods which we are apt to lose if we do not continually fight for them. But a sober examination of the historical facts shows that the extent to which the Church has actually hindered scientific activity has been grossly exaggerated. Numerous and atrocious have been the persecutions for theological, as for political, heresy. But so far as I know, the proposition that the earth revolves about the sun is the only proposition of modern science officially or semi-officially condemned by the authority of the Church, and on this the latter has had to yield and withdraw. (Of course individual theologians have raved at different doctrines of modern science, but so have statesmen, literary critics, and patriotic citizens generally—and with equal futility.) On the other hand, Professor Curtis himself admits that the Church made possible the return of scientific thinking (p. 49) and that the modern universities arose in intimate union with the scholarly activity of the Church, following the general revival of Western Europe. Despite his main thesis that the decline of science was due to the Church and theology (pp. 4, 48) we learn incidentally that the decline of science was *not* due to the prohibitions of theologians, but to general intellectual backwardness (p. 46). The latter is much nearer the actuality. Science, like a plant, may be hindered by external obstructions, but the main fact is the positive energy within it and the general intellectual life in which it has its roots. Where a vigorous intellectual curiosity or desire for truth exists, prohibitions against its satisfaction will generally be overcome. We need not, therefore, be surprised that periods of vigorous development in theology are also periods of great creative activity in science—witness the thirteenth, sixteenth, and seventeenth centuries.

When we come to the third part, dealing with the general significance of science, Professor Curtis's account suffers not only from the absence of any special knowledge or humility in regard to the complexity of the social problems to which science is to be applied, but even more by the failure to ask what it is that distinguishes science from ordinary human thought. Science, we are told, is but the application of reason to natural phenomena, and that is precisely what everyone does who carries on his business carefully. But, if this is so, may not a lawyer, or a critical historian like Thucydides, who examines his evidence with critical care, be much more representative of the scientific spirit than an uncritical zoologist?

To enumerate all the questionable assertions on philosophy, psychology, economics, etc., which Professor Curtis accepts as unquestionable truth, would be to give a list of nearly all the superficial commonplaces which pass as axioms in our popular intellectual milieu. Comment on a few of them, however, may not be out of place. Thus to the confident assertion that the economic problem is no longer how to produce goods but how to distribute them (p. 265), it may be remarked that the problem how to produce economic goods without deadening human life is precisely the economic problem that natural science has not yet solved. To Professor Curtis the social good is identical with open-mindedness, and the latter means the acceptance of the *new*. But it seems never to occur to him that skepticism may be a good thing not only when applied to established tradition but also when applied to unbaked remedies for intellectual or social difficulties. Indeed, despite his constant glorification of skepticism, Professor Curtis does not hesitate to accept the fashionable American will-to-believe attitude in condemning *moral* skepticism and in telling us that in the issue between mechanism and vitalism we should prefer the latter for moral reasons. Perhaps even more significant is the way the thin truism that "things change" is made the basis of an attack on legalism as the adherence to precedents—ignoring all the time the fact that the law must serve not only new needs but the old needs as well. Would not the ignoring of all precedents be the same as the scientists' ignoring of all past observations? The fashionable and complacent use of the shibboleth "dynamic and not static" should not blind us to the existence of relatively permanent human interests.

To refuse acceptance to a zoologist's unproved assertion that the actual teachings of Jesus were not theological (p. 43), that the external world is the creation of the mind (p. 230), or that democracy is necessarily friendly to science (p. 287), does not involve a rejection or distrust of science. But the reflections here adduced may help us to see that the study of any one science, and even the enthusiastic preaching of universal skepticism, will not necessarily guard us against unwarranted dogmatism. The career of the great Descartes shows how futile is the exhortation to universal doubt, since our prejudices are precisely the "clear ideas" which it never occurs to us to question. Effective skepticism is the result, not the beginning, of organized and cumulative knowledge. The heights of science are, of course, free and accessible to all, but only at the price of an arduous toil that few at present can afford. Hence not only the multitude but even teachers of science are ready to believe uncritically in the name of science if not in the name of theology. Indeed, if we relied solely on the facts of our direct personal experience only an infinitesimal part of science would be open to us for direct verification. But while we cannot effectively question all things and must rely on the reports of others, it is a good thing to hold that nothing is above question. This means intellectual tolerance for those who reject our fundamental beliefs, even while we hold on, as we must, to that which we deem good, as the necessary zest of life. Something like this, to be sure, was said long ago by a theologically-minded Jew of Tarsus. But, despite the invaluable progress of science, life is still somewhat of an adventure and not yet altogether a demonstrable theorem.

50

THE OPEN MIND

THOSE who genuinely value the freedom of the human mind will always speak with respect of the great rationalists of the eighteenth century. It is they who broke the back of ecclesiastical and political restraints on science and renewed the old faith in the dignity and brotherhood of man. But we cannot withhold a smile at their naïve faith that the Age of Reason was actually at hand when they merely replaced the old dogmas with new ones. The most noteworthy of the new dogmas was the belief that the whole universe is a mechanical contrivance in which nothing can happen except in absolute accordance with the eternal and unalterable laws of mechanics. It was indeed a most useful dogma, for it helped to banish the open belief in magic and witchcraft and in antiquated moral codes based on the authority of miracles. But the social utility of a belief is not the same as its physical proof, however much we are inclined in our weaker moments to blur over the distinction.

There are enlightened brethren who will at once jump at this and exclaim: "Who is this obscurantist that dares cast doubt on the reign of law which modern science has so clearly proved?" Peace, brethren! Which modern science has proved, or can prove, the impossibility of chance happenings in this world of ours? There is not a single law of nature that can be verified with absolute accuracy, for the simple reason that we have no instruments that can measure with absolute precision. Ask a

Published in *The New Republic*, Vol. 13, p. 191 (December 15, 1917), as a review of Emile Boutroux, *The Contingency of the Laws of Nature*.

chemist whether he ever gets exactly twice as much hydrogen as oxygen from the decomposition of water, or in fact whether he ever gets exactly the same result repeating itself, and he will tell you: "Well, no—but the variations are so small that they may be neglected for practical purposes." Observe that chance variations which may be neglected for practical purposes are not proved to be nonexistent. Of course, you meet the scientist who will tell you: "The chance variations are all due to us. The object in itself never varies its conformity to law." But this is a respectable philosophic belief, not a scientific demonstration; for when you press your scientific friend, he knows little of the *object in itself* apart from his measurements of it. On the other hand, you will meet with scientists of the titanic breed who frankly speak of scientific truths in terms of greater or less probability or as statistical averages. You may, if you like it, believe that every particle of matter attracts every other particle precisely as the products of the masses and inversely as the square of the distance between them. But careful scientists like Poynting and J. J. Thomson will warn you that none of our evidence rules out the possibility that on some kinds of matter the attraction is greater and on some less. All we know definitely is that when we take the enormous masses represented in the planets the average conforms to our law. If in the whole world the number of men and women were equal, it would not follow that they were equally distributed in every family. Science therefore has not disproved the existence of absolute or spontaneous chance. The most original of our American scientific thinkers, Charles S. Peirce, boldly defended the priority of chance and regarded law as a sort of general habit which things have accidentally acquired. Boltzmann, one of the leading physicists of the last century, made it the principal business of his long scientific career to suggest that the presence of regularity in the world was due to the fact that as the world-mixture was being thoroughly shaken up, the various elements were approaching a more uniform distribution; but that this did not preclude the remote probability of the world process reversing itself (water starting to run uphill, etc.), and of the whole world order in which we live returning to the chaos and night whence it sprung. If you think this is altogether too fanciful, study the Brownian movements and you will see something like it under the microscope. In brief, the account which science keeps of the world is not yet closed. You may, if you like, jump to the conclusion that the total universe is an eternal machine that never wears out. But you have no more right to do so than the one who thinks that it is like a tree that grows or dies by imperceptible degrees.

None of this, of course, disturbs the genuine natural scientist. Approximate or probable truths are good enough for him. The philosopher, however, is as a rule not content to live in an unfinished world. There must be no open windows or draughty cracks to disturb his cozy reflections, and he will not tolerate the thought that the world is not a docile pupil incapable of turning up anything contrary to the rules laid down for it. But as philosophy has never entirely ceased to be the auxiliary of theology, it has always felt called upon to invent some device whereby a supernatural influence may enter an eternally closed system of nature. Many systems of philosophy may thus be characterized as elaborate devices whereby a *deus ex machina* may be freely introduced into a closed, airtight temple.

It is curious to note that France, which produced in Laplace the archpriest of the closed view of the world, produced in Cournot and Boutroux the two foremost opponents of this view. While Cournot, like our own Peirce, assumed this position simply out of logical or purely intellectual motives, Boutroux does so clearly in the interest of humanistic and thinly veiled theologic ones. Like Bergson and other French writers, Boutroux relies more on the piling up of suggestions than on the close concatenation of arguments. This rhetorical method of exposition allows a good deal of appeal to such edifying but unilluminating distinctions as that between the "higher" and the "lower," and in general to doctrines which are plausible and widely accepted but not accurate or readily demonstrable. Nevertheless this book does abound in shrewd insights and in keen criticisms of the half-baked monistic philosophy which underlies current popular science.

As an antidote to current deterministic mythology, such as

the economic determinism of Marx or the psychologic determinism of Freud, the reading of this book may be highly recommended. But the critically-minded will not be satisfied with M. Boutroux's account of the part that necessary law does play in the natural world. His systematic disparagement of logical, mathematical, and physical law does not do full justice to these elements of exact science. The world may not be in all respects subject to fixed law; and what exists may be more than what is necessary. But necessity is, after all, a genuine part of the world stream.

XII

EPILOGUE

51

THE FUTURE OF AMERICAN
LIBERALISM

I

To affirm a faith in liberalism may seem quixotic at a time
when the word "liberalism" is commonly associated either
with an outmoded individualistic theory of economics or with
a political trend that shuns clear thinking and seems to offer
a special haven to those mushy-minded persons who, rather than
make a definite choice between Heaven and Hell, cheerfully
hope to combine the best features of each. But liberalism and
liberal civilization may be conceived more generously. For my
part I prefer to think of the liberal temper as, above all, a faith
in enlightenment, a faith in a process rather than in a set of
doctrines, a faith instilled with pride in the achievements of the
human mind, and yet colored with a deep humility before the
vision of a world so much larger than our human hopes and
thoughts. If there are those who have no use for the word
"faith" they may fairly define liberalism as a rationalism that
is rational enough to envisage the limitations of mere reasoning.

Liberalism is too often misconceived as a new set of dogmas
taught by a newer and better set of priests called "liberals."
Liberalism is an attitude rather than a set of dogmas—an attitude that insists upon questioning all plausible and self-evident
propositions, seeking not to reject them but to find out what
evidence there is to support them rather than their possible
alternatives. This open eye for possible alternatives which need
to be scrutinized before we can determine which is the best

grounded is profoundly disconcerting to all conservatives and to almost all revolutionaries. Conservatism clings to what has been established, fearing that, once we begin to question the beliefs that we have inherited, all the values of life will be destroyed. The revolutionary, impressed with the evil of the existing order or disorder, is prone to put his faith in some mighty-sounding principle without regard for the complications, compromises, dangers, and hardships that will be involved in the adjustment of this principle to other worthy principles. Revolutionaries and reactionaries alike are irritated and perhaps inwardly humiliated by the humane temper of liberalism, which reveals by contrast the common inhumanity of both violent parties to the social struggle. Liberalism, on the other hand, regards life as an adventure in which we must take risks in new situations, in which there is no guarantee that the new will always be the good or the true, in which progress is a precarious achievement rather than an inevitability.

The fanatic clings to his one principle and in its defense is ready to shut the gates of mercy on mankind, precisely because he cannot see any alternative to it except utter chaos or iniquity. Rational reflection, however, opens our minds to other possibilities. It enables us to see that most of the "yes or no" questions on which political debate centers at any given time involve false alternatives and unduly narrow assumptions that unnecessarily limit the scope of possible solutions. Thus the liberal, while generally provoking the hostility of both sides in any current dispute, sometimes develops a solution which shows that the dispute was a mistake. How many issues have arisen in our own generation which were supposed to be so critical that a wrong response would condemn us to unending suffering and a correct response would bring us a heaven on earth! And how often these issues have been resolved or forgotten without bringing the blessings or the tragedies that were anticipated by both parties to the dispute!

Liberalism has been viewed historically as that philosophy which regards the exercise of human energy as in itself a good, which becomes evil only when it becomes self-defeating. It is opposed to the view that regards the natural desires of the flesh as inherently evil and justified only under certain restricted and properly sanctioned conditions. Liberalism is thus a reaction against all views which favor repression or which regard the denial of natural desires as in itself a good.

Liberalism so conceived is concerned with the liberation of the mind from the restraints of authoritarianism and fanaticism. As opposed to the policies of fear and suppression, based on the principle that nature is sin and intellect the devil, the aim of liberalism is to liberate the energies of human nature by the free and fearless use of reason. Liberalism disregards rules and dogmas that hinder the freedom of scientific inquiry and the questioning of all accepted truths. Prophets, priestly hierarchies, sacred books, and sanctified traditions must submit their claims to the court of human reason and experience. In this way mankind wins freedom from superstitious fears, such as that of magic or witchcraft, and from arbitrary and cruel restraints on human happiness. Liberalism in general thus means the opening up of opportunities in all fields of human endeavor, together with an emphasis on the value of deliberative rather than arbitrary forces in the governance of practical affairs.

It is characteristic of the liberal temper that it combines generosity towards ideas with a sense of discrimination. To be generous towards all ideas is an attitude possible only for barbarians to whom few ideas are revealed. At the opposite extreme of intolerance lies the realm of the fanatic to whom all that lies outside a single doctrine is false. Those of us who are not of the Moslem faith can afford to smile at the narrowness of the Mohammedan who observed that it is unnecessary to read current literature because either all the ideas contained therein are already contained in the Koran, in which case the new books are superfluous; or they are not contained in the Koran, in which case they must be false. But most of us are not so sensitive in detecting the absurdity of our own fanaticisms.

Ultimately civilization, like life in general, involves a balance between the expansive or centrifugal forces which make for diversity and adventure, and the constraining or centripetal forces which make for organization and safety. Life, in point of fact, is impossible without both of these forces. Without the expansive forces we should not be able to adjust ourselves to an ever changing environment. But without the restraining forces which originate from fear we should rush headlong into ruin. Human impulses going in diverse directions would disintegrate life. Nor can we afford to forget that animal drives lead not only to the preservation of life but also to inevitable death.

The life of civilization, like the life of each organism, oscillates between opposite extremes. The law of life is not a law of constant and inevitable progress but rather a law of rhythm, of growth and decay, of anabolism and katabolism. At certain points in world history liberal civilization has flowered: in shifting parts of Western Europe and America since the Renaissance, in China in the age of Confucius, in Egypt in the Alexandrian period, in India in the period of the rise of Buddhism, and again in the period of Akbar and the Mongol Emperors, but above all, and most brilliantly, in Greece during the age of Pericles. But these periods are, typically, preceded and superseded by ages of immobility or retrogression. One may find in the life of the race an analogy to the change of seasons. Liberalism is the springtime, and our hopes flower when sunshine and warm rains fructify the soil, but the Olympian gods of the sky and clouds come after the chthonic or underground deities and they are in turn followed or overthrown by Dionysius or Pan, the source of panic. To discover the calendar or formula that governs human history is a task to which scientists, philosophers, prophets, and poets have devoted much high aspiration and generous effort. I have no ambition to compete with such a prophet as Spengler, who not only is certain that the civilization of the West is doomed but has figured out the exact date of its destruction. My purpose is less subjective and more limited; in pursuing it, therefore, one can be a little more attentive to evidence. In seeking to trace the course of liberalism in America it is possible to isolate a few of the basic characteristics of the civilization that has flourished in this country since the days of George Washington, and to note the ways in which changing years have strengthened or weakened our traditional faith.

II

One may well contend that there was nothing remarkably liberal in seventeenth-century America when Governor Berkeley of our largest colony thanked God that there were no printing presses or public schools in his domain. Nor would it appear that the Puritan North with its theological narrowness and intolerance offered much that could genuinely be called liberal. Yet the seeds of liberalism were there, first in the custom of choosing local officials by ballot. Then also in religious life the laymen naturally began to play a larger role in determining church policies. There was also, even in the stern Calvinism, a liberal element in so far as it cut the ground from under all ideas of aristocracy or snobbery by reducing all human beings to the same level. The Puritan who said when he saw a man led to the gallows, "There, but for the grace of God, go I," had in him the most fruitful source of the democratic spirit, which regards externals of rank and the like as of no inherent importance. Moreover, even in the seventeenth century, men like Roger Williams began to lay down explicitly one of the principles that we now regard as essential for any true liberalism, namely, the separation of Church and State. This religious liberalism became a dominant note in American life with the deism of the eighteenth century. And though the various Evangelical movements have brought at times a reaction against this, the ideas of tolerance developed by Locke have remained dominant.

What are the fundamental characteristics of American civilization as the Founders of our Republic conceived it? The first essential point, I think, is the view that people have a right to govern themselves, to change their form of government by a revolution and to establish their independence—what we call today the right of self-determination. The old idea was that government rested on divine authority and that all resistance to it was sinful. The Colonists asserted the rights of man as opposed to the rights of kings, insisting that the just powers of any government rest ultimately on the consent of the gov-

441

erned; and, hence, that the people have a right to rebel against an unjust government.

That is a right which Americans have claimed for over a hundred and fifty years. This conception of the right of revolution as based on the rights of man is part of the classic tradition and of the liberal philosophy of the eighteenth century. The American Revolution was an expression of it, both in theory and in practice. We generally associate Thomas Jefferson, the author of the Declaration of Independence, with that theory, but George Washington certainly represents the practical side of that movement for independence and self-determination. The influence of the Declaration of Independence and of the agrarian democracy of Thomas Jefferson has been so attuned to the conditions of independent small property owners thinly spread over a wide land that this has become the basic stream of American political thought. Even in the South the existence of slavery could not overthrow this ideology. The extension of the suffrage and the custom of frequent elections have strengthened the feeling that every man has a right to participate in the government and at least to run for office, if not to hold it. Political liberalism has thus also included the right to criticize not only government officials but also the methods of administration.

Closely connected with the conception of independence and self-determination was the policy of isolation—of "no entangling alliances." That meant that since the European monarchies were too much wedded to the old ways, we as a nation, having been conceived in liberty and the rights of man, were to go our own way. Washington's Farewell Address is the classic expression of that point of view. This ideal of isolation, of separateness—a kind of political holiness—was undoubtedly a dominant idea of American civilization for the first hundred years of our national existence.

Connected with this conception of the right of revolution, the rights of man, the right of independence, and the right to be an isolated nation, there were other policies which were a part of our traditional liberalism. The first in time of these was complete subordination of the Army to the civil authorities.

Washington, as Commander-in-Chief, did his part in disbanding the army and having its members re-enter civil life. As President, he also stood for the same policy of subordination of the military to the civil authorities, and in the main this has been the policy of the United States. We did not believe in standing armies at the time when all European nations had them. We did not believe in conscription.

Recently there has been considerable agitation on the point, and some people think that we have made a mistake. In other words, the position of traditional American liberalism on this point has been challenged. People think we need a stronger navy and a larger army. The traditional idea that we do not need a large army and conscription was aided by the idea of isolation: if we do not covet our neighbor's goods, our neighbor will not attack us. That is one way of putting the traditional American liberal policy.

Connected with this was also the conception of separation of Church and State. The connection between Church and State in Europe is largely political. In France, for instance, there are a large number of people who feel that France should be a Catholic nation, but that it is not important for a man to believe in the dogmas of the Catholic Church. A man can be, like Charles Maurras, an unbeliever or an atheist and a Catholic. But to be a patriotic citizen one must belong to the National Church.

Such a conception of the relation between Church and State is the direct opposite of the conception which prevailed in the United States for the first hundred years. The separation of Church and State, of course, was largely due to historical conditions, to the fact that there were different churches in the different colonies. Nevertheless, one point cannot be disputed, namely, that the separation of Church and State became a part of our traditional liberal civilization.

One of the most basic elements of American liberalism has been the ideal of federalism. The United States is the only great world power that has assumed the form of a federal republic, but few seem to realize how profoundly this is reflected in our whole life. For not only in the legal and political realm, but in

443

our religious and cultural life as well, we have been a free federation aiming not at a monarchic uniformity, which is jealous of all diversity, but rather at a unity which encourages the freest development of the component states.

States that value military efficiency above all else are ruthless in their pursuit of a unity which excludes all internal differences; hence the frightful persecution of all dissenters by Nazi Germany, of Finns, Jews, and Poles by the Russian Czars, and of the Slavs by the Magyars of Hungary. In opposition to this tendency, which, when successful, leads to a dead uniformity, we have the centrifugal tendencies of dissenting minorities or nationalities who will not abdicate one iota of their peculiarities. The history of the Balkans, of Poland, or of heretical sects generally, shows the anarchic and disintegrating results of this tendency. Obviously human welfare requires neither bare uniformity nor mere diversity but a wise use of both. Wisdom, however, is a rare attainment. The history of philosophy shows that those who have been delegated to pursue wisdom have, in their disputes about the one and the many, simply duplicated in the intellectual realm the devastating struggle between the fanatical worshipers of unity and the blind worshipers of diversity or independence. From this point of view, therefore, our federal system appears as a remarkable achievement in human wisdom.

When our Federal Constitution was adopted, all parties regarded it as a poor compromise—it satisfied neither those who wanted a strong national government nor those who were anxious to preserve the independence of the states. But precisely because merchants and farmers, descendants of Cavaliers, Puritans, Dutch, and Scotch-Irish were all willing to compromise, the constitution proved a remarkable working plan of government. It broke down temporarily when people refused to compromise on the question of states' rights which involved the basic issue of slave vs. free land economy. The outcome of the Civil War showed that the United States was a real union, and the readmission of the revolting states on a footing of political equality with the loyal states emphasized its character as a union of states.

444

Our federal system has, at least until very recently, persisted in its hostility to undue centralization. It has emphasized the value of local autonomy and self-expression, and this political and religious federalism has been hostile to what has been the greatest enemy of democracy in Europe—namely, large standing armies with a sharp distinction between commissioned officers coming from the upper classes and the plain soldiers representing the masses.

The conditions of American economic life also have been unfavorable to any artificial restraints on commerce between the different parts of the country. Americans have been opposed to monopoly and in the main have felt that everyone should have an opportunity regardless of pedigree.

The fear of overcentralized government is still a powerful sentiment in this country. The prevailing sense of the American people will not allow a uniform or national divorce law, or a national system of education, any more than it will allow a national church. The principles of states' rights and home rule are still very much alive. Under the pressure of military demands we have had to increase the powers of the central government. For this, federal legislation in the last four decades on questions of railroads, banking, pure food, labor relations, and social security has prepared the way. But in trying to defend our national life the danger is that we may sacrifice those liberal traits which have made it so well worth defending. The greatness of America has been largely based on the fact that it has been a land of opportunity—spiritual as well as material. It has allowed the various constituent groups to develop freely and make their distinctive contribution to the common life. The ideal of "E Pluribus Unum" is realized not by a melting-pot where all diversity of form is lost, but by a thoroughly trained orchestra where each in a distinctive way contributes to the common end.

I might mention other elements of what we have called American liberal civilization. But the upshot of it all is a certain glorification of freedom. That glorification showed itself in different forms. For instance, it glorified the United States as a haven of refuge for the oppressed of all nations. All were wel-

445

come here, especially those who had fought for republicanism against monarchy. Our immigration laws were liberal—almost anybody could come in. We prided ourselves upon the fact that we did not suppress differences of opinion. Anybody who wished to preach any particular doctrine—"Single Tax," Christian Science, "No cooked food," anything at all—was allowed free opportunity. We prided ourselves upon various other forms of complete freedom: freedom of the press, no government press, no government censorship, and so on.

All these things were an integral part of a certain complex of institutions which might fitly be called the traditional American liberalism. At the beginning of this century this traditional American liberalism was pronounced dead by a great American philosopher, William James. In addressing the Anti-Imperialist League he said in effect: We had better disband. We have been fighting to preserve the peculiar traditional American liberalism, which is inconsistent with imperialism. That liberalism, based on isolation and a free land economy, is dead. We have, for good or evil, entered into the arena with other nations. We are producing goods for other nations. We are going to have investments abroad. We can no longer maintain our isolation. We might as well recognize this and join with our natural comrades in other nations in the fight which is raging all over between liberalism and its enemies.

That was a startling remark to make at the beginning of the twentieth century. But the development of the following decades demonstrated its profound wisdom. There is no doubt that we have become imperialistic. We have had a number of wars now in which the President of the United States, without the consent of Congress, has invaded the territory of other nations. During President Wilson's administration, our armies invaded Mexico, and practically made war on Russia. Our invasion of Mexico was ruled by the War Department itself to have been a war. The official name for the shooting in Nicaragua is as yet undetermined, but it was in fact a war of invasion.

If my points are well taken, it is evident that as a nation we have lost faith in our old liberalism. We are in the process of losing respect for the right of revolution. Revolutionists are not in good repute. Though we talk of protecting the rights of minorities, there is a strong tendency to establish uniformity in all fields, to wipe out cultural differences. A certain disrespect has developed for the rights of man, and for liberties which formerly were regarded as sacred. For instance, one of the fundamental political rights, which the Constitution guarantees to every citizen of the United States, is the right to petition Congress. And yet, during the First World War, a great university, which naturally upholds the Constitution, dismissed a professor because he wrote a letter to Congress asking that conscripted men be not sent abroad. I do not believe that this was the actual reason for his dismissal, but it was the reason alleged. And it is most significant that the Board of Trustees of a great university had not sufficient respect for the Constitution to know that by acknowledging that reason they were throwing the Constitution to the wind. In recent years we have had people arrested for reading the Declaration of Independence in public. All such things, of which examples could be multiplied indefinitely, indicate a general disinclination on the part of the public to take the old rights very seriously.

There are many indications of a declining faith in the republican form of government—certainly a declining enthusiasm for it.

When a republic was first established in Hungary, our State Department characterized the Russian attempt to suppress it by force as criminal and offered to provide a warship to bring its first president, Kossuth, to our shores. Kossuth's visit to the United States was a national occasion for the display of our sympathy for republicanism. He was almost universally acclaimed in all parts of America. Contrast with this the fact that the second president of the Hungarian Republic, Count Karolyi, was not even allowed to enter this country! The United States was the last nation to recognize the Republic of Portugal, and we helped Hitler and Mussolini crush the Spanish Republic by preventing the sale of arms to the people, who, after an orderly election, had set up the Republic of Spain, although we were in treaty bound to full and free trade relations, and the republic was ready to pay in gold for all goods sent to it.

Hence an historian, looking at the history of American civilization in a large perspective, might well say that since the Spanish-American War there has been a decline in faith in the old liberal American civilization. After that war came the conquest of the Philippines, which had almost succeeded in overthrowing the yoke of Spain. Annexation was principally dictated by expansion of American trade and all the involvements that go with it. That interpretation of our history, I think, would be very just and significant. Civilizations frequently change by conquest even more than they are changed by being conquered. For instance, Greek civilization was profoundly transformed by the conquest of Asia. Spanish civilization was profoundly transformed, and for the worse, because of the conquest of America. Portuguese civilization was paralyzed by the conquest of Africa. And so on! Civilization changes not merely by growth within, but also by contact with others. There is no doubt in any case about the radical transformations which may be called the "fall" of the liberal civilization that prevailed in the first century of our history. It has certainly disintegrated. It may revive; it may not. It seems to me it cannot revive in its old form because it was based upon a free land economy and isolation from foreign countries, both of which are physically impossible today. Therefore, I entirely agree with William James that that form of liberal civilization is dead.

III

We are now entering into the world arena, and the question is no longer that of the special type of liberal civilization which once existed in the United States, but whether any type of liberal civilization can exist in our America. Liberal civilization has existed in many forms in many nations. What is its essence? Here again it is safer to indicate realities and let the result coin its own definition.

Liberal civilization came to the fore in Europe in the middle of the eighteenth century. It was a movement which banished the Inquisition, abolished the despotic power of kings, and broke up the system of censorship and of political and economic privilege in relation to taxation, trade, and obedience to oppressive laws. It was necessary to wage a long fight before monopoly privileges were taken away from the old aristocracy. The movement to extend education to everybody came to full force only in the nineteenth century. It was the nineteenth century that saw the removal of limitations on the suffrage as well as those on holding public office: property qualifications, religious affiliations, and the like. The liberal movement was directed to the wiping out of such restraints. The emancipation of women and their final admission to the privilege of the suffrage has occurred within our own day.

If a formula is necessary for all this, I would suggest that liberalism means a pride in human achievement, a faith in human effort, a conviction that the proper function of government is to remove the restraints upon human activity. The philosophy back of that is summed up in two great faiths or beliefs: the belief in progress, and the belief in toleration. I think those are the two fundamental ideas of liberalism.

The idea of progress can hardly be understood unless we have in mind the ideas against which the idea of progress was a reaction. The people who were in favor of progress had some definite objective. They were opposed to the old attitude which we associate with Calvinism, but which existed even in large sections of the Catholic Church, as well as in non-Christian groups. This was the view that human nature is profoundly and radically sinful and corrupt. Therefore human beings cannot be trusted to fulfill their natural inclination. Nature is sin. To indulge our natural impulses is sinful. That is an idea which is easily recognized; it has not yet died.

As a consequence of the idea that the human flesh is corrupt and our nature sinful, there was the necessity of relying upon authorities and magistrates, rules and blue laws. The excessive regulation of life by governments, such as we had in some of the Puritan colonies, was a natural consequence of that belief.

The belief in progress was a reaction against such a point of view. The believers in progress said: "No, human flesh is not originally corrupt. To be sure, man commits sins and crimes. You cannot deny that. But that is due to the bad institutions under which we live. If you could only wipe out the evil institutions under which man has lived, human nature would assert itself." This is the idea that underlies almost all of Shelley's writings—an idea that he got from Godwin.

There is something very beautiful and noble about that idea. There are, to my knowledge, few parallels in human history to the nobility of Condorcet in the shadow of the guillotine. He was hiding in a garret in Paris; his life was hanging on a thread; and yet he was writing a marvelously enthusiastic sketch of the progress of the human race, anticipating for the human race an indefinite advance towards perfection.

The only fit parallel that I can find to the nobility of that act is Socrates discussing the immortality of the soul, just before drinking the hemlock, or Jesus saying, "Father, forgive them, for they know not what they do," during the crucifixion.

The idea of progress took root as a creed of hope and a fighting faith. In the course of time, however, progress came to be a shibboleth for a fatalistic optimism or meliorism. The notion that man inevitably progresses through the centuries came to claim the support of science under the name of evolution. But there is no evidence in science or history for the assumption that human nature is bound to become perfect as it develops in time.

There is no proof that human history is a simple straight line upward and onward, and there can be no such proof. For one thing, there are no clear meanings that can be assigned to the terms "upward" and "onward." Upward, of course, was a very definite idea under the old Ptolemaic astronomy. But under modern conditions one has to define "upward" with regard to standards. Unfortunately, people who talk glibly about progress and evolution generally have no very definite conception of any final goal or standard, or even of any definite direction.

Let us, however, go on to some of the more concrete expressions of this idea of progress. One of the ways in which the doctrine of progress is justified is by pointing to the history of mechanical inventions and to the growth of science. It is undoubtedly true that science has made rapid strides, but it is not true that all people today are more scientific than people were a hundred and fifty years ago, or three hundred years ago, or one thousand years ago: and on that point, I think, reflection will show that there is a very great deal of loose talk. Is it true, for instance, that a man who believes that the earth goes around the sun is more scientific than one who believes that the sun goes around the earth? If he has no reason, I fail to see that one belief or the other is scientific. How many college graduates are there who can prove that the earth does go around the sun? Having taught college students for many years, I venture to say that there are no more than two in a hundred who can offer a logical proof. And any such proofs are bound to be inadequate. This can be affirmed without any hesitation because it is a matter of mathematical demonstration. Motion is relative, and therefore there can be inherently no such thing as proof of the fact that the earth goes around the sun. All you can prove is that a certain system of equations will explain planetary motions and other physical phenomena better than other systems do. And that, of course, is a matter that can be proved to all who know mathematics. Obviously that applies to a very small portion of the educated public.

For that matter, most of popular science is just a new form of superstition. What evidence is there that, because a man has read something about the romance of the atom, he really understands the world better; that he has attained a more scientific turn of mind? What evidence is there that because a man talks freely about psychology, or psychoanalysis and complexes and libidos and things of that sort, he really has scientific detachment and a sense of scientific evidence and scientific method? I should say that changes of lingo and various exercises of technical vocabulary do not indicate any growth of science—though the body of knowledge available today is larger than it was. People who want to use the material of science certainly have a better chance. But that does not mean that the great body of people today are more scientific than they were before.

Belief in gradual and inevitable progress becomes more and more difficult to maintain, in the face of the carnage and destruction of two world wars and the failure of two victories to achieve the high objectives upon which so many wartime hopes were pinned. The kind of liberalism that was associated with this faith in progress through piecemeal cumulative reform has little appeal today and may well have less tomorrow. But is the liberal attitude necessarily dependent upon confidence in the inevitable success of our efforts? Many stout champions of the liberal cause have been frank to admit their inability to predict the future. Why can we not risk our lives in struggles of uncertain outcome? I am inclined to think that the faith in progress which is essential to the liberal attitude is not a faith in the inevitability of progress but rather a faith in its possibility.

That faith requires us to admit that we do not already possess the absolute truth. Such an admission runs counter to the religious, political, or economic convictions of many men and women. But it may be that the same catastrophes and failures which are destroying the faith in inevitable and gradual progress may also undermine the absolutisms that block the development of a liberalism fitted to the problems of our American future.

Today as in the time of Jesus those who seek the truth are the lovers of freedom. Conservatives and Communists generally do not seek the truth in social questions, because they already have it, or think they do. The peddlers of various brands of racial and national hatred do not seek the truth, because they fear it. Many more people do not seek the truth because they do not know how or lack the energy or time or skill demanded by the quest for knowledge. And, of course, there are many scholars and pedants who seek the truth only in narrower and narrower fields. But the man who can strive, with Ulysses, "to follow knowledge like a sinking star, beyond the utmost bound of human thought," who accepts no limitations on what he may study or question, to whom every endeavor of the human spirit is deserving of critical consideration, is the true liberal.

Liberalism can move forward, like science, because it embraces self-correcting principles which permit the correction of error and partial truth without an overthrow of the system that makes such correction possible. Like science, liberalism is based on the faith that other human beings can carry forward, by rational methods, the gains that we have won in human understanding. The faith of the liberal, as of the scientist, grows out of a deep

452

humility which recognizes the limitations of mortal finitude and acknowledges the impossibility of any individual's attaining correct answers to all the problems that he faces. But this humility is combined with a hope that, through rational communication and collaboration among individuals, a living body of common thought may be created which will more adequately answer the problems of an age or society than can any individual, whether he be a scientist or a dictator. In the long run, liberal democracy may outlast any form of dictatorship because the strength of a liberal democracy is not bounded by the prowess of any one man or party. The strength of liberalism lies in the fact that it enables each of us to rise above the limitations of our hereditary class prejudices and to contribute toward a body of *ideas and aspirations in action* that may incorporate more understanding than is vouchsafed to any single mortal. In the end, there is no way in which people can live together decently unless each individual or group realizes that the whole of truth and virtue is not exclusively in its possession. This is a hard lesson to learn, but without it there can be no humane civilization.

Let us take the other great belief of liberalism: the belief in tolerance. This is very closely connected with scientific method. Unless one has a certain amount of skepticism in one's system, one cannot possibly believe in tolerance. What does tolerance mean? Tolerance means that we shall give our enemies a chance. If we are secure and we know that our enemies cannot hurt us, we may be willing to give them a chance. But suppose that we believe in a certain sacred truth—say the truth of the Messiah, or the truth of a certain economic order, or the truth of certain constitutional doctrines—and some scalawag preaches that these are not true. Shall we be tolerant to untruth? That seems to me to be the crux of the whole question of liberalism. The true liberal has a certain amount of skepticism. The true liberal, being impressed with scientific method, says: "Certainly we should, for, although I am convinced that what I believe to be the truth is the truth, the other man may have something to say which I haven't heard yet, or the other man may have a point of view which is worth investigating. On the whole, in

453

the conflict of opinions, more truth will thus come out than if there is suppression."

This attitude involves a number of things which are generally not recognized. It involves not only a certain amount of skepticism in our own fundamental conviction, but a certain amount of detachment which very few people have. It is a rare gift to be able to be tolerant in that sense, because if we are pressed, if the enemy has the sword at our throats, we are not tempted to play fair and play according to the rules. We will do anything in our power to kill our assailant—or, at any rate, to get the sword away. And in general, people are not tolerant under stress, in periods of great passion, in periods of compulsion. Tolerance is a virtue that seems to thrive only in a certain leisure, in a certain cultivation. The people who show it best are the philosophers, because they thrive on diversity; or scientists, who also thrive upon the skepticism that is inherent in scientific method: "Come on with your doubts, everybody; the more the merrier." The scientific method is largely a method that consists in the development of the consequences of different hypotheses. It seems self-evident that from a point outside of a straight line only one parallel can be drawn. Along comes the Russian, Lobachevsky, and says: "I can conceive a point outside of a straight line through which more than one parallel can be drawn." Or the German, Riemann, who says: "No such line can be drawn through any point."

What is the attitude of the scientist? His business is primarily to develop the consequences of every one of these possible hypotheses. It is only because of that, because he is interested first of all in the play of ideas according to the rules of the game, that he can afford to be tolerant—to be hospitable to all sorts of denials and doubts.

In matters of religion we cannot so easily be tolerant. Suppose I know on the authority of the Koran that certain things are true, and somebody comes along and doubts it. I cannot listen to his doubts forever. Heretics generally talk too much anyway. The most important thing is that the true faith shall be maintained. Tolerance appears to be a sin under those conditions.

So it is with other matters of great importance, e.g., economic interest. Where the pressure is strong upon us, tolerance is not an easy thing to practice. And so what you have is that, in the course of various civilizations which have appeared in history, the fine flower of tolerance has appeared only rarely, and I do not think it is likely ever to become a permanent acquisition of human nature. Tolerance is the result of unusually favorable circumstances and training. Where a man can afford to care more for the rules of the game than for any particular result, he can be tolerant. The chivalrous knight and the genuine scientist show how this attitude is conditioned.

Can such a thing become universal? I do not think so. Consider, for example, the scientists as a body of citizens. Could it be said, for instance, that a group of scientists are politically more liberal than other men? I think on the whole they divide like the rest of us. Are the scientists as a body more liberal on the subject of religion? Perhaps a little, but not very much. After all, even a scientist devoted to the search for truth is tolerant only in those particular scientific lines in which he happens to be an expert. He knows the difficulty of being certain about the complex facts he has studied, and therefore he has a certain amount of skepticism; but outside of his own field he is as dogmatic as anybody else, because he is likely to know as little.

So it seems to me that since a generous stock of ignorance is one of the fundamental equipments with which the Creator has endowed all human beings, tolerance will always be a very rare phenomenon. Therefore, a civilization that depends upon tolerance is always in a very precarious condition. It may thrive for a hundred years or more, but it is inherently frail like the bloom of a flower.

The enemy of tolerance is fanaticism, the opposite of liberalism. The root of fanaticism is impatience with contradiction, and that impatience goes very deep into the roots of human nature. Watch boys in New York, for instance, on the 16th of September and their attitude towards the man who persists in wearing a straw hat. Or suppose somebody were to appear in the streets of Washington wearing clothes such as respectable senators wore in ancient Rome: irritation would soon express itself. It is to be seen when somebody pronounces words in an unaccustomed way. In our elemental reactions we are irritated by the unfamiliar, the uncouth, the unknown. We do not feel at home and are thrown out of gear by departures from the usual order of things. Such irritations may accumulate and lead to an explosion, especially if someone comes along and capitalizes—or certain widespread experiences capitalize—them.

Once, as I was sitting in a car, a young man back of me—a very tall and handsome man—was talking to a girl, and he was complaining very bitterly that there was no chance for anybody who was not a Jew to get along in New York City. I sympathized with him very much because he really felt deeply distressed. He had to explain to this lady why he was not so successful as she would like him to be. Here was an occasion in which all the irritations of his daily life were capitalized and accumulated, and the explosion was noticeable and voluminous. This seems to me to be the kind of stuff out of which race or group conflicts are made. Such irritations become organized as economic conflict, or religious conflict, or something of that sort. They form the substance which explodes if some one issue arises to touch off the fuse.

That is, in general, why I believe that civilization of the type that I have called liberal has no assurance of survival.

Human history shows the precariousness of liberal civilization. As the curtain of human history rises, we see at first Oriental monarchies. What is the typical way in which these Oriental monarchies show themselves? Consider their wisdom. Its essence is conformity. The fear of the Lord is the beginning of wisdom, and, alas, also the end. Fear and conformity are therefore the dominant rules. Morality consists in obedience to the law of God, and this is generally identical with the customary. We see this in the picture of Egyptian life. Everything is fixed—art, morals, and all human activities follow a fixed pattern. Everything has a fixed place, and to depart from it is to venture into the unknown, the strange and the unfamiliar, the uncouth. In contrast with this is the typical view of the Greeks, which begins with the adventures of the Argonauts, subsequently typified by Ulysses, whose venture beyond the Pillars of Hercules is characteristically condemned by Dante, who puts him in Hell for venturing beyond prescribed bounds.

The Greek invention or discovery of mathematics is perhaps the most characteristic expression of the free mind. Nothing is left to authority, to mere belief. Every proposition is freely questioned until we come to propositions that no one can question. And this free inquiry is extended to religion, morals, and politics.

We see this spirit manifested by the Ionian philosophers Thales and Pythagoras as early as the sixth century B.C. These men followed in the wake of Greek merchant adventurers. Thales and Pythagoras seem themselves to have been extensive travelers, and these travels seem to have disintegrated accepted traditional ideas and made free inquiry possible. This freedom puzzled the wise men of Egypt, who remarked to Herodotus, "You Greeks are children." And indeed the Greeks were, like children, free inquirers, until the growth of dogma produced the effects of dogmatic education. The best example of this spirit of free inquiry is perhaps Xenophanes, a wandering bard who observes that Ethiopians make their gods with snub noses and kinky hair, while the Thracians make theirs with blue eyes and flaxen hair, from which he concludes that if oxen made gods they would make them in the shape of oxen. This is an idea that would not occur to anyone living in a fixed community of agricultural piety.

We see this spirit in the teaching of philosophy by dialogue. Socrates proves propositions to a slave boy not by telling him on the authority of his own wisdom but by showing him that this truth is obtainable by clear thinking. This spirit of free inquiry led to the humanizing of religion—e.g., the gradual elimination of human sacrifice among the Greeks. It led to the liberation of medicine, the substitution of free inquiry into natural causes of disease, leaving the gods out of account. Thus priestly magic was rendered unnecessary for cures. In the political life it means democracy opposed to the divine right of kings or hereditary aristocracy. Perhaps the simplest outer expression of this is the fact that the Greeks were the first to

457

introduce town planning. Cities were to be built on a rational plan instead of being allowed to grow in helter-skelter fashion as is the case with all Oriental cities. Perhaps the most characteristic expression of this, however, is to be found in the Greek conception of ethics. The conduct of life is to be regulated not by taboos, or traditional superstition, or any arbitrary prohibitions. Life is to be regulated by considerations of wisdom. Man can plan his life within certain limits of nature, and when nature makes of life a smoky room, he may leave. We do not, therefore, have to be slaves if we are intelligent. Even in the decline of the Greek tradition the philosopher Plotinus can still contrast the life of reason with the life governed by belief in magic.

Now, it is well to note that the liberalism of the Greeks depended in a certain sense upon what we may perhaps call imperialism. The Greek philosophers from Thales and Herodotus were travelers. The safety of their travel depended on the peace preserved by the Persian Empire, which found its successors in the Macedonian and the Roman Empires. Freedom of motion depends on established roads that are well policed. The fitful tides of human life need channels. Greek civilization was liberal because it had the spirit of adventure, and this spirit of adventure is in one sense a harmony, or at any rate a balance, between caution and heedlessness.

Life brings illusion. Many of the new ideas that occur to us must be faulty and contradict each other. Hence the notion that mere change or mere novelty is the root of truth cannot be maintained.

The Greeks developed the scientific spirit because they struck the happy medium between fear and the spirit of adventure, carrying the latter into the intellectual realm. But when they conquered the Near East, the Oriental attitude diluted the Hellenic elements. I do not say the latter died, because in certain corners, in certain unforeseen places, it persisted in some way or other in a shell—until it blossomed out in the form of the Arabic civilization, which during the ninth and tenth centuries contained certain elements of liberalism. There again you had a certain glorious opportunity, because of favorable historical conditions. That is the course of civilization. It blossoms out, dies down, and then blossoms out again.

The revival of learning opens a new era—the Renaissance, which restores man to his natural place and turns its back upon the old formula that nature is sin and intellect the devil.

We have elements of liberal civilization in the Italian city-states of the later Middle Ages and early Renaissance. There we see again this balance between conformity and the spirit of adventure. It begins with the Crusades; it is typified by such adventurers as Marco Polo and the pioneers of modern science. It is curious that most of the great predecessors of Newton in laying the foundations of modern science were connected with Padua. This was the university of Venice, and the Venetians used to say, "We are first Venetians and then Christians." They resisted the authority of the Pope. It was not profitable for Venetian trade to exclude Turks, Greek Orthodox, or Protestants from its university town. Thus trade leads to a liberal attitude toward students of the different nations, and thus you have within Padua the free development which we call modern science. Padua declines when Venetian trade declines.

Similar remarks can be made about the great Dutch universities which served as models for the liberally inclined universities of other European countries at the end of the seventeenth and the early part of the eighteenth century.

The disintegration of traditional restraints upon human thought and energy has generally been the effect of commercial contact between different peoples. Today, however, the conditions that made commerce such a liberalizing influence in the past no longer operate so forcefully. In the first place, modern machinery and the easy means of travel and communication have reduced the diversity of life in different countries—and ideas, like clothes, are almost everywhere of the same pattern. The American who actually travels to Europe sees little more than the one who stays at home. While free thought is still of some advantage to commerce—to the extent that scientific discoveries may increase the volume and value of goods produced and exchanged—the commercial interests are more concerned to defend private property against all thought which may seriously modify it. Romantic nationalism in the economic field, of the type represented in economics by Fichte, Gentz, Adam Miller, and List, has become dominant, and our commercial classes are more fearful of internal insecurity than of the loss of international trade.

If commerce can no longer guarantee free trade in ideas, can we perhaps find guarantees for the future of liberalism in the forms of democracy? It is generally assumed that democracies are necessarily liberal. But while liberalism does tend to promote democracy—it has certainly been responsible for the extension of the suffrage and of the opportunities for education—democracies are not always liberal.

Rather obvious reasons for this are the intellectual and material conditions which democracies breed. Our own democracy has been liberal in supporting our school system, and our Western states have been generous in supporting state universities; but it is well to inquire whether we really want our children to learn new ideas. While democracies are always ready to follow leaders, these leaders are seldom intellectuals or men who demand intellectual discipline on the part of their followers. King Demos wants to be flattered rather than intellectually trained, and it is easier to gratify the former want than the latter. I think it was King Ptolemy who asked to have geometry made easier for him. His geometry teacher, who happened to be a genuine Greek, said, "There is no royal road to geometry." But there are not many such Greeks living today. When King Demos says, "I want an easy way to the quantum theory, or to Einstein's relativity theory," hundreds of popular accounts are written, which do not really help King Demos to get very far along these roads. How much nonsense is written about evolution! Of course everybody believes in it. But ask your neighbor what it is that he believes and what the evidence for it is. You will then find that what most people believe and most of what is written about evolution is just arrant nonsense. In the hands of some of the high priests of science—of men like Osborne, Conklin, and others of that type—it is just Christian theology translated into scientific lingo. Experimental biology does not really use the concept of evolution, because it is too speculative and too vague. But popular audiences are not interested in such critical reflection. They crave something constructive.

What is the demand for something constructive? It is, after all, a demand for some symbol to which we can cling, some picture that will make things easier and rosier. Now, most of us have other things to do besides studying science. Most people have certain work to achieve, and the amount of time and energy they can give to popular science is limited. Hence the important thing is that the author should be able to sell rather than know his subject.

Certainly, if people can be flattered into believing that they understand, they are not going to take the painful trouble of thinking. I do not say that aristocracies are superior in this respect, but they realize more readily the importance of training and discipline to keep themselves in power.

I have already alluded to the importance of a certain amount of material comfort and leisure as a condition of liberal civilization. But when the hunt for material things becomes excessive, you have what has been called barbarism rather than liberalism. That is to say, you have an absorption in material things which prevents the development of free personality. Attention to inner needs and inner judgments is necessary for the kind of detachment and degree of aloofness which a liberally civilized life demands. And in this respect democracies are not always favorable. In a democracy, where there are no impassable class divisions, most people want to appear wealthier than they are. For where the basis of distinction is only the attainment of wealth, everybody tries to appear on a level higher than his own. And this tends to increase the desire for material accumulation and expenditure for display rather than for the satisfaction of more substantial needs.

Under an aristocracy this does not happen, since it is just as unseemly for the commoner to act like an aristocrat as for the aristocrat to act like a commoner. Where class lines are sharp, morality consists in conformity to class mores.

There is one other element that ought to be mentioned in this connection: the element of stimulation. Every human being, of course, needs some stimulation, and for a good deal of it we are dependent on others. We need a certain amount of sociability. Nevertheless too much sociability is inimical to thought. Men may act in crowds, or run in crowds, but they do not think in crowds. There is a certain distraction which comes from excessive sociability and too much absorption in practical activity, which is the death of thought, and with it necessarily the death of a liberal attitude. We may view this from the purely physical side. Thought requires a certain energy. That energy is not generally available when our organism is responding to a large number of small stimuli all the time. The tendency of modern civilization is to stimulate the organism constantly with all sorts of sounds, motions, or colors. A man goes out to the country away from the hurry and bustle of the city and from its bewildering sights and motions, and he feels a great relief. A great deal has been written about sex stimulation producing nervous strain. But the more ordinary stimulus of cupidity—the excitement of seeing other people becoming wealthy, and trying to imitate them—is a constant factor of no less importance in preventing us from having any leisure for quiet reflection. And whatever militates against free thought is profoundly inimical to the continuity of a liberal civilization.

IV

The difficulties that stand in the path of American liberalism today are many and various, and the charting of them is a hazardous task. But against the background of history four special dangers cast foreboding shadows. First of these is the shadow of militarism. Our traditional American liberalism was closely associated with the fact that we had no large standing army, no peacetime conscription, and even no wartime conscription in our earliest struggles to win and maintain independence. Along with our dislike of military regimentation there grew up a certain glorification of personal freedom, free economic enterprise, freedom to believe in and preach unorthodox views, and a general irreverence towards the authority of parents, policemen, legislatures, and other traditional repositories of wisdom and power. All this is somewhat shocking to foreign visitors, but it has certainly played its part in the development of modern invention, which is stimulated by disrespect for authority, and in the advancing living standards which are so largely based on advances in technology and economic enterprise. This disrespect for authority has also stimulated our national intellectual life; and, while much of the result is shoddy, there are fields, such as anthropology, jurisprudence, and formal logic, where in recent years the lead in world scholarship has passed to the United States. But disrespect for authority is the one thing that the military mind cannot permit. And it is natural that a generation that has gone through many years of warfare in which the survival of freedom was thought to be at stake should develop a great respect for the military virtues and the military system. The imitation that arises out of conflict is one of the most potent forms of conversion, and it is only natural that constant comparison of our efficacy in warfare with the efficacy of our enemies should lead to the adoption of the things that made our enemies powerful and incidentally of the things that made them our enemies. As an old Chinese proverb has it, the first result of any war is that the adversaries exchange vices. And just as the Axis powers have taken over some of the worst features of American mass-production and advertising, so the danger is that we shall copy the militarism that corrupted Germany and Japan.

Only less important than the influence of our enemies is that of our allies. If we are to co-operate with other militarized nations, it will be very easy for us to slip into their way of action. Either that, or we shall have to persuade our allies and associates to adopt our ways of acting—which will require a faith in democracy that is very rare.

Alongside the danger of militarization looms the danger that the growth of governmental power may lead to an American form of dictatorship. The opposition to governmental power which was once so strong a part of Jeffersonian democracy is increasingly rare, except among malefactors of great wealth who would like to exercise their own forms of dictatorship. The tradition of keeping governmental powers weak and widely diffused has given way to the glorification of efficiency. From the standpoint of efficiency, government should be centralized and all checks and balances are as unnecessary as they would be in a corporate board of directors. Whether enough vitality remains in the traditional Jeffersonian democracy to check the growth of executive government and to bring about a revival of federalism and the diffusion of governmental powers remains a serious question.

The prospect of increased concentration of economic sovereignty in corporate directors is as large a danger as the prospect of political dictatorship. Indeed the differences between the two prospects are relatively unimportant. Government is no less dictatorial because its orders are sealed with the dollar sign rather than with the national emblem. It may be that old-fashioned liberals of the Brandeis school are right in thinking that the interests of efficiency will curtail the growth of economic power before it endangers our liberties. But I think liberals stand on firmer ground when they insist that economic efficiency must give way to other intangible values when the accumulation of wealth threatens the decay of men.

Finally there looms the danger that our natural disposition to look on the world as a fight between pure light and utter darkness will be so intensified by the experiences of war that men will tumble wholesale into the folds of those faiths that purport to have the answers to all problems, and that in the warfare between these faiths, or in their union and alliance, the voice of liberalism will be drowned out.

Can America realize the liberal vision that dogged its youth, now in the days of its maturity and power? None of us knows the answer to that question. Perhaps it is enough that each of us who holds to the liberal faith shall, in his own way, give his strength to the defense of the ancient and ever new ideal of liberal civilization.

V

The hasty conclusion that liberalism is dead has been given currency by the passionate and uncompromisingly ruthless war spirit, common to Communists and Fascists. But I do not believe that liberalism is dead, or that it has outlived its day. There still seems to me enough human reason left to which to appeal against reckless fanaticism.

Fanaticism is prone to belittle the gains that have come to mankind from the spirit of free inquiry, free discussion, and rational accommodation. So long as human beings lack omniscience, society can only suffer serious loss when one group suppresses the opinions and criticisms of all others. Liberalism, conceived as the spirit of free inquiry, free discussion, and rational accommodation, can continue to appeal to the conscience of men as long as the world offers visible proofs of the blindness of all illiberal power philosophies.

Liberalism, so conceived, may take forms very different from those with which the word has been traditionally associated in the popular mind. Traditionally, liberalism has been conceived as a form of individualism. Liberalism in economics has been associated with opposition to collective controls over production and distribution. In politics liberalism has been historically associated with the supremacy of individual rights. Neither of these beliefs has a very bright future.

Just now individualism is admittedly bankrupt throughout the world in the industrial field. In this country we have no national plan to overcome the obvious and simple stupidity of a system that periodically has too much food on the one hand, and want, bordering on starvation, on the other, without being able to bring the food from those who wish to sell it to those who need it. The economics of individualism, with its assumption of pre-established harmony, is as intellectually discredited as the belief in witchcraft.

Thoughtful people today can no longer hope for salvation through economic warfare and anarchy. There is a general consensus that some social plan of production for the needs of a community, rather than for individual profit, is necessary if the routine of civilized life is to continue. The real question is: Shall the planning be done by some irresponsible dictatorship, or by democratic representatives whose acts are subject to discussion and criticism?

My own belief is that increased governmental participation in our economic life is desirable and necessary if we are to avoid the greater evils of economic anarchy and corporate despotism. And such an approach to the problem of economic controls can be made entirely within the framework of liberalism. I do not challenge the right of those who oppose this tendency to invoke the name of liberalism. Liberals may disagree with each other on all kinds of vital issues. But if liberal individualists and liberal collectivists disagree with each other they do not need to resort to guns to settle their differences. Like scientists they can argue and exchange evidence and arrange crucial experiments; and, though these methods cannot be relied upon to produce immediate unanimity on all issues, they do, in the long run, bring substantial agreement on most issues which have been examined in a scientific spirit over a considerable period. And the problems that have been thus solved, whether in the field of mathematics or in the field of penology, are more likely to stay solved than those settled by guns.

Liberalism cannot be confined to individualistic doctrines in the field of politics any more than in the field of economics. The classical defense of human freedom in terms of the inherent rights of the individual gave us, in earlier days, our bills of rights, which are the best monuments of liberal individualism. But the idea of the superiority of the individual to society came in later years to serve as the stock justification for all sorts of immoral and unsocial activities on the part of privileged groups and vested interests. Thus today a philosophy of liberalism that minimizes the social interest in individual conduct, particularly in economic fields, may appeal to conservatives and reactionaries but will hardly serve as a weapon of democracy. But, though liberalism in modern times is deeply rooted in the philosophy of individualism, the essentials of the liberal attitude are entirely compatible with a belief that the growing interdependence of men in an industrial age calls for an increasing scope of governmental activity in fields once left to private charity and private initiative. The defense of free speech can be more effectively waged today in terms of the social importance of full exploration and exposition of alternative views than in terms of the sanctity of individual error. Just as mathematics proceeds by tracing the consequences of erroneous views, so public enlightenment must proceed by the analyzing and debating of false and threatening opinions. From the standpoint of society, it is essential that misguided individuals have every opportunity to develop in discourse the consequences of their errors, though the safety of society may require that such individuals be locked up when they begin to put into practice ideas that violate human decency.

The defense of individual liberty in these social terms may carry greater weight than either the appeal to "natural rights" or the argument that suppression is self-defeating. History gives little support to the doctrine that suppression is always ineffective. Of course, all human arrangements succumb to the attrition of time. But, taken over a limited period, which is generally as far as human prevision can go, suppression has often achieved its goal. Paganism was suppressed in Christian lands, and so were various forms of heresy. Spain got rid of Protestants as well as of Jews and Moors, and France achieved unity by suppressing the Huguenots. The ruthless eradication of the Paris Communards by the Versailles troops of Thiers, of the Socialists in Finland by the counterrevolutionaries, and of all liberal and dissident parties by the Bolshevik, Fascist, and Nazi governments, are a few of the examples that can be cited of the successful achievement of unity by deliberate and systematic suppression.

The real evil of suppression is not that it is ineffective but that it deprives the society that practices it of the opportunity to enlarge its vision of the good life and to realize its best potentialities through processes of peaceful change.

The importance of encouraging rather than suppressing diversity extends beyond the realm of discourse. All fields of life are impoverished by the monistic mania for uniformity which serves as the background for the ridicule and persecution of that which is peculiar.

A narrow conception of integration is illustrated in the conception of Americanization as the utter abandonment of any loyalty to foreign cultural traditions on the part of the foreign-born. Those who preach this do not realize how it would impoverish America if our immigrants did not contribute from their own tradition to the common stock of American civilization. Our political parties seeking to attract the votes of the foreign-born do much more to Americanize them by giving their representatives a place in our political life. There is little reason to believe that all abilities are homogeneously distributed in the different groups. On the contrary, there is a good deal of evidence to indicate that, for historical reasons, certain nationality groups send more than their proportionate share of able men into the maritime occupations, others into the civil service and engineering fields, others into the police and fire departments of our larger municipalities, and others into law and medicine. To ignore this and restrict any group to any fixed quota is thus to deprive the community of the best obtainable service.

The concept of federalism still has an important role to play in national as well as international affairs, and in cultural as well as political activities. The unity that a great society requires is the unity of a symphony or a drama, not the unity of a monotone or of a vaudeville actor who endlessly repeats the same good or bad joke.

There remains the inevitable question: Is it worth while to try to perpetuate liberal civilization? Perhaps most people, if pressed to state their real attitude, would say it is not. For liberal civilization, after all, is based upon (or can be expressed in) the Greek motto: "What is important is not life, but the good life." Many of our current opinions seem to me to be contrary to that. They seem to assume that life as such is more important than the good life. That seems to me the real issue, and one of the most fundamental issues we can face. The reasons that lead the Catholic Church to condemn birth-control; the reasons that make so many lovely, sentimental people condemn the death penalty for criminals—all these reasons seem to me to go upon the assumption that life as such is sacred, and the human beings must not lay their hands upon the gates of life and death. If you really believe that, then the question of liberalism is a minor matter. The important thing is: "Keep your hands off from the gates of life and death."

The real liberal takes a very different attitude. He believes that life is important only as the condition or opportunity for

468

the good life, and prefers not to live at all if he must live as a slave or in degradation.

History has no end, and I do not pretend to be able to predict the future. But I do think it worth while to reiterate my general disbelief in the doctrine that history is just one continuous line of progress onward and upward; or even in the more ancient view of Aristotle, the Hindus, Vico, and Nietzsche, that history is a series of repeatable cycles. I accept neither of these views because I do not believe history is as simple as that. In fact, I do not believe that if we take the whole complex of history we can form any adequate symbol for it. What we can do is to consider certain phases of it.

Suppose we stood outside of the earth and actually saw its motion. It would appear even more irregular than that of the other planets. We obtain some clarity by decomposing the concrete reality into elements. So it is, I think, with regard to history. We have to decompose the various elements which enter into history, and trace each one of them separately. When we do that it seems to me that we have to fall back upon a general view which may be called the polarity of nature, i.e., the two-sidedness of things. In the physical realm there is always action and reaction. There is no one force acting, but always many forces acting in opposite directions. So, in life, there is growth and decay. In human history there are ups and downs. There are periods of flowering and periods of decay. There is no use, it seems to me, in thinking that any one movement of history, or of human life, will continue forever.

So I come back to the notion of Goethe—that if you could say to one moment, "O stay, thou art so fair," that would be the end.

INDEX

INDEX

Abraham, 349
absolute truth—*see* truth
Abyssinia, 402
academic freedom, 280-81
accommodation and compromise, 117, 183, 262
accuracy, qualifications for the sake of, 138
Adam, 236, 421
Adams, Brooks, 219
Adams, Charles Francis, 63
Adams, Henry, 219
Adams, James Truslow, 256-61
   The Adams Family, 256
   The Epic of America, 256
   The Founding of New England, 256
Addison, Joseph, 224
Adler, Felix, 78-84, 365, 403
   An Ethical Philosophy of Life, 78
administrative posts in colleges, 284
aether, theory of the, 51
Agag, King, 349
Age of Reason, 430
aggressiveness, American, 259-60
agrarian party, 254
agricultural interests—*see* farmers
agriculture, 403
Ahad Ha'am, 327

Akbar, 440
Albigenses, 350
Alcibiades, 372
Aldobrandi, 240
Aldrich, Thomas Bailey, 250
   The Story of a Bad Boy, 251
Alexander II, Czar, 264
Alexander VI, Pope, 324
Alexander the Great, 371, 390, 440
algebra, 378
altruism, 127-29
Amendments, Constitutional, 114-15, 254; Fifth, 33, 37, 154, 178; Fourteenth, 23, 33, 37, 154, 164, 177, 178
American dream, the, 257
American history, 256-61
American liberalism—*see* liberals and liberalism
American Philosophical Association, 292, 365
American Revolution, 112, 220, 225, 402, 442
American traits, 259
"Americanism" as interpreted in Europe, 289
Amor Dei Intellectualis, 307, 313, 316, 317, 319
Amos, 352
Anaximander, 297
Anderson, Sherwood, 223-24

473

Andreyev, A. A., 266
Anglo-Saxons, 125, 258
Anshen, ed., *Freedom: Its Meaning*, 161
anthropology, 138, 140-41
anthropomorphism, 5-7, 19, 52, 308-309, 341
Anti-Imperialist League, 258, 446
anti-Semitism—*see* Jews
Antikolski, 329
Apollo, 343
Appellate Division, N. Y. C., 208, 209
Aquinas, St. Thomas, 350 n., 368, 383, 399
Arabian Nights, 251
Arabs, 400, 458, 467
Archimedes, 87, 291, 409
architecture, classic, 334
Argonauts, 457
argument, its effect on changing one's religion, 358-59
Argyll, Duke of, 296
aristocracies, 18, 113, 187, 449, 461
Aristotle, 13, 80, 81, 88, 94, 234, 291, 316, 335, 348, 368, 370, 371, 372, 373, 383, 469
Ark, the, 344
armies, standing, 445, 462
Army, subordinated to civil authority, 442-43
Arnold, Matthew, 307
Arnold, Thurman, 136-48
The Symbols of Government, 136
Articles of Confederation, 190
artificial in society, the, 275
artistic pursuits in a democracy, 286, 289, 290
arts, fine and industrial, 154-55, 357, 368

asceticism, 310-11
Asquith, H. H., 181
astrology, 404
astronomy, 140, 404
atheism, 309, 384
atoms, 6, 372, 404, 451
Augustine, St., 84, 350 n., 374, 402
Austin, John, 137
Austin, O. P., 168
Australian Blackfellows, 78
authority, irreverence toward, 462-63
Averroes, 374
Axis powers, 463
Ayres, Clarence, 296-98
Huxley, 296

Babbitt, Irving, 231
Bach, Johann Sebastian, 94
Bacon, Francis, 47, 69, 70, 374
Novum Organum, 70
Baer, Karl Ernst von, 374
Balfour, Arthur, 300, 301
Defence of Philosophic Doubt, 301
Foundations of Belief, 301, 358
Balkans, 444
"ballot," 259
Bancroft, George, 256
bankers, 153, 254
banknotes, state, 177
barbarism, 461
Barlow, Joel, 225
baseball, 334-36, 351
Bastiat, Claude Frédéric, 253
Beard, Charles A., 186-87, 279
An Economic Interpretation of the Constitution . . ., 187 n.
Bebel, A., 160
Becket, Thomas à, 352
Beethoven, L. van, 94, 368

behaviorism, 297
beliefs, 428; acting on, 4; religious, 340, 359-60; cherished, 404, 453; primitive peoples', 420
Benn, W. W., 345
Bentham, Jeremy, 60, 141, 190
Berger, Victor, 250
Bergson, Henri, 85, 300, 329, 379, 381, 384, 399, 403, 405, 432
Berkeley, Bishop George, 60, 299, 372, 394
Berkeley, Sir William, 441
Bernard, Claude, 393
Beveridge, *Life of Marshall*, 179 n.
Bible, 125, 189, 290, 302, 343, 344, 420, 421, 426
    infallibility, 346, 359
    criticism and interpretation, 26, 298, 345, 346, 393
    stories and citations from, 27, 125, 309, 345, 346, 349, 354
Biklé, Henry W., 32
Bill of Rights, 163, 181
biology, 383-84, 426, 460; transformist or evolutionary, 140
birth control, 356-57, 385, 468
Bismarck, Otto von, 33 n., 243
Black, Justice Hugo, 180
Blackstone, Sir William, 183
Blair, *Rhetoric*, 221
Blanc, Louis, 253
"Blue Sunday" laws, 351
Board of Estimate, N. Y. C., 208
Board of Higher Education, N. Y. C., 199 n., 200-210
Boas, Franz, 297
Boccaccio, 347
Boehme, Jakob, 381
Bohemia, 350
Bohr, Niels, 55
Bolsheviki, 467 (*see also* Russia)

Boltzmann, Ludwig, 431
Book of Enoch, 320; of Job, 348, 354; of Judges, 354; of Kings, 331, 349, 354; of Proverbs, 321; of Psalms, 321; of Samuel, 343, 354
books, reviewing, 32
Borah, Senator William E., 255
Boudin, *Government by Judiciary*, 182 n., 184 n.
bourgeoisie, 113-14, 261
Boutroux, Emile, 432-33
    The Contingency of the Laws of Nature, 430
Bourne, Randolph, 252
Bowditch, Nathaniel, 252
Boyle, Robert, 409
Bradlaugh, Charles, 337
Bradley, F. H., 70, 303, 319
Bradley, Justice Joseph P., 176
Brahe, Tycho, 48
Brandeis, Justice Louis D., 26, 32-39, 163, 164-65, 176, 180, 464
Bright, John, 39
Brith Shalom, 330
Bronx borough, N. Y. C., 104-105
Brown, Dr. John, 374
Brownian movements, 432
Brunetière, F., 228, 229, 230
Bruno, Giordano, 80
Bryan, W. J., 70, 426
Bryce, James, 255, 278
Bucci, Mr., 200, 207
Buddha and Buddhism, 52, 88, 94, 285, 310, 352, 440
Bulwer Lytton, *Pelham*, 301
bureaucracy, 137
Burke, Edmund, 91, 190, 222
Burns, Robert, 134
Burr, Aaron, 179, 216
Bush, 403

business—freedom in, 137 (*see also
    under* government); Ameri-
can worship of, 396
businessman, status and character
    of, 102, 103, 152, 153, 402
businessmen in Europe and Amer-
    ica, their age at retiring, 286
Butler, Justice Pierce, 176
Butler medal, 403

Cabell, Branch, 249
Cabinet, whether to make it re-
    sponsible to Congress, 171
Calas, Jean, 194
Calvin, John, 340, 349
Calvinism, 26, 27, 60, 72-77, 162,
    253, 441, 449
Cambridge Modern History, 268
Cambridge Platonists, 222
Cambridge University, 420
Campbell, *Rhetoric*, 221
canonization, 337
cant, 137
Cantor, Georg, 410
Capaneus, 235
capital and capitalism, 26, 34-36,
    63, 93-119 *passim*, 165, 169,
    187
Cardozo, Justice Benjamin Na-
    than, 40-45
Carlyle, Thomas, 303
cartels, 63
Casaubon, Isaac, 344
cases:
    Adair, 36, 186
    Adkins, 36
    Burns Baking Co. v. Bryan, 186
    child labor, 186
    civil rights, 186
    Consolidated Gas, 44
    Coppage v. Kansas, 36, 186

cases: (Cont.)
    Danbury Hatters, 28
    Dred Scott, 186
    Gold Cases, 25, 164
    Jones & Laughlin, 164
    Marbury v. Madison, 178, 179
    Muller v. Oregon, 37
    Munn v. Illinois, 36
    Northern Securities, 28
    Oklahoma Ice, 33
    Oregon Telephone, 183
    Ribnik v. McBride, 186
    Tyson v. Banton, 186
caste system, 129-33
categorical imperative, 314-15
catharsis, 335
Cather, Willa, 250
Catherine II, Empress, 263, 372
Cavaliers, 444
celibacy, 356
censors of books, judges as, 203-204
censorship, 357, 448
Cervantes, 225
Chamberlain, *Foundations of the
    Nineteenth Century*, 328
chance, 396, 430-31
Chase, Chancellor H. W., 204
Chase, Justice Samuel, 176, 179,
    180 n.
Chase National Bank, 35
chemical processes, 431
"Chicago School" of philosophers,
    386
Chicago, University of, 295, 297
child labor, 177; Amendment, 254
China and the Chinese, 102, 134,
    135, 356, 440
Christian Church, 118-19, 189, 353,
    400-401 (*see also* Roman
    Catholic Church)

Christian ethics as promoting unity, 400
Christian Fathers, 234
Christian Science, 446
Christianity, 337-61 *passim*, 390, 400-402
Church of England, 301, 358
Church and State, separation of, 304, 329, 441, 443, 445
Cicero, 85, 88, 189, 224, 374
city government, 102-103
civil liberty, 128, 163 (*see also* freedom *and* rights)
civil service examinations, 202-203
Civil War, 259, 444
civilizations, how changed, 448
Clapp, Professor, 172
Clark, J. M., 166
class conflict, 113-14, 130-33
class divisions, 101-102, 130-33
class power, 113
"classicism" in literature, 221, 224-25
Clayton Act, 258
clergy in colonial America, 285
Cleveland, Dr., 170-71
Code Napoléon, 267
Cohen, *Law and the Social Order*, 31 n.
Coke, Sir Edward, 25, 91, 182
Colbert, J. B., 114
Colenso, Bishop, on the Pentateuch, 298, 345
Coleridge, S. T., 307
   Biographia Literaria, 222
collective farms in Russia, 114
collectivism, 35, 59-67 *passim*, 96, 107-108, 168
College of the City of New York, 198-210 *passim*, 293-94, 409
colleges, 276, 284-85, 293

Columbia University, 279
commerce, international, 168, 459
common law, 32, 33, 43-44, 178
communal organization as an identifying mark of religion, 353
Communism and Communists, 93, 110-19, 243, 302, 339, 452, 464 (*see also* collectivism *and* Socialism)
Communist leaders, 115-16
Communist party in Russia, 118, 261
competition, 28, 33, 34, 38-39, 63, 150, 191
compromise and accommodation, 117, 183, 262
Comte, A., 297, 410
Condorcet, Marquis de, 341, 450
conflict, social, 119-36; whether good or evil, 120-22; among races, 122-23; predisposition to, 123-25; how suppressed, 125-29; among castes and classes, 129-31; methods of reducing, 131-36
Confucius, 440
Congress, 36, 164, 171, 182-85, 446, 447; "lame duck," 179
Conklin, Edwin Grant, 460
conquest, its influence on civilizations, 448
conscription, 443, 462
conservatism, 8, 24, 70, 438; in accepting new sciences, 140; and new ideas, 187
Considérant, *Principes du Socialisme*, 111
Constitution, the, 22, 24, 36-37, 43, 113, 137, 163, 175-93, 259, 444; interpretation of, 36, 153-54,

176 (*see also* judges *and* Supreme Court)
Constitutional Convention, 178
constitutional liberty, 163
constitutional rights, 186-91
consuetudo, 189
contemplative life, 288-91
contingency in natural laws, 430-33
contract, original, 402
Cooke, Jay, 249
Cooley, T. M., 252
Coolidge, President Calvin, 258
co-operation vs. individualism, 34-35
Copernicus, 60, 69, 140, 147, 318, 374
Corn Laws, 28
Corporation Counsel of N. Y. C., 200-210 *passim*
corporations, increasing power of, 464
Corwin, Professor, 163
cotton gin, 400
Cournot, A. A., 432
Court of Appeals, N. Y., 202, 206
courts—*see* judges *and* Supreme Court
creeds, religious, 54-55, 360
crime, opportunities for, 102
crime and punishment, 238-39
criticism, literary—American, 213-27, 249-55; impressionism and authority in, 227-33
Croce, Benedetto, 162, 379
cruelty in religion, 349-51
Crusades, 459
Cudworth, Ralph, 222, 344
currency, stabilizing of, 172
curses, 356

Curtis, W. G., 425-29
Science and Human Affairs, 425

Dante, 13, 80, 94, 225, 234-41, 316, 325, 347, 368, 457
Convito, 235
Divine Comedy, 241
Inferno, 235, 239, 240
Paradiso, 214
Purgatory, 235
Darwin and Darwinism, 26, 29, 94, 291, 296-98, 359, 410, 426
The Descent of Man, 87
David, 421
De Leon, 250
Debs, Eugene V., 250
decisions, reliance in judicial, 44-45
Declaration of Independence, 71, 165, 442, 447
Declaration of the Rights of Man, 71
Defoe, *Moll Flanders*, 223
degeneration, 421-22
degrees, college, 281
deism in the eighteenth century, 253
Delaware & Hudson Railroad, 280
Delphi, oracle at, 343
democracy, 17, 18, 34, 400, 429, 453, 457, 459, 460; scientific examination of, 155-61; oligarchic tendency in, 157-60; how efficient, 170-71
democratic education, its failure to maintain high standards, 286
democratic leaders, 460
Democratic party, 254
Democritus, 6, 297, 348, 370, 372
Demogue, 141

demons and demoniac possession, 342-43, 344, 356
De Morgan, A., 138, 309
Demosthenes, 372
Demikin, A. I., 261
Dernburg, H., 136
Descartes, R., 51, 60, 69, 304, 371, 373, 429
  Discourse on Method, 69, 70
  Geometry, 70
  Optics, 70
despotism—*see* dictatorships
determinism, 121, 218-20, 250
Dewey, John, 252, 317, 369, 371, 385, 403
  — and Kallen, eds., *The Bertrand Russell Case,* 198
Diaspora, 330
Dickens, Charles, 207
dictatorships, 17, 111, 162, 400, 463
dietary laws, 353, 423
Dilthey, Wilhelm, 389
Diogenes Laertes, 374
Diophantus, 409
discipline and self-control, 76, 277
discrimination in loving, 10
Disraeli, Benjamin, 285
dissenting minorities, 444
divorce, 205
divorce law, 445
dogmas, 339, 356, 439, 457
Domesday Book, 181
Dostoievsky, F. M., 266
doubt (skepticism, challenging accepted truths, etc.), 9, 14, 15, 24-25, 341-42, 345-46, 428, 429, 453-54
Draper, J. W., 341, 345, 426, 427
Dreiser, *An American Tragedy,* 223

Dreyfus, Alfred, 193, 194, 198, 389
Driesch, Hans, 410
Dryden, John, 224
"due process," 178, 184, 200
Duhem, Pierre, 374
Dunne, Mr. Dooley on "The Education of the Young," 277
Dutch, 444
Dutch universities, 459

"E Pluribus Unum," 445
earth's revolution, 427
easy ways of learning, 460
economic conception of history, 121-22
economic determinism—*see* determinism
economic interpretation of constitutional rights, 185-86
economic reform, 61-62
economic waste, 63-64
economics viewed pragmatically, 148 ff.
Eddington, Sir Arthur S., 46, 303, 381
Edison, Thomas A., 284
education, 134, 191, 260, 273-78, 285-86, 293, 304, 445, 449; Greek, 293
Edwards, Jonathan, 72, 251, 340, 360-61
efficiency engineering—*see* scientific management
efficiency, glorification of, 463, 464
efficiency of workmen, 100
egocentric thinking, 4-5
Egypt, 440, 456
Ehrlich, Dr. Paul, 329
Einstein, Dr. Albert, 46-56, 139, 410, 460
  The World As I See It, 46

élan vital, 405
electoral system, 259
electromagnetism, 374
Eliot, George, 205
Eliot, President C. W., 391
Ellsworth, Chief Justice Oliver, 178
embryology, 374
Emerson, R. W., 25, 219, 220, 222
emotional side of religion, 354-57
Empedocles, 374
Encyclopedists, 263
enemies—killing off, 125; love of, 55, 127; and allies, their influence on us, 463
Engels, F., 116, 217
Enlightenment, 55, 189, 253, 400
enterprise, private, 97, 100, 149-50, 462
Epicurus, 6, 84, 341, 354
epiphenomenalism, 299
equality, 18, 243; among nationalities and individuals, 164-65
Erasmus, 322-26
Erie Railroad, 63
error, tolerance of subversive, 14-15, 128-29, 453-54
Esmein, 141
esthetic function of literature, 214, 215
eternity—distinguished from time, *see* time; from "the everlasting," 312
ethics, 81, 143, 385-88, 400 (*see also* good *and* morality)
Eucken, Rudolf, 403
Euclid, 189, 224, 233, 367, 379, 409
Europe, population of, 402
euthanasia, 356
evolution, 6, 297-98, 405, 426, 460-61

examinations for teachers, 202-203
exchange, international rate of, 172

factory conditions in England, 62, 399
factory legislation, 60, 116, 191, 353
facts, before or after assumptions, 139
fairy-tales, 424
faith, effect of destruction of, 300-301
false opinions, tolerance of, 14-15
fanaticism, 39, 117, 119, 351, 438, 439, 455, 465
Faraday, Michael, 291, 303
Farinata, 235, 236, 240
farmers, 113, 187, 254
Fascism, 106, 111, 116, 119, 129, 464, 467
fear—as basis for morality, 348-49; in religion, 355-56
Federal Reserve Act, 254
federalism, 165-66, 443-45, 464, 468
Federalist, The, 184
Federalists, 179, 187, 254
fetishes, 344
Fichte, Johann, 460
fideism, 359
Field, Justice Stephen J., 252
Fielding, *Tom Jones,* 223
Finland, Socialists in, 126, 467
Fisher, Irving, 172
Fiske, John, 251, 279
Flettner ship, 47
Flexner, Dr. Abraham, 329
Florentine Academy, 282
Folquo, 236
Fontenelle, Le Bovier de, 297
foreign teachers, 202

foreign-born in America, 260, 468
foreigners, 123-24, 133
Founding Fathers, 42, 163, 441
Fourier, F. M. C., 111
Fraenkel, Osmond K., 193-98, 201
   The Sacco-Vanzetti Case, 193
France, Anatole, 60, 228, 229, 230, 231
   Les Dieux ont soif, 84
Franco-Prussian War, 87, 243
Frankfurter, Justice Felix, 32, 33, 36; ed., *Mr. Justice Brandeis,* 32
Franklin, Benjamin, 42, 252
Frazer, Sir James G., 24, 344, 384, 420-24
   The Golden Bough, 420
   Studies in Comparative Religion, 420
Frederick II, Emperor, 237
Frederick the Great, 371
freedom—of the will, 19; of thought, discussion, and inquiry, 38, 111, 175, 456-57; in business, 137; meaning analyzed, 161-67; why sometimes given up, 162-63; of speech, 466-67
Frege, 393, 410
French Constitution, 185
French Revolution, 112, 114, 163, 190, 229, 263, 328, 372
Freneau, Philip, 225
Fresnel, A. J., 50
Freud, Sigmund, 213, 313, 433
Freund, Professor, 179
   Standards of American Legislation, 179 n.
Friedman, ed., *American Problems of Reconstruction,* 167
frontier life in America, 259-60

Fuller, Governor A. T., 196
Fundamentalism, 298, 339, 346

Galen, 81, 374
Galileo, 49, 50, 69, 80, 94, 147, 318, 370, 374, 381, 417-19
   Dialogues Concerning Two New Sciences, 417
Gallican Church, 443
Gandhi, 95
Garland, Hamlin, 250
Gauss, K. F., 291
genius—*see* literary genius
"genteel" tradition, 213, 226
Gentz, 460
geocentric conception, 51
geology, 140
geometry, 404 (*see also* Euclid)
geometry, non-Euclidean, 140, 378
German people, 33 n., 85
German revolution of 1918, 163
Germany, 52, 81, 241-45, 444, 463
gerrymanders, 187
Gibbon, Edward, 230, 341
Gibbs, Willard, 252, 284
Gierke, J., 329
Gilbert, William, 374
Gladstone, W. E., 291, 301
God, 26, 29, 235, 307-19, 346, 354; the term, 309, 338; problem of nature and existence of, 384; personal, 302, 309, 310, 341; anthropomorphic, 19, 309; intellectual love of, 307-19
Godkin, E. L., 250, 251
gods, the, 72, 352, 354
Godwin, William, 450
Goethe, 46, 138, 242, 243, 307, 469
Golden Rule, 10
Goncharov, *Oblomov,* 60

good (and evil), 75, 78, 120, 142-43, 276 (*see also* morality)

"good will," the, 82

Gorky, M., 266

Gould, Jay, 63

government—the best that governs least, 187, 190; symbols of, 136-48; function of, 449; centralization of, 445, 464; reform of, 144; its authority strengthened by sentiment, 191-93; its responsibility and authority in our industrial system, 153; its powers increased, 445, 463, 466; its interference with the individual, 60; with business, 137, 153, 465-66; vs. individual control of industries, utilities, etc., 66, 102-105, 169, 170 (*see also* State)

graft, 103-104

graven images, 357

Gray, "Elegy," 257

Greece and the Greeks, 440; adventurous spirit, 456-57, 458; democracy, 371; drama, 335; religion, 348, 349; philosophy, 458 (*see also* Socrates, Plato, Aristotle, etc.); ethics, 458; scientific spirit, 458

Greek Orthodox Church, 339, 459

Green, T. H., 303

Grotius, 14, 188, 189, 325

guesswork, 74

Guyau, M. J., 81

Halley's Comet, 355-56

Hamilton, Alexander, 184 n., 216

Hamilton, Walton, 32, 148

Hannibal, 269

happiness—defined, 94-95; as the end of man, 314-15

Harding, President Warren G., 258

Hartshorne and Weiss, eds., *Collected Papers of Charles S. Peirce*, 391

Harvard Law Review, 163, 199

Harvard University, 295, 392

Harvey, William, 46, 69, 374

hatred in religion, 350

Hay, John, 250

"Little Breeches," 251

"Jim Bludso," 251

Hebrew prophets, 352, 401

Hegel, F., 60, 113, 217, 243, 297, 368, 370, 371, 372, 373, 374, 383, 399, 410

The Phenomenology of the Spirit, 87, 291, 372

Heine, Heinrich, 241-45, 307, 329

Hell, 234-36, 239, 240, 325, 350, 354, 355, 360, 457

Hennequin, 232

Henry, Joseph, 252

Heraclitus, 120

heredity, Mendelian, 389

heresy and heretics, 38, 134, 137, 236, 279, 342, 349, 351, 427, 444, 454

Hergesheimer, Joseph, 249

Herodotus, 354

high schools, 263, 276

highway billboards, 289

Hill, James J., 285

Hindus and Hinduism, 128, 339, 340, 349, 469

Hinton, Judge, 197

Hippocrates, 374

history, 401; philosophy of, 388-91

Hitler, A., 52, 192, 332, 447

Hobart, 182

Hobbes, Thomas, 15, 25, 297, 311, 409

Hobhouse, *Democracy and Reaction,* 126 n.

Holmes, Justice Oliver Wendell, 20-31, 32, 33, 37, 39, 40, 65, 97, 121, 136, 141, 176, 185, 187, 252; on doubting one's principles, 9; on "the life of the law," 25
    Collected Legal Papers, 22 n., 29 n., 30 n., 109, 185 n.
    The Common Law, 24

Holt, 182

Holy Alliance, 267

Home Rule Bill, Irish, 181

Homer, 80, 94, 241

Hoover, Herbert, 117

hope, 354

Horace, 224

Howells, William Dean, 250

Hoxie, Robert F., 100; report, 38, 151
    Scientific Management and Labor, 100 n.

Hughes, Chief Justice Charles Evans, 32, 178, 180

Huguenots, 126, 467

human consciousness, 299-300

human institutions, 449-50

human nature, sinfulness of, 449

human sacrifice, 349, 457

Hume, David, 60, 265, 304

Hungary, 447

Husserl, Edmund, 395

Hussites, 350

Hutchins, Robert M., 142

Hutten, Ulrich von, 323

Huxley, Aldous, 301

Huxley, T. H., 26, 63, 296-304, 358; works, 302, 303

hypotheses, 66-67, 68, 69, 117

ideas—their prestige in America, 283-87; in Plato's and Kant's sense, 381; socially effective, 399; discriminating among, 439; in action, 453; how affected by travel, 457

ignorance and bliss, 7, 310

illusions, pleasant, 4, 354

immigrants to America, 133, 165, 332-33, 445-46, 467-68

immigration laws and quotas, 165, 202, 332-33, 356

imperialism, 258, 446

impressionism in literature, 214, 227-33

income, earned and unearned, 170

income tax, 178, 254

independence for nations, 165

indeterminism, 396

India, 440 (*see also* Hindus)

individual, interests of the, 132-33, 159-60

individualism, 59-67, 68, 465-66; economic, 29, 34-35, 37, 59-67, 95-96, 93-109 *passim,* 117, 168, 465

indulgences, sale of, 324

industrial breakdowns, 150

Industrial Revolution, 152

industrial system (American) analyzed, 148-52, 169-70; discipline needed, 152-55; woman in, 172

industrialism, 95

Ingersoll, Robert, 337

initiative, the, 254

Inquisition, 38, 236, 350, 351, 448

insurance policies, 177
integration of groups and peoples, 131-33
"intellect" in Spinoza's sense, 309
intellect, its products not highly esteemed, 283-87, 289
intellectual vision, 289
intellectuals and anti-intellectuals, 25, 71, 283, 401
intolerance—see tolerance
intuition, 406
intuitional philosophy, 191, 221, 384
inventions as proof of progress, 450
Irish, 130, 302
irrationalism, 67-71
irrigation works, 254
Isaiah, 52, 352
Islam—see Mohammedanism
isolationism, 442-43, 446
Italian city-states, 459

Jackson and Frankfurter, eds., *The Letters of Sacco and Vanzetti,* 198
Jacksonian era, 113
Jacob, 420
James, brother of Jesus, 320
James, Henry, 249
James, William, 95, 299, 310, 335-36, 358, 359, 360, 361, 365, 369, 379, 391, 392, 396, 446, 448; on changing one's opinions, 8; definition of metaphysics, 70; on success, 95; on the essence of philosophy, 366
"A Moral Equivalent for War," 335
"The Will to Believe," 358
Japan, 85, 102, 463

Jastrow, Joseph, 393
Jaurès, J., 160
Jay, Chief Justice John, 185
Jefferson, Thomas, 33, 42, 190, 219, 253, 259, 400, 442
Jeffersonian democracy, 33, 34, 214, 255, 463-64
Jeffersonian Democrats, 254
Jehovah's Witnesses, 128
Jena, battle of, 87, 291, 372
Jenks, 92
Jenner, Dr. William, 267
Jesus Christ, 52, 54, 72, 88, 94, 95, 234, 310, 320-22, 343, 346, 349, 352, 429, 450
Jewish dietary laws, 353, 423
Jewish orthodoxy, 294, 423
Jewish tradition, 54-55, 294
Jewish University, 330
Jews, 124, 130-31, 134-35, 347, 349-50, 352-53; discrimination against, 53, 328, 456; persecution of, 53-54, 444, 467 (*see also* Judaism *and* Zionism)
Jhering, R. von, 136, 141
John the Baptist, 321
Johns Hopkins University, 295, 392
Johnson, Dr. Samuel, 205 n., 224
Josephus, 320, 331
Joshua, Rabbi—see Jesus Christ
Judaism, 53-55, 94, 326-33 *passim,* 339-60 *passim,* 390
judges, 22-23, 32, 37, 40-45, 137, 153-54, 176, 180, 187, 188, 203-204, 254 (*see also* Constitution *and* Supreme Court)
judicial review, power of, 164, 182-86
judiciary, British, 181
Judiciary Repeal Act, 179

jurisprudence, 141
jury trial, 92
Juvenal, 138

Kames, *Elements of Criticism*, 221
Kant, Immanuel, 13, 50, 60, 79, 81, 94, 229, 243, 265, 308, 354, 368, 369, 370, 371, 372, 373, 381, 382
Karolyi, Count Mihály, 447
Katkoff, M. N., 328
Kay, a Mrs., of Brooklyn, 200, 201, 206
Keats, John, 30
Kelsen, Hans, 141, 142
Kemmerer, Edwin W., 170
Kepler, J., 48, 69, 94, 318, 381
Keynes, J. M., 138
kings—despotic power of, 448; divine right of, 457
knowledge, 405-406
Kolchak, A. V., 261
Koran, 346, 357, 439, 454
Kossuth, Louis, 447
Ku Klux Klan, 351

La Guardia, Mayor F. H., 207-208
labor—hours of, 64-65, 116; rate of work, *see* speed-up; division of, 86; future elimination of any need of, 154
labor (as a class), 38-39, 169-70, 256; and capital, 28, 169; skilled and unskilled, 151; exploitation of, 191
labor contract, 60
Labor Party, British, 116
labor-saving devices, patents on, 63-64
laborer, insecurity of, 169
Ladd Franklin, Christine, 393

laissez faire, 33, 61-62, 107, 142, 149, 163, 166, 171, 190, 254
Lamartine, A., 231
Lane, Franklin K., 171
Langdell, C. C., 252
language and logic, 376
Laplace, Pierre de, 291, 432
Lassalle, F., 116, 219, 243
Latin language, 277, 282, 293, 366
Latini, Brunetto, 240
Latter-Day Saints, 128
law—true character of the, 25, 41-42; function of, 143-44; enforcement of, 139; moralistic veneer of, 25; writings on, as part of American literature, 252
law schools, 23, 42, 285
lawlessness in America, 260
laws—in philosophy, 312; of nature, 430-31; sumptuary, 16; oppressive, 448-49; declared unconstitutional, 37; obedience to, 18
lawyers, 26, 43, 188-89, 191, 254, 402
Lea, Henry C., 256
leadership, 132, 158-59
League of Nations, 87, 88
Lecky, W. E. H., 301, 341, 345
Leconte de Lisle, 231, 307
lecturing, college, 282
legal history, 24, 27
legislation—factory, 60, 116, 191, 353; tariff, 254; "Blue Sunday," 351
Leibniz, G. W. von, 13, 26, 60, 61, 314, 368, 373, 393
leisure, 154-55, 257-58, 286
Lemaître, Jules, 230, 231
Lenin, N., 105, 116, 219, 340

Leo X, Pope, 357
Leonardo da Vinci, 88, 368
Lerner, Max, 32, 35-36, 38
Lessing, G., 54, 55, 243, 307
Levi-Civita, T., 47
Lewes, George Henry, 205
Lewis, John, 117-18
Lewis, Sinclair, 249
liberals and liberalism:
  general position defined, 3-10, 28, 437-39, 449; contrasted with conservatives and radicals, 438; disagreeing with each other, 466
  general tenets—see accommodation; caste system; dogmas; freedom; individualism; openmindedness; progress; rationalism and irrationalism; reason; rights; tolerance; Zionism
  history of, 38-39, 71, 440 ff.; in America, 165, 253, 255, 332, 400, 441-48; in Europe, 33, 263, 448-49
  what it has accomplished, 38-39, 71
  chances of survival, 448-69; precarious, 38, 456-57; difficulties, 462-63; hope, 116-17, 119, 464-69
Liberia, 330
libertarianism, 17
liberties, clash of, 166
liberty—meaning of, 178, 184; civil, 128; industrial, 165 (see also freedom and rights)
Liebknecht, Karl, 116
life, literature as expressing, 216
Lilly, 300
Lincean Academy, 282

List, G. F., 460
literary criticism, 213-33, 249-55
literary genius, factors governing, 218-20, 250
literature—what concerned with, 251-53; as belles-lettres, 214; as any printed matter, 250-51; the law in, 252; journalistic manner in, 257
Livy, 237
Lobachevsky, N. I., 265, 454
Locke, John, 60, 244, 253, 308, 396, 441
Loeb, Jacques, 297, 422, 426
logic, 28, 375-81, 404; symbolic, 377
Logicismus, 380
London Times, 291
Longfellow, H. W., 216
  "A Psalm of Life," 314
Loree, President, 280
Lorentz, H. A., 47
Loskii, 266
lottery tickets, 177
Lotze, Rudolf, 374
Louis XIV, 263
Louis XV, 263
"love," the word, 127
love, 10, 236, 239; of enemies, 55, 127; of neighbors, 10, 127-28, 314; of God, 307-19
Lowdermilk, Land of Promise, 333
Lowell, Abbott Lawrence, 196, 280
Lowell committee, 196
Lowell, James Russell, 217, 220, 225
Lowie, R. H., 297
Loyola, The Spiritual Exercises, 355
Lucretius, 6, 52, 297, 341, 354
Lunacharsky, A. V., 105

Lusitania, 85
Lusk Committee report, 69 n.
Luther, Martin, 243, 322-26
Luxemburg, Rosa, 116
Lvov, Prince Georgi, 262
Lyell, Sir Charles, 26
lying, 346

McGeehan, Judge, 199, 200-208
McNulty, Professor, 199 n.
McReynolds, Justice James C., 176
machinery, 95, 100, 151
Mach, Ernst, 47, 49, 50n., 406, 410
Madison, President James, 163, 179, 184, 190 n., 259
magic, 14, 344-45, 424, 430, 458
Magna Charta, 91-92, 181, 182, 200
Magnes, Dr. J. L., 330
Magyars, 444
Maine, Sir Henry, 24
Maistre, J. M. de, 358
Maitland, F. W., 390, 424
majority in a democracy, 158
Mallock, 300, 301
Malthus, Thomas R., 29, 30, 402
Manning, Bishop William, 200
Marco Polo, 237, 459
Marconi, G., 284
Marshall, Chief Justice John, 21, 36, 176, 178, 179-80, 183, 184, 219
Marx, Karl, and Marxism, 81, 111, 113, 116, 213, 217, 218, 219, 243, 313, 329, 433
    Communist Manifesto, 111
    Das Kapital, 110, 134
Mary, Queen, 349
Masaryk, *The Spirit of Russia*, 265
materialism, 299, 311

mathematics, 49, 50-51, 290, 291, 312, 406, 457, 466
Maurras, Charles, 443
Maxwell, James Clerk, 291, 376
Mayflower Pact, 258
Mead, Acting President, 199
measurement, units of, 172
mechanics, non-Newtonian, 140, 378
medical schools, quotas in, 131
medicine, how influenced by philosophy, 374, 457
medieval theology, 235-41
Meinong, A., 395
melting-pot, 445
Mencken, H. L., 227
Mendel, Abbot, 303, 389
Mendeleief, D. I., 265
Mendelssohn, Moses, 55
Mengenlehre, 383
mental automatism, 297
Mephistopheles, 289
mercy, deeds of, 352-53
Meredith, George, 31
Messiah, 320, 453
metaphysics, 375-85, 401 (*see also* philosophy)
meteorological events as portents, 345
Methodist Church, 400
Mexican War, 293
Mexico, 349, 353, 446
Micah, 352
Michels, Robert, 155-61
    Sociology of Political Parties, 105, 155
militarism, 17, 52-53
militarization, danger of, 463
military virtues, 463
Mill, John Stuart, 21, 44, 47, 48, 60, 61

Miller, Adam, 460
Miller, Justice Samuel F., 164, 252
Millikan, Robert A., 46, 298, 339
mill-owners, 256
Milton, John, 72
minorities, 444, 447
miracles, 345, 356, 430
modernism, religious, 302, 346
Mohammed, 52, 136, 233, 235, 341, 352
Mohammedan sects, 350
Mohammedanism, 94, 338, 339, 340, 341, 343, 348, 350, 354, 355, 439
Moloch, 349
Molokans, the, 338
monasteries and monastic life, 356, 357
money, cheap, 254
monism, 145
Monroe, President James, 259
Montesquieu, C. de, 26, 188
Moore, Professor, 142
Moore, Dr. George Foot, 281
morality, 314-15; defined, 75-76, 347, 456; conventional, 279, 301, 395; based on fear, 348-49; based on rewards, 75; medieval, see Dante; modern, 240; sexual, 301; how affected by discrediting of mythology, 300
morality and religion, relation between, 347-53, 456
More, Paul Elmer, 72-77, 230, 231
  Platonism, 72
  Shelburne Essays, 73
More, Thomas, 344, 390
Morelli gang, 197
Morley, John, 230, 285
Mosaic cosmogony, 297, 300, 359

Mosaic law, 321, 344, 349
Moscow, University of, 263
Moscow uprising, 112
Moses, 52, 94, 297, 421
Mosheim, J. L. von, 346
Motley, John Lothrop, 256
Müller, Johannes, 374
municipal administrations, 102-103
Münsterberg, Hugo, 389
Murphy, Dr., 199 n.
Mussolini, B., 192, 447
myths, 420, 422-23, 426

Nairne, Lady, 134
Napoleon, 242, 266-69, 368
National Labor Relations Board, 164
nationalism, 54, 132, 225-26, 242-45
nationality groups, 130, 468
"natural philosophy," 409
"natural rights," 164, 166, 175-93
  passim
naturalism vs. spiritualism, 308, 310, 314, 317
"nature," the word, 274
Nazism, 121, 129, 467
Negro, status of, 122-23, 165, 178, 329-30
neighbors, love of, 10, 127-28, 314
neo-Platonism, 69, 309, 312, 318, 381
New Deal, 166
New York City—boroughs, 104-105; Board of Higher Education, 199 n., 200-210
New York Times, 204
Newcomb, Professor, 199 n.
Newcomb, Simon, 252

Newton, Isaac, 46, 49, 50, 51, 88, 94, 244, 285, 291, 318, 367, 368, 381
Principia, 51, 373
Nicaragua, 446
Nicholas I, Czar, 264
Nicolson, Dr. Marjorie, 204-205
Nietzsche, F., 30, 61, 81, 120, 300, 410, 469
Nihilists, Russian, 262
Nisard, Désiré, 231
Nobel Prize, 160
nominalism, 312, 372
nonconformity, 167 (*see also* heresy)
normative and existential, 142
Norris, Frank, 224
Norwegians, 130
NRA, 34, 37
Nuremberg laws, 332

oath of obedience to the Constitution, 182-83
Oersted, Hans Christian, 374
oleomargarine, 177
oligarchic tendencies in democracy, 157-60
omniscience impossible, 4-5, 6, 44, 117, 407, 452-53
open-mindedness, 430-33
opium, 135, 262
optimism, 259-60, 314-15
optimism and pessimism in literature, 253
Orientals, European hatred of, 123
Osborne, T. B., 298, 460
other-worldliness, 310-11, 391
Outlook, 194
Overstreet, Professor Harry, 199 n.
Owen, Senator R. L., 172

Owen, Sir Richard, 296
Oxford University, 420

pacifism, 52-53
Packard, Lotta, 195
Padua, University of, 374, 459
Paine, Tom, 253, 338
Palestine—*see* Zionism
panaceas, 160
Panama Canal, 338
Paolo and Francesca, 235, 239
Paracelsus, 297
parallel lines, 454
parcel post, 254
Paris Commune, 87, 112, 467
Parker, Justice, 180
Parkman, Francis, 256
Parliament, 181, 182, 302
Parmenides, 372
Parrington, Vernon, 216, 221, 249-55
The Beginnings of Critical Realism in America, 249
Main Currents in American Thought, 214-15, 249
Partington, Mrs., 231
party organization, 158-59
Pascal, Blaise, 358
"passion," in Spinoza's sense, 316
Patten, Simon N., 149
Paul, St., 27, 60, 320, 429
Pavlov, I. P., 265, 297
Peano, Giuseppe, 393, 406
peasant revolts, 112, 323, 324
Peirce, Benjamin, 252
Peirce, Charles S., 232-33, 279, 299, 304, 376, 391-97, 431, 432
Collected Papers, 391-97
Pericles, 372, 440
Perkins, George W., 167-68

persecution and suppression, 53-54, 125-26, 351, 427, 444, 467 (*see also* tolerance *and* Jews)

Peter of Abano, 344 n.

Peter the Great, 265

Peterson, Houston, 298-302
Huxley, Prophet of Science, 296

Petrarch, 239

Phidias, 94

Philippines, 448

Philo, 320, 321, 329

philosophical terms, changes in their meanings, 308

"philosophy," meaning and use of the word, 25, 409; "moral" and "mental," 409

philosophy—history of, 370-75; as a separate study, 409-12; modern, 312-13; teaching of, 292-95; taught by dialogue, 457; true purpose of, 404; the "practical" in, 412, 413; ethical neutrality of, 404; ethical and social issues in, 385-88; in the modern curriculum, 408-14; as a *Lebensanschauung*, 385; vision and technique in, 365-91; intuitional, 191, 221, 384; the poet's, 239; of history, 388-91; scientific method in, 405-406, 411-12, 413; its relation to the sciences, 410; to medicine, 374; to psychology, 374 (*see also* logic *and* metaphysics)

"phonograph theory" of the judicial function, 43-44, 176

phosphorous matches, 64

physics, 47-51, 172, 374, 406, 409

physiology, 374

Pickering, E. C., 252, 284

Piero delle Vigne, 239

Planck, Max, 47

planning, social and economic, 39, 93-95 (*see also* collectivism, individualism, *and* Socialism)

Plato and Platonism, 29, 72-77, 85, 88, 94, 236, 291, 343, 368, 371, 373, 381, 383, 397, 406, 414
The Republic, 75

Plotinus, 458

Plucknett, Professor, 182

Plutarch, *Lives,* 269

Poe, Edgar Allan, 219, 220, 222

Poincaré, Henri, 47

Poincaré, Raymond, 171, 406

Poles and Poland, 53, 85, 444

political parties, 155-61

Pope, Alexander, 224

Popular Science Monthly, 233, 252

population, increase in European, 402

Populist party, 254

Portugal, 447

Portuguese civilization, 448

Positivism, 314

postal-savings banks, 254

Poynting, J. H., 431

practical vs. theoretical in living, 289

prayer, 341, 343, 344, 352, 355, 356

predestination, 238, 239

Prescott, W. H., 222, 256

Priestley, Dr. Joseph, 304

priests, 343, 344, 424, 439, 457

primitive peoples, 78, 420, 423

principles in the law, constructive value of, 144-45

private enterprise, 97, 100, 149-50

private ownership, 169

Privy Council, 188
probability in natural laws, 431
Proctor, Captain, 195
production of goods, 63-64, 149, 169, 428; for profit, 52-53, 150, 465; restricted and unrestricted, 63, 95, 97, 99-100
profit, private, 53, 96-97
profit motive, 65, 96-97, 150
profits, 63-64
progress, 61, 94, 129, 422; belief in, 449-53; mechanical law of, 290
Prohibition, 97, 351
propaganda in literary criticism, 253
propertied class, 254 (see also aristocracy)
"property," meaning of, 178, 184
property—ownership of, 29, 30-31, 117, 402; conventional ideas of, 302; socialization of, see Socialism
Protestants, 59-60, 130, 351, 467
Proudhon, P. J., 253
Proust, Marcel, 101
    A la recherche du temps perdu, 60
Psalms, 321
psychoanalysis, 136, 451
psychology—popular, 138, 451; Kantian, 406; how influenced by philosophy, 374
Ptolemaic system, 51
Ptolemy, King, 460
public office, qualifications for holding, 449
public utilities, management of, 103-104
punishment, divine, 348

Puritans and Puritanism, 26, 60, 87, 213, 250, 259, 289, 350, 441, 444
Pythagoreans, 73, 457

quantum theory, 303, 460
questioning—see doubt

racial antagonism, 122-23
racial equality, 165
railroad coupling devices, 177
Raphael, 94
Rasputin, G., 264
rational motivation of conduct, 423
rationalism, 15, 313, 430 (see also irrationalism)
rationality, 8-10, 146-47
rationalizing, 70
realism and the realistic movement, 145, 147, 221, 222-24, 249-55
"reality," the word, 375
reality—independent, 49-50; changing of, 56
reason, 70-71, 404; use of, 14; distrust of, 70
reasoning—legal, 191; logical, see logic
reasons, "good," 70
recall, the, 254
referendum, the, 254
Reform Bill of 1832, 113
Reformation, the, 59-60, 322-26
relativity, 50, 139, 460
religion—defined, 19, 52, 339-40; absolute claims, 351; dark side of, 337-61; cruelty and hatred in, 349-51; emotional side of, 354-57; defense of, 357-58; changed because of

argument, 358-59; philosophy of, 384-85; in America, 258; relation to science, 5-6, 302, 308, 339, 341-42, 345-46

religious antagonism and repression, 124-26

religious beliefs, 340, 359-60

"religious experience," 384

religious creeds, 54-55, 360

religious practices, cruel, 349-51

religious revivals, 355

religious thought, literature of, 251

Renaissance, 240, 293, 440, 458

Renan, E., 72, 307

Renouvier, C. B., 391

research, free, 279-82

revenge and cruelty, 133

revivals, religious, 355

revolution, right of, 446-47

revolutions, 112

Reynolds, Mrs., 216

rhythm in life, 440

Ricardou, 232

Ricci, C. G., 47

Richardson, Professor, 197

Richberg, Donald R., 32, 34-35

Richelieu, Cardinal, 114

Rickert, Heinrich, 389

Riemann, Georg, 454

rights—absolute, 166; natural, 164, 166, 175-93; civil, 21, clash of, 166; constitutional, 175-93; of revolution, 446-47; of minorities, 447; to petition Congress, 447

risks, taking, 16, 438

rituals to appease supernatural beings, 343, 352, 420

rivalry and competition, 120-21

Roberts, Justice Owen J., 176

Robespierre, M. F. de, 105

Robinson, James Harvey, 68-70, 142

The Mind in the Making, 69

Roman Catholic Church, 15, 124, 128, 147, 166, 324, 337, 339, 344, 347, 359, 427, 443, 449, 468 (*see also* Christian Church)

Roman religion, 348

romantic criticism, 222

Romantic movement, 60, 316

"romanticism" in literature, 221, 222, 225

Roosevelt, President Theodore, 35, 70, 102, 150, 254, 290, 338

Root, Senator Elihu, 43

Rousseau, J. J., 95, 229-30, 274-75, 293, 400

Émile, 274-75, 293

royal road to geometry, no, 460

Royal Society, 282, 406

Royce, Josiah, 353, 365, 391, 392, 396

rural influence in American literature, 254

Ruskin, John, 334

Russell, Bertrand, 6, 165, 318-19, 383, 393, 396, 403-407, 410, 420

"A Free Man's Worship," 318

Our Knowledge of the External World . . . , 403

Principles of Mathematics, 406

Russia and the Russians, 62, 85, 101, 105-106, 107, 112, 113, 149, 330, 338, 400, 446, 467; absence of liberalism, 261-66; social traits, 262-63; thought and literature, 262-64, 266;

agriculture, politics, education, 264-65

Russian Revolution, 112, 114, 118, 163

Rutgers College, 280

Rutherforth, 188

Ryan, Father, 166

Sabbath, 352, 353

Sacco, Nicola, 193-98

sacraments, 339

Saint-Simon, Comte de, 111

Sainte-Beuve, C. A., 232

saints, 344, 350, 352

Samson and Delilah, 421

Santayana, George, 3, 317, 318, 425

The Life of Reason, 294, 317

Saracens, 124 (*see also* Mohammedans)

Saturday Evening Post, 223

Savigny, F. K. von, 24

scenery spoiled for utilitarian reasons, 289-90

Schelling, F. W. von, 113, 368

Schiller, *The Ring of Polycrates*, 354

Schlegel, F., 222

Schneider, H. W., 161, 167

scholarship, 279-82, 285

Scholasticism, 366, 370, 419, 426

Schopenhauer, A., 60, 314

Schwab, Charles M., 172

science—essential character of, 428; methods and limits of, 69, 407, 410, 425, 453, 454; as providing a vision, 49-50; reliability of its results, 380-81; dogmatism in, 401, 425-29; law and probability in, 430-31; procedures in, 48-49, 138-42,
409, 421; its effect on the medieval view, 237-38; origin of modern, 69, 409; popular, 23-24, 284, 303-304, 357, 421, 451, 460-61; utilitarian, 49-50, 284, 287, 289, 290-91, 396, 404; official leaders of, 298; influence on American thought, 251-52; in universities, 282-83, 409; relation to philosophy, 373, 409-10; to religion, 5-6, 302, 308, 339, 341-42, 345-46, 426-27; growth of, as proof of progress, 450

scientific management, 37-38, 64, 100-101, 150-51

scientific, whether men today are more, 450-51

scientists—their efforts in philosophy, 5; and philosophers, 48; dogmatic, 401; honest, 426; their liberalism, as a body, 455; methods and attitudes in, *see above,* science, methods and limits of

Scotch-Irish, 444

Scots, 130

self-control—*see* discipline

selfishness, group, 133

self-torture, 352

Seligman, E. R. A., 170, 178

Sellar and Yeatman, *1066 and All That*, 125

Senators, popular election of, 254

Seneca, 386

separation of powers, 183

serfs, 400

Servetus, Michael, 349

Seventh-Day Adventists, 128

sex element in religion, 355

sexual morality, 301

Shakespeare, William, 46, 88, 94, 215, 216

Shaw, G. B., 216, 244

Sheldon, Professor, 365

Shelley, P. B., 6, 52, 214, 307, 340, 450

Sherman, Stuart, 231

Silva, 194-95

Simms, W. G., 220

sin, 355, 357

Single Tax, 446

Sisson, Mr., 168

skepticism—*see* doubt

slacking in wartime, 84-88

slavery, Negro, 81, 259, 353, 399-400, 444

Smith, Adam, 61

Smith, Alfred E., 255

Smith, Benjamin, *Der Vor-Kristliche Jesus,* 320

Smith, Bernard, 213-27
   Forces in American Criticism, 213

Smith, Robertson, 421, 423, 424

Smith, Theobald, 284

sociability, 462

social classes, 101-102, 130-33

social conflict, 119-36; differences (speech, dress, etc.) as predisposing cause, 123-24

Social Democratic Party (Germany), 105, 160, 336

social forms, adjustments to, 129-30

social justice, 353

social order, fixed, 129-30

social reform, legislation for, 24-25, 29, 36, 144

social righteousness, 352-53

social sciences, 140-41, 409, 420-24

social security, 445

social settlements, 253

Socialism, 93-109, 160, 261; arguments against, 95-105; limitations, 105-109

society, adjusting to, 275

socio-economic aspects of literature, 217-18

sociology in American literature, 253

Socrates, 88, 94, 236, 285, 389, 414, 450, 457

Solomon, 94, 236

Soloviev, S. M., 265

Song of Songs, 251

Sophocles, 256, 266, 388

soul, idea of the, 399, 400

South, the, 259, 353, 400, 442

space, concept of, 50 n.

Spain, 448, 467

Spanish-American War, 258, 448

Spanish Republic, 447

Spartacists, 261

special creation, theory of, 301

speed-up, 100, 117, 151

Spencer, Herbert, 37, 61, 163, 251, 299, 303, 381, 405, 410, 422

Spengler, Oswald, 440

Spingarn, Joel E., 227

Spinoza, B., 6, 13-19, 50, 52, 94, 285, 307-19, 328, 329, 338, 348, 371, 372, 373, 386
   Ethics, 308, 310, 314
   Logic, 319

spiritualism vs. naturalism, 308

standard of living, American, 164-65

standards of literacy, 286

State, the, 15, 17, 166, 169, 372 (*see also* government)

state bonds, 178

State Department, 447

state legislative acts, 185
state legislatures, 163-64
states, the, 36, 185
states' rights, 259, 444, 445
stimulation, 461-62
Stoic philosophers, 321, 371
Story, Justice Joseph, 21, 176
Strachey, John, 116
Strachey, Lytton, 298
strenuous life, 289, 290
Stuarts, the, 402
subconscious, the, 313
sublime, the, 418
suffrage, universal, 304, 449
suicide, 356
Sunday, observance of, 350-51
supernatural, the, 300, 310
supernatural beings, 343, 344, 423-24
superstition, 14, 300, 341-47, 423-24, 458 (see also demoniac possession, magic, witchcraft)
suppression—see persecution
Supreme Court, 23 n., 32, 37, 43, 164, 176, 179, 180-81; voiding power, 182-86 (see also judges)
surplus production, 63; and starvation, 26, 465
survival of the fittest, 63, 300
"survivals" in anthropology, 421-22
suttee, 349
Swiss constitution, 185
syndicalism, 159

taboo, 423
Tacitus, 321
Taine, H., 218, 232, 249, 307
Talmud, 41, 294, 423
Tammany Hall, 130

Taney, Chief Justice Roger B., 21, 176
tariff legislation, 254
Tatars, 263, 402
taxation, 170, 448
Taylor, Frederick Winslow, 64, 151
Taylorism—see scientific management
Taylor, Henry Osborn, 256
Taylor Society, 38, 151
teachers—licenses for, 201; freedom for, 279-80; made administrators, 281; their responsibility for students' indifference to ideas, 284; their overwork, 284-85
technique in philosophy, 366-91
Tennyson, The Passing of Arthur, 275
Tertullian, 350 n.
Thales, 372, 457
Thayer, Judge, 195, 196, 197
Thayer, Professor J. B., 188
theism, 384-85
theology, 405, 427; in conflict with science, 341
theoretic pursuits, 85-88
theory, its value in living, 289
Thiers, L. A., 126, 467
Thomas à Kempis, 386
Thomson, J. Arthur, 284
Thomson, J. J., 431
Thoreau, H. D., 217
Thorndike, E. L., 403
Thucydides, 343
time and eternity, Spinoza's distinction between, 308, 311-13
Titanic, 257
Tocqueville, A. de, 255

tolerance and intolerance, 21, 53, 117, 119, 125-26, 144, 342, 351, 427, 449, 453-56; of contrary opinion, denial of known truth, etc., 14-15, 128-29, 453-54

Tolstoi, L., 72

Torquemada, 340

torture, 344

Tourtoulon, 136

town planning, 458

trade—see commerce

trade unions, 151, 165, 177, 353

Transcendentalists, 219, 220, 222

travel, its effect on ideas, 457-59

Treitschke, H. von, 242

trial by peers, 92

Trotsky, L., 105, 116

trustees of colleges and universities, 280-81

trusts, 63, 150

truth, search for, 74, 85, 280-81, 370-71, 373, 404, 427, 452

truthfulness, 346

Tugwell, Rexford G., 148-55

Turgeniev, A., 266

Turks, 400, 402

Turner, *The Frontier in American History*, 259 n.

turning the other cheek, 127

Twain, Mark, 244, 251, 253
Innocents Abroad, 225

Ugolino, 240

Ukrainians, 53

Ulysses, 236, 240, 457

Unamuno y Jugo, Miguel de, 236, 350 n.

unemployment, 38

unions—see trade unions

Unitarians, 128

United States as refuge for oppressed, 445-46

United States Post Office, 104

unity and diversity, 7, 145-46, 381-82, 444

unity promoted by Christian ethics, 400

universe—total, 381; a mechanical contrivance, 430

university, the, 278-83, 285, 288

"upward," meaning of, 450

U'Ren, 252

utilitarianism—as an end in science, 49-50, 284, 287, 289, 290-91; in nature, 299

Utopias, 390-91

Vanderlip, Frank A., 172

Vanzetti, Bartolomeo, 193-98

variations in natural law, 430-31

Vattel, E. von, 188

Veblen, Thorstein, 138

Venice and the Venetians, 459

Vesalius, 69, 374

Vico, G. B., 469

Victorian age, 296, 301

Virgil, 237

Virginia, 441

Voltaire, 138, 244, 263, 337, 341, 358, 374, 400, 427

wages, 118, 133, 148

Wagner, Richard, 243, 368

Waite, Chief Justice M. R., 176, 252

Waldenses, 350

Wallace, *Russia*, 338 n.

Wallas, *Human Nature in Politics*, 156

Wallis, John, 409

Ward, Lester, 252

wars, 111-12, 119-26, 168, 351, 446, 451, 463

Washington, George, 178, 179, 440, 442, 443

Farewell Address, 442

Watt, James, 267

Weale, *The Conflict of Colour*, 123 n.

wealth, its use for philanthropic purposes, 286

Wehle, Mr., 169

Wells, David A., 253

West Point, 409

Western Philosophical Association, 204

Weyl, Walter, 252

White, Andrew D., 341, 345, 426, 427

Whitehead, Alfred North, 383, 398-403, 406

Whitman, Walt, 217, 250, 253

Whitney, Mr., 64

Wilberforce, Bishop Samuel, 296, 301

Wilcox, Ella Wheeler, 216

Wilhelm, Kaiser, 242

will to believe, 428 (*see also* James, William)

Williams, Roger, 441

Wilson, James, 42, 190

Wilson, President Woodrow, 150, 258, 446

Windelband, Wilhelm, 389

witchcraft, 14, 38, 343-44, 430

woman, American, 172, 260

Woodbridge, F. J., 292, 365, 403

Woolsey, Theodore S., 252

words, their meanings in modern philosophy, 308, 375-76

work—skill and speed in, 100, 118; joy in, 154

workmen's compensation laws, 22

world trade, 168 (*see also* commerce)

World War, First, 135, 168, 243, 257, 258, 389

Wright, Chauncey, 139

Wright, Harold Bell, 217

Xenophanes, 72, 341, 457

xenophobia, 123-24

Yale University, 295

Youmans, E. L., 252

Zabarella, 374

Zeno, 383

Zionism, 53, 326-33

Zola, Émile, 231

Zulus, 125